Holidays
and Other Weird Events

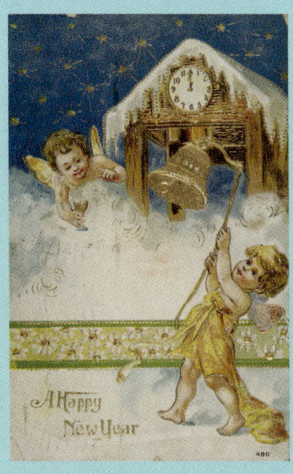
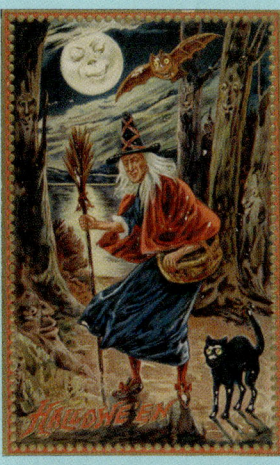
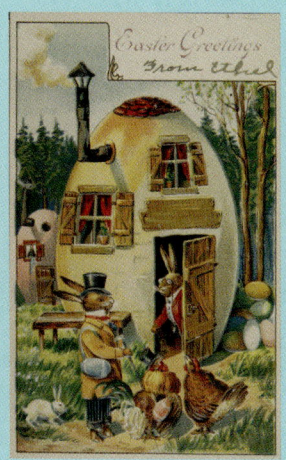
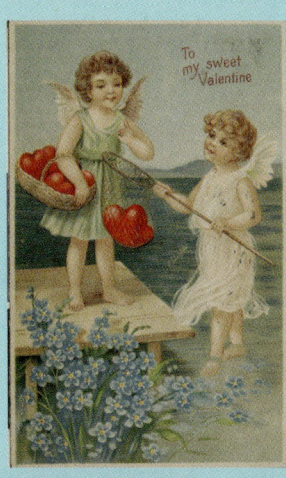
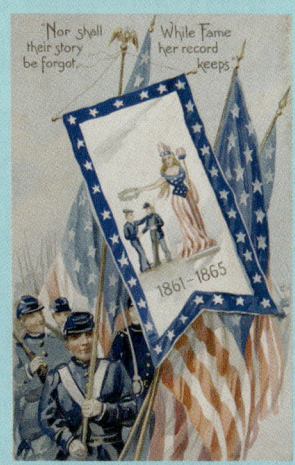
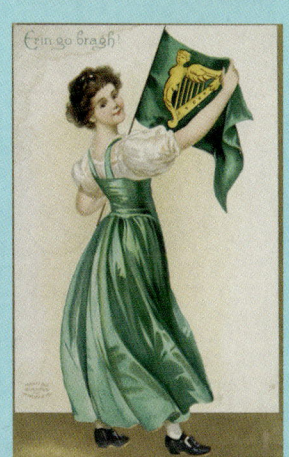
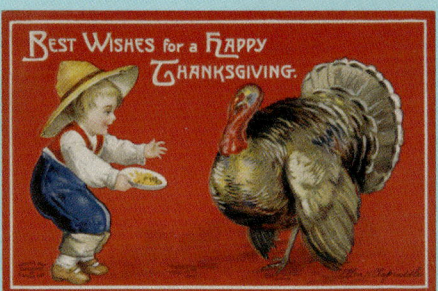
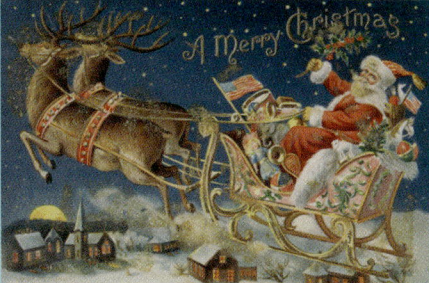
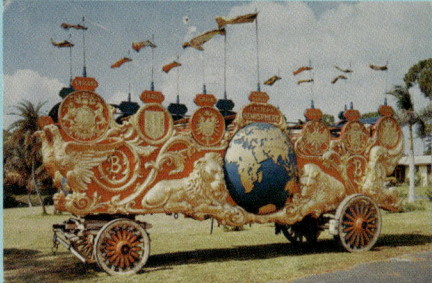

Featuring the Collection of the Landis Valley Museum

Irwin Richman

Schiffer Publishing Ltd
4880 Lower Valley Road, Atglen, PA 19310

Dedication

My family has shared holiday seasons and miscellaneous weird events with me over various periods of time. Claiming the longest tenure is my wife, Dr. M Susan Richman. The rest of the time voyagers are our children, daughters-in-law, and grandchildren. Our eldest son, Dr. Alexander E. Richman, a mathematician, and his wife, Elana, are Pennsylvanians. Our younger son, Dr. Joshua S. Richman, a medical researcher, and his wife, Kristin, are parents of our grandchildren, Benjamin David and Zoë Elizabeth Anne. Our honorary son, Oscar D. Beisert, Jr., is an architectural historian.

Copyright © 2009 by Landis Valley Associates
Library of Congress Control Number: 2009929683

All rights reserved. No part of this work may be reproduced or used in any form or by any means—graphic, electronic, or mechanical, including photocopying or information storage and retrieval systems—without written permission from the publisher.
The scanning, uploading and distribution of this book or any part thereof via the Internet or via any other means without the permission of the publisher is illegal and punishable by law. Please purchase only authorized editions and do not participate in or encourage the electronic piracy of copyrighted materials.
"Schiffer," "Schiffer Publishing Ltd. & Design," and the "Design of pen and ink well" are registered trademarks of Schiffer Publishing Ltd.

Designed by John P. Cheek
Type set in Grasshopper/Zurich BT

ISBN: 978-0-7643-3362-0
Printed in China

Schiffer Books are available at special discounts for bulk purchases for sales promotions or premiums. Special editions, including personalized covers, corporate imprints, and excerpts can be created in large quantities for special needs. For more information contact the publisher:

Published by Schiffer Publishing Ltd.
4880 Lower Valley Road
Atglen, PA 19310
Phone: (610) 593-1777; Fax: (610) 593-2002
E-mail: Info@schifferbooks.com

For the largest selection of fine reference books on this and related subjects, please visit our web site at
www.schifferbooks.com
We are always looking for people to write books on new and related subjects. If you have an idea for a book please contact us at the above address.

This book may be purchased from the publisher.
Include $5.00 for shipping.
Please try your bookstore first.
You may write for a free catalog.

In Europe, Schiffer books are distributed by
Bushwood Books
6 Marksbury Ave.
Kew Gardens
Surrey TW9 4JF England
Phone: 44 (0) 20 8392 8585; Fax: 44 (0) 20 8392 9876
E-mail: info@bushwoodbooks.co.uk
Website: www.bushwoodbooks.co.uk

Contents

Acknowledgments — 4

Preface — 4

1. **Holidays Are Weird** — 5
2. **New Years**: New Lives — 6
3. **Valentine's Day**: Hearts and Little Naked Kids — 18
4. **Easter**: Religion and Rabbits — 35
5. **St. Patrick's Day**: We All Turn Green — 59
6. **Patriotism**: Celebrations and Memorials — 66
7. **Halloween**: Talking Pumpkins and Witches — 81
8. **Thanksgiving**: Pilgrims and Prescient Turkeys — 97
9. **Christmas**: More Religion and a Strange Man in the House — 114
10. **Weird Events**: Can You Believe These? — 131

Sources and Suggestions for Additional Reading — 143

Index — 144

Acknowledgments

Whenever I am involved in a project I realize how wise John Donne was to observe, "No man is an Island." Steve Miller, my friend and the immediate past Director of the Landis Valley Museum (he has since moved to a higher sphere) has been a major facilitator. I am also proud to claim him as a former graduate student. An effective administrator, he has helped make the museum the vital entity it is. Bruce Bomberger and Nicole Wagner are the professional guardians of the postcard collections at Landis Valley and they have always been helpful. Dr. Russell Eaton, is a retired physicist who, as a volunteer, has undertaken the ongoing, almost Herculean, task of organizing the huge Landis Valley postcard collection. He always shares his knowledge and enthusiasms with me. Privately a very selective collector of postcards, he has kindly lent me cards, which enhance those gleaned from the Museum's holdings, to include in this book. Two others have also loaned images. Mike Emery, Landis Valley Museum Educator and Volunteer Coordinator, an avid collector of books, paper, and photographic memorabilia, has volunteered cards reflective of his specific interests. Washington, D.C. based architectural historian, Oscar D. Beisert, Jr., has shared Texas views, some of which are probably unique. My other colleagues at Landis Valley have helped whenever they could. Thank you Donna Horst, Tim Essig, Will Morrow, Joyce Perkinson, Cindy Reedy, Joe Schott, and Trish Frey. As always, the Penn State Harrisburg Library staff have performed their magic for me.

I am a technological idiot. Thankfully, kind people have taken pity. At the office, Mike Emery always helps me with computer issues. I do not know, however, if I could function in this increasingly complex world without my wife, Dr. M. Susan, a mathematician and retired university dean. She is my major technology enabler and she has voluntarily transcribed the manuscript from my inelegant scrawl into useful and improved typescript. She, blessedly, is touched with the work ethic of her Pennsylvania German forebears.

Over the years I have worked with and been inspired by many historians who have encouraged my interest in the visual. Some were my teachers and some were friends, while some were both. I especially pay homage to Wood Gray, Wallace Davies, Manville Wakefield, and Russell Weigley. They made a difference.

Preface

The most difficult task in creating this book was selecting the limited number of postcards that could be included. The number and variety of holiday cards is phenomenal. Weird cards also exist in astounding numbers. Early in the 20th century almost anything was fair game for the postcard makers. Many had a wide commercial distribution and were printed in the hundreds, thousands, or even more. Others were privately distributed in very small numbers. A few were probably unique. As indicated above, while some cards included here are the property of private collectors, most are from the collections of the Landis Valley Museum in Manheim Township, Lancaster County, Pennsylvania, where the author is Director of Research and Development for the Heirloom Seed Project. This book is compiled for the benefit of the not-for-profit Landis Valley Associates, whose mission it is to help maintain and develop the Landis Valley Museum.

The Cottage
Bainbridge, Pennsylvania
2008

1
Holidays Are Weird

'Weird' is a wonderful word. It is rich in both denotation and connotation. Commonly, 'weird' is often a synonym for 'strange' or 'unusual': "Man that's weird!" But historically, weird events are those involving fate, destiny, prophecy, witchcraft, and the unearthly.

Holidays in contemporary America are generally days of commemoration or, even better, days of celebration marked by an exemption from labor – no work today! Alas, most of us have to work on Valentine's Day, St. Patrick's Day, and Halloween. The origin of the word 'holiday' comes from Holy Days, which, of course, were and are religious feast days. While the faithful would bristle at most of the meanings of weird being applied to their faiths/beliefs, most would agree that religion is of a higher order and is truly unearthly. Skeptics more readily see relationships between some religious beliefs and the weird.

In America, important holidays that are religious in origin often have become secular and their religious message tamed or blunted to become popular events. Ellen Litwicki, in her book *America's Public Holidays, 1865-1920*, also notes that:

> Between 1865 and 1920 Americans invented more than twenty-five holidays. Some, such as Memorial and Labor Days, became a permanent part of the nation's holiday calendary, while others, such as Constitution and Bird Days, never really caught on. Some holidays, such as Confederate Memorial Day, remained regional. Still others, such as Tadcusz Kosciuszko's Birthday or Emancipation and Haymarket Martyrs' Days, remained particular to ethnic, racial, or ideological groups. In addition to creating these new holidays, Americans in this period breathed new life into older ones, including the Fourth of July, Washington's Birthday and St. Patrick's Day.

Why was this so fertile a period in the creation of holidays? The answer is complex and relates to the Civil War, Emancipation, Immigration, and the Labor Movements… all great events and movements which had to be domesticated and brought into the mainstream of American life as American identity was redefined.

Postcards

The surge in holiday-making and redefinition overlaps with the development of the postcard, which becomes our first mass-produced popular greeting card. The years 1900 to 1918 are generally considered the golden age of postcards. Postcard entrepreneurs encouraged people to send cards for all events and on all occasions. Some holidays became card-generating machines. Most did not. By the 1920s more modern greeting cards became increasingly popular and most messages were enclosed in envelopes.

One major American, card-generating holiday did not emerge until after the decline of the golden age of the postcard. That is Mother's Day, which was first given national recognition by President Woodrow Wilson in 1914 but did not become a major holiday until the mid-1920s. The holiday's first emphasis was on flowers, with cards developing later. Newer holidays have also emerged. "Presidents' Day" is a modern construct that combines two older days of commemoration, Washington's and Lincoln's birthdays, so that room could be made for the newest legal holiday, Martin Luther King Jr. Day, formally proclaimed by Congress in 1988.

The King holiday is solemn and most Americans don't quite know how to observe it. This unease says volumes about white/African-American relationships. One sign that social equality has been achieved may appear when the market feels comfortable in finding commercial and/or entertaining ways to observe the holiday. Ads unashamedly inviting you to "Come to the Poconos for a King-sized, King Day Weekend" or "Be King for a Day at Smith Furniture's King Day Sale" would be indicative. Even more than the election of President Barack Obama.

While many people enjoy a vacation from work on Martin Luther King Day, even more celebrate the unofficial mid-winter holiday, "Super Bowl Sunday." This is, in some ways, the ideal American observance – having a completely commercial genesis, widely promoted by television, sports fans, and the makers of snack food. Inclusive, it welcomes all: sports enthusiasts, onlookers, boozers, eaters, or the merely social. Select your own ritual!

Memorial Day, like Martin Luther King Day, was originally solemn, but it has been transformed into a day of patriotic parades, cookouts, and sales marking the beginning of summer. Labor Day was a lofty celebration of the working man. Today it is a picnic-enhanced day marking the end of the summer season.

For a true appreciation of the weirdness of holiday recognitions, think of the images of a kid in a diaper kicking out an old bearded man, turkeys dancing, chickens nodding to rabbits, and strange men dropping down chimneys to make children happy. The weird is integral to American holidays. Suspend your disbelief and come explore with me.

2
New Years

New Lives

In ancient times New Years was celebrated in March. It wasn't until 1752 that Great Britain and its colonies adopted the New Style, or Gregorian, calendar with the New Year beginning on January first. The Puritans in New England, finding any association with the pagan god Janus repugnant, ignored the date's new significance and referred to January mearly as "First Month."

Our New Years Eve customs are indirectly descended from the ancient Roman Saturnalia, a pagan celebration held around the time of the winter solstice, when rules governing the ordinary norms of behavior were suspended. New Amsterdam (later New York City) was famed for New Years Eve celebrations which occasionally became especially raucous. With adaptations, New York City's New Year celebrations are still famous. The glittering apple descending from a rooftop high above Times Square is televised worldwide. Sometimes in New York, as well as other eastern cities, including Boston, Philadelphia and Baltimore, there were street demonstrations and violence with groups of men and boys roaming the streets, fighting, making noise, often blowing tin horns, setting off firecrackers, tearing down fences, and breaking windows. Street thugs were even known to force their way into rich homes and demand food or money!

In popular culture the old year has come to be characterized as a bearded old man; the New Year by a newborn baby. Traditionally the baby reflects both the religious symbol of the Christ Child and the more secular pagan-inspired symbol of rebirth and renewal. As this infant emerges in the world of postcards, he often loses his innocence and is transformed into a symbol of fun, pleasure and, in violation of modern liquor laws, a tippler.

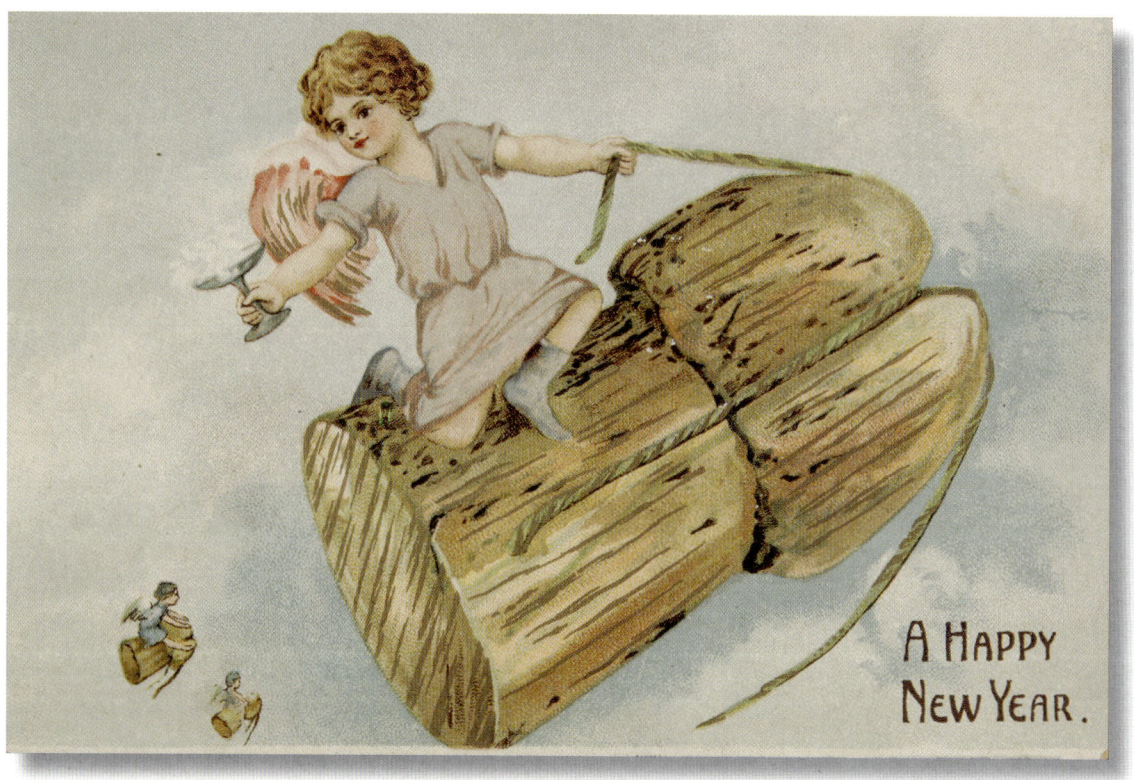

The New Years infant has been transformed into a young goblet-bearing angel, who, along with his comrades, is transported through the heavens on a champagne cork. The card was printed in Germany, *circa* 1905. Did the pre-Freudian, pre-rocket age artist understand the imagery of the ride as we do?

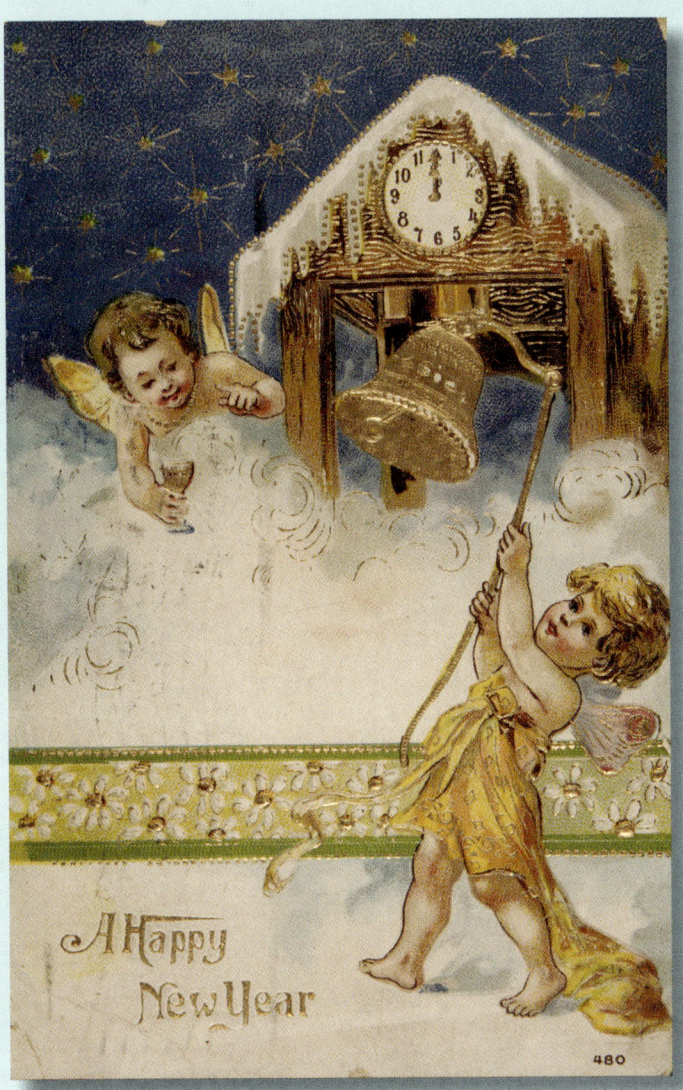

Stars glisten above partying angels on New Years; one rings the bell at Midnight, watched over by a drink-bearing companion. A friendly moon smiles down on cherubic stars organized on ribbons of gossamer. Both cards are German, *circa* 1910.

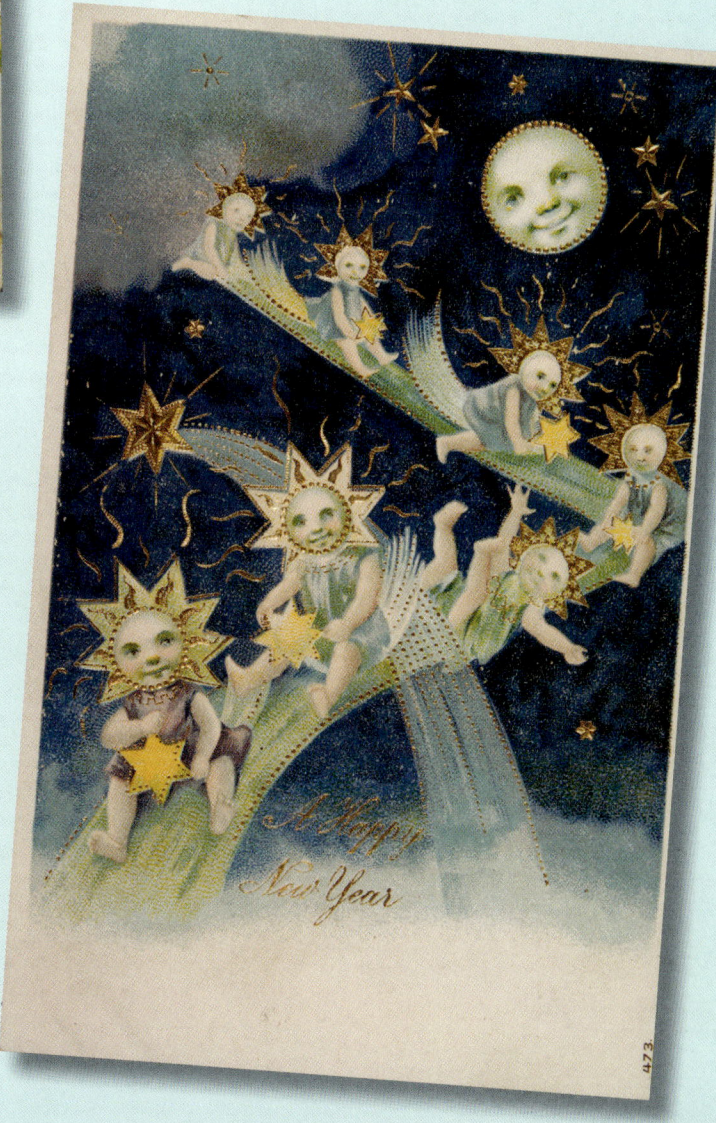

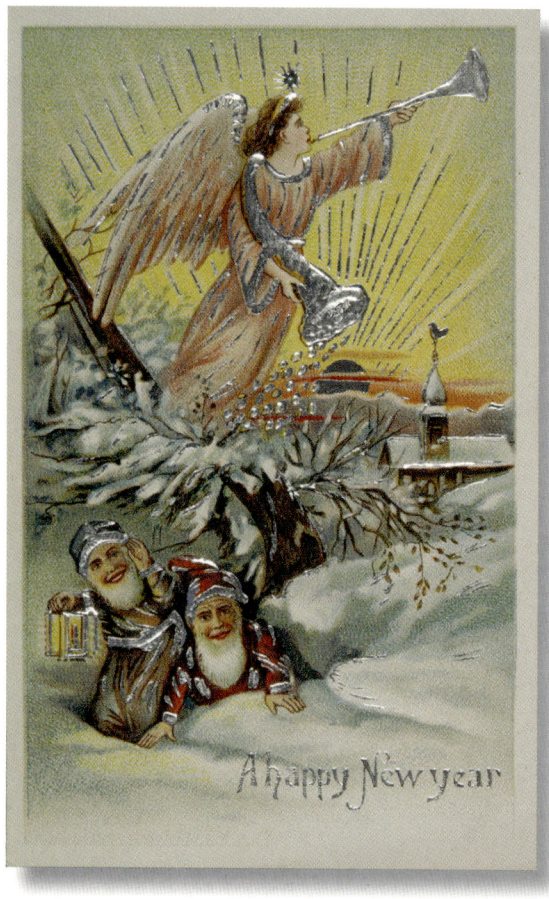
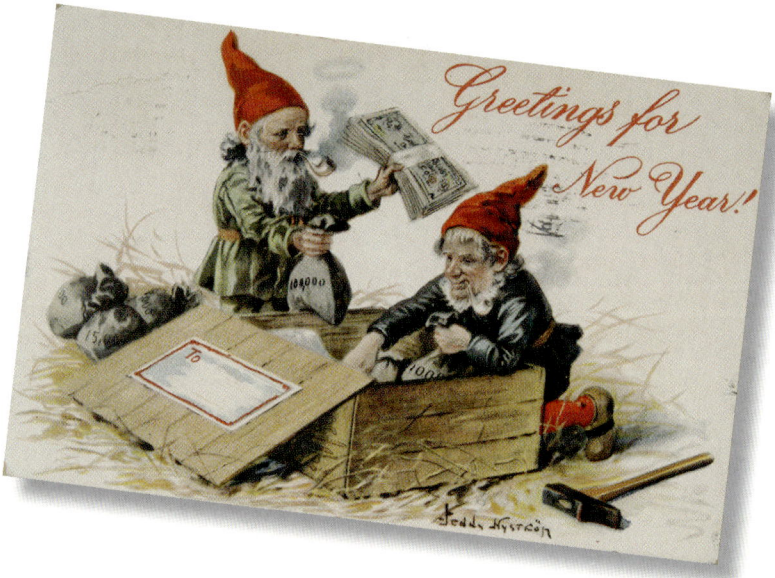

Gnomes and elves regularly appeared on New Years cards. A very Christmas-like angel heralds the New Year in a snow-covered landscape above two Santa-like elves, one of whom carries a lantern. A pair of elves is helping to insure a prosperous, as well as a happy, New Year by packing a box of money for some lucky recipient. Their card is signed by artist Teddy Nystcön.

Prepubescent boys often replace the newborns as harbingers of the New Year. Naval symbolism was also popular. How did epaulettes attach to bare shoulders? The scantily clad lad also sports a sword and a plumed hat. He makes his fully clothed compatriot seem bland.

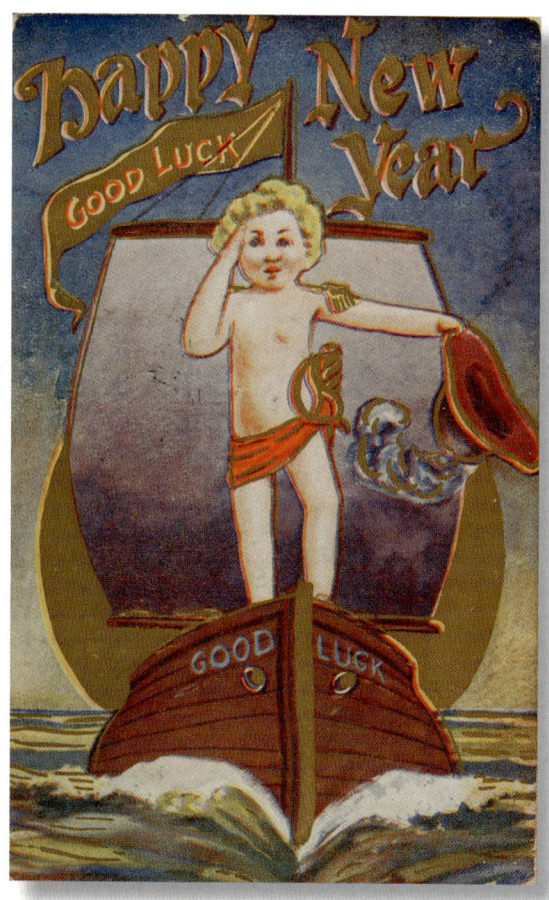
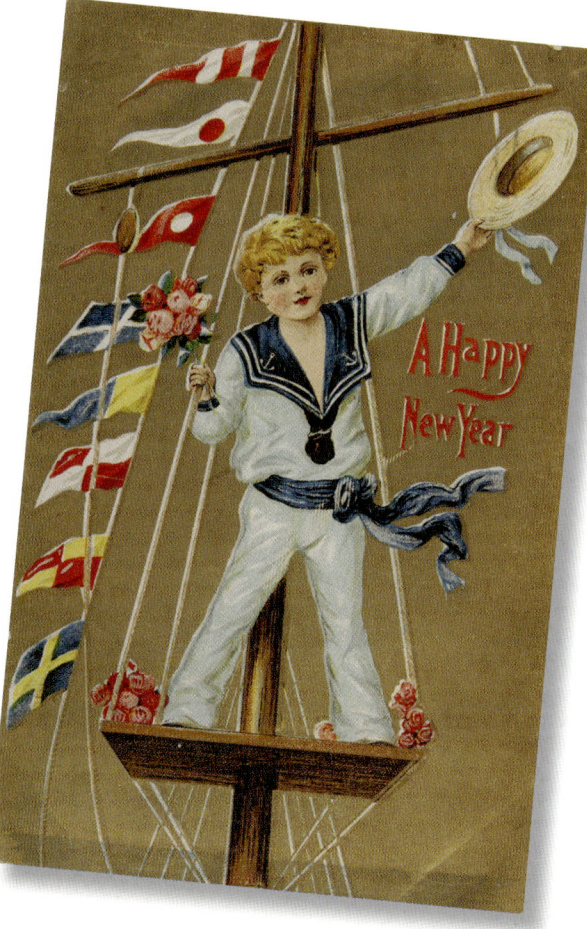

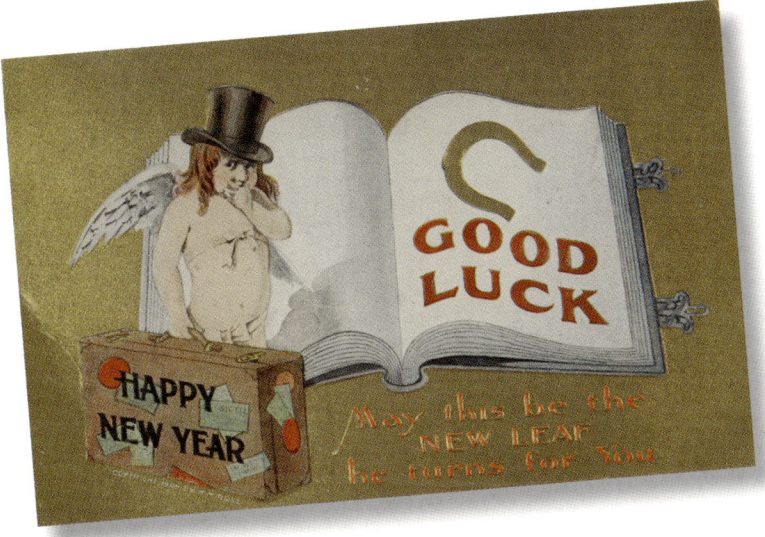

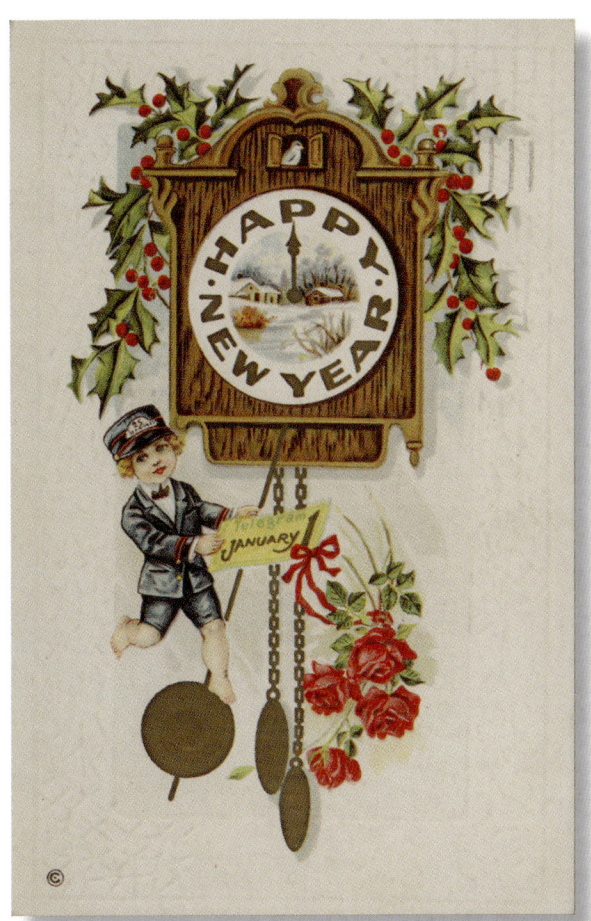

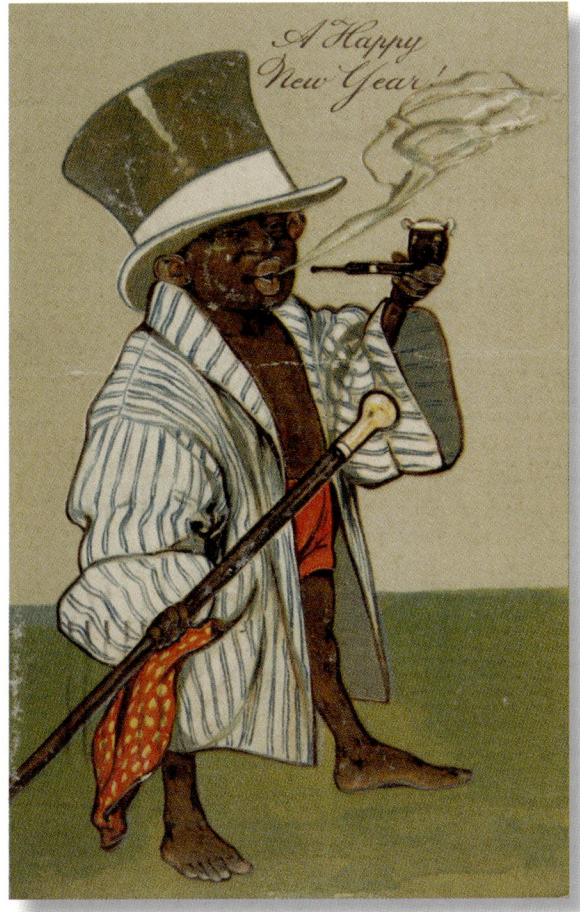

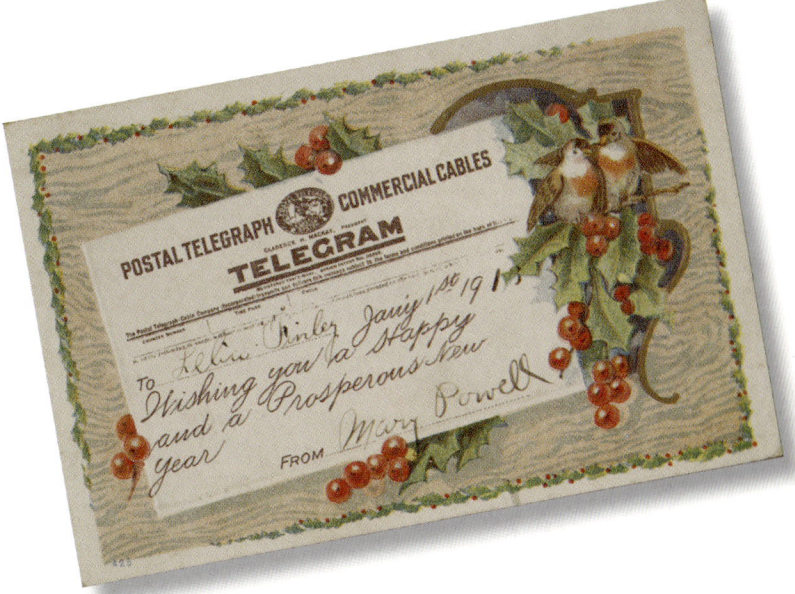

Not all young males representing the New Year are innocent or cherubic. Dapper in top hat and wings, a rather unsavory young angel arrives holding a well-used suitcase wishing you "Happy New Year." A pipe-smoking lad, wearing an oversized top hat and robe over red shorts, carries a man-sized walking stick. The polka dot bandana streaming from the pocket reinforces early twentieth century racial stereotypes.

Getting a telegram in 1910 or 1913 was, for most people, a rare and special event. Postcards could be inexpensive substitutes. The holly berries on both cards bespeak the holiday season. The message on the reverse of the clock card thanks the Howes of Cedar Rapids, Iowa, for, "… our lovely Christmas gifts." Clocks and clock faces are common devices used on New Year cards. Perhaps unique, our New Year boy is dressed as a Western Union (telegraph) messenger.

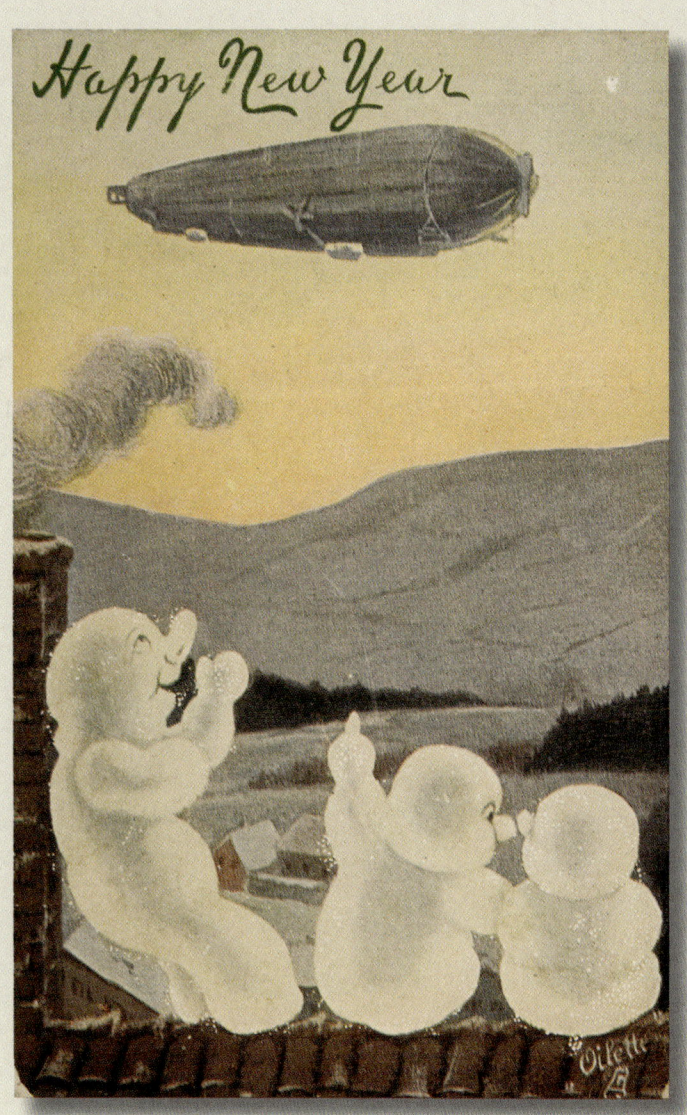

Dirigibles were the high tech air machines before the Wright brothers' flight. Anthropomorphic snow men, improbably seated next to a heated chimney on a rooftop, wave as a lighter than air craft floats over a snowy landscape. Two richly clad, impossibly perfect, children ride in (and, indeed, one steers) the vehicle's gondola. *Snowman, Collection of Dr. Russell Eaton*

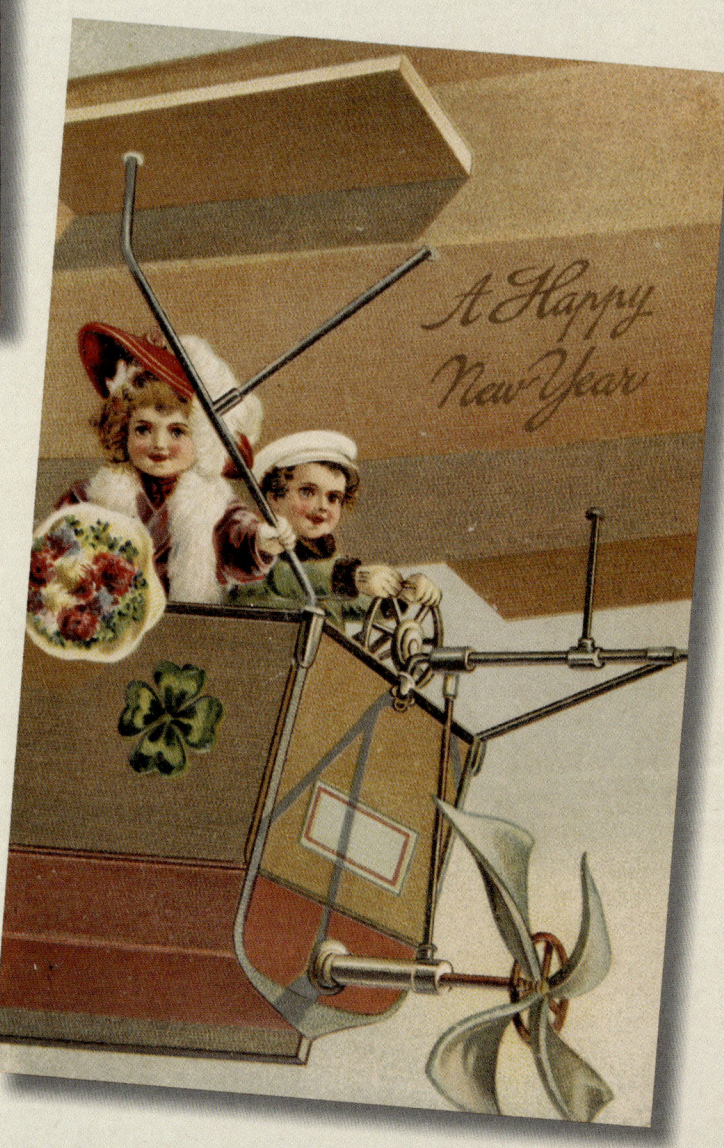

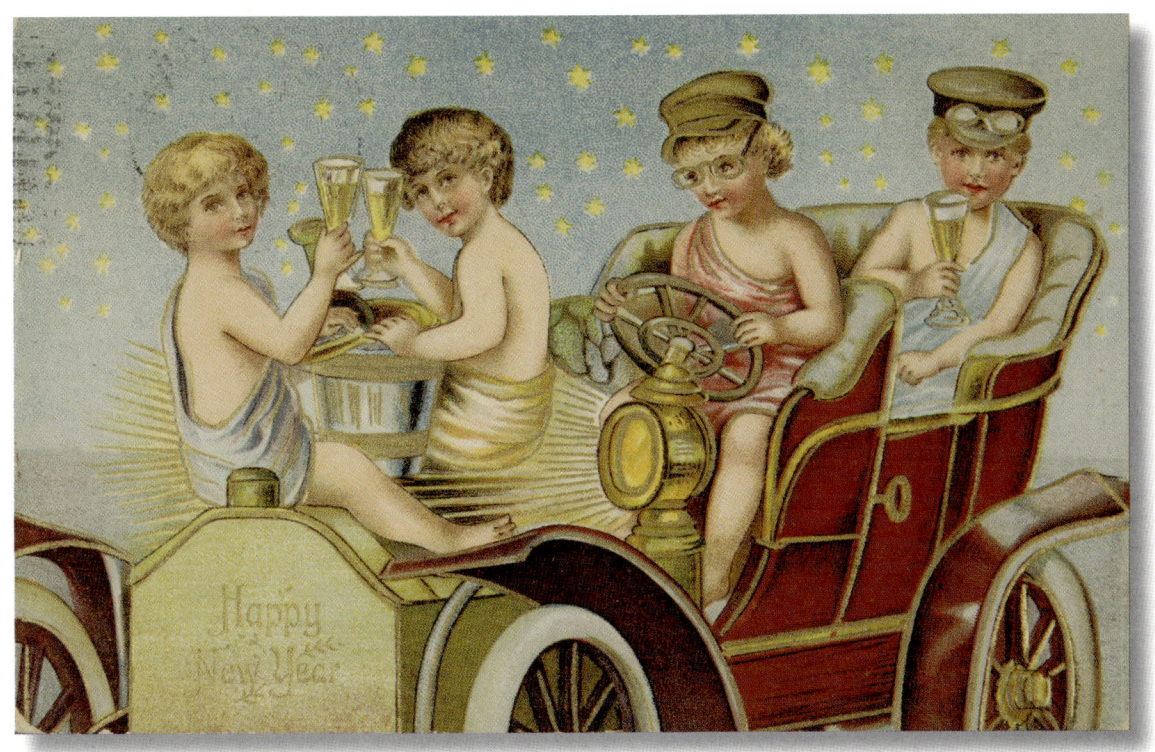

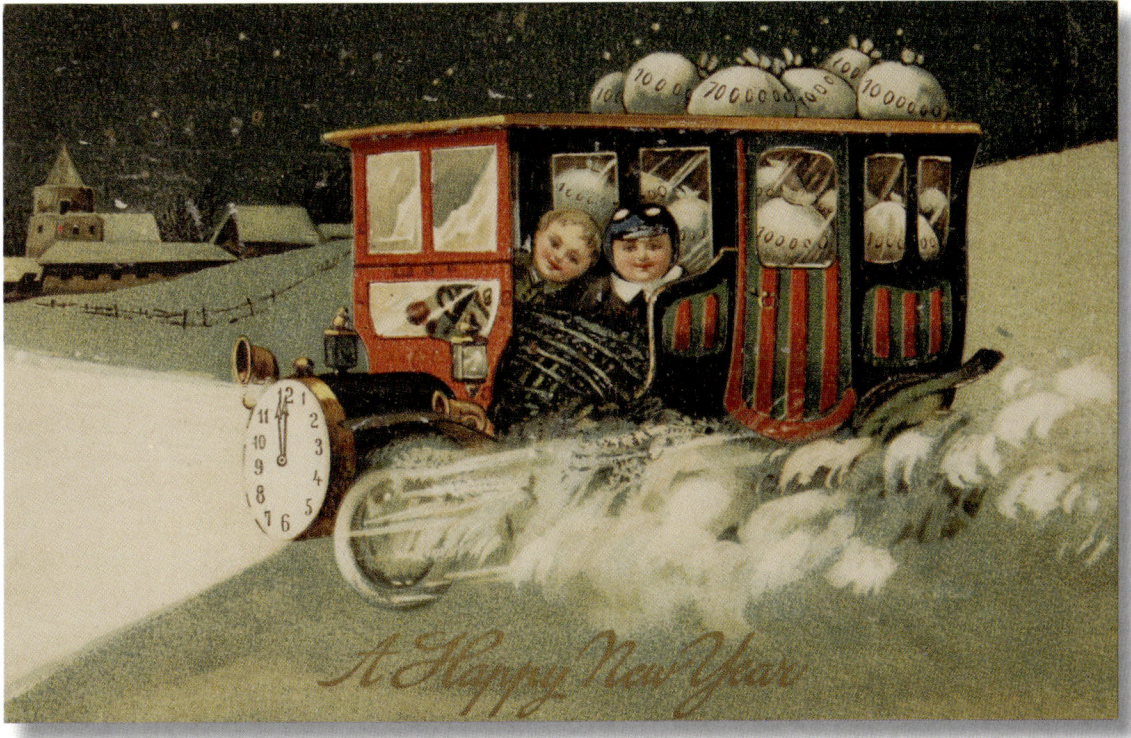

Automobiles were new, luxurious, and auto-related liquor regulations were non-existent in 1909 when the happy foursome drove in the New Year. Note the driver wearing goggles. His alternate has his goggles on his cap. In the age before windshield wipers, the driver and his friend look out the side door as they drive their clock-fronted station wagon loaded with cash – each bag is marked $70,000. The year of the card is 1907: a very prosperous New Year wish, indeed!

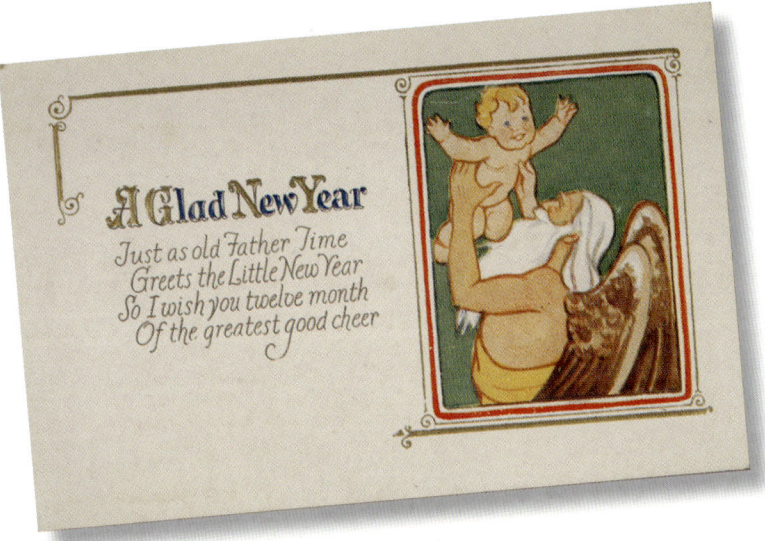

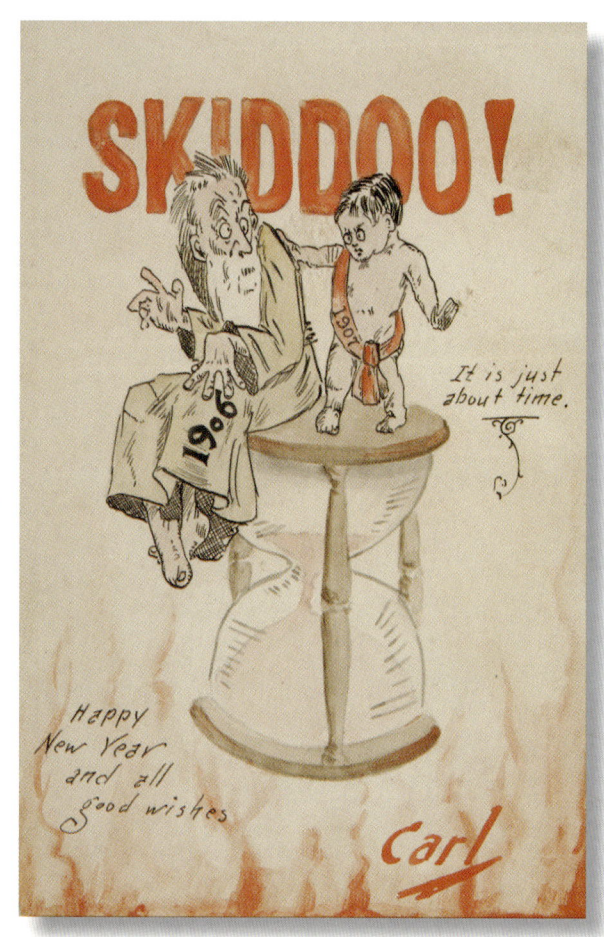

The relationship between the old year and the new, age and youth, is varied. A kindly, celestial "Old Father Time Greets the Little New Year" in a traditional way. More unorthodox is the nasty little 1907 pushing out a startled, weary 1906 as the sands of his time literally runs out. This is a unique hand-drawn and -painted card signed "Carl." Several of this artist's creations are in the Landis Valley Museum collections. They were all sent to Miss Gussie Palmer of "Lancaster, PA."

The image of the New Year and new life go hand-in-hand. Where does the stork find the babies he delivers? Why, in a pre-existence lily pond, where young boys, all clad in Teutonic helmets denoting different occupations, vie to be born. Will the stork choose to deliver "A Butcher, a Baker, or a Candlestick Maker? Interestingly, this card was printed in America. [Note the cattails, a native American plant.]

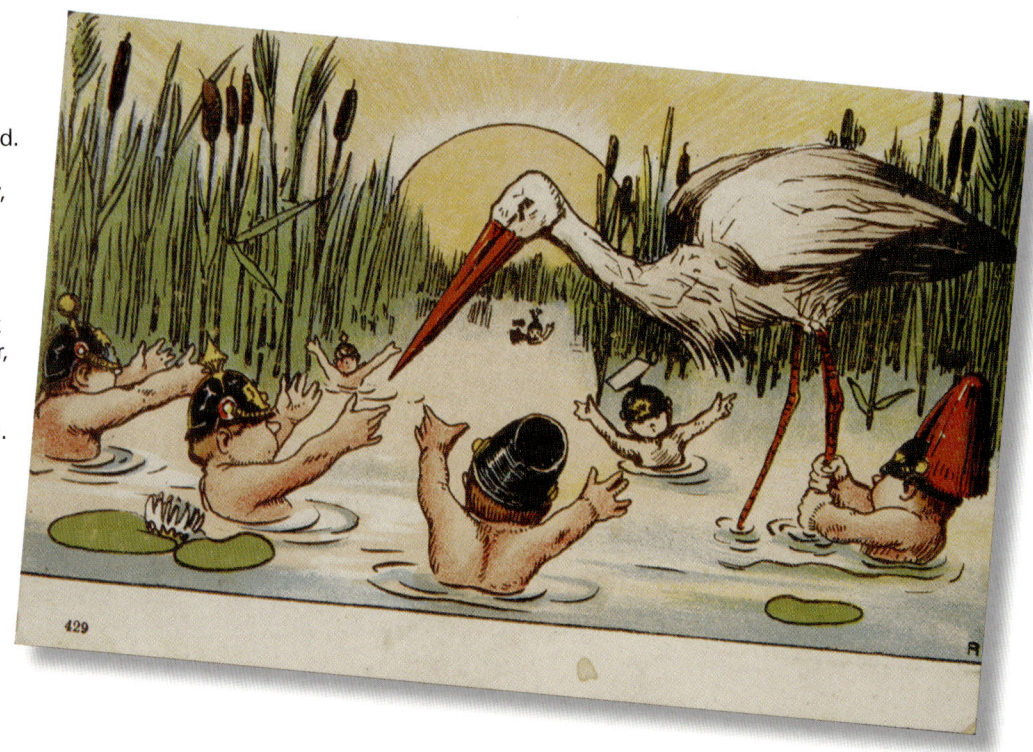

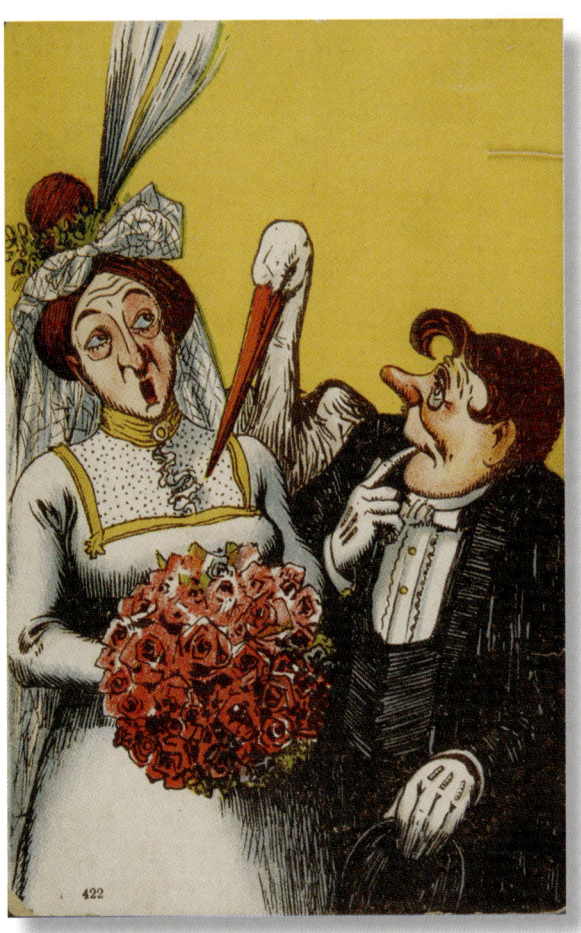

The stork's presence was not always welcome … certainly not at a wedding where the bride's bouquet is of red roses – not exactly the symbol of purity. The fashionable society matron, based on the art of Charles Dana Gibson's famed "Gibson Girl," snubs an unhappy stork with his unopened sack. Is there a whiff of birth control here?

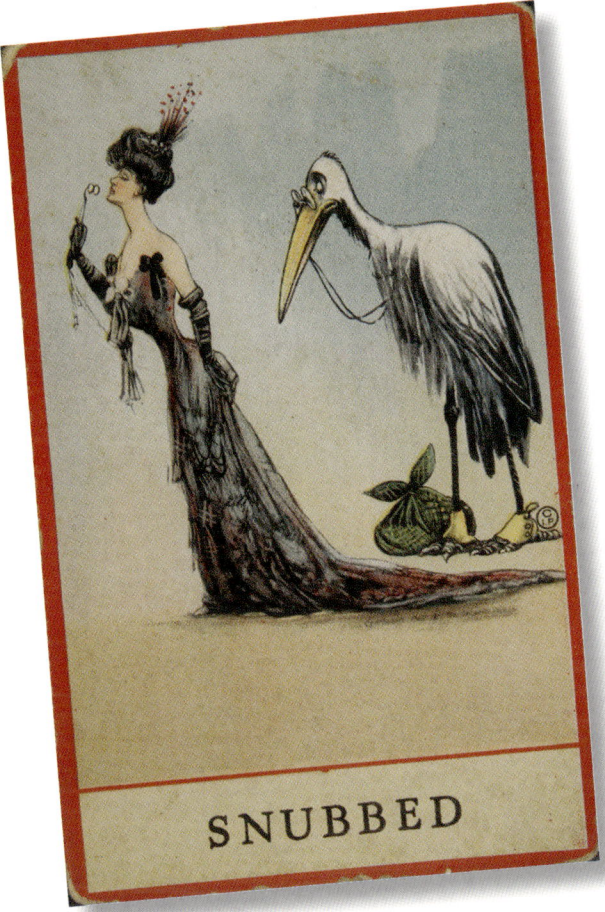

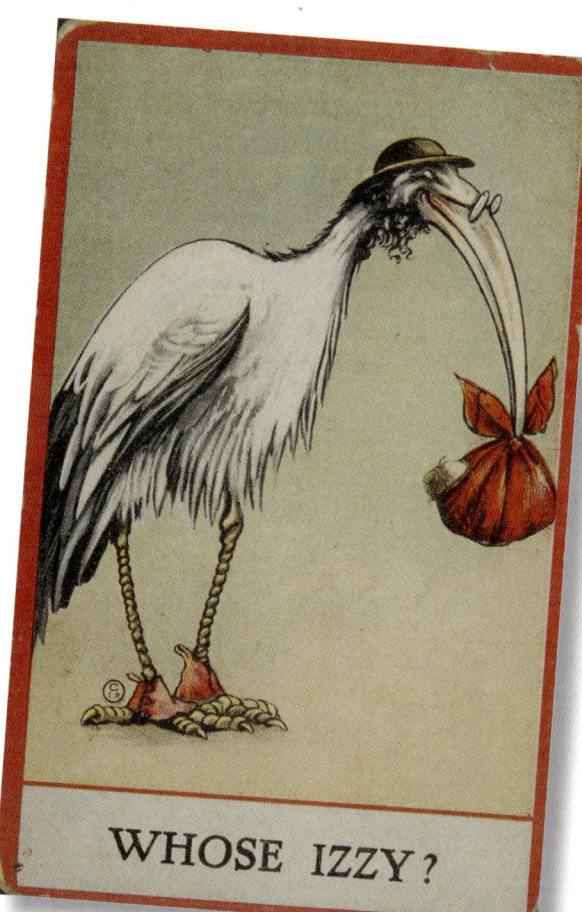

Ethnic stereotyping was often obvious on early 20th century cards. The stork's physiognomy has been given a decidedly Hebraic cast as he delivers his red swaddled bundle of joy. Observe his snazzy red spats. Only suspect men – gamblers, swindlers, or outsiders -- wore brightly colored spats.

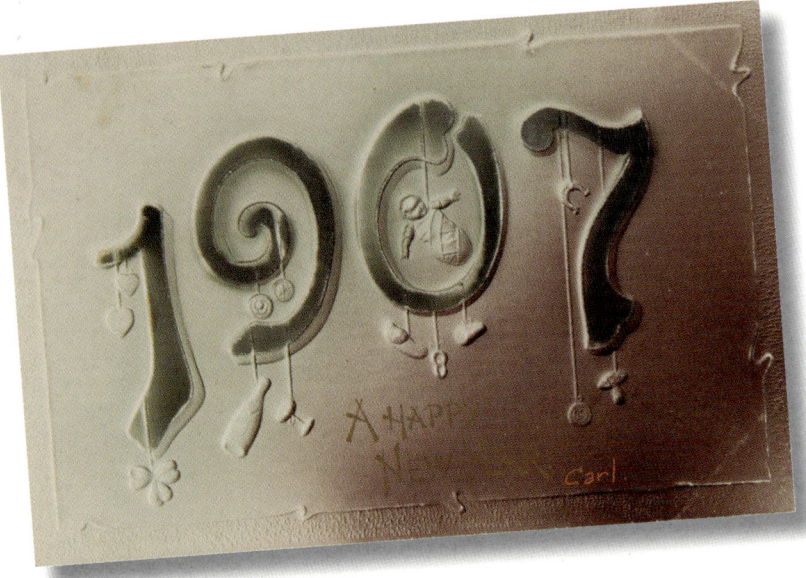

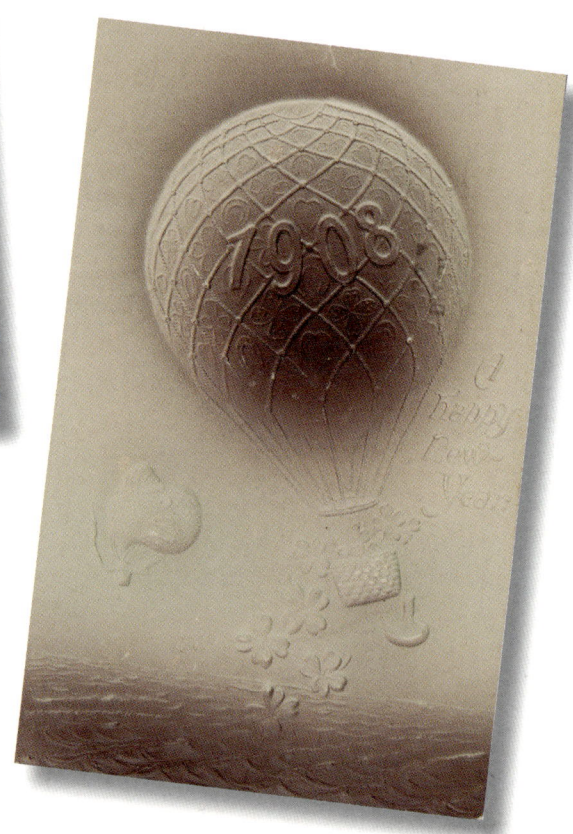

Sending subtly toned embossed cards was a popular way to announce the New Year. The 1907 card has the requisite baby suspended in the "O." 1908 is heralded with a hot air balloon scattering four-leaf clovers and a jettisoned champagne cork. A deflated 1907 balloon drifts toward earth.

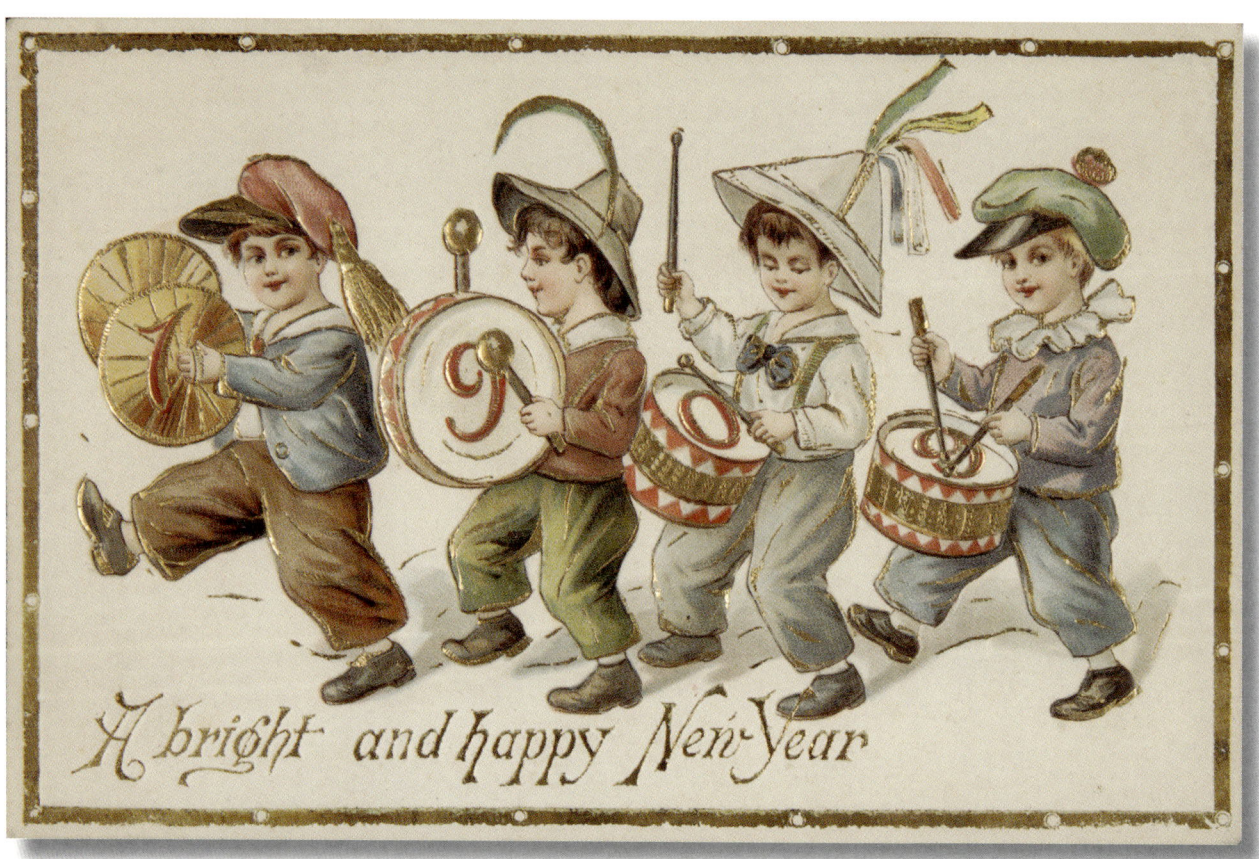

Looking like an innocent 1909 precursor to "The Village People," kids in fancy clothes and headgear joyously parade.

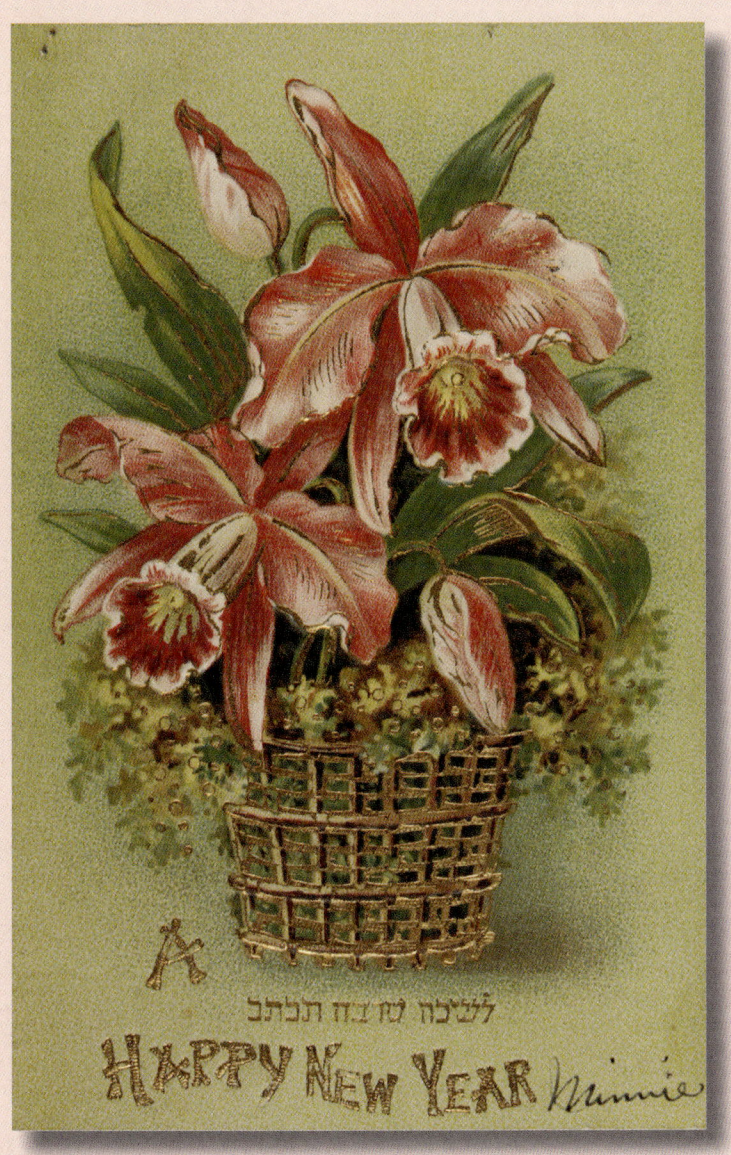

The large influx of Eastern European Jews into America in the late 19th and early 20th centuries was traumatic for both the transplants and the older stock. As the Jews Americanized, they started sending New Year cards in great abundance, but these were for the Jewish New Year (*Rosh Hashanah*) rather than the secular one celebrated by the general populace. According to the Hebrew calendar, this religious holiday is celebrated on the first and second days of the month *Tishrei*; this usually falls in September of the common calendar. Orchids were a symbol of prosperity also found on secular cards. The flower-embellished scroll is much more religiously specific.

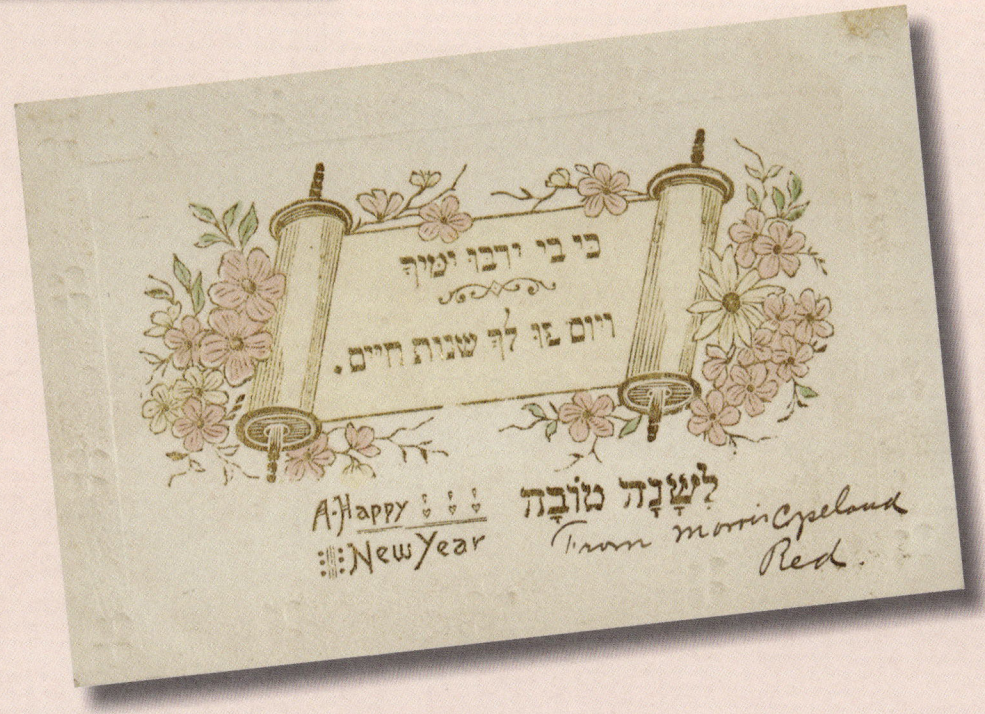

Every four years, New Year brought a special meaning because it heralded Leap Year, when women were given leave to turn the tables on established custom and ask men to marry them. Originally the freedom was only allowed on Leap Day, February 29, but the license was expanded over the whole year. Man did not have a chance. Climbing a tree was no escape! The image of the ideal man appears in milady's fireplace topped with feminine bric-a-brac, especially vases. The dreamed image of a future bride appears within a young swain's hearth. He is, however, romantically inclined. Note that his pipe rack is shaped like TWO hearts! The animals shown on the cards are curious. Usually men are shown owning dogs and women cats.

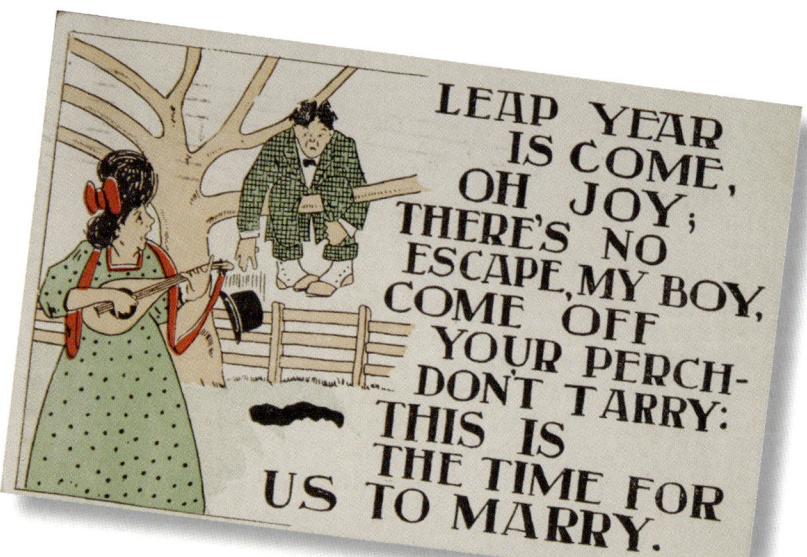

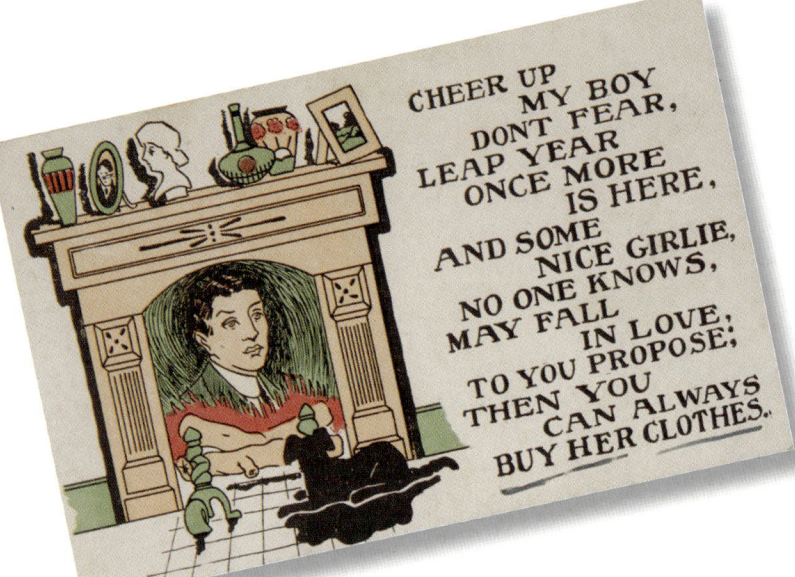

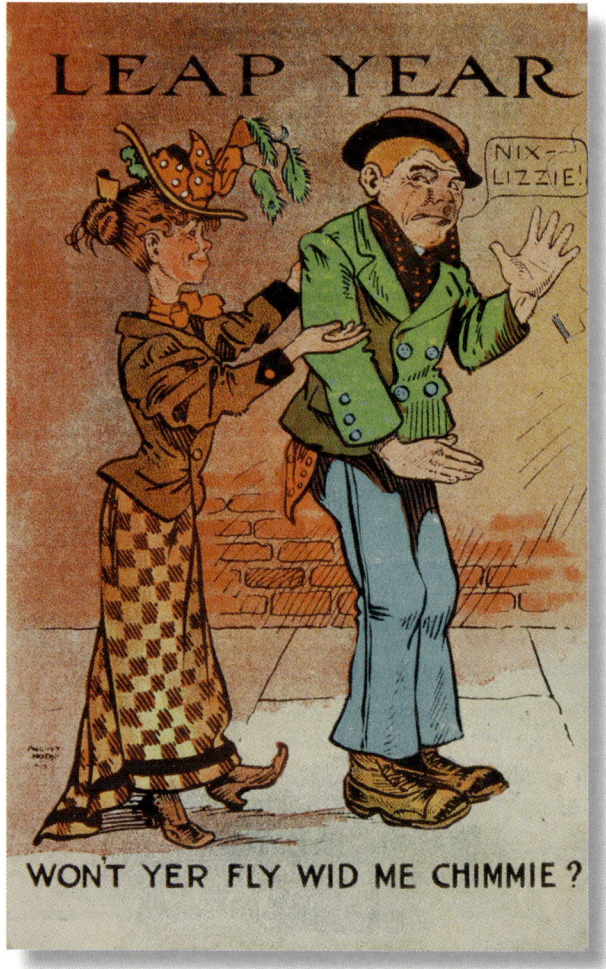

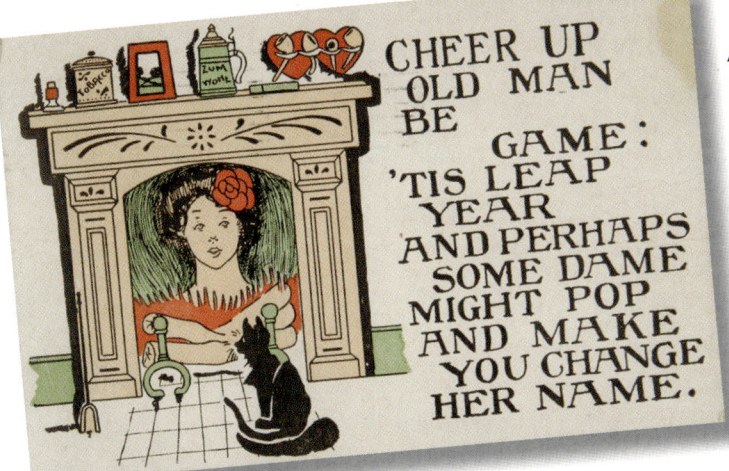

An Irish stereotypical male isn't at all interested in getting married. Perhaps the artist knew that this was true to the history of Leap Year, which can be traced back to the fifth century and involves St. Patrick and St. Bridget. Bridget complained that her nuns were unhappy that they had no chance at marriage. [Celibacy in religious orders was then based on private vows rather than church law.] St. Patrick eventually agreed that women be given the right to propose to men every four years. Bridget then immediately proposed to Patrick, who said, "No," but instead gave her the promise of a kiss and silk gown!

During Leap Year, women lay in wait behind every tree to snare an eligible single male. But not every man was judged to be suitable – even then there were rejects.

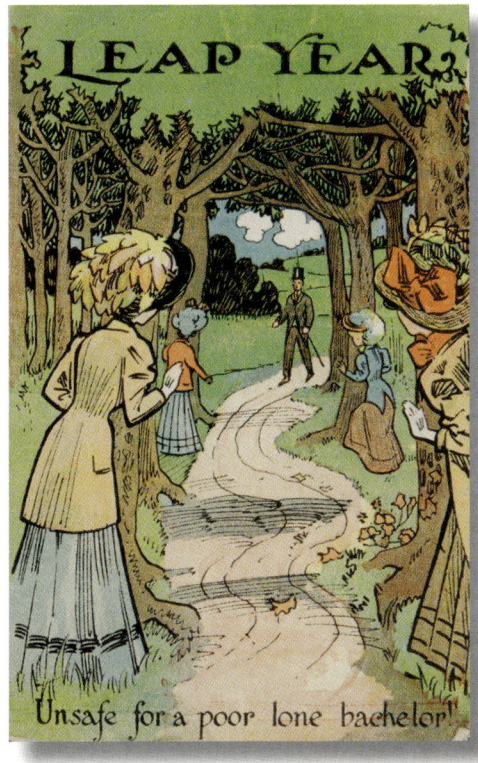

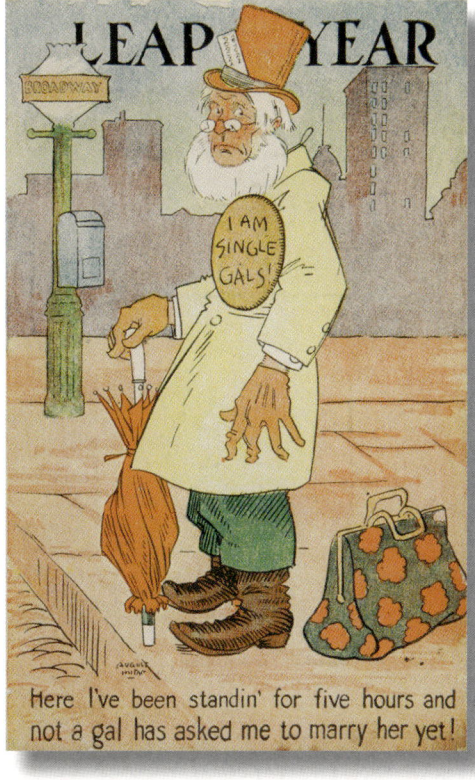

Should the opportunity be missed, there were "After Leap Year" cards like this one sent to lifelong bachelor, George Diller Landis, with the cryptic, "Compliments, Sincerely, Y.W.C." Those not inclined toward marriage could sigh with relief as the Leap Year tradition slowly died out in the early 20th century. However, a variant was reintroduced in the 1950s by cartoonist Al Capp for his comic strip "Li'l Abner." Named "Sadie Hawkins Day," it was observed each November 9 and featured a foot race in which all the eligible men of fictional "Dogpatch" ran from all the maiden ladies. If the man was caught he was quickly carried off to "Marry'n Sam," the local clergyman. This day, allowing for the reversal of traditional gender roles, became a mock popular holiday. Many towns featured "Sadie Hawkins Day Dances." The rise of feminism has banished the observance as archaic. Every year can be Leap Year or any day, Sadie Hawkins Day.

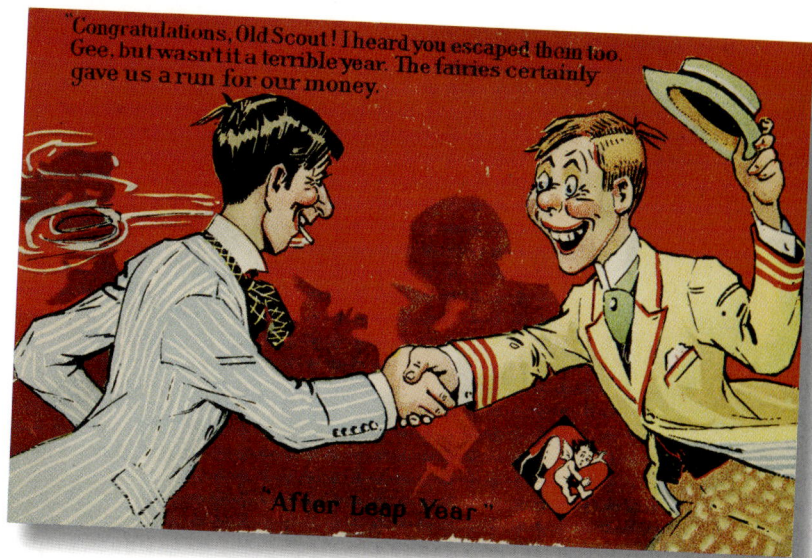

3
Valentine's Day

Hearts & Little Naked Kids

Mid-February arrives seven weeks after the Winter Solstice, a landmark in the progression from winter to spring, which is traditionally regarded as a time of the awakening of fertility. The Romans celebrated Lupercalia on February 15. This began as a fertility ritual but soon became a lovers' holiday, whereby Roman boys chose their celebratory partners by drawing names from a container, often an urn. During the festival the newly joined couples would exchange gifts. When the armies of Rome conquered what would become Britain and France, they brought Lupercalia with them and the transplant grew vigorously.

With the rise of Christianity, the Church consciously worked to put a Christian face on many pagan holidays. In 459 A.D. Pope Gelasius proclaimed February 14 as the Feast of St. Valentine to honor a young Roman who was martyred on February 14, 270 A.D., for his refusal to abandon his Christian beliefs. Among the miracles traditionally ascribed to the martyred saint was that he restored the sight of his jailer's blind daughter. They, of course, fell in love and on the morn of his execution he sent her a farewell note signed, "From your Valentine."

Lupercalia and the Feast of St. Valentine merged to create our secular, romantic Valentine's Day, encrusted with symbolic cupids, hearts, arrows and lovebirds. Even before the boxes of candy there were the Valentine cards, which appeared in America as handcraft, around 1740. Beginning in the 1880s the first commercial cards were introduced and were the harbinger of the postcard explosion.

As the modern age has come upon us, Valentine's Day has become a bit more edgy. One of the best reflections of this can be seen in a week of "Cathy" cartoons in which the insecure, then single, heroine lamented:

> I bought sultry lingerie but I'm too embarrassed to wear it. I bought a suggestive card, but I'm too embarrassed to send it… I bought a provocative gift, but I'm too embarrassed to give it. I thought of renting a sexy move, but I'm too embarrassed to go pick one out and even if I did, I'd be too embarrassed to admit I had it. I'm beginning to understand why red is the color of Valentine's Day.

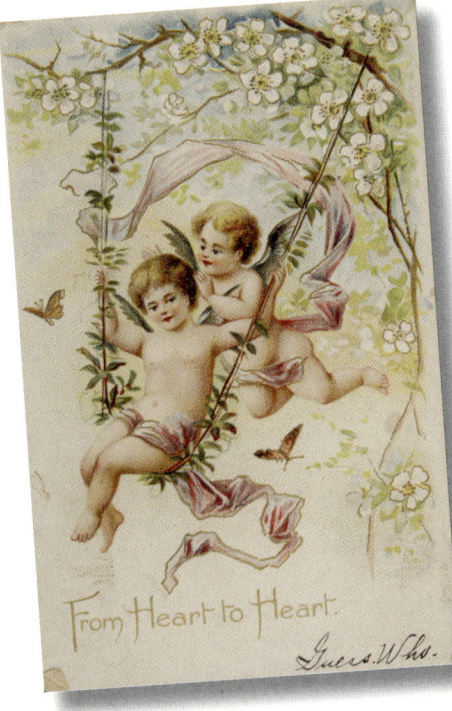

Hanging from an impossibly frail flowering branch, a leafy swing provides a perch for a curiously sensuous cherub with the presumed body of a child, but the face of an adult – and the very decided suggestion of breasts to come. It was sent to "Miss Carrie Lynch of Bausmans Penna." by "Guess Who in 1907."

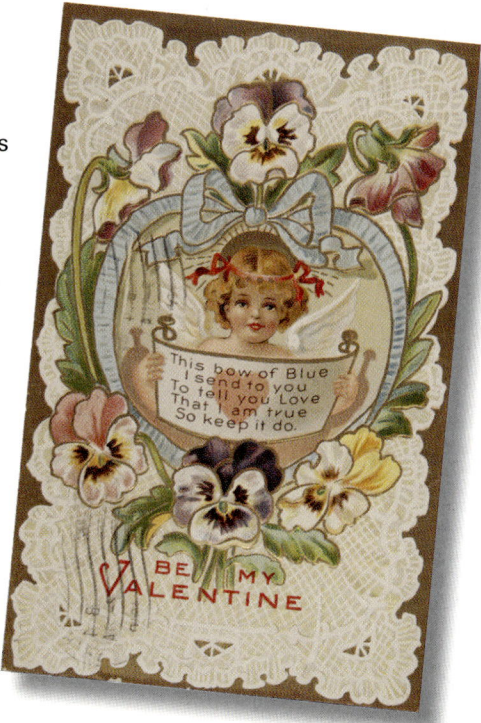

The absolutely safe card for a husband to send to his wife is a pledge of eternal fidelity delivered by Cupid, himself, surrounded by a bouquet of pansies. Once flower-giving became commercialized the Valentine's day flower, *par excellence*, became the red rose.

18

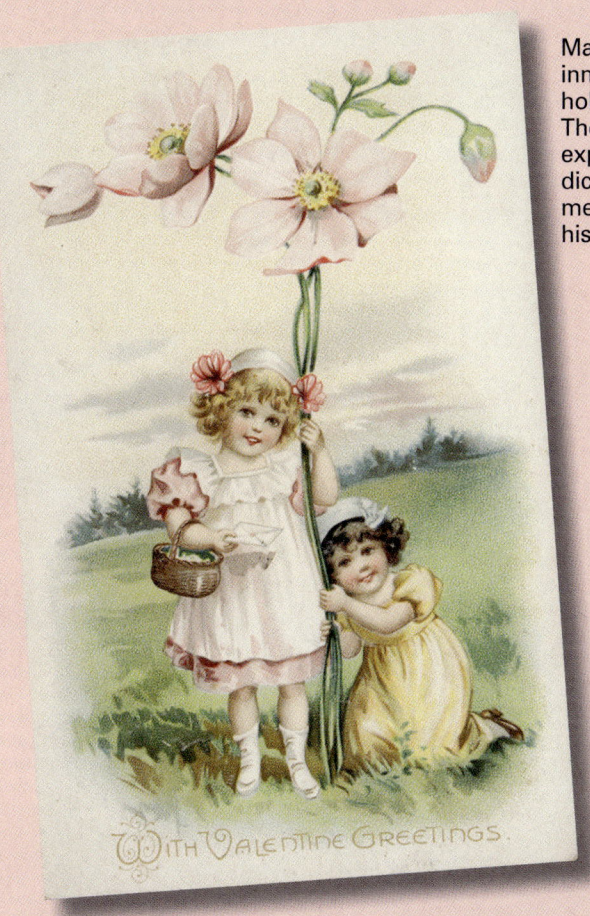

Many Valentine greetings combine a message of youthful innocence with flower iconography. Two cherubic little maids hold giant stems of an unlikely flower, the autumn anemone. The sweet card was sent, "To Lizzie from Sister Rachel." More expected is the daisy which, of course, is endowed with predictive qualities. Pluck petals reciting alternately, "She loves me", and "She loves me not." Cupid has stacked the deck with his daisy. The remaining petals read, "You Are My Best Love."

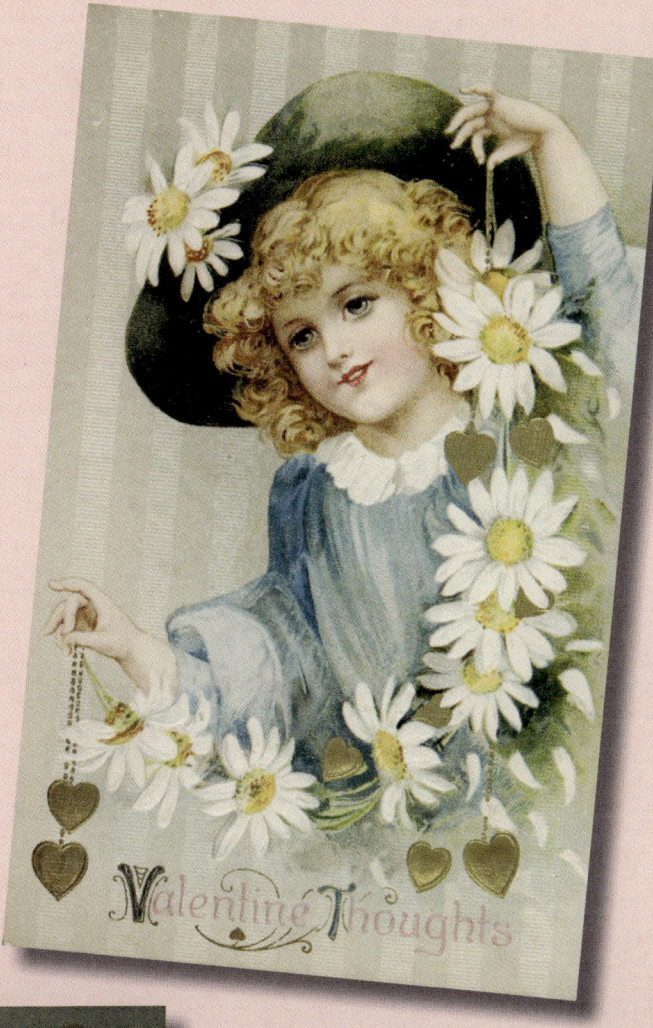

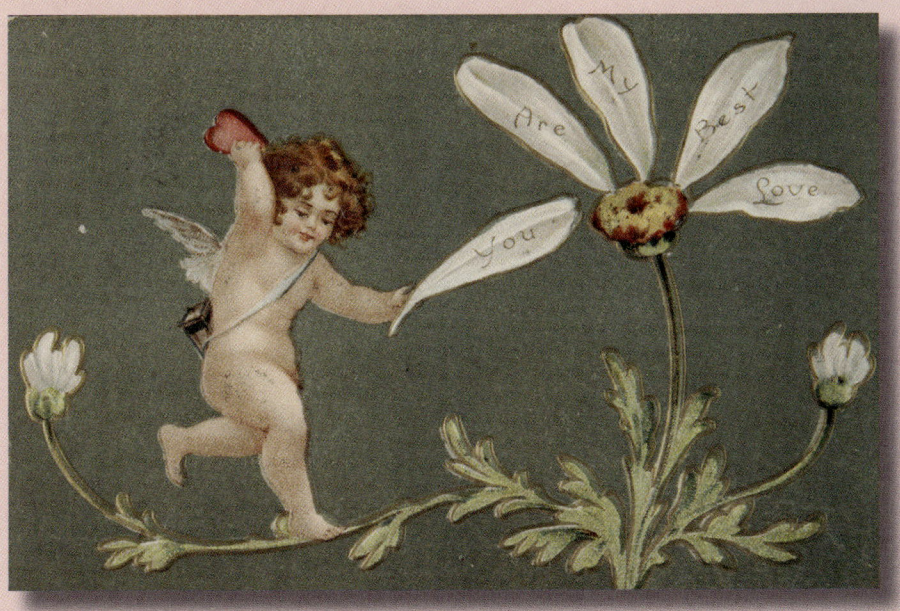

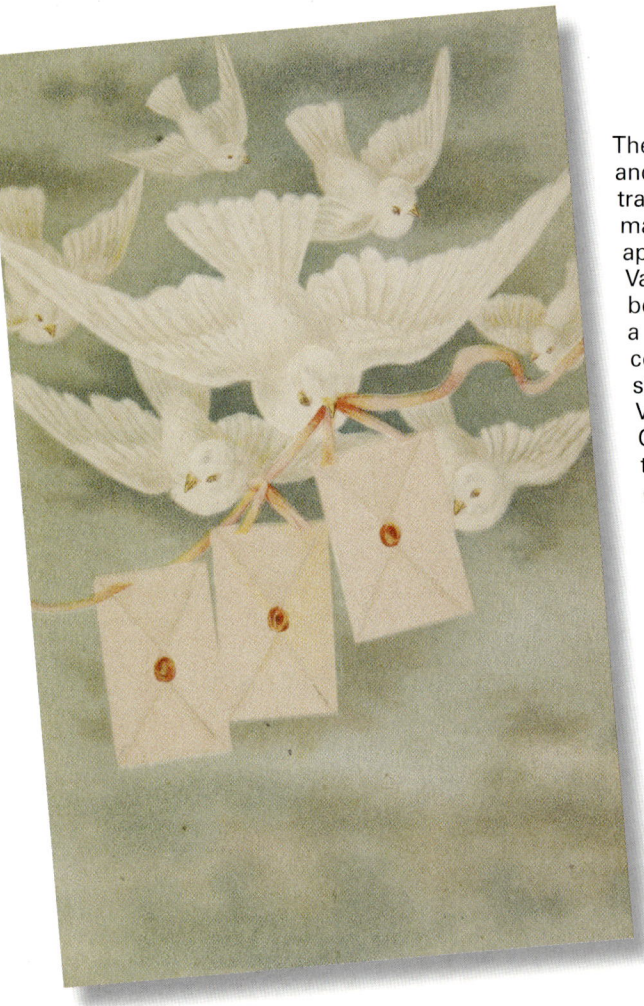

The dove was sacred to Venus, the goddess of love, and to other romantic deities. This, combined with a traditional medieval belief that the birds chose their mates on February 14, made these creatures, also appreciated for their "billing and cooing," popular Valentine symbols. A flock of doves carry three beribboned Valentine messages, as depicted on a card delivered in Cincinnati, Ohio. An angelic color-coordinated young lady spinning flax while sitting in a field of forget-me-nots received her Valentine message from a single descending dove. One wonders if J. K. Rowling was influenced by this avian imagery when she replaced doves with owls as mail deliverers in her writings centering on Harry Potter.

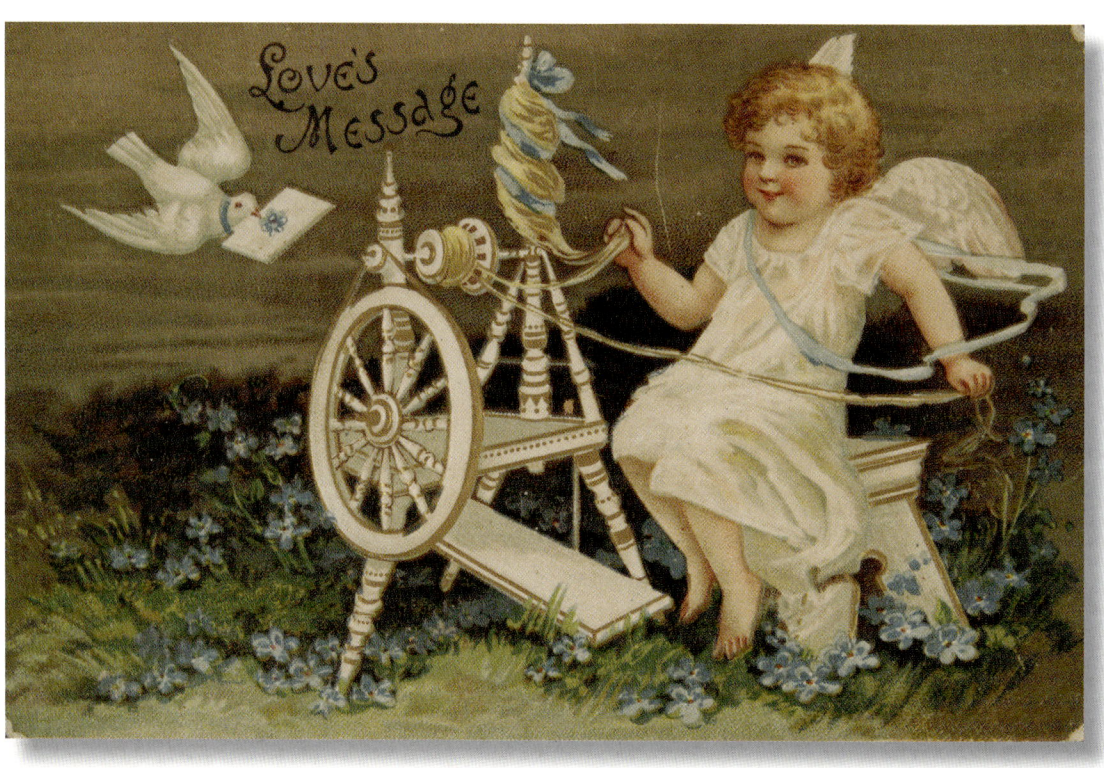

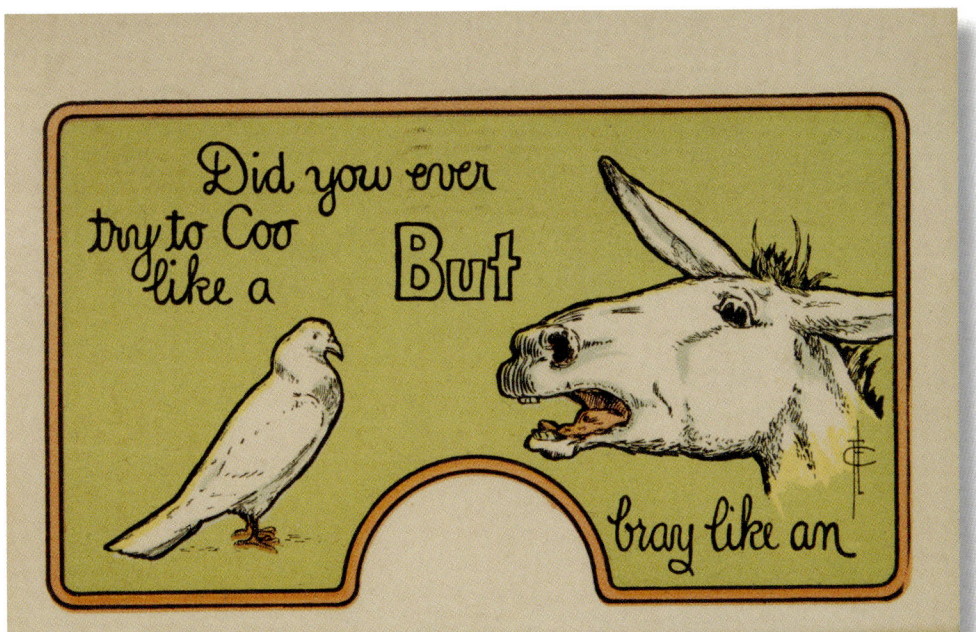

Sometimes romance goes awry in the voice of an inept would-be lover who would want to coo like a dove but rather brays like a jackass.

No one would consider an anatomically correct heart to be romantic and, had this butcher boy presented one to the young miss she would probably have recoiled in horror. As early as the 12th century, the heart was believed to be the center of love and affection, but that certainly wasn't today's conventional heart shape -- symmetrical and tapering to a sharp point. Speculation holds that our cardiac image is representative of the human buttocks or of the primitive Venus/Earth Goddess figure of a female torso with large breasts and a narrow waist.

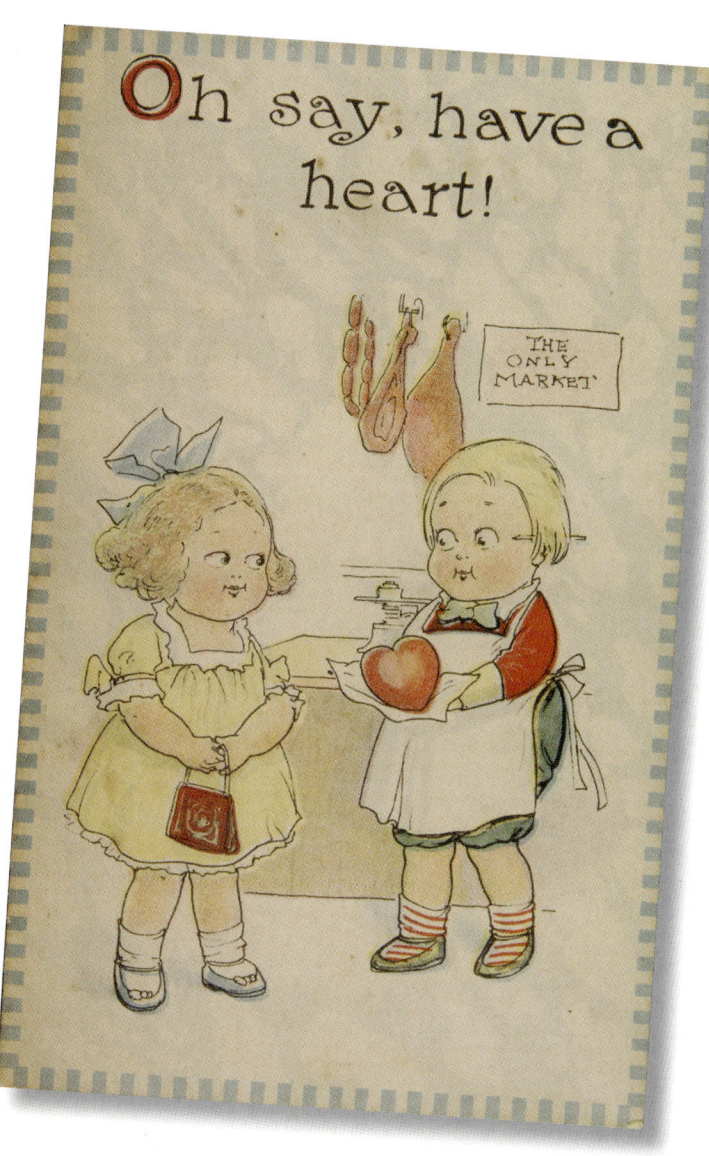

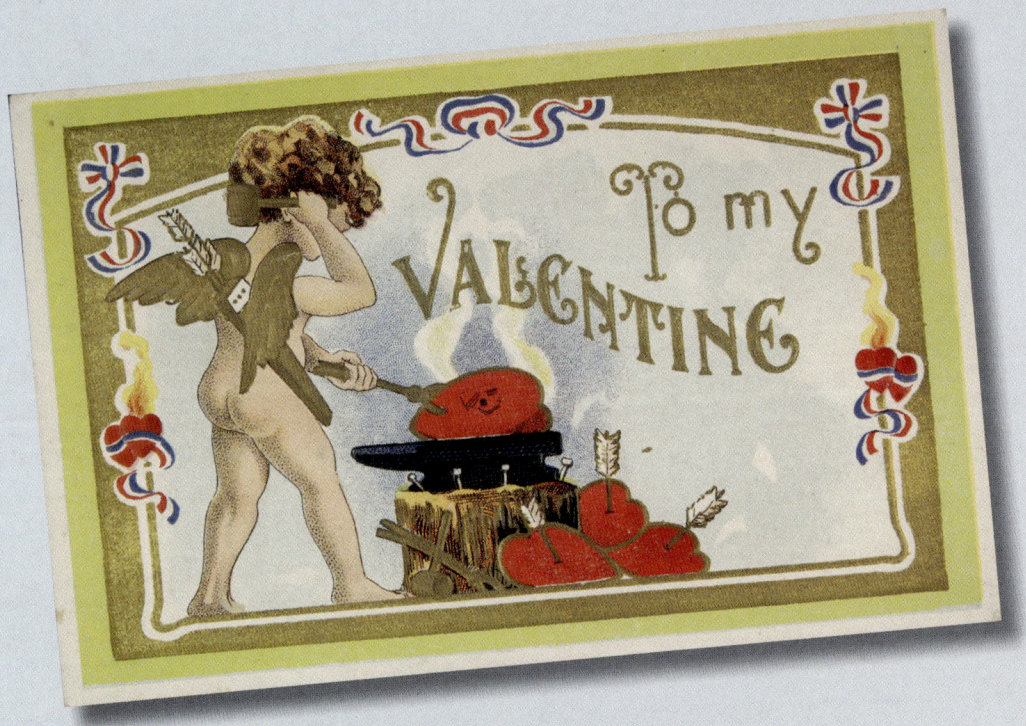

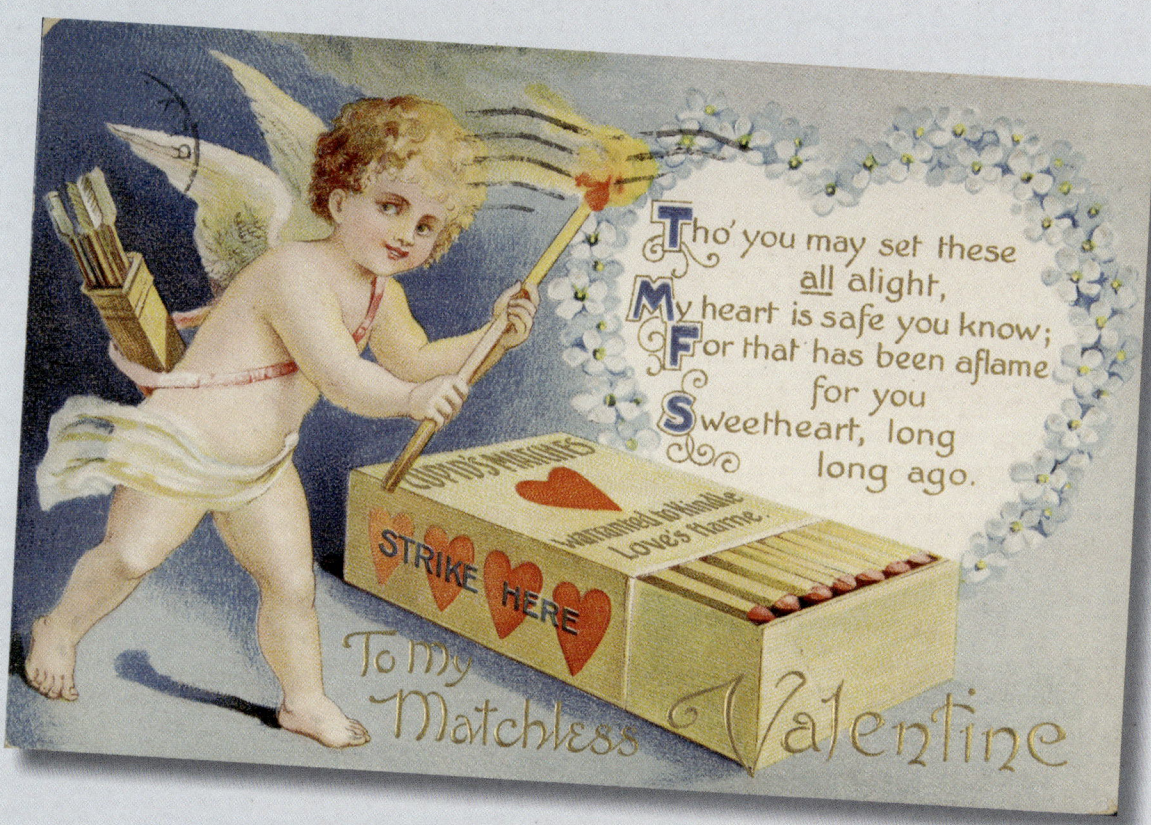

Cupid, the Roman God of Love, is one of the most important symbols of Valentine's Day, but his image has changed greatly over time. In classic and neoclassic art Cupid is depicted as a handsome young man who, befitting a God of Love, has a sexual identity. The myth of the love of Cupid and Psyche has provided many artists with classical erotic subjects, most notably French artist Jacques David (1745-1825), whose "Cupid and Psyche" was widely known and admired throughout the 19th century. The classic Cupid was too dangerous for middleclass Victorian taste, and he was transformed into a prepubescent and, occasionally a pudgy or androgynous, child. In these cards. As we first formally meet Cupid; he is in the guise of his brother god Vulcan at the forge, but instead of weapons, he is forging a heart. Next we see him as Bacchus, the god of wine and revelry, goblet in hand, improbably surrounded by a shower of four-leaf clovers and hearts. A more domesticated Cupid is using sealing wax to affix hearts inscribed with "Amor" to a letter. The most modern of the Cupids has arrows at his disposal, but he chooses to use a contemporary invention, the safety match, to light a passion as depicted on a card mailed in 1911.

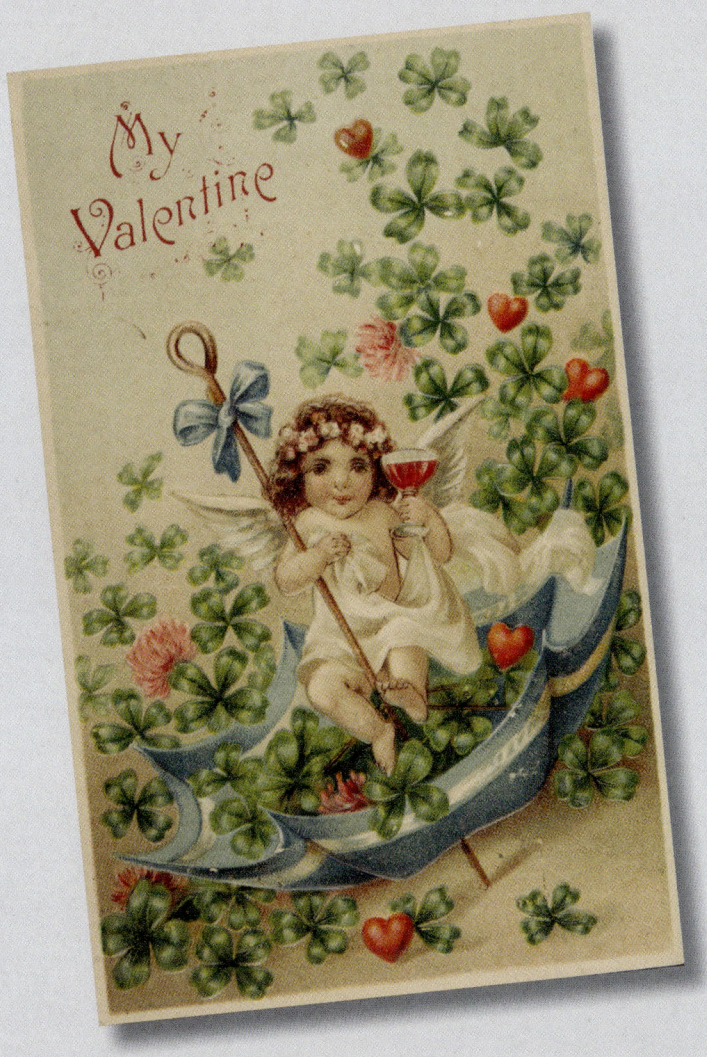
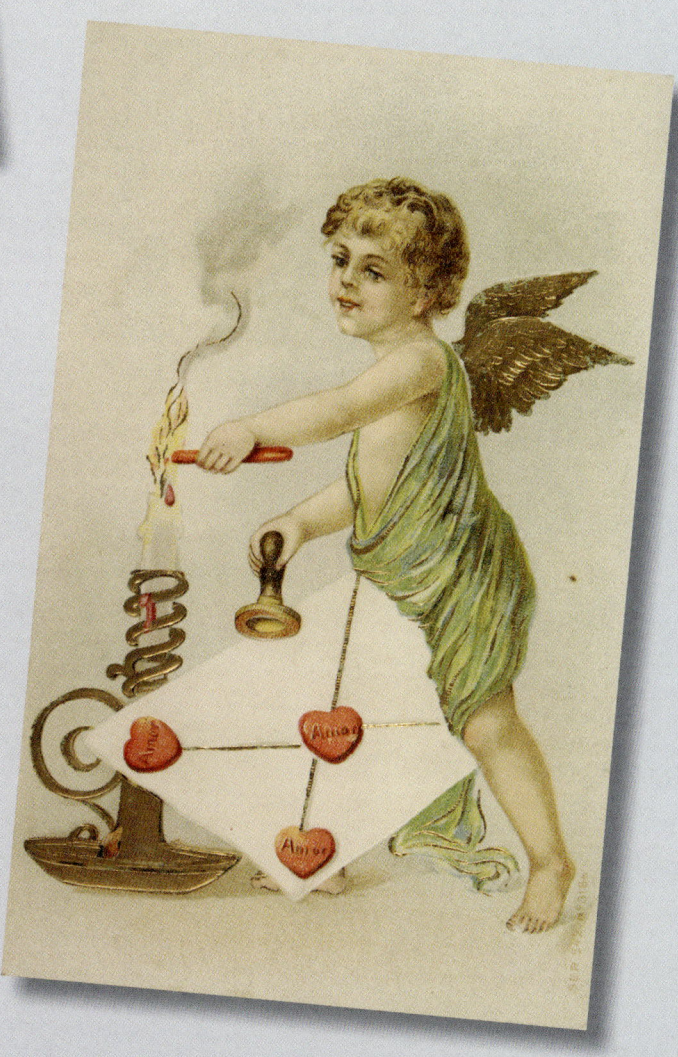

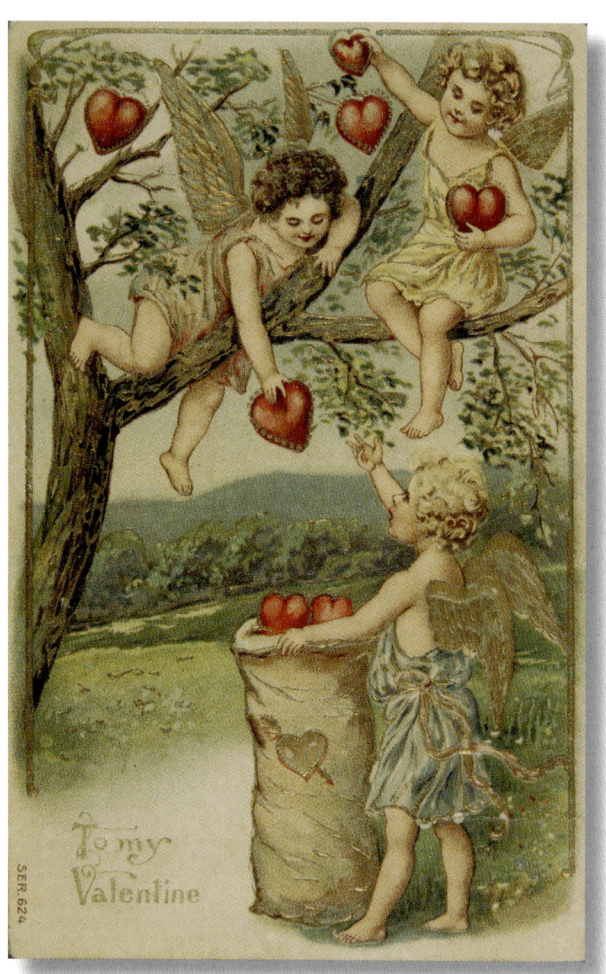

The heart iconography is multifaceted. Sometimes only a single heart is shown: a symbol of devotion. Multiple hearts are more common. Their meanings can be obtuse. Hearts grow on trees. Does the man or woman who gathers or receives the biggest bag win at love? Hearts, like crabs, can easily be netted in shallow waters. How many are enough? Or you can go heart shopping? Madame, using a lorgnette, the eyewear of choice for upper class ladies, inspects hearts spread out on a peddler's table. A servant carries her previously wrapped purchases, presumed to be hearts, under both arms and in a basket. The rich can be choosy, but they are also greedy.

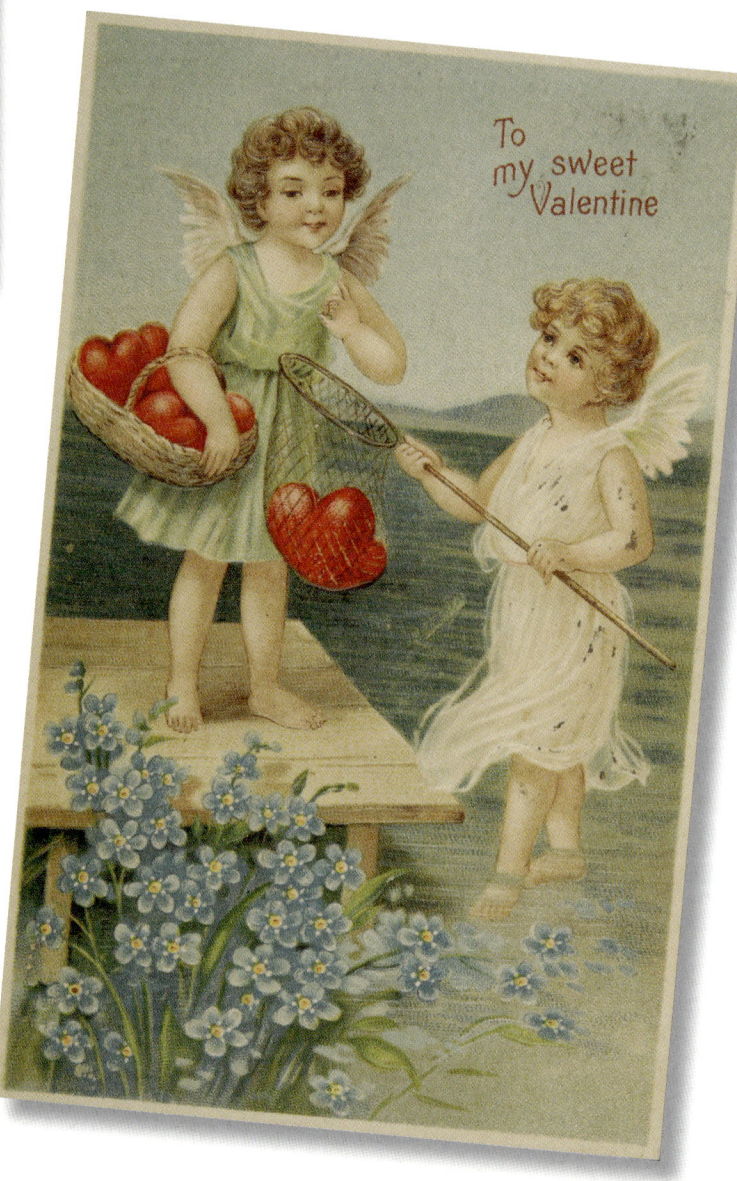

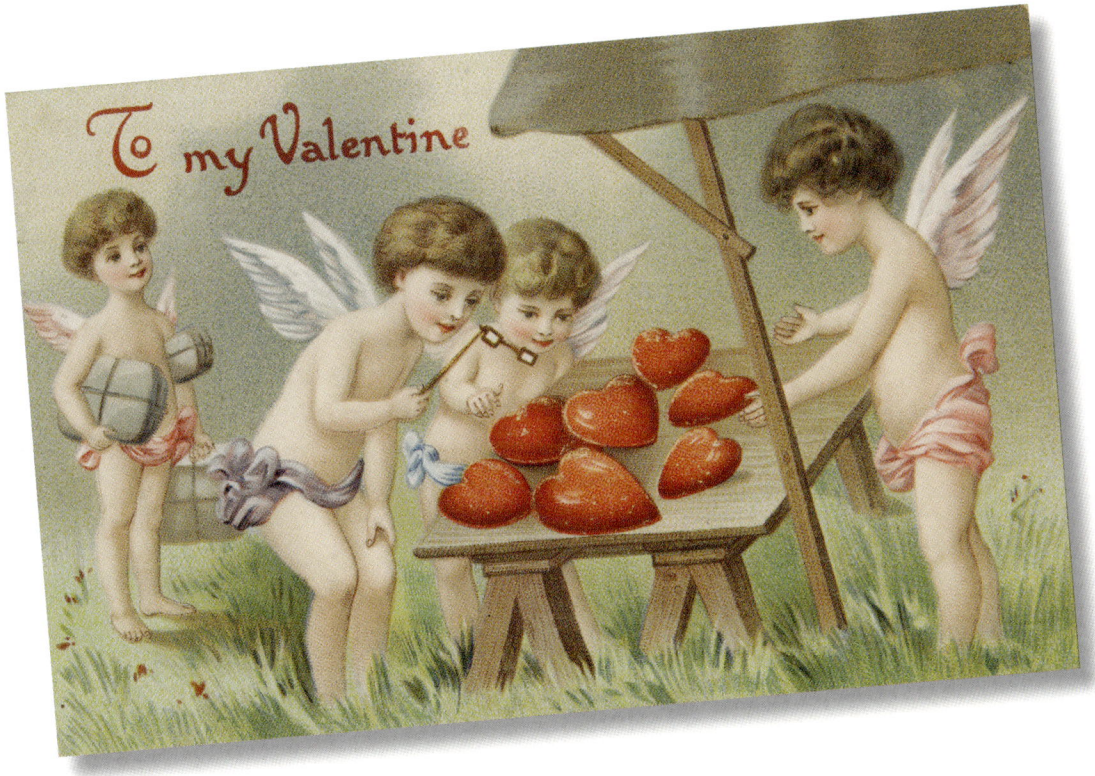

Is love a game of tennis? Is the "Message of True Love" that your heart may be in play with a racket?

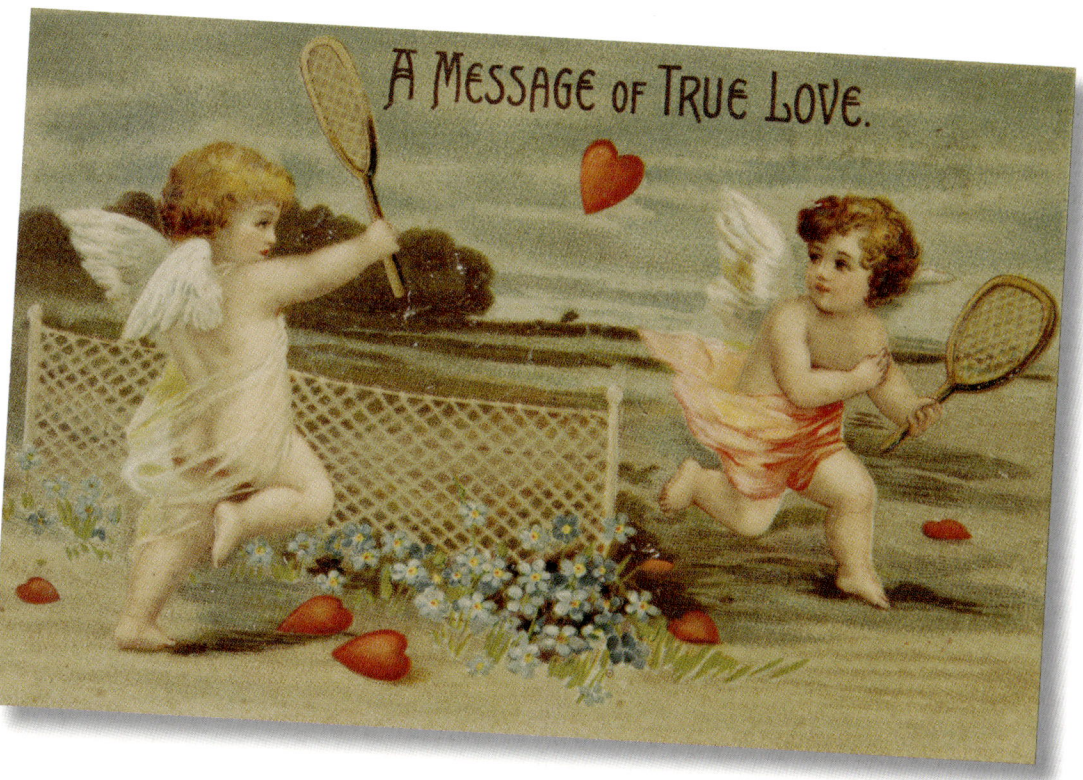

25

Hearts are easily broken and mended, sometimes simultaneously. But, as the legend on the card with the large taped heart reads, "Don't despair as yet broken heart Cupid in patching it will make a new start." For the do-it-yourselfer there is always a pot of glue and role of tape.

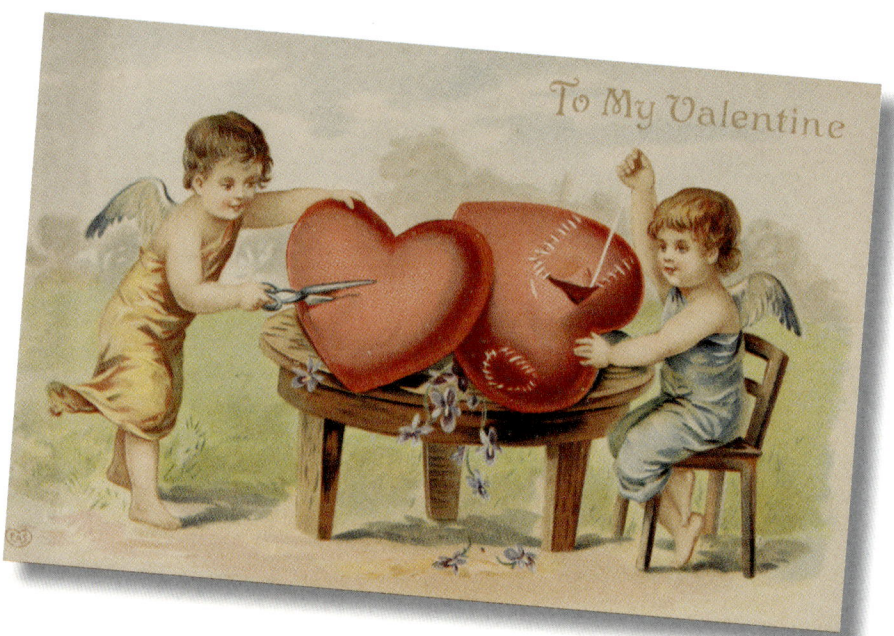

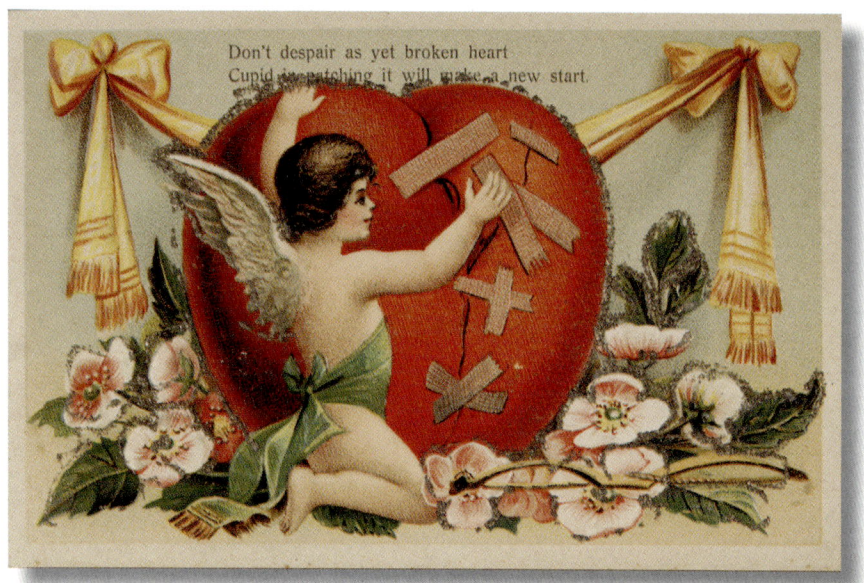

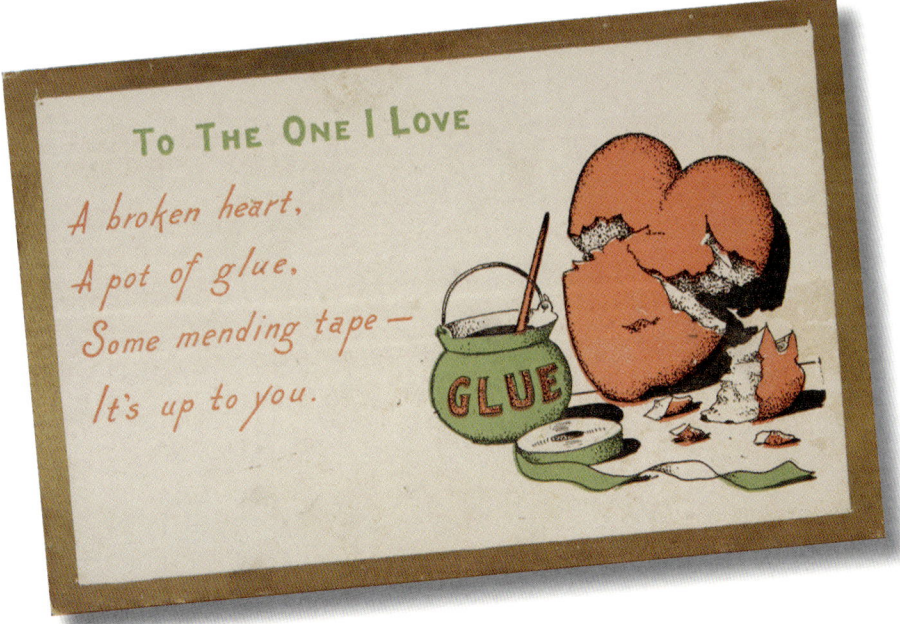

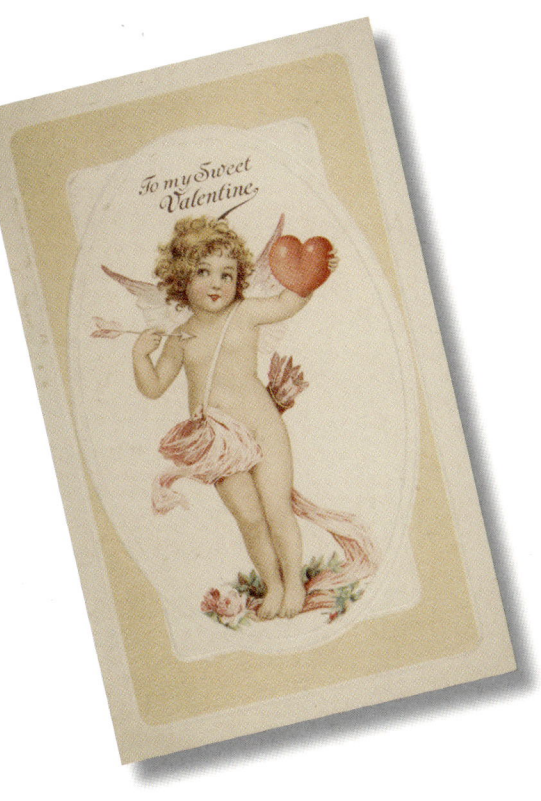
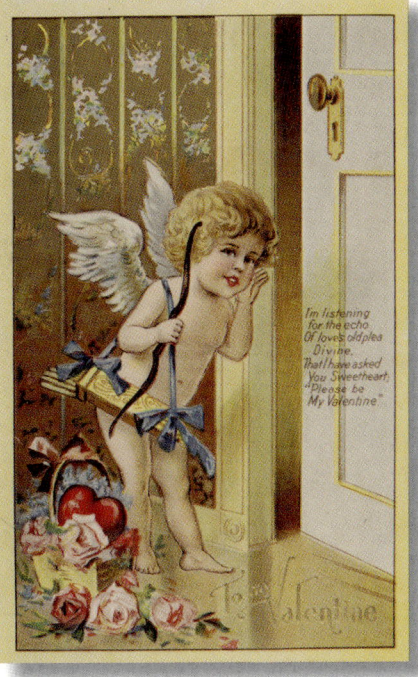
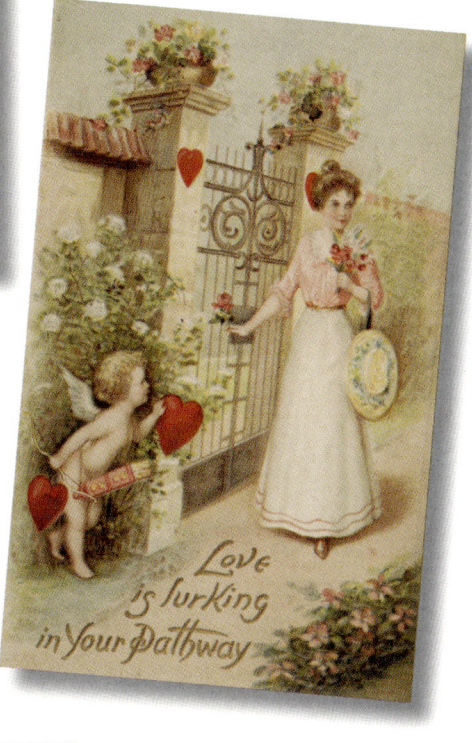
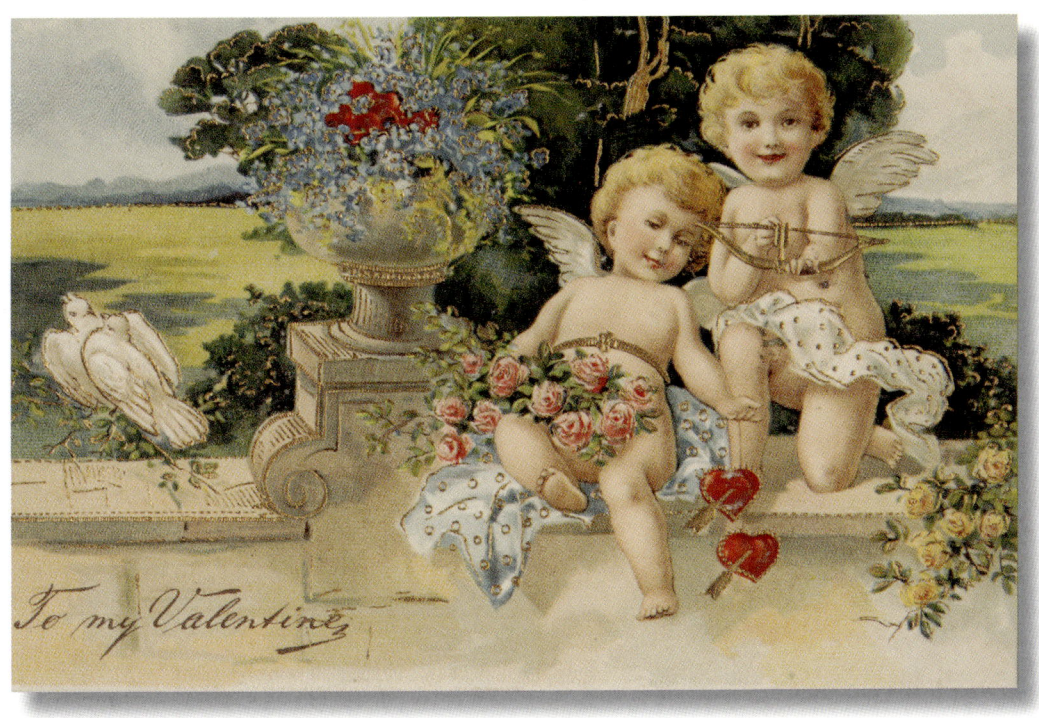

As a Greco-Roman god, Cupid had some disagreeable habits, including whetting his arrows with the blood of innocent babies. But the Victorians helped clean up his act. The Romans believed his arrows to be invisible – and his victims, both gods and mortals, literally didn't know what hit them when they suddenly fell in love. It's hard to imagine any of these androgynous entities as being symbols of passionate or tender love. Playful, perhaps.

The heart pierced by an arrow symbolizes vulnerability as well as love. Sending a Valentine is taking a risk – your love might be rejected. Some go to extraordinary trouble to keep their hearts intact.

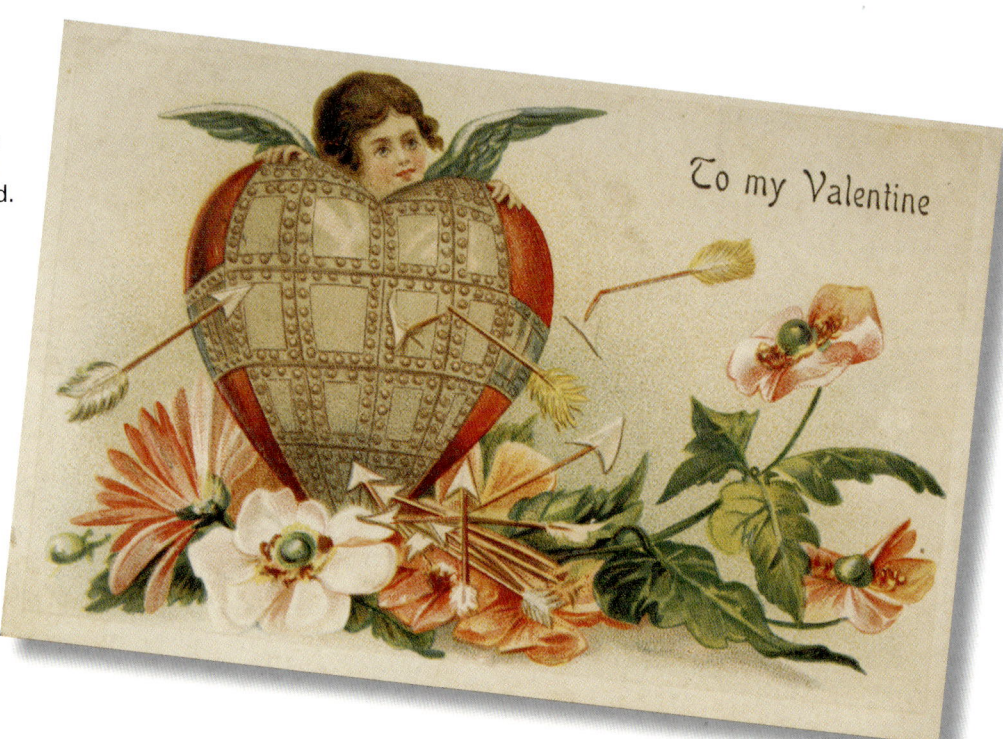

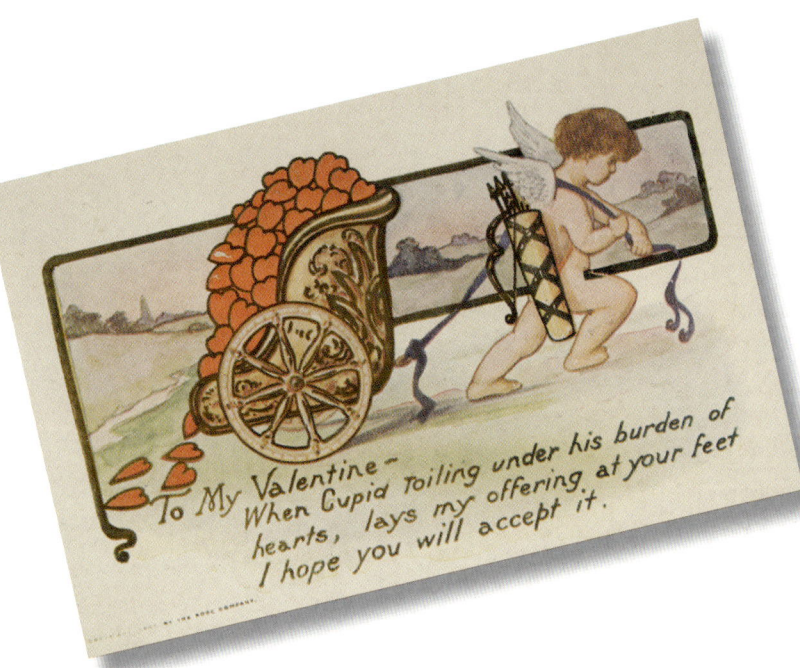

Cupid as delivery man: Santa-like he dutifully pulls a chariot filled with "a burden of hearts." Wearing nifty green shorts, he delivers a single heart while tobogganing downhill.

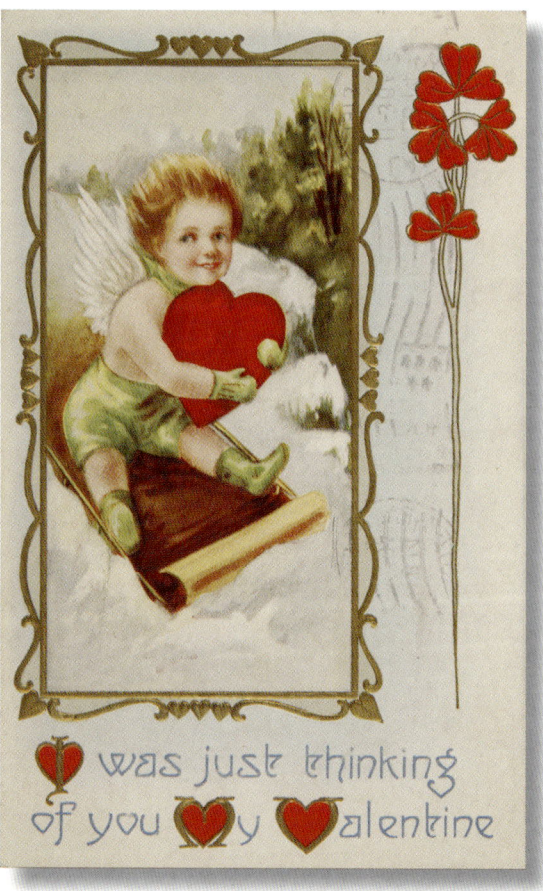

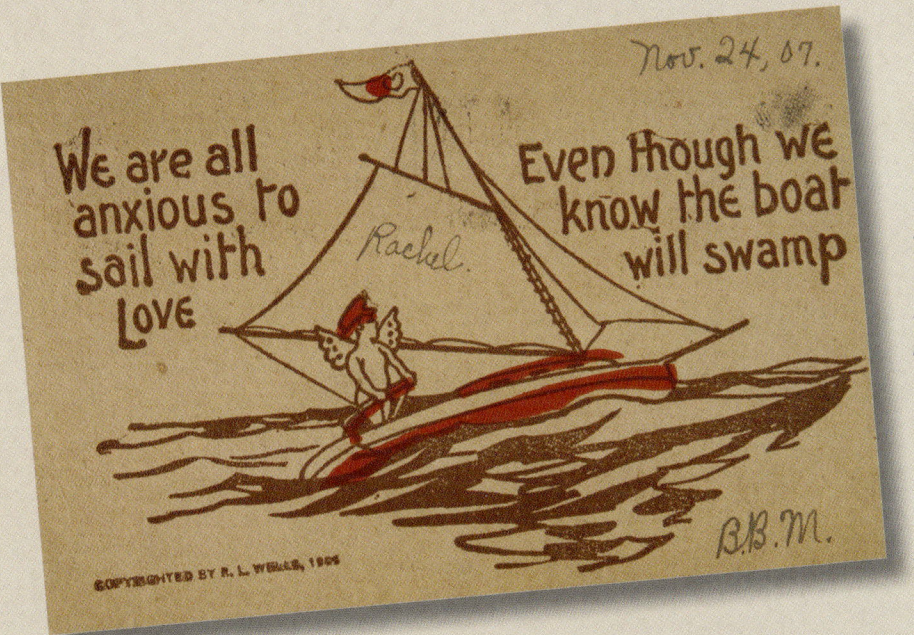

Love takes to water, be it in a sailboat with Cupid at the helm or in varieties of steam-driven vessels. An improbable vessel laden with giant-sized violets and encrusted with four-leaf clovers, sails on calm water. A red rose-decorated, proudly American "Love Boat" sails the sea of amour complete with floating roses. *Love: collection Dr. Russell Eaton.*

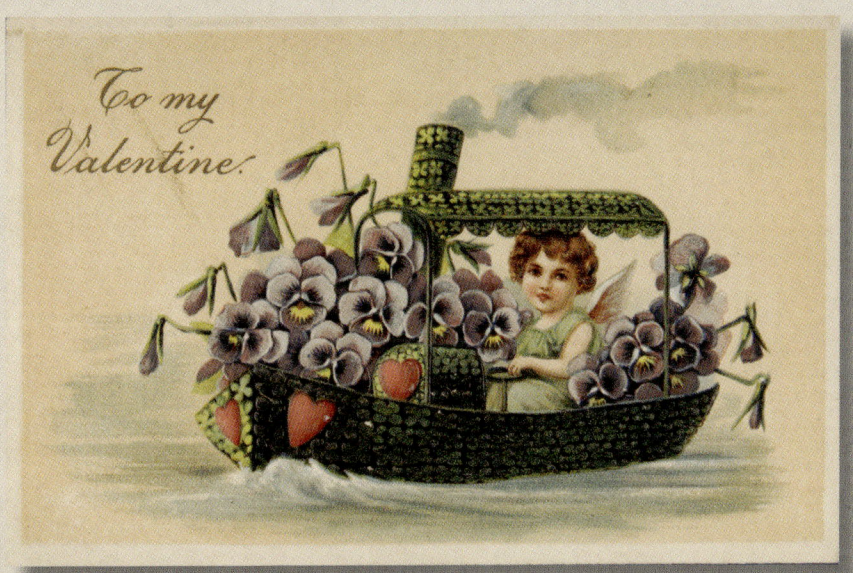

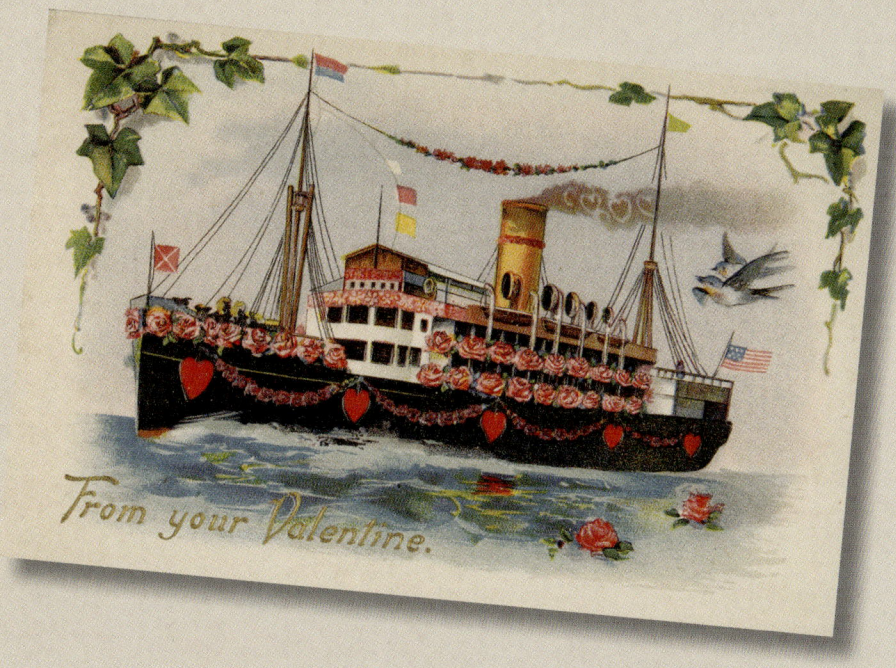

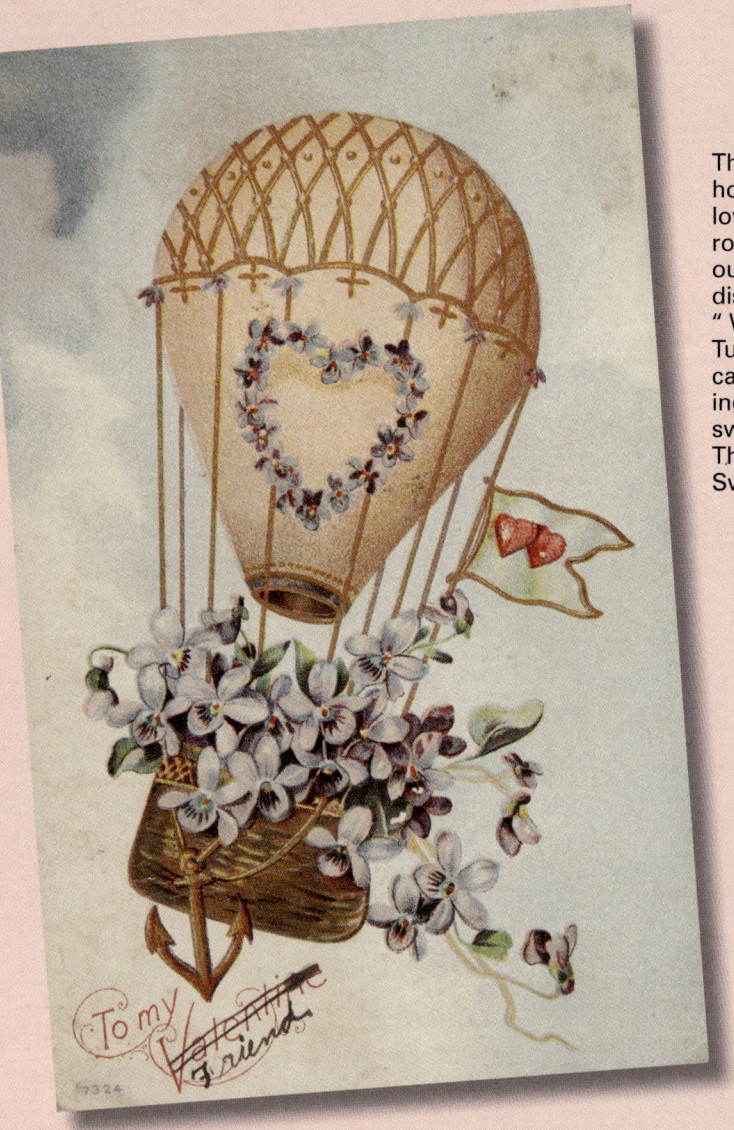

The image of love floating through the air is delicious. A hot air balloon embellished with violets flies a banner of love. Its crosses are a motif rare on Valentine cards. The romantic illusion is shattered with "Valentine" crossed out, replaced with "Friend." The message on the back dispels any notions of a lovers' quarrel. Annie sends it, " Well hello Pearl – I suppose you are going to the Party Tuesday Night. I expect to go if it is nice. Excuse this card." Annie apparently had an overstock. Two charming children in pseudo-colonial garb ride a violet-edged swing descended from a similarly decorated balloon. The poem reads: "My heart is light, My heart is free, My Sweetheart is bright, She'll ever love me."

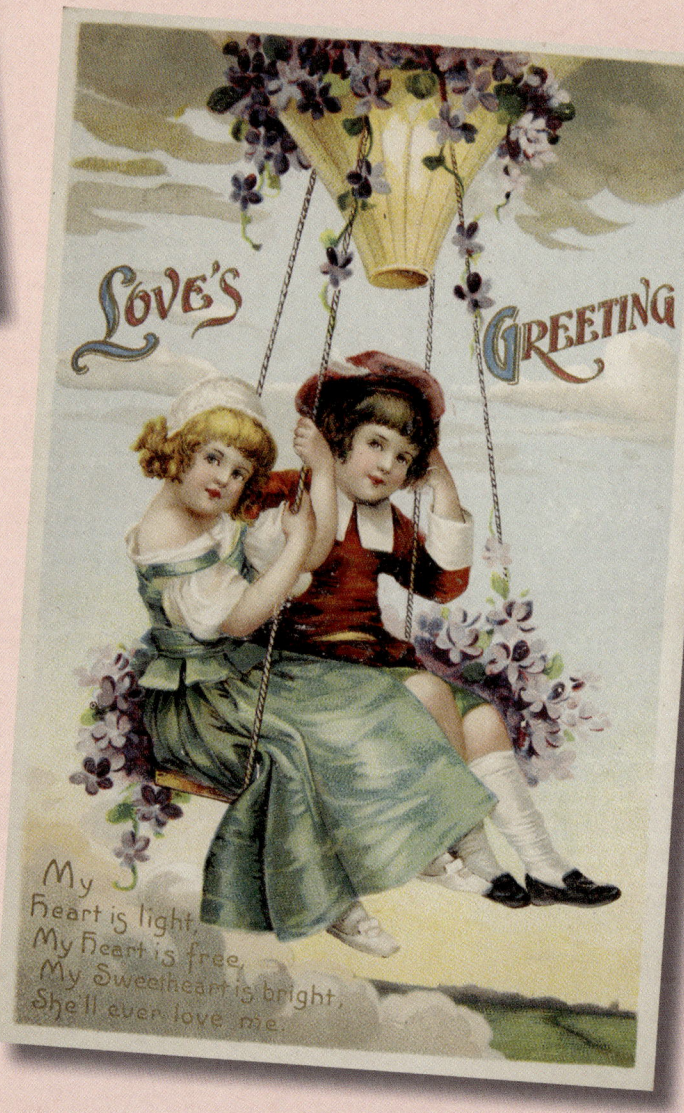

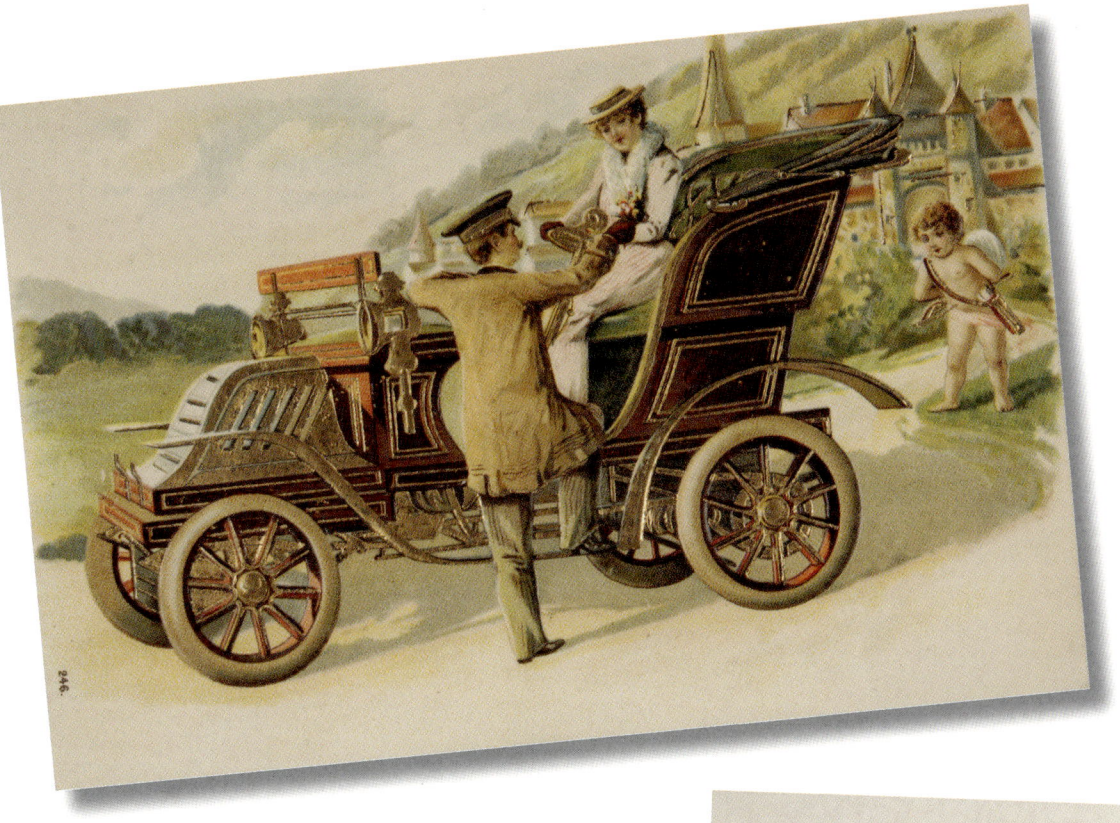

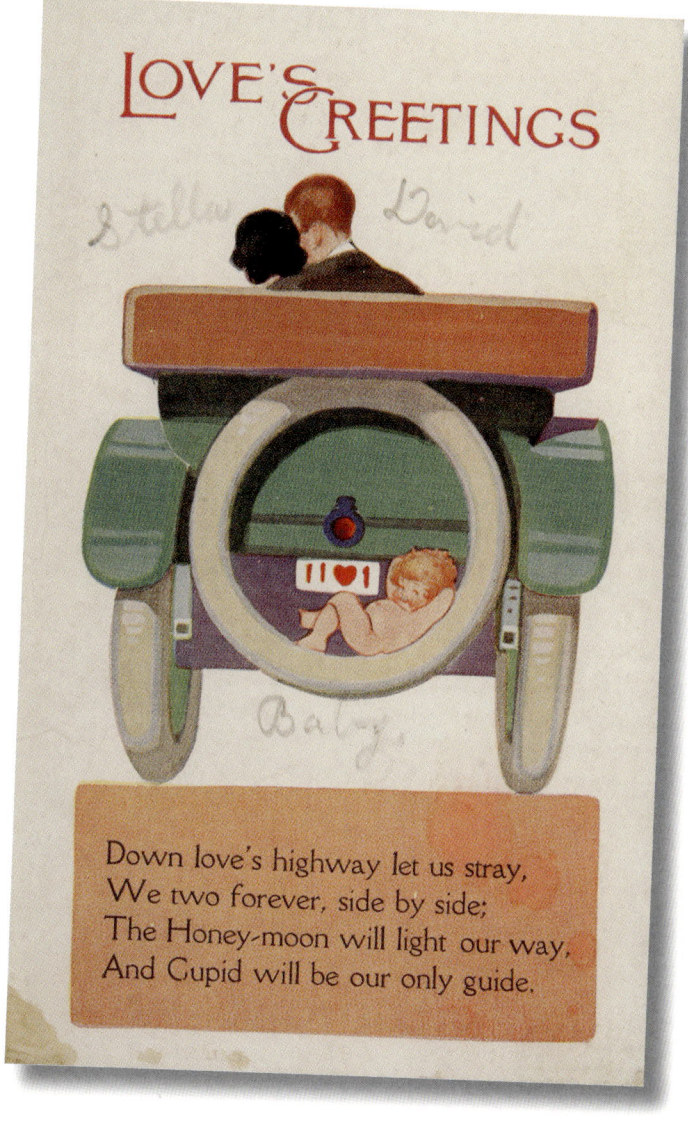

Automobile imagery is rare on Valentines. The implied message of the young lady in the grand car is especially interesting. What is Cupid's intent? Is this card the precursor to *Lady Chatterley's Lover* with a chauffeur replacing a gardener? Cupid has been transformed from the God of Love to the fruit of love by the sender of the second romantic image.

Then romantic, now environmentally destructive, the undeniably image of young love was given to "Mr. J. G. Westafer, Elizabethtown Pa.: by "Vera."

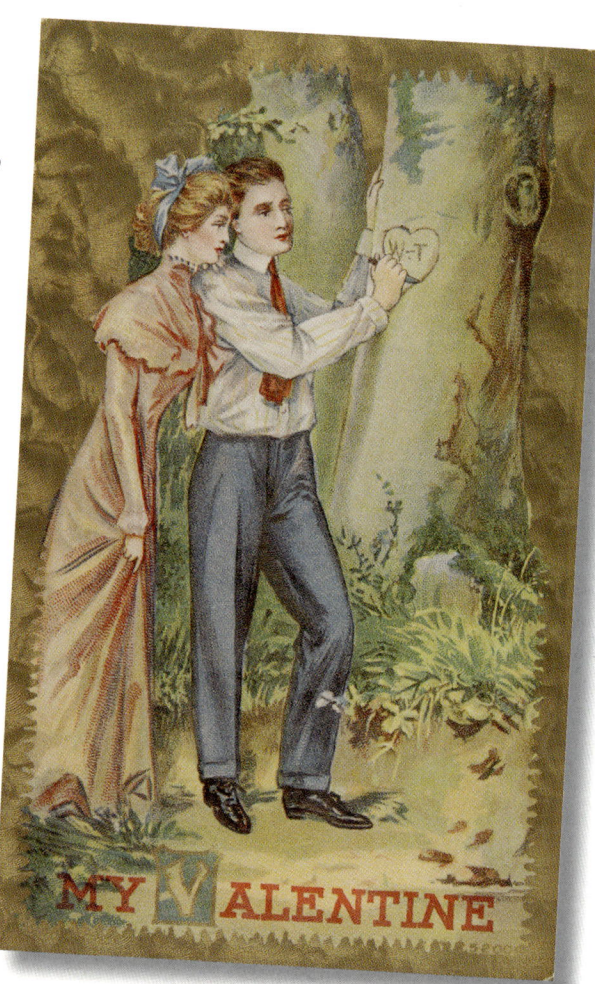

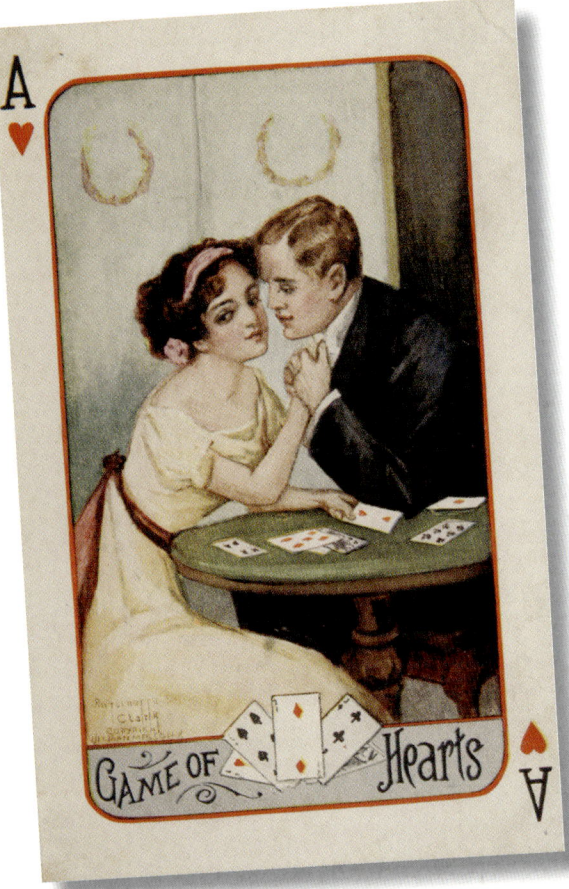

Love as a "Game of Hearts." The message on the back is enigmatic: "Dear S. How about this. I thought it very good. N"

In this charming "old fashioned" card a key, in the hand of a muff-wearing young lady, replaces Cupid's arrow but the symbolism is the same. The key or the arrow and the heart represent the yin and yang, the union of male and female.

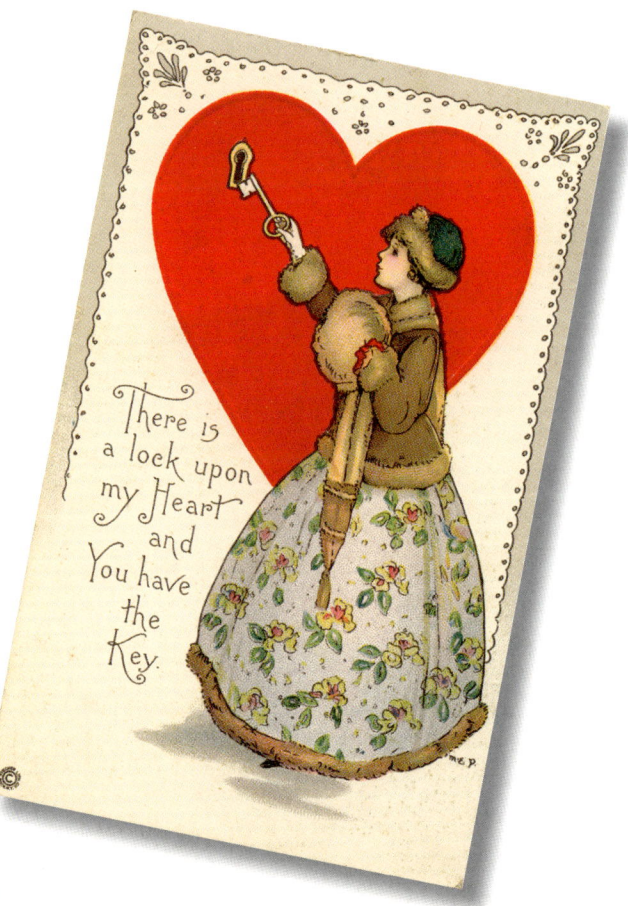

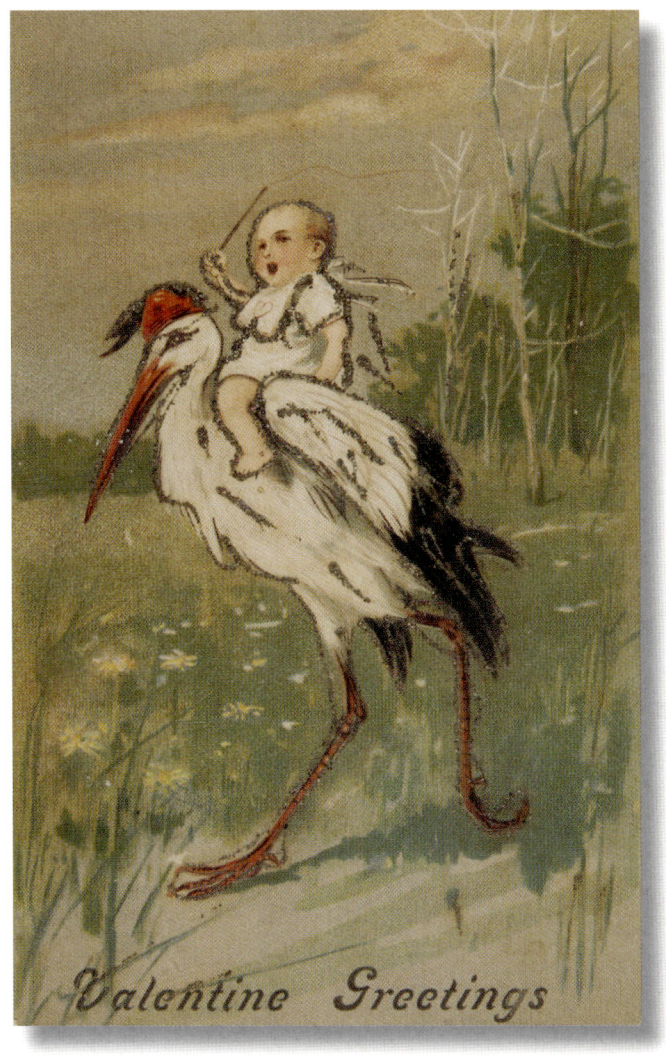

Valentine Greetings

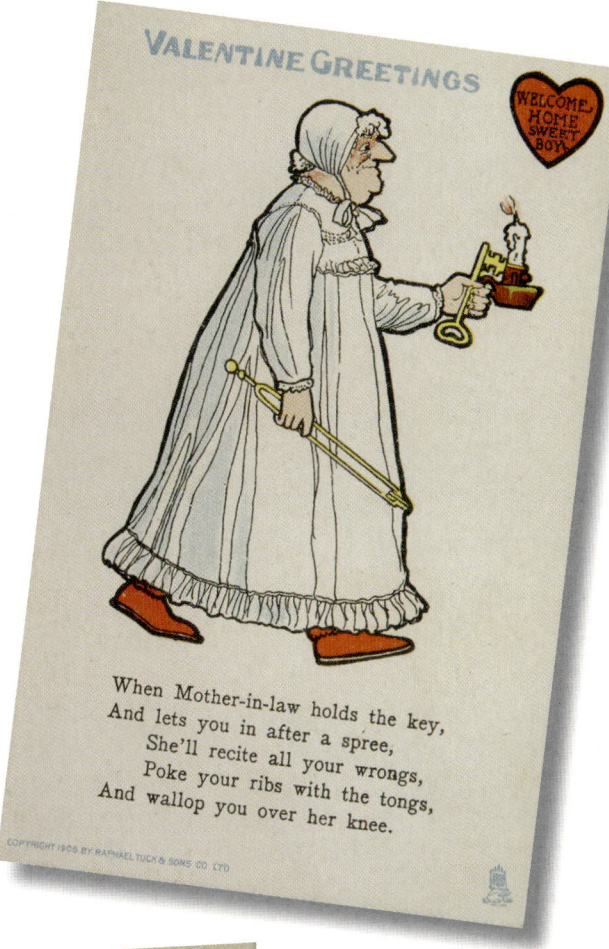

VALENTINE GREETINGS

WELCOME HOME SWEET BOY

When Mother-in-law holds the key,
And lets you in after a spree,
She'll recite all your wrongs,
Poke your ribs with the tongs,
And wallop you over her knee.

COPYRIGHT 1906 BY RAPHAEL TUCK & SONS CO. LTD

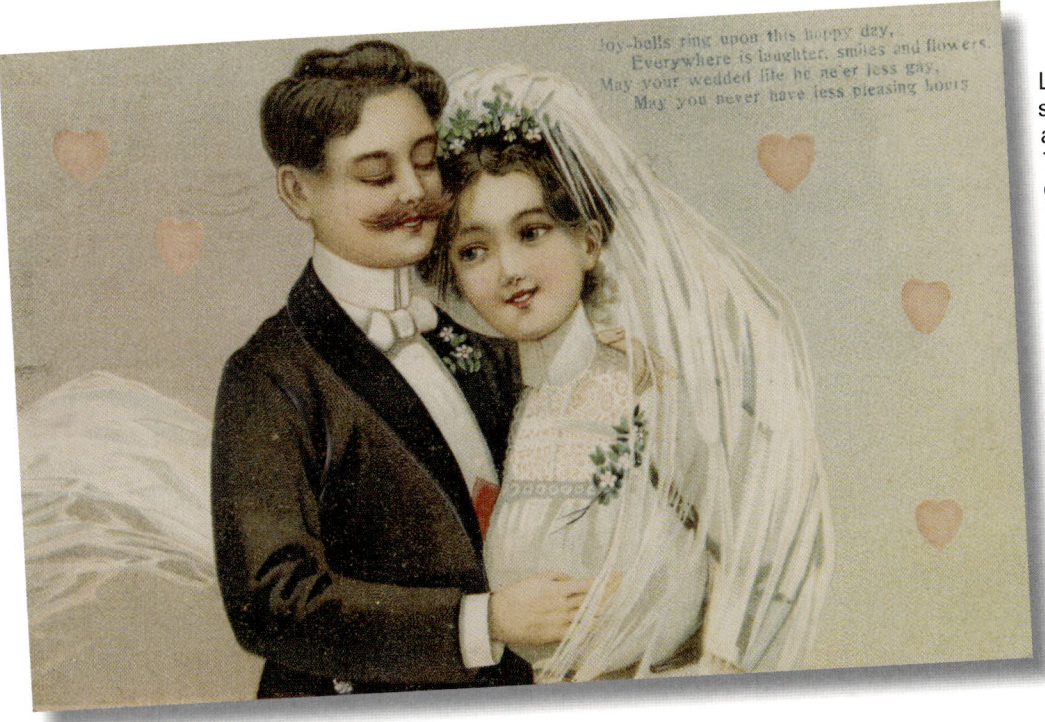

Joy-bells ring upon this happy day,
Everywhere is laughter, smiles and flowers.
May your wedded life be ne'er less gay,
May you never have less pleasing hours

Love and marriage and the subsequent consequence are observed in three cards. The message on the back of the romantic card sent to "Dr. J. L. Hertz" reads, "Leap Year, Will you meet me some time!" The sender's motives were clear. The baby riding a stork was clearly meant to be sent to a married woman, in this case, "Mrs. Emma Seidel," of "Reading Pa" by "Darwin." It would have been considered indecent sent to a maiden. Ultimately we meet the "Mother-in-Law from Hell," who clearly threatens son-in-law with abuse or something kinky.

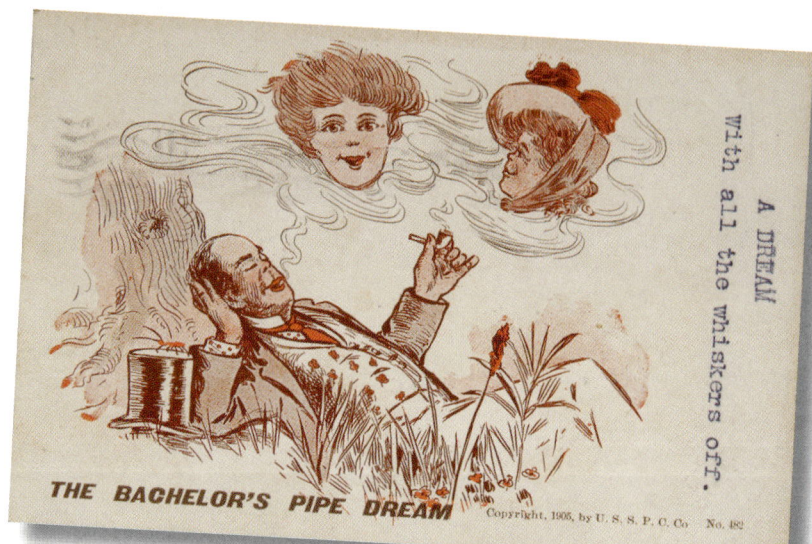

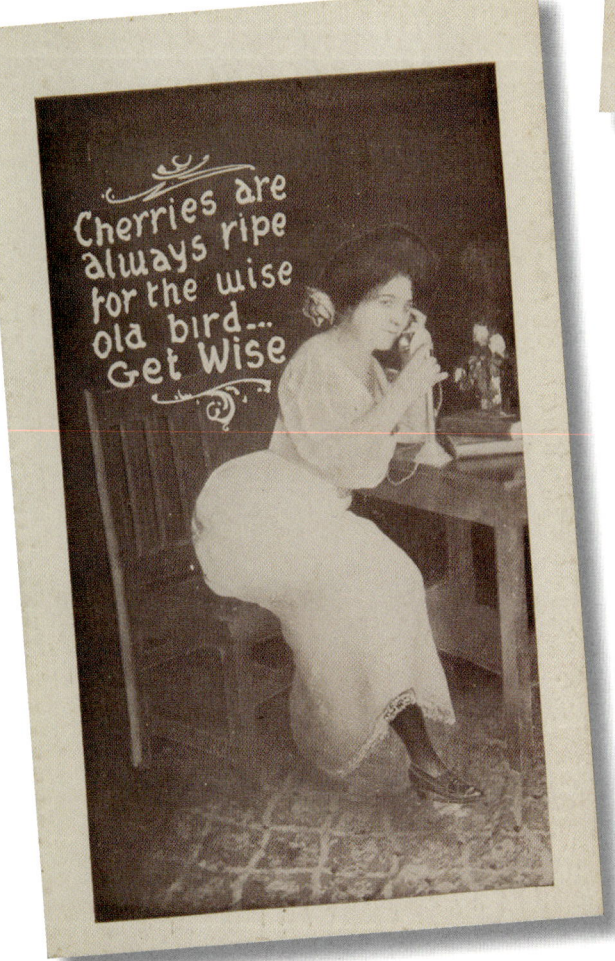

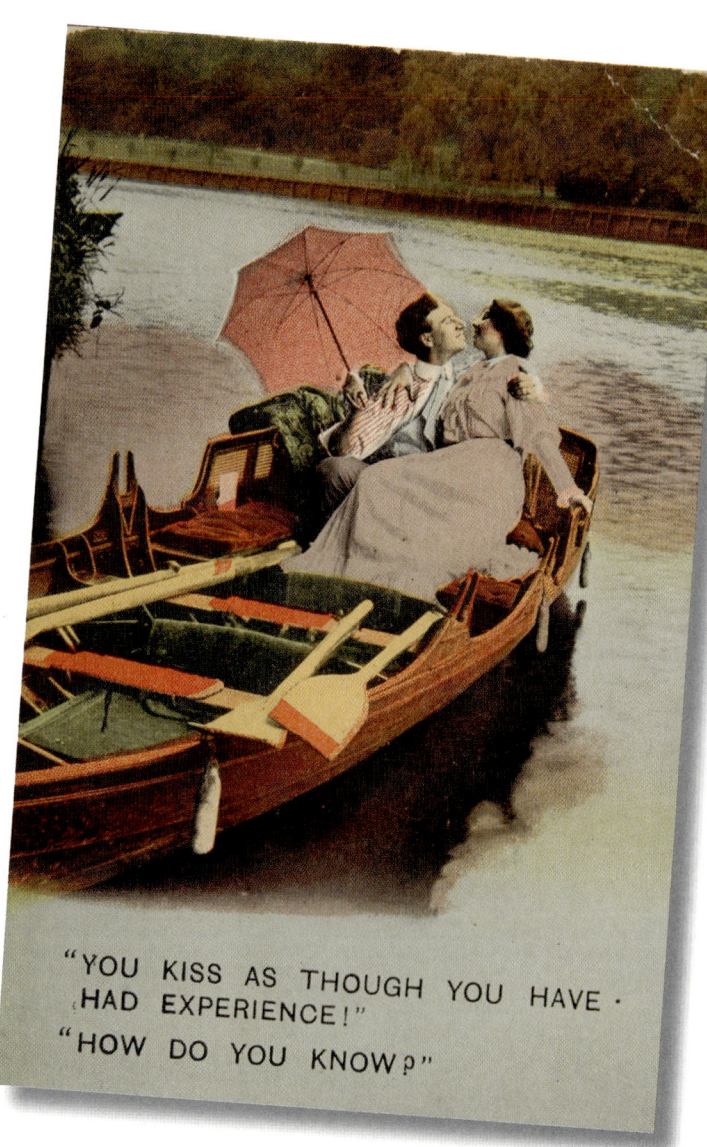

Not Valentines, but images of romance nevertheless. A bachelor dreams of beautiful faces, a forward modern woman uses the telephone while showing some ankle, and a couple begins a debate on experience. Happy Valentine's Day!

4
Easter

Religion & Rabbits

Easter is the principle feast of the Christian year, celebrating the Resurrection of Jesus Christ. Many of the pious resent that, in America, the face of the holiday is more commonly represented by the Easter Bunny than by Jesus. Like many holidays and festivals observed in the West, Easter is a combination of pagan and Christian events and customs. Traditionally, the crucifixion of Jesus Christ is identified with March 25, a date probably chosen in the hope that a commemoration so timed would replace ancient pagan festivals honoring the Vernal Equinox, observations which often involved feasting, sexual merriment, and the adoration of flowers. Essentially, these were celebrations of the rebirth of life after winter. The very name "Easter" is derived from the goddess Ostara, a Saxon deity whose springtime feast was a proclamation of renewal and fertility.

Most of the common Easter commemorations are exploited on postcards, with a few exceptions. Easter bonfires, never popular in America, were commonly lighted on the Saturday evening (Holy Saturday) before Easter Sunday. Deriving from the pagan past when people believed that fire came from the sun and that flames were both the givers and destroyers of life, the ashes from Easter fire were often spread on gardens to assure bountiful harvests. For centuries, the Pennsylvania Dutch have spread wood ash on their four-square gardens on Ash Wednesday.

In Jerusalem, "the Illumination" was derived from the custom of building bonfires. Here the lighting of a large candle, the Paschal Candle, on Saturday evening heralded the beginning of a vigil that would end at sunrise, commemorating the traditional time when Jesus' followers went to his tomb, only to find it empty.

Sunrise services became very important. The Moravians, a small German church, brought the custom to America, along with brass, usually trombone, and choirs. Most Protestant churches would adopt the practice *sans* horns. The religious and the secular love of spectacle often merge into massively attended Sunrise Services being celebrated in huge man-made or natural venues, including the Grand Canyon, New York's Central Park, and the Hollywood Bowl.

Deriving from Easter being a time of renewal, the holiday has become the time to wear new clothes. In the United States wearing a new hat to church on Sunday was important to many women. Indeed, after church and before dinner many families would promenade so that everyone could enjoy the millinery spectacle. "The Easter Parades," as they came to be known, were a community fixture. New York's, held on fashionable Fifth Avenue, became nationally famed. The phenomenon was enshrined and celebrated in our anthem of the holiday, "Easter Parade," written by Irving Berlin in 1933. While Easter bonnets may have gone out of fashion, many Easter symbols and customs endure: Easter lilies, lambs, chicks, kittens, and, inevitably, rabbits and colored eggs.

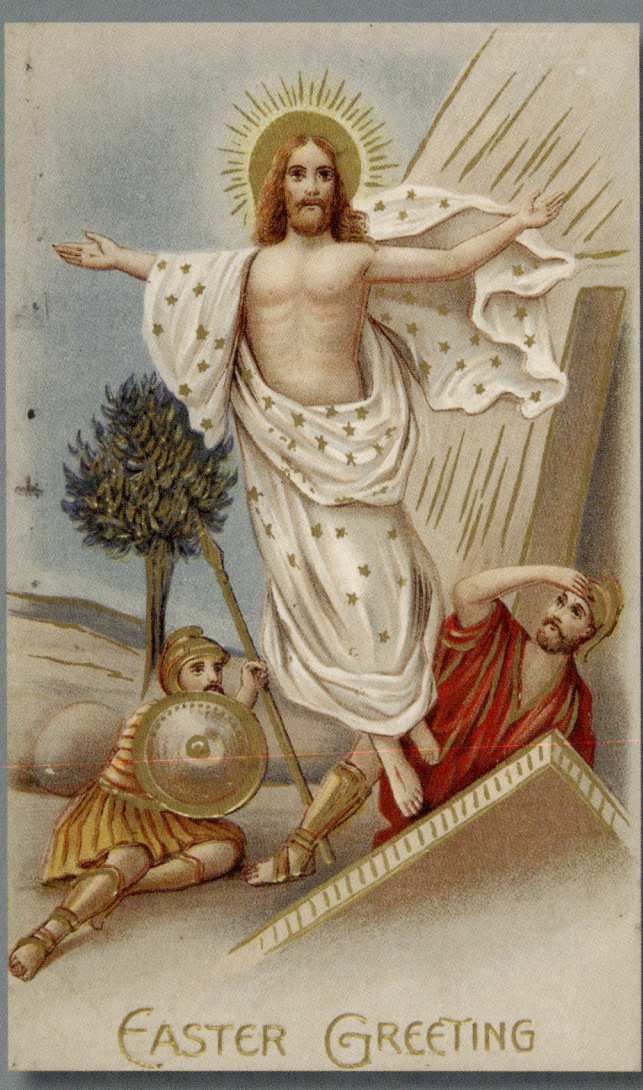

Religious traditionalists favored cards celebrating the Resurrection, which is central to Easter. Here Christ, in a star-spangled robe, ascends to heaven while Roman soldiers look on in awe.

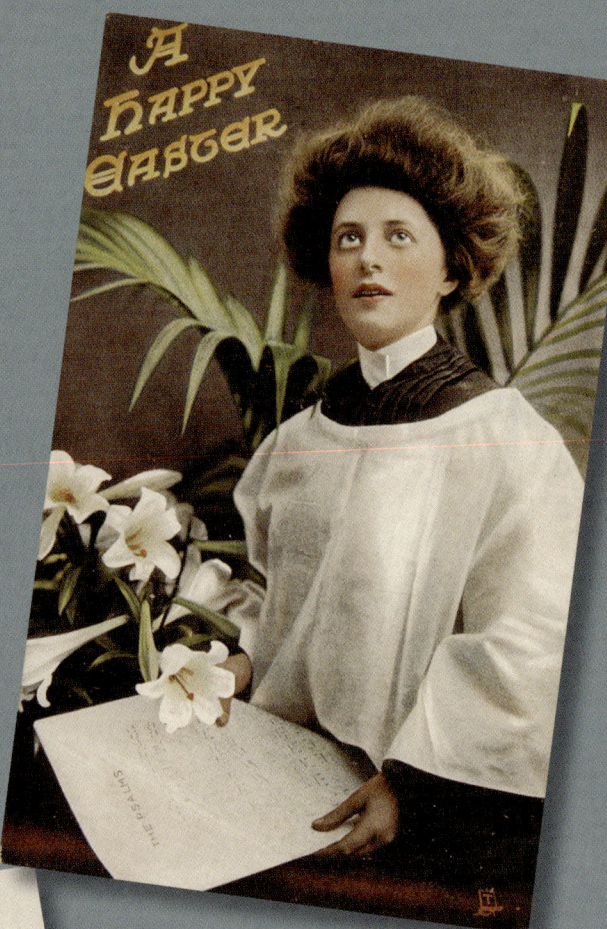

To go to church on Sunday was admirable; to be surrounded by Easter lilies was symbolic but not ancient. While the lily is mentioned in the bible as representing beauty, goodness and perfection, our modern Easter lily was only introduced into the United States in 1880 from Bermuda. An instant sensation, it grows from a buried bulb and then is reborn as a wondrous flower in time for Easter. Scented trumpet-shaped blooms recall the angel Gabriel's horn. For many of the contemporary pious, Easter without the lily is unthinkable. A choir of dew-faced lads in Roman collars and robes sing surrounded by Gothic glories and lilies. A similarly attired young lady, in ecstasy, looks to the heavens. She is backed by palms, embraced by Easter lilies, and she holds "The Psalms" in her hands.

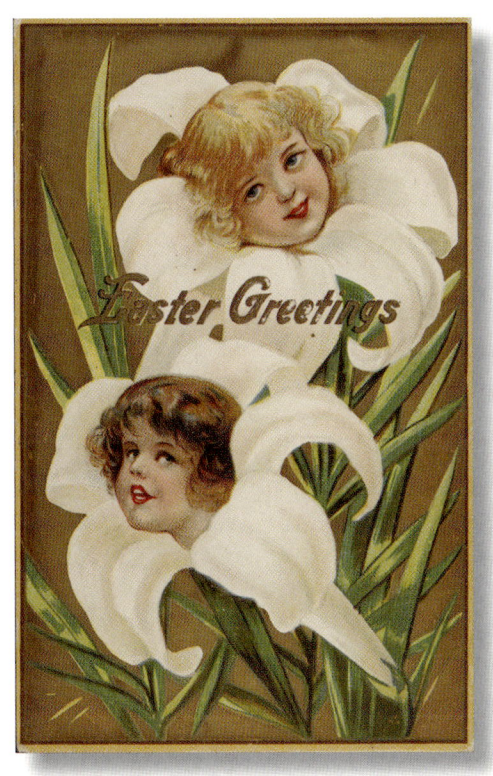

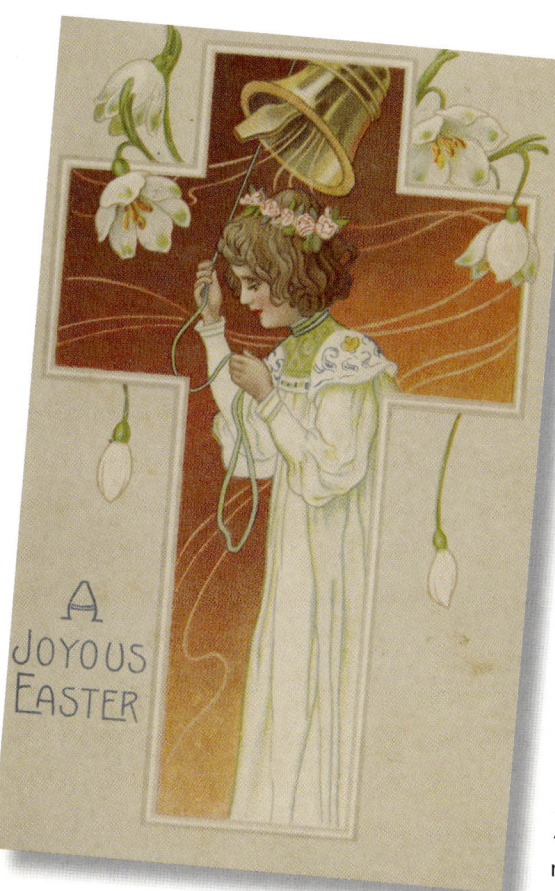

A JOYOUS EASTER

Flowers, closely associated with the *Vernal Equinox*, were adopted as a symbol of Easter. Blooming plants are frequent Easter gifts. Cards celebrating Easter often included floral imagery: sometimes heavy on religious symbolism, other times sweet and amusing. Lovely girl heads emerge from Easter lilies – one blond, one brunette. A similar duo embellish a cross of jonquils bordered by pussy willows. A rose-crowned young lady rings an Easter bell, surrounded by ambiguous flowers that are a cross between fruit tree blossoms and snow drops. Two angels stand amidst a bed of lilies-of-the-valley while one holds an anchor "the anchor of her faith," made of forget-me-nots.

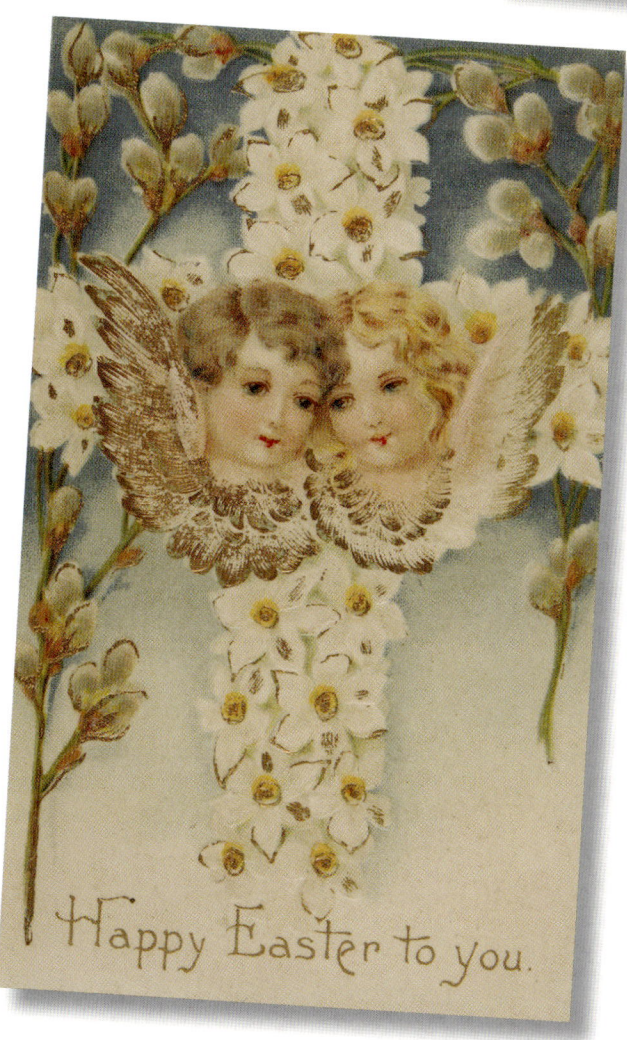

Happy Easter to you.

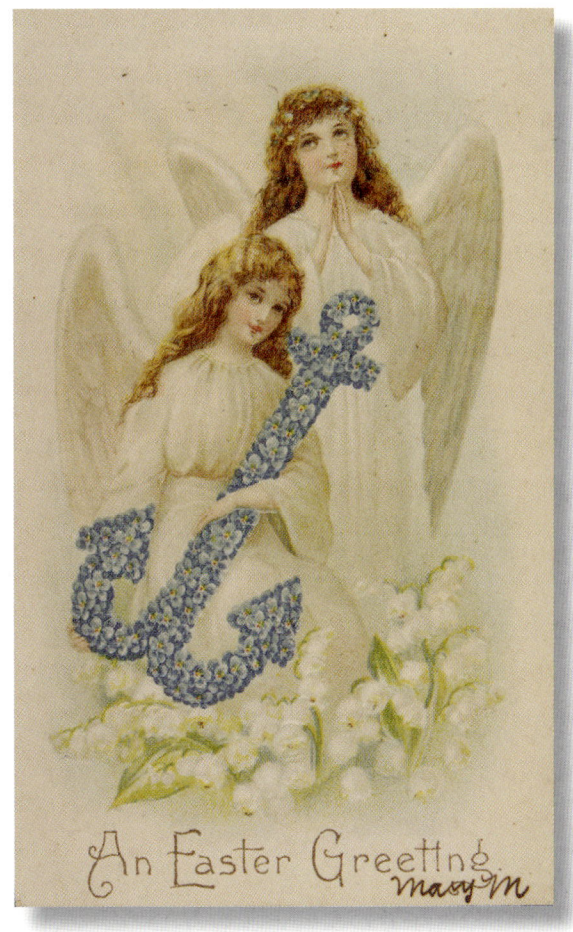

An Easter Greeting

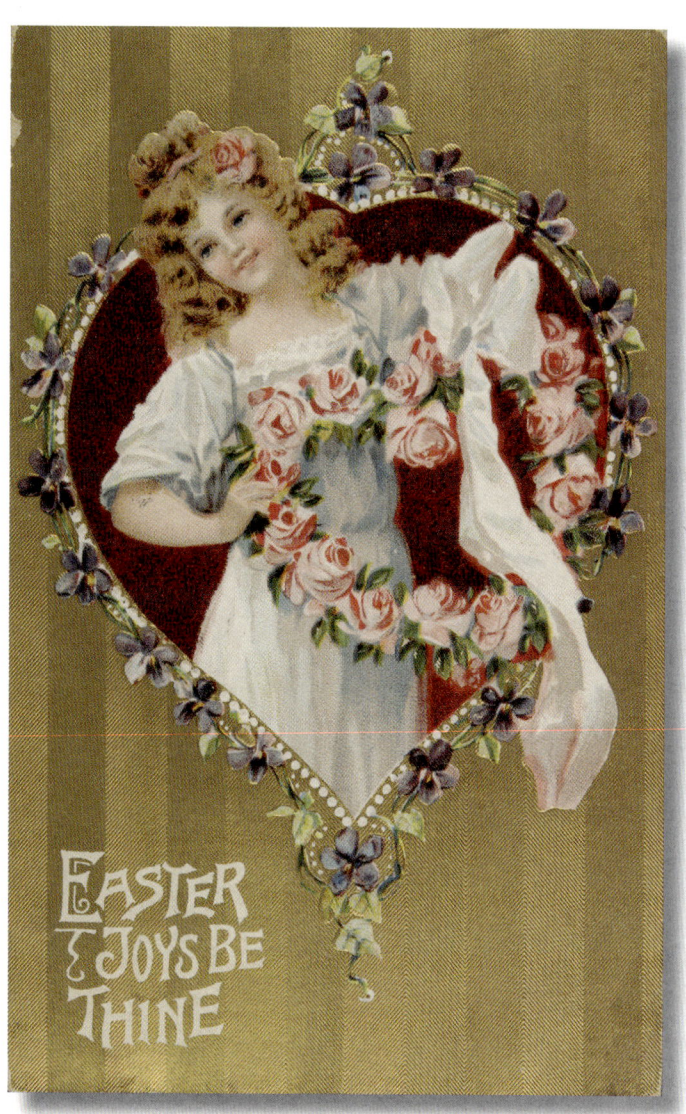

Some card motifs were recycled from holiday to holiday to holiday. The charming lady within the heart obviously started life gracing a Valentine card. Other motifs were reused -- with changes. The two doves probably held baskets of flowers on a Valentine card – and pussy willows are a new addition.

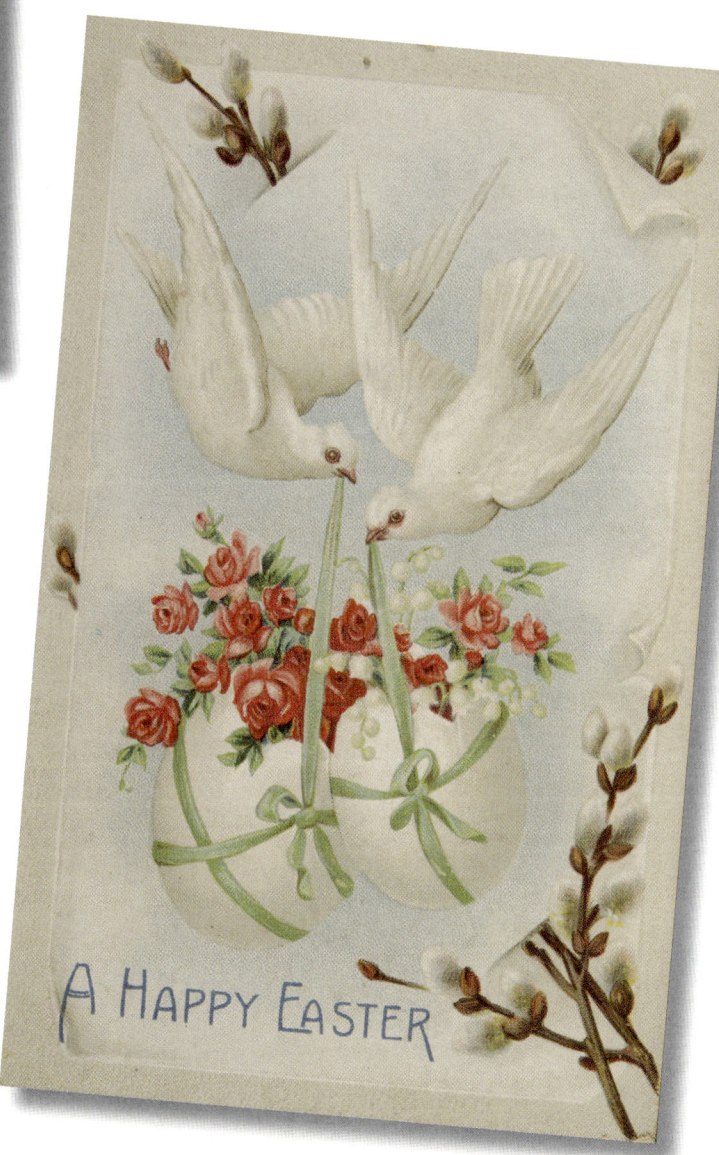

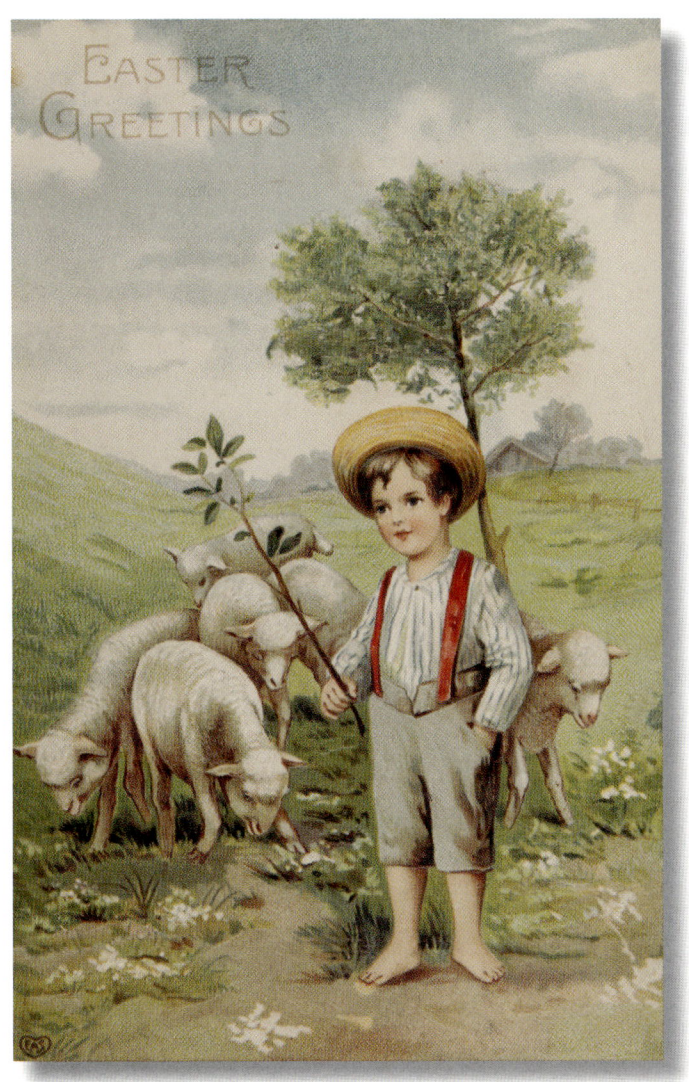

The lamb is often as a symbol of Easter. The Paschal Lamb, a fusion of aspects of the Jewish Passover festival and Christian Easter, is the animal traditionally sacrificed on the eve of Passover. It was later associated with the "… Lamb of God, which taketh away the sin of the world," according to John 1:29. Additionally, John the Baptist had been a shepherd in his youth. On one card an Americanized "St. John" watches over his flock. On another, two sheep pull a peculiar chariot, one bearing a giant Easter egg.

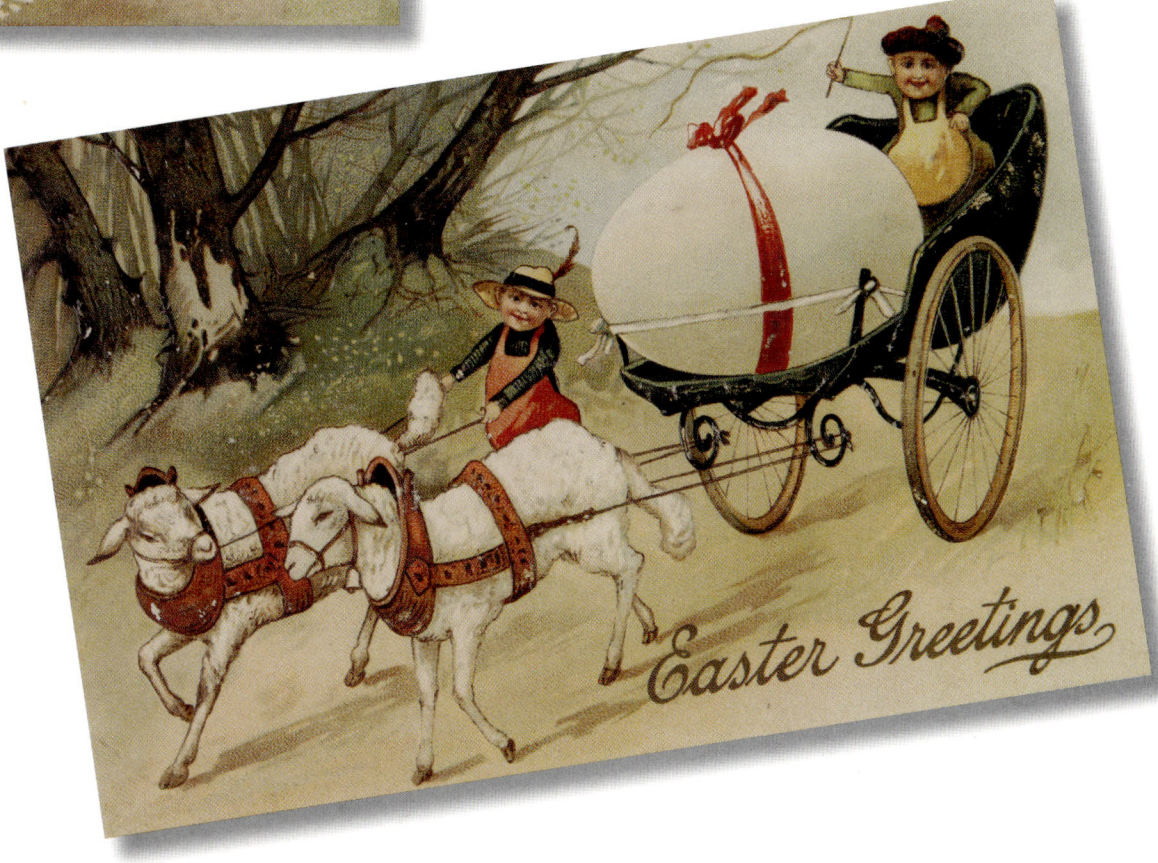

In a picture of piety, a young boy, presumably in his new Easter suit, holds a prayer book. An angel literally has her hand on his shoulder. An Easter lily blooms on the left.

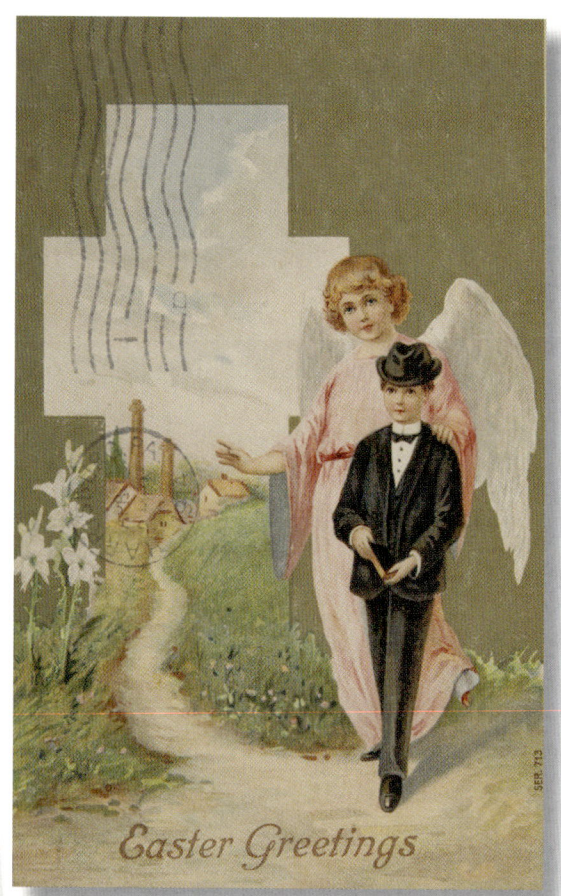

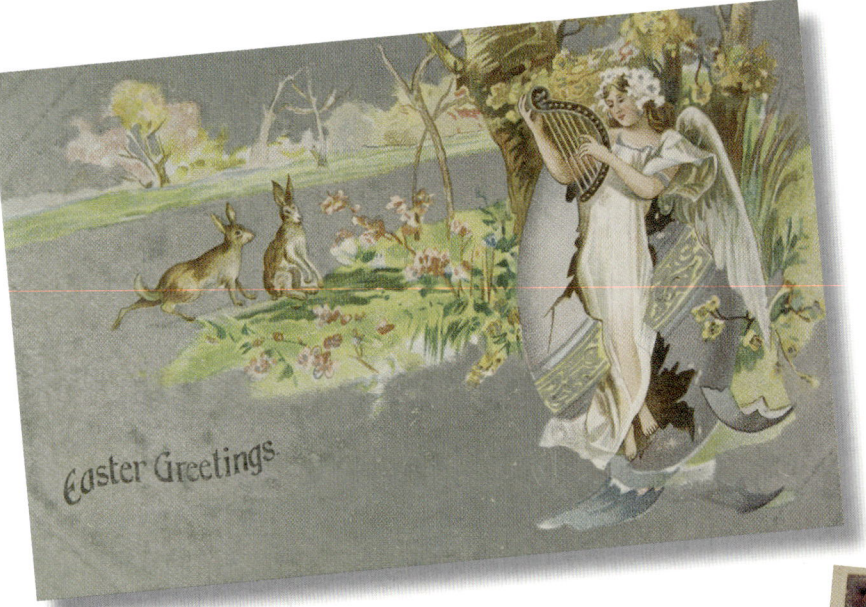

The pagan goddess Ostara, after whom the Germanic spring festival *Ostern* (the possible origin of the word Easter) was named, was usually shown with a hare, possibly the ancestor of the Easter Bunny. Our lyre-playing angel/goddess is more Grecian.

Pussy willows, a harbinger of spring, and colored eggs are often shown on Easter cards. The egg is a universal symbol of fertility and rebirth. Coloring eggs is ancient, but any symbolic value of the colors is lost in America. In Russia, however, eggs colored red, commemorating Christ's blood, are exchanged on Easter Day.

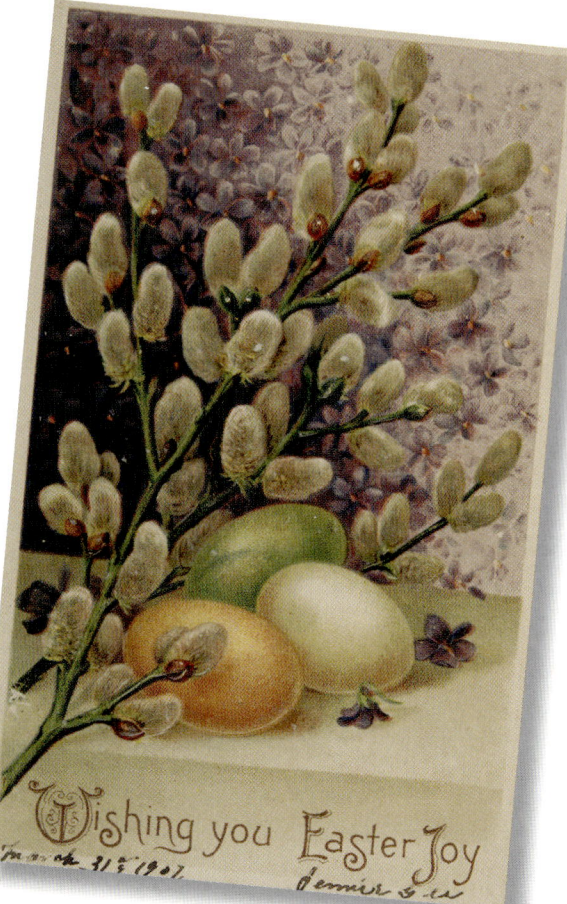

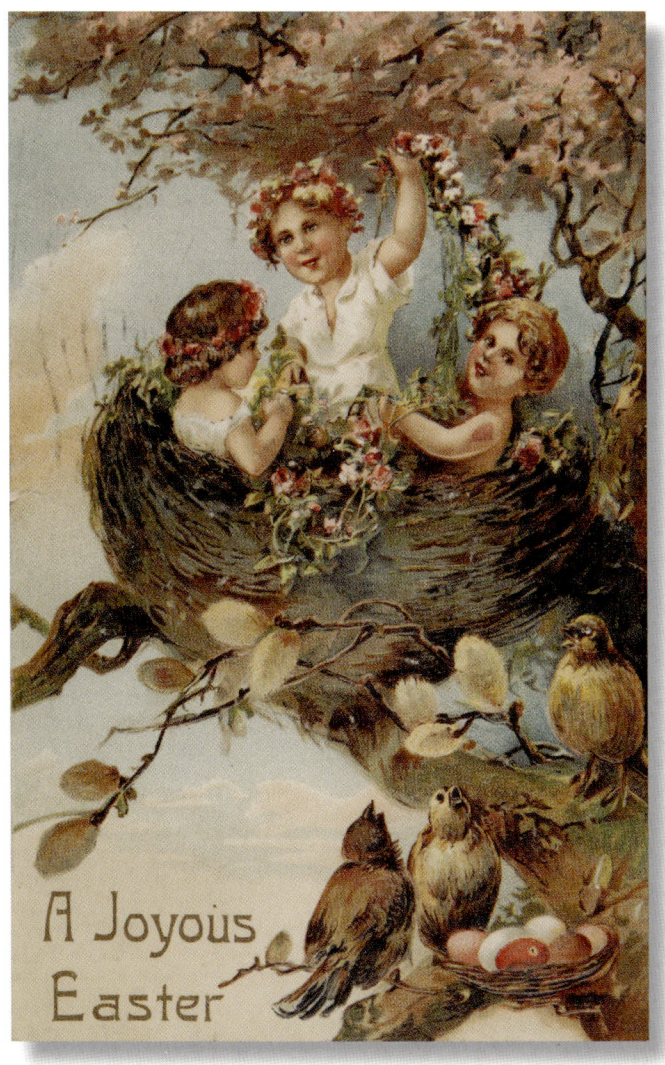
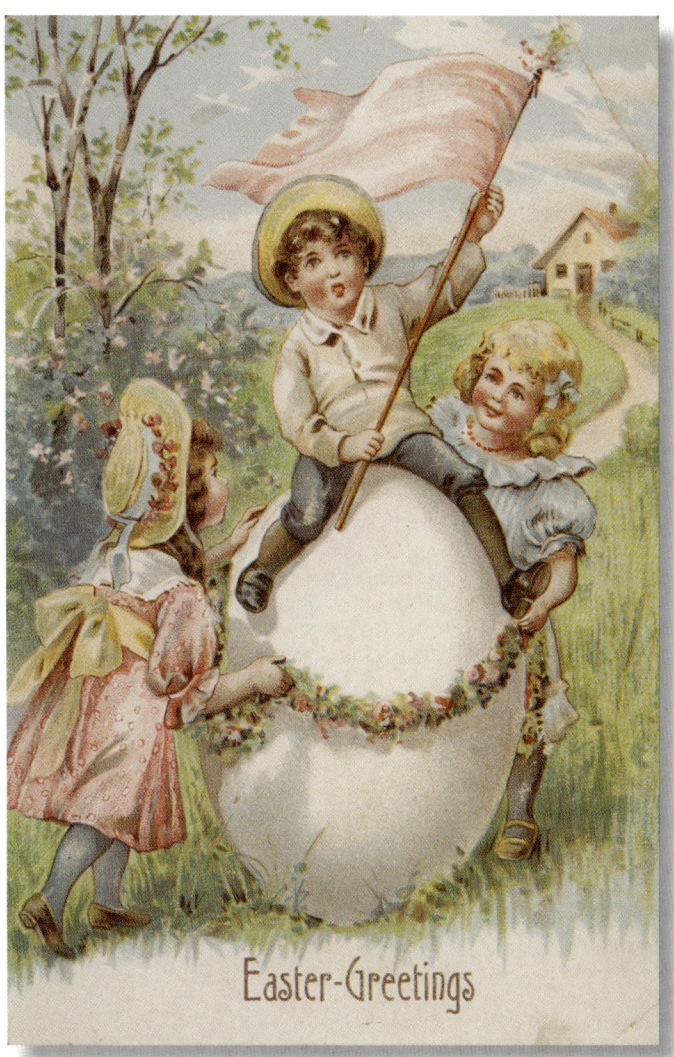
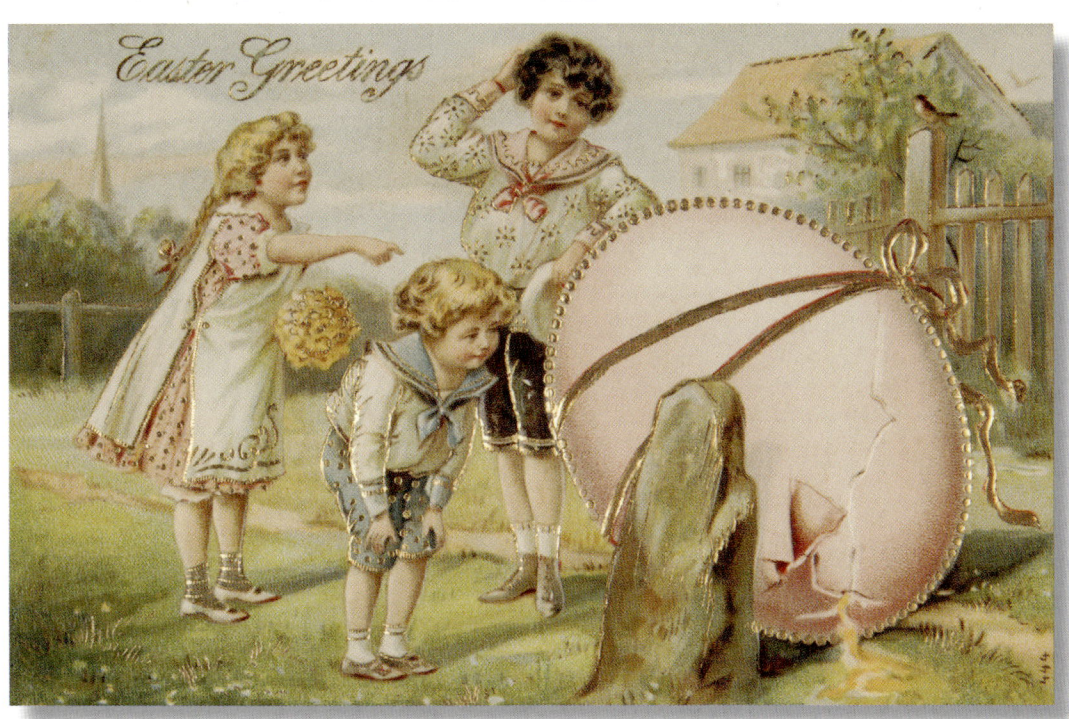

Arrangements of children, eggs, rabbits, flowers, nests, and birds are often bizarrely mixed on Easter cards. Three young children sit in a nest. Below them are birds with a clutch of varicolored eggs. A flag-waving boy sits atop a giant egg adorned with a garland held by two girls. Children and a rabbit watch as a baby bunny emerges from a pink egg.

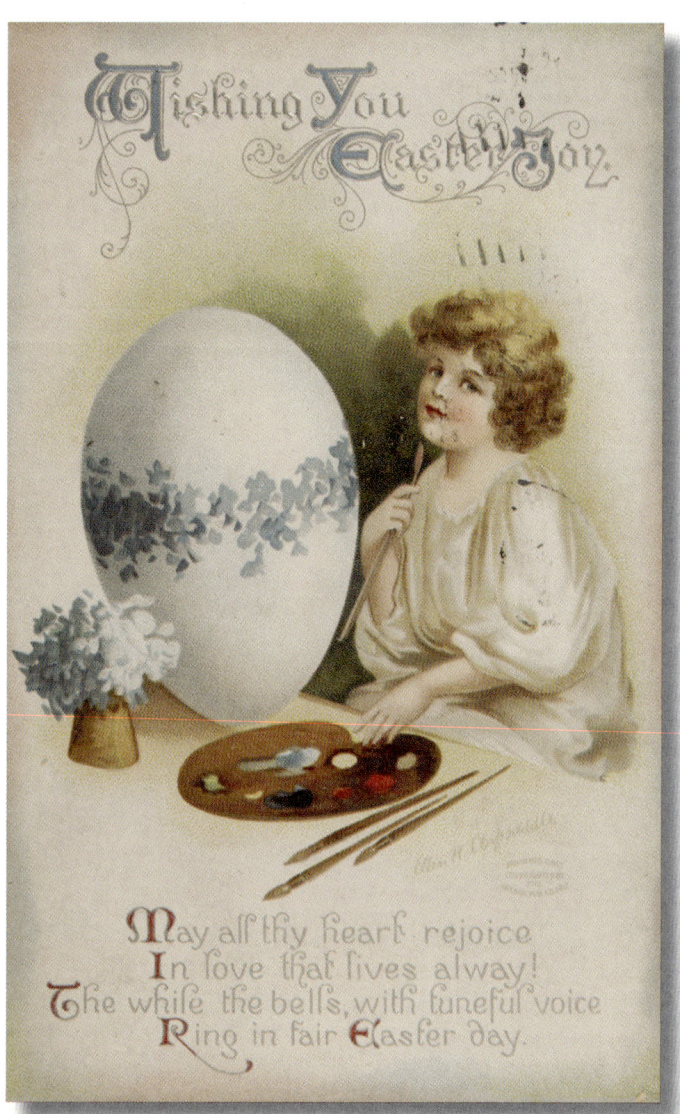

Sweetness personified: an angelic artist decorates an extraordinary egg. Was there a sighting of a Roc, the mythic giant bird?

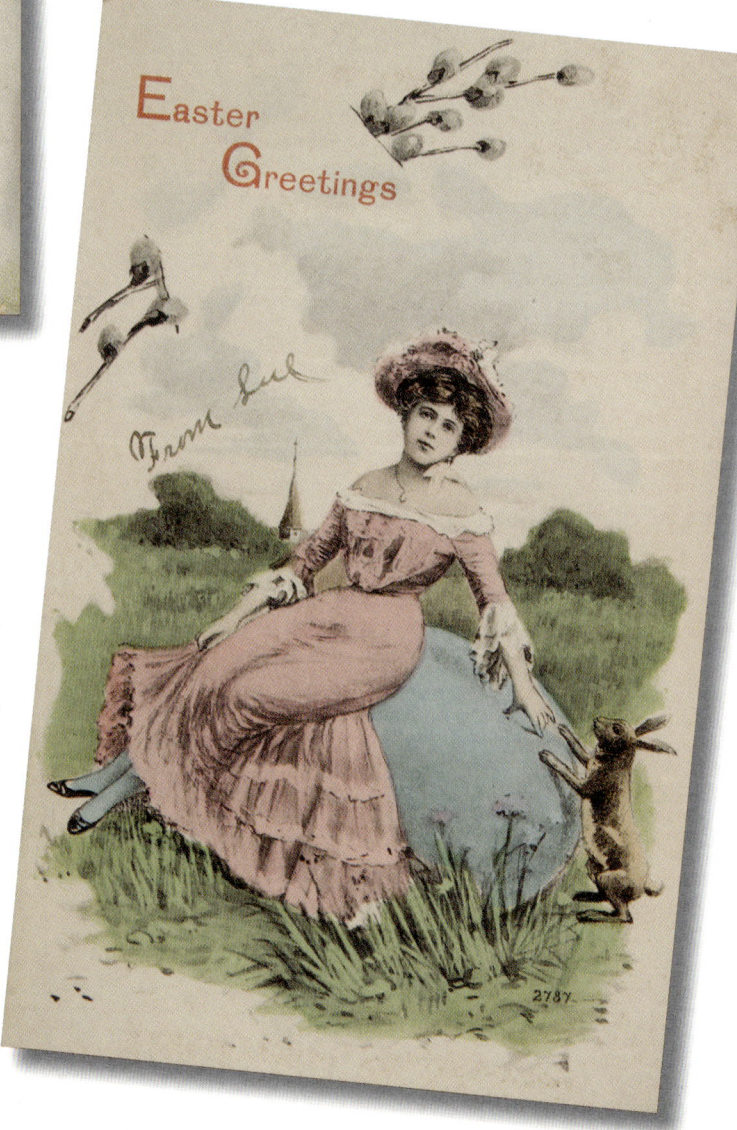

An Easter pinup. A very immodest young lady shows her stockings in a decidedly non-"blue stocking" pose. She sits on another "Roc" egg. A rabbit, a church and pussy willows enhance the holiday imagery. Curiously, the card was given to "Stella" "From Sue."

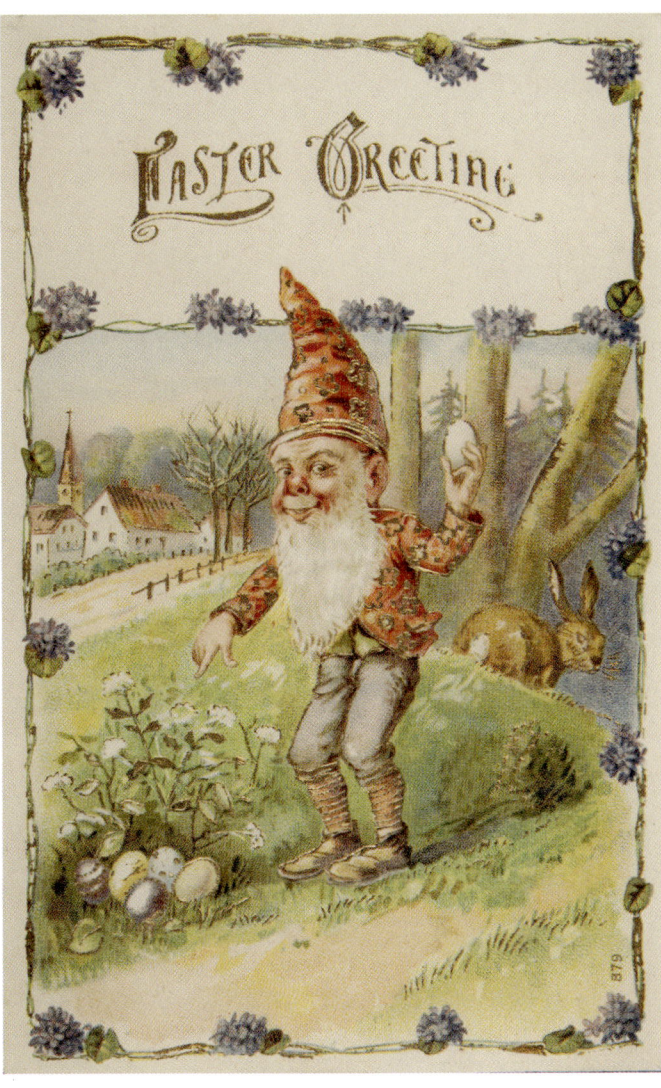

Easter elves? Why not? A pleased little fellow has just found a cache, presumably laid by the unhappy-looking rabbit at the right. Three nasty elves torture a Humpty Dumpty-sized egg on the ground.

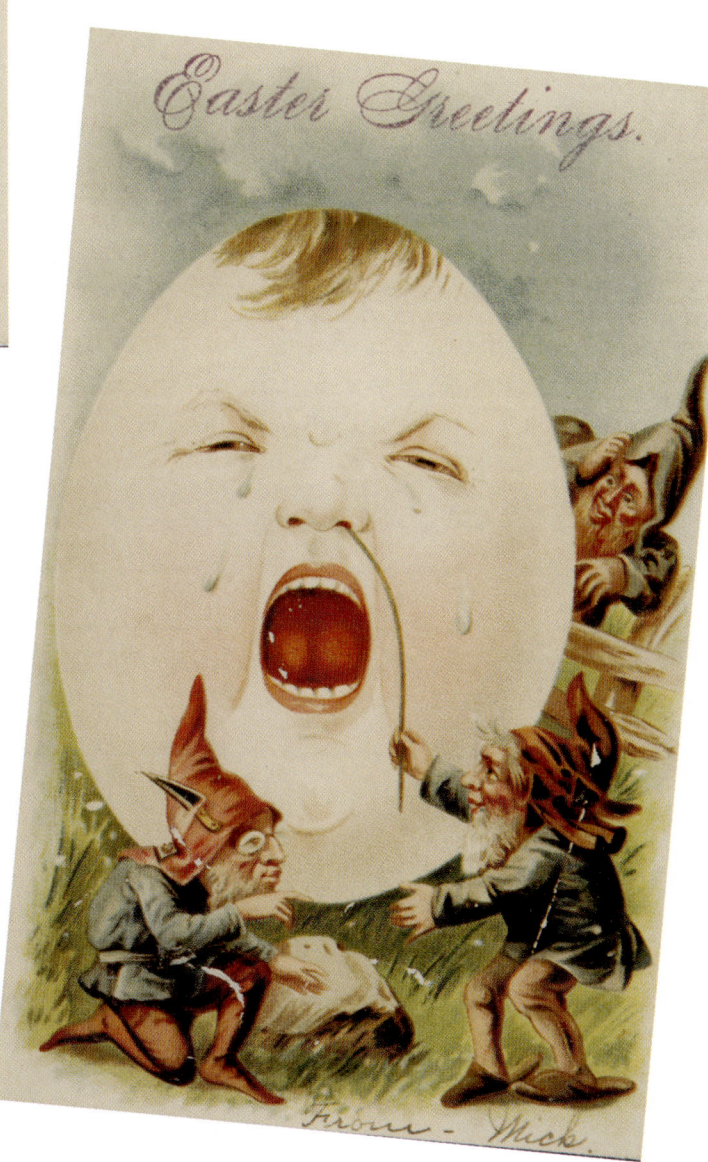

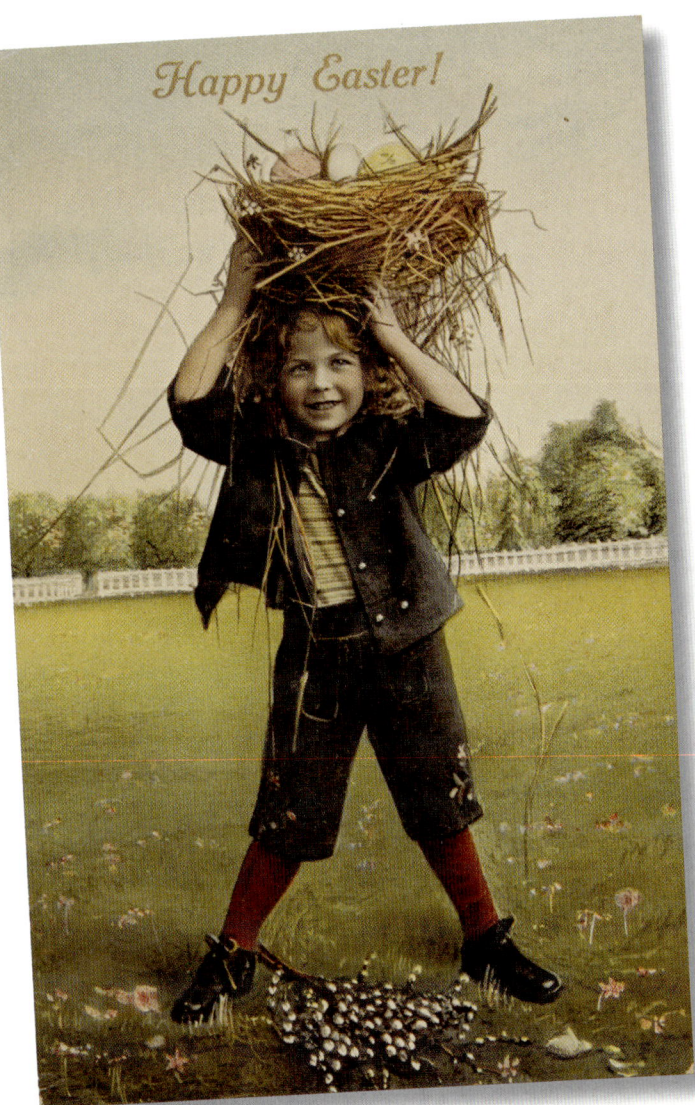

Early in the last century children left empty nests for the Easter Bunny to fill. Baskets didn't become common until the 1920s. This happy lad has a full complement of eggs in his nest!

"Don't put all your eggs in one basket" remains good advice.

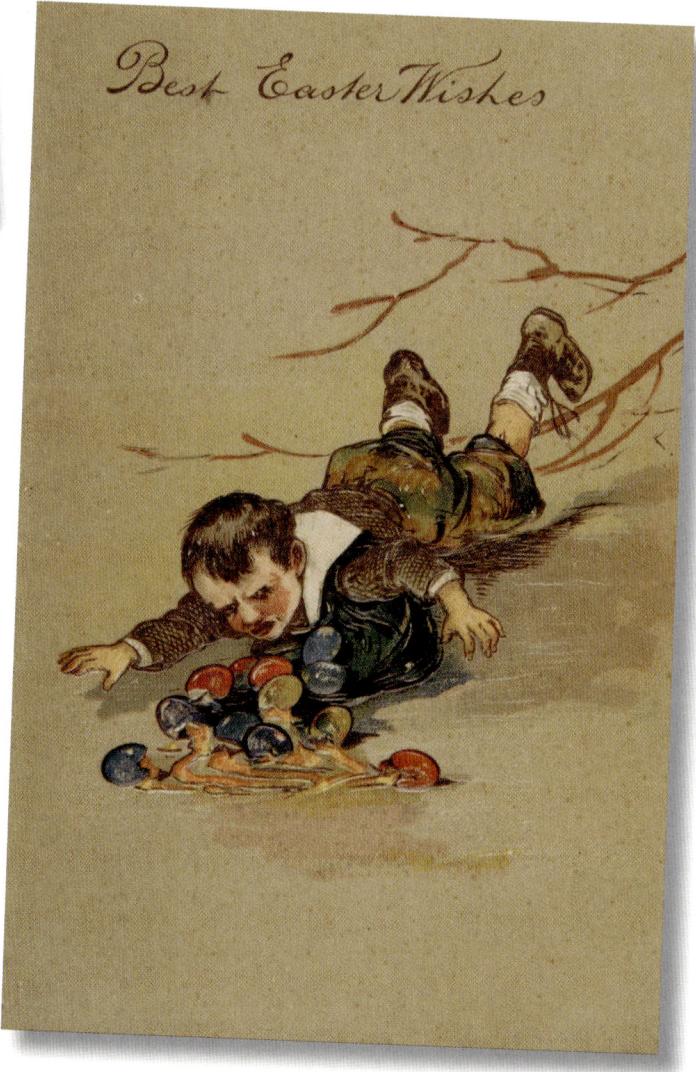

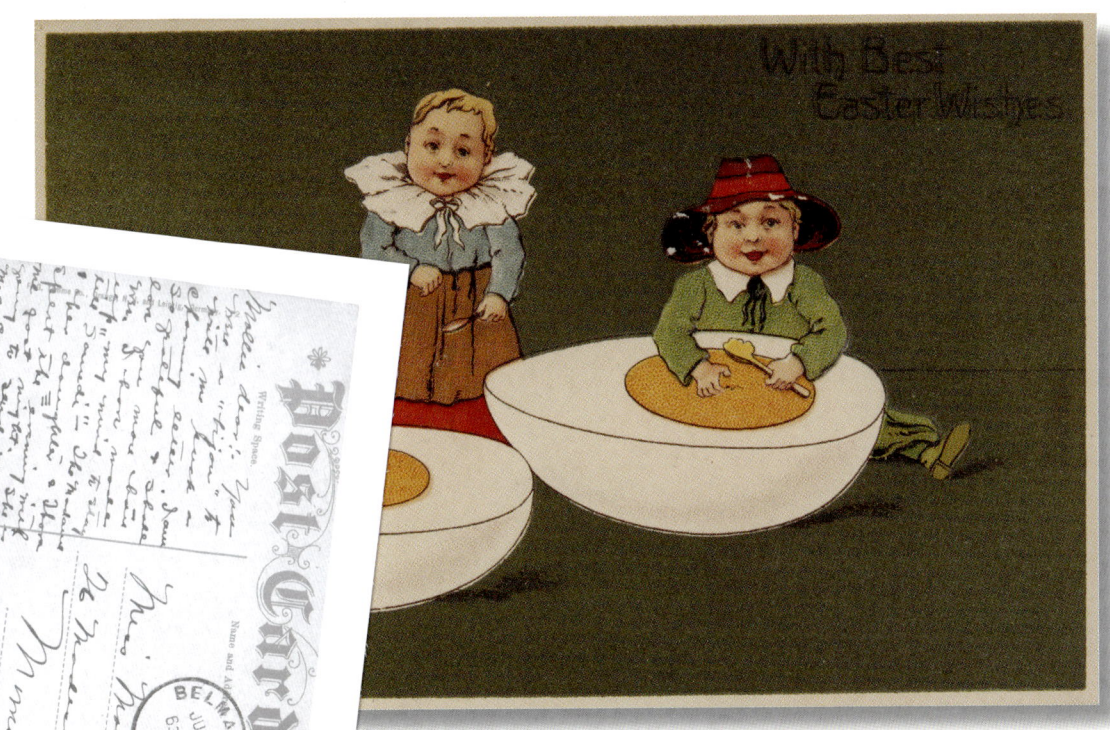

Showing eggs as hardboiled is rare. Showing them being eaten is rarer still. In 1908, Henry Landis sent this card from New York City to his brother George at Landis Valley. The message on the reverse is humorous: "Humpty Dumpty had a hot time – Humpty Dumpty round as a dime. Now, all the Kings [sic] wisdom and all the Kings [sic] men can't fix him up so he'll run again."

…ogically probable, a hen and a …ster are responsible for a clutch …eggs. Their attire is weird as is …e airborne egg to the left.

Ready to Write a Book?

Do you collect images of your town or county? Are you passionate about local history, and eager to share what you've learned? If you or your organization always dreamed of writing a book, we would love to hear from you. We are eagerly seeking authors to write illustrated, regional history and guide books. We'd love to hear more about the images you have access to, and the audience you are writing for.

Email your book idea to info@schifferbooks.com, write to Acquisitions, Schiffer Publishing, Ltd. 4880 Lower Valley Rd., Atglen, PA 19310 USA, or call 610-593-1777 to make an appointment to speak with an editor.

Normal animal instincts are suspended at Easter as placid kittens passively watch a chick hatching. Five chicks emerge -- from brown wrapping paper rather than from egg shells.

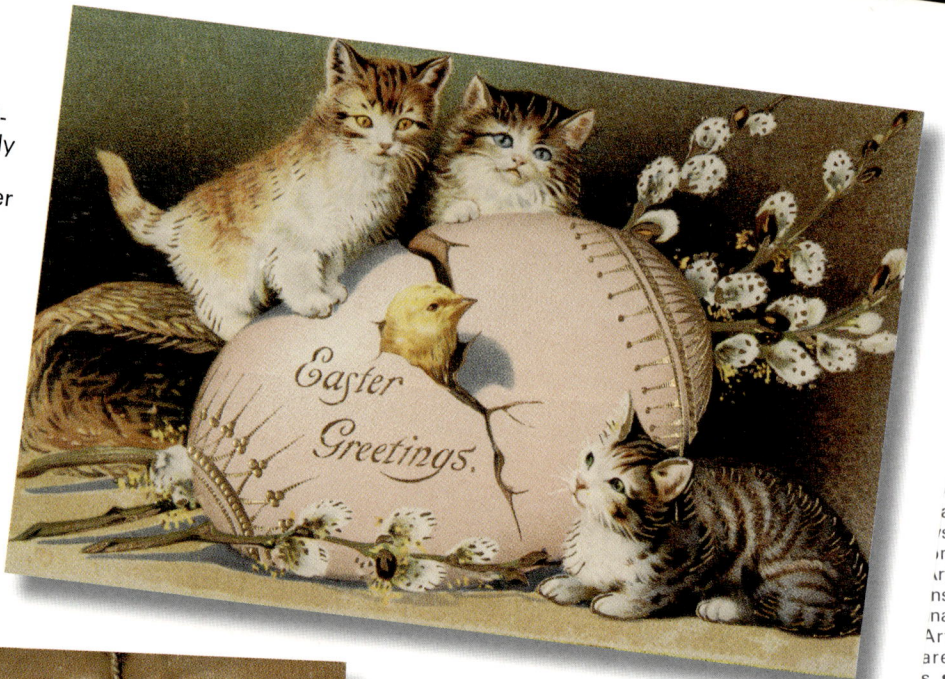

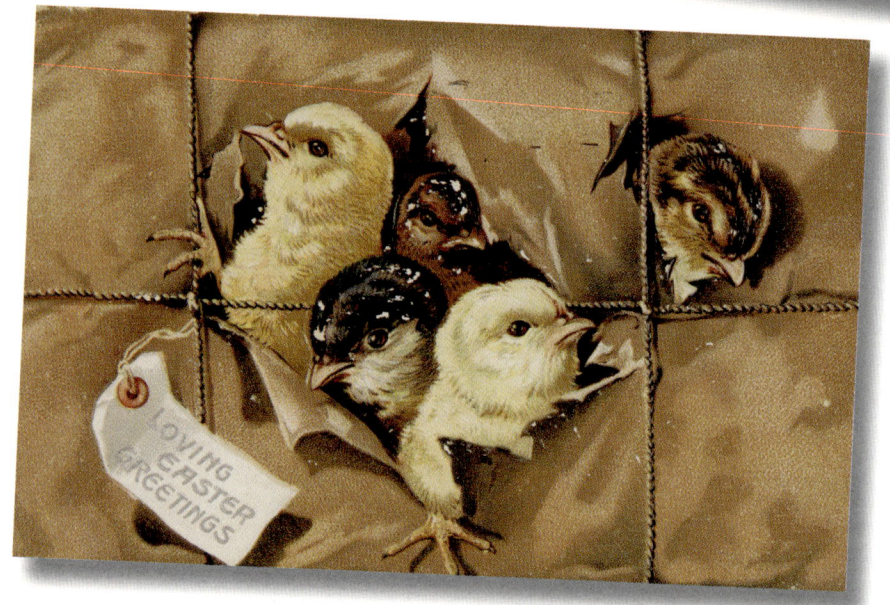

On rare occasions ducklings emerge from colored Easter eggs.

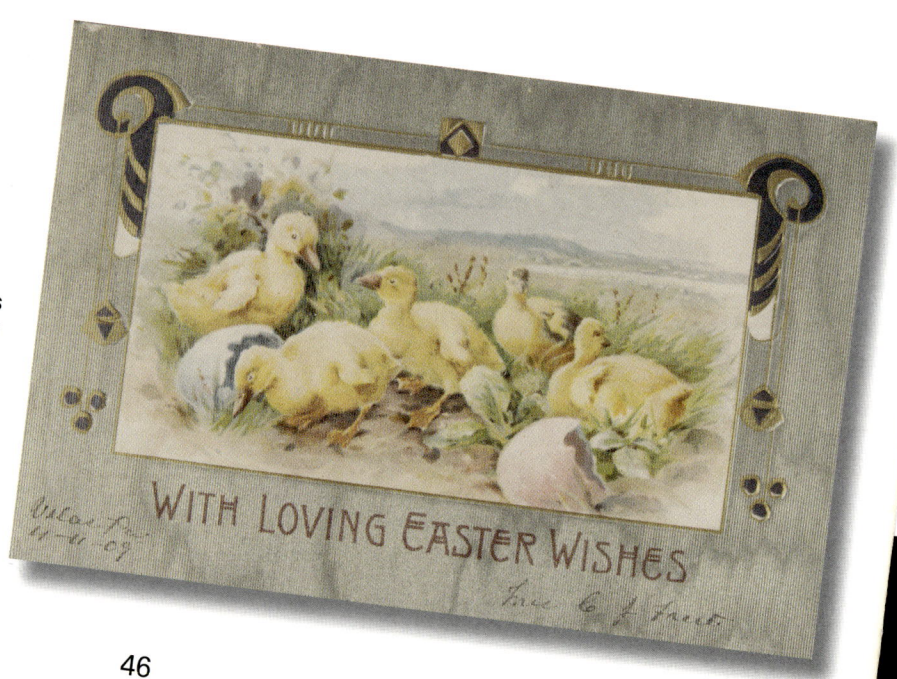

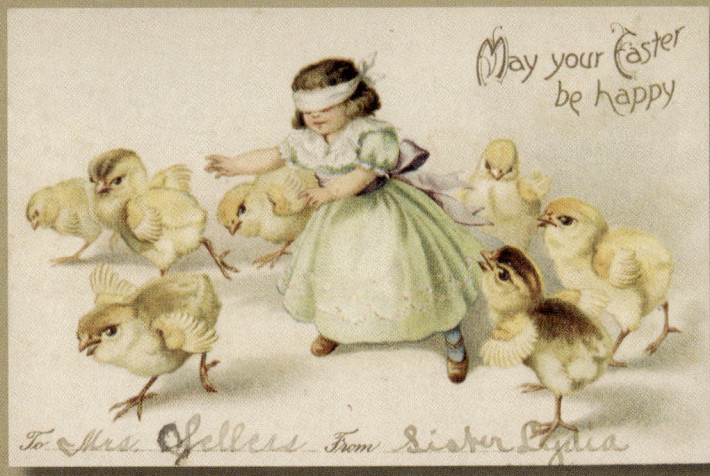

Newly hatched chicks have various quirks, uses, and talents. They are very good at playing blind-man-bluff and they literally feed on books. A very dexterous chick uses a telephone while epaulette-wearing chicks deliver eggs by boat – complete with a chick-headed figure head.

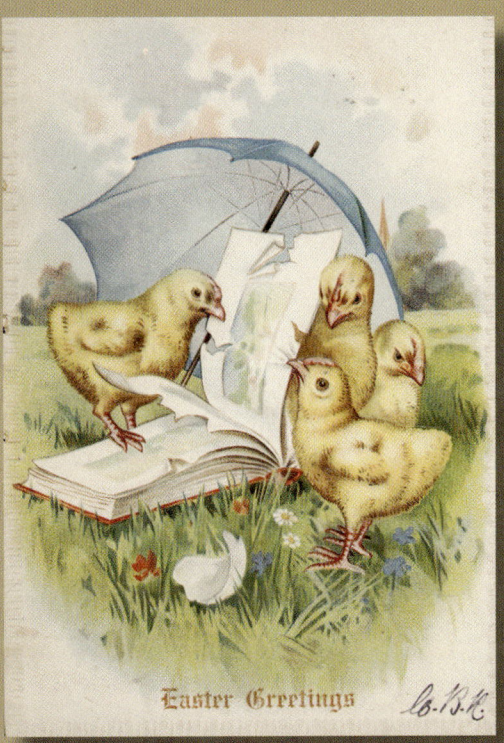

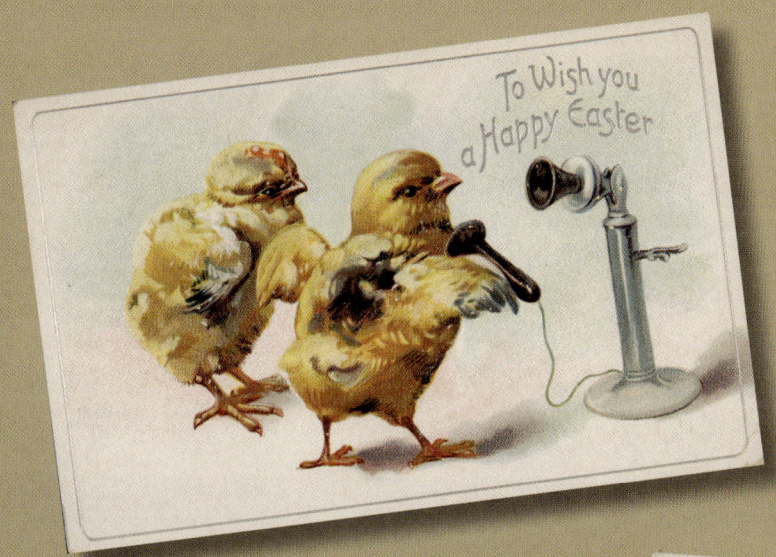

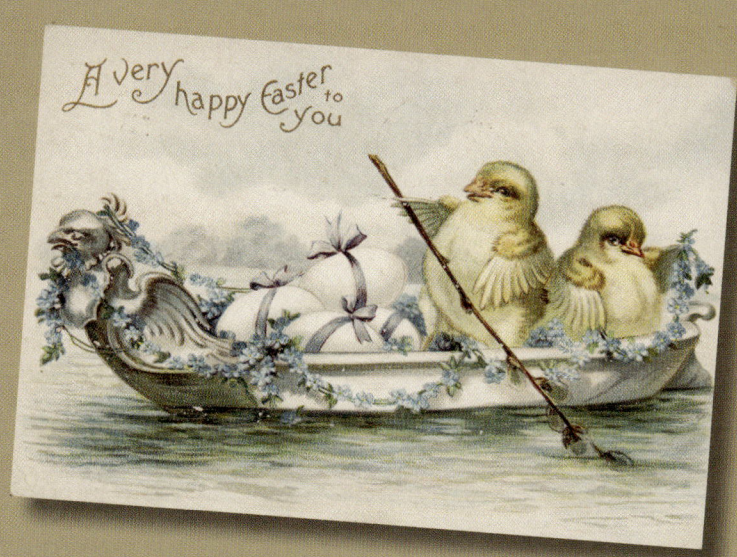

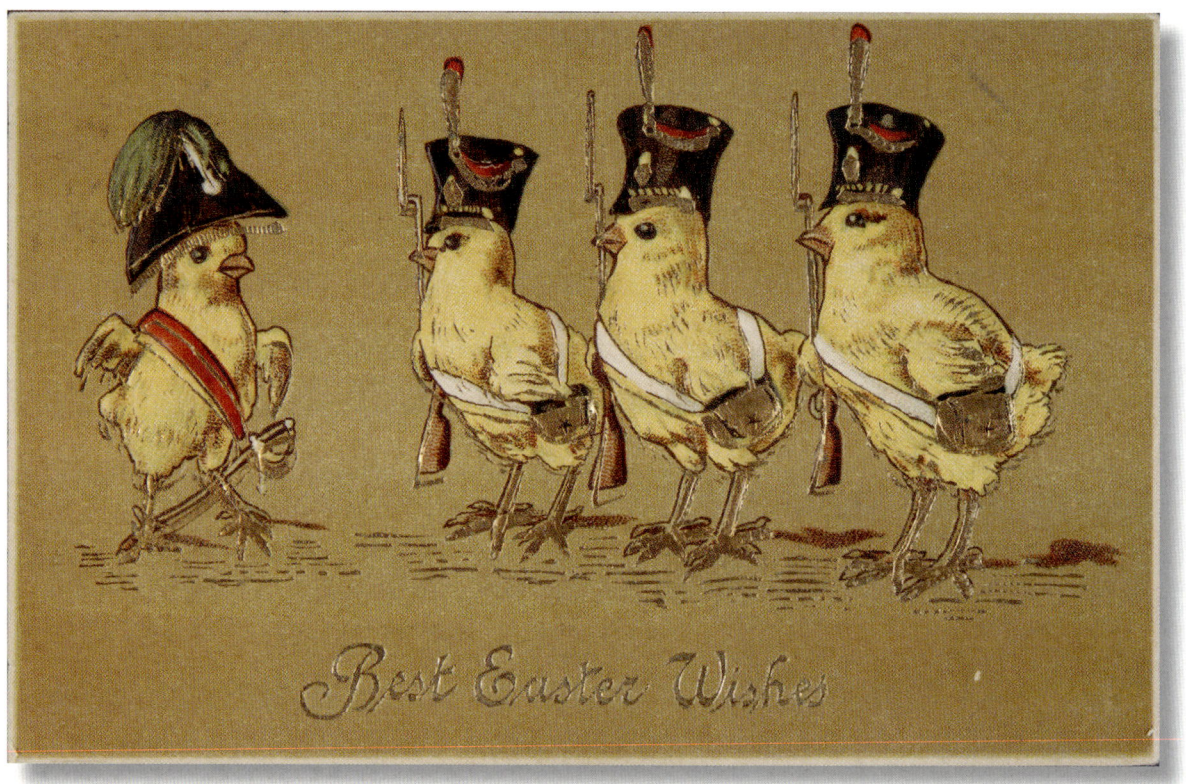

When chicks prepare for war! This is one of a number of oddly bellicose Easter greetings published in Germany in the years leading up to World War I. *Collection Mr. and Mrs. Michael Emery*

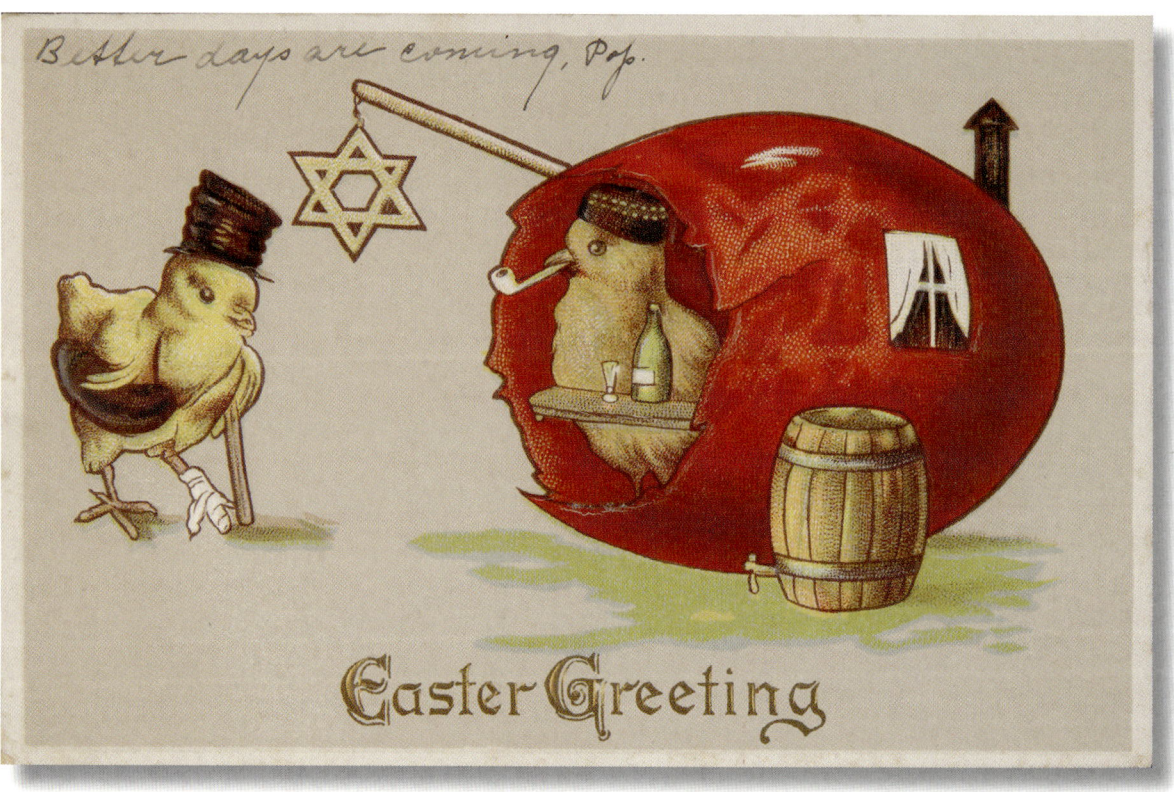

The wounded chick limping to a tavern fashioned out of a red Easter egg is probably the most esoteric Easter card the author has encountered and highlights the fact that almost nothing is known about the background of most artists who created postcard illustrations. It is likely that this card's creator was of Eastern European origin. Red is the color most associated with Russia, where eggs are tinted to commemorate Christ's blood. That the tavern sports a Star of David is emblematic that in most small towns in the countryside tavern-keeping was one of the few occupations allowed to Jews.

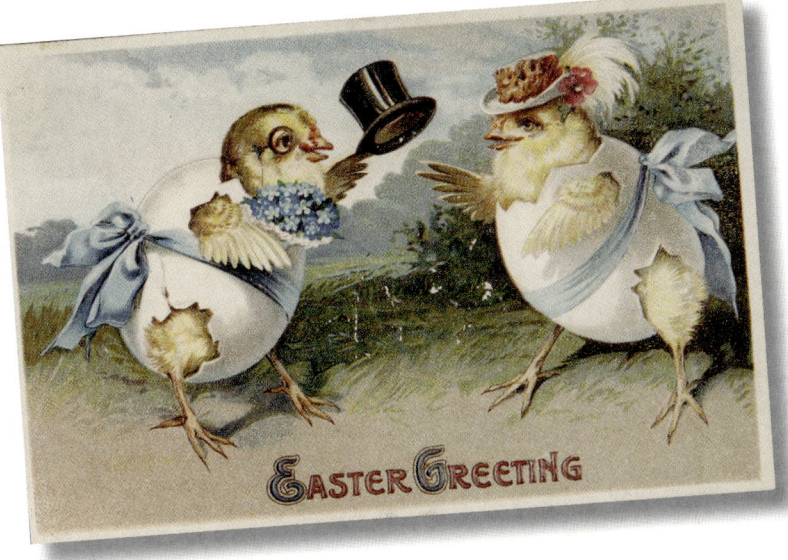

Occasionally chicks were presented as affected adults. While colors of flower and sashes vary, as do the greetings, these amusing cards are from a larger series of German chromolithographed cards, none of which had been sent. This suggests that these were purchased for their humor and added to a personal collection.

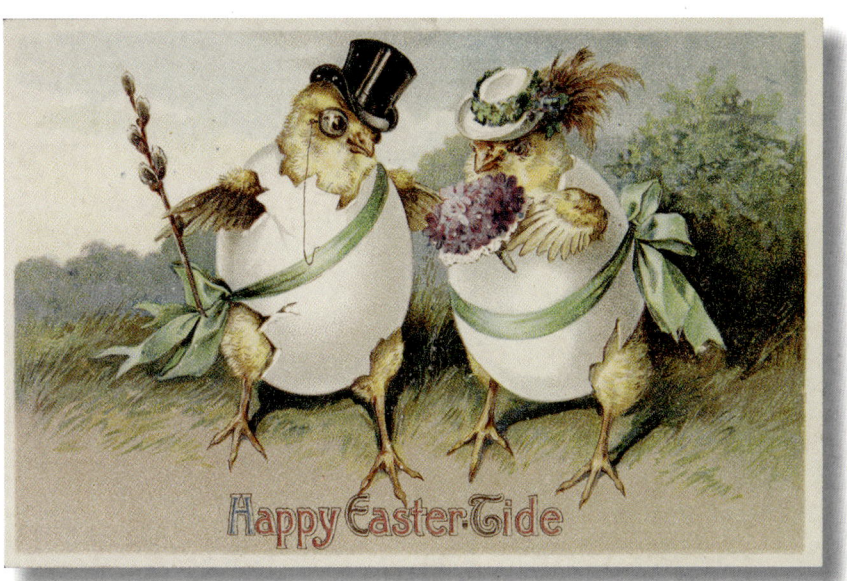

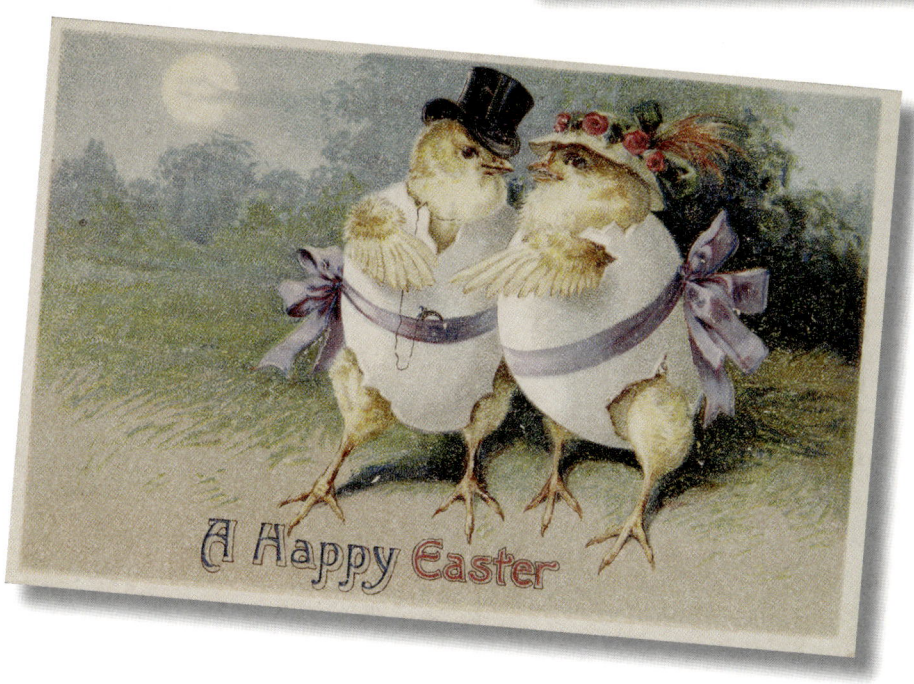

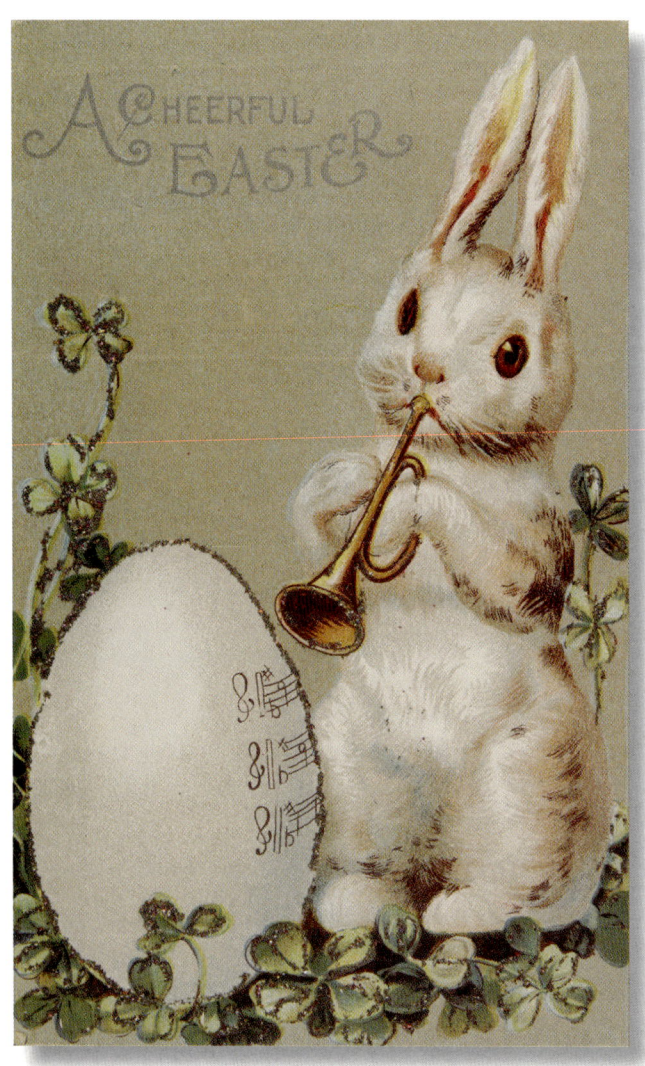

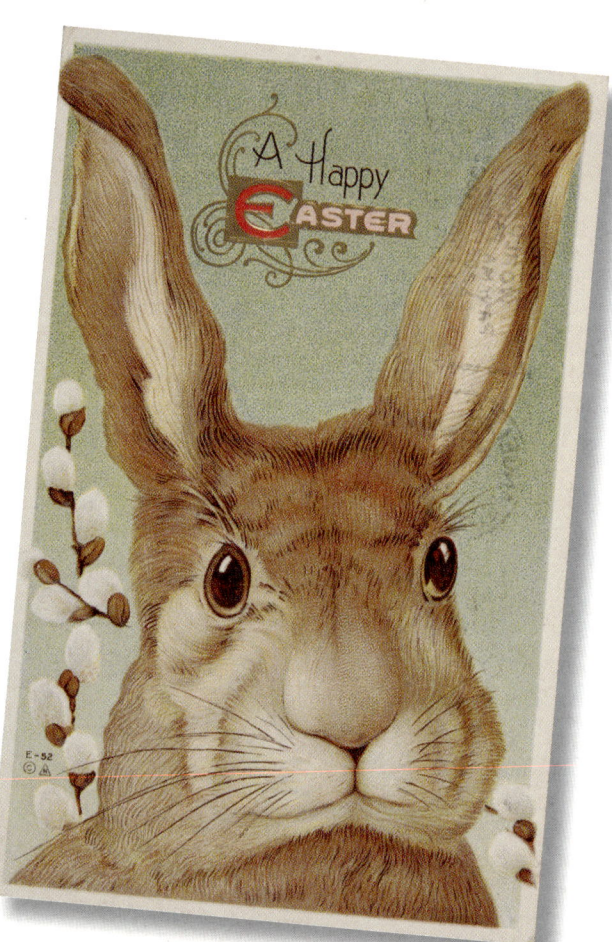

Rabbits have never had any Christian symbolic value, but they are important in pagan fertility lore, where they are emblematic of abundant new life. Trying to put a Christian face on the creature's symbolic value some hold that the rabbit in emerging from his burrow, is like Christ emerging from the tomb. The Easter Bunny arrived in America *via* the Pennsylvania Germans with the earliest known surviving illustration being done before 1812 by artist Conrad Gilbert (1734-1812) of Berks County. To the early German settlers the Easter Bunny is *"Oschter Haws."* Bunnies are usually appealing especially paired with pussy willows or sitting on a log. An anthropomorphic rabbit plays a horn; is he heralding the coming of Easter? *Rabbit portrait courtesy: Dr. Russell Eaton*

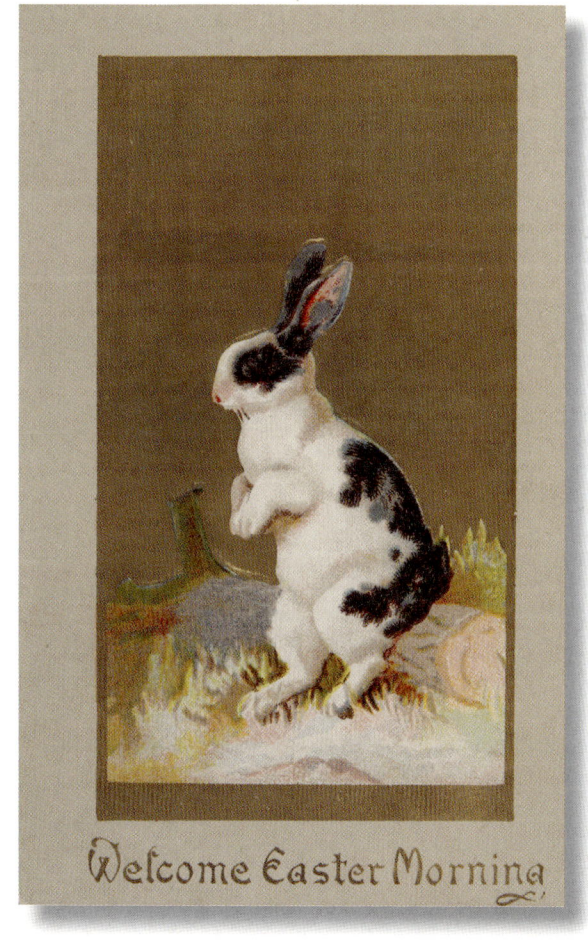

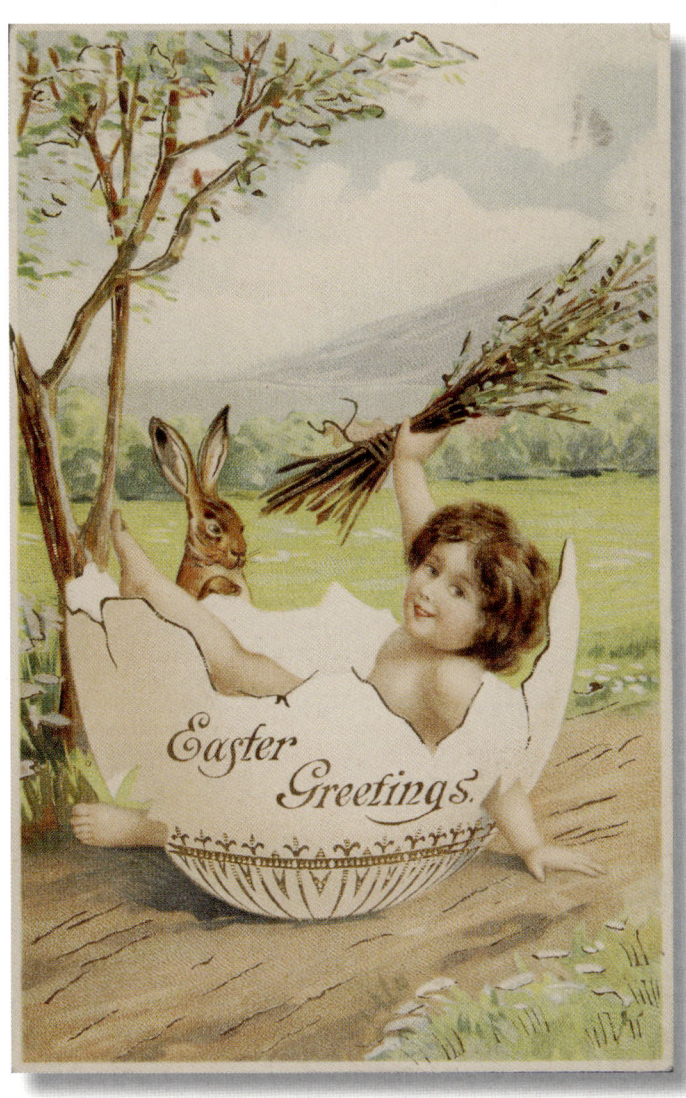

Wonderfully bizarre mixed metaphors abound on Easter cards. A young child happily sits in (or emerges like a god from) a giant egg, holding a sheaf of pussy willows, while a somber-looking rabbit observes. Two similar rabbits pose next to a giant pink Easter egg decorated with a spray of pussy willows and violets while the Paschal lamb obligingly poses.

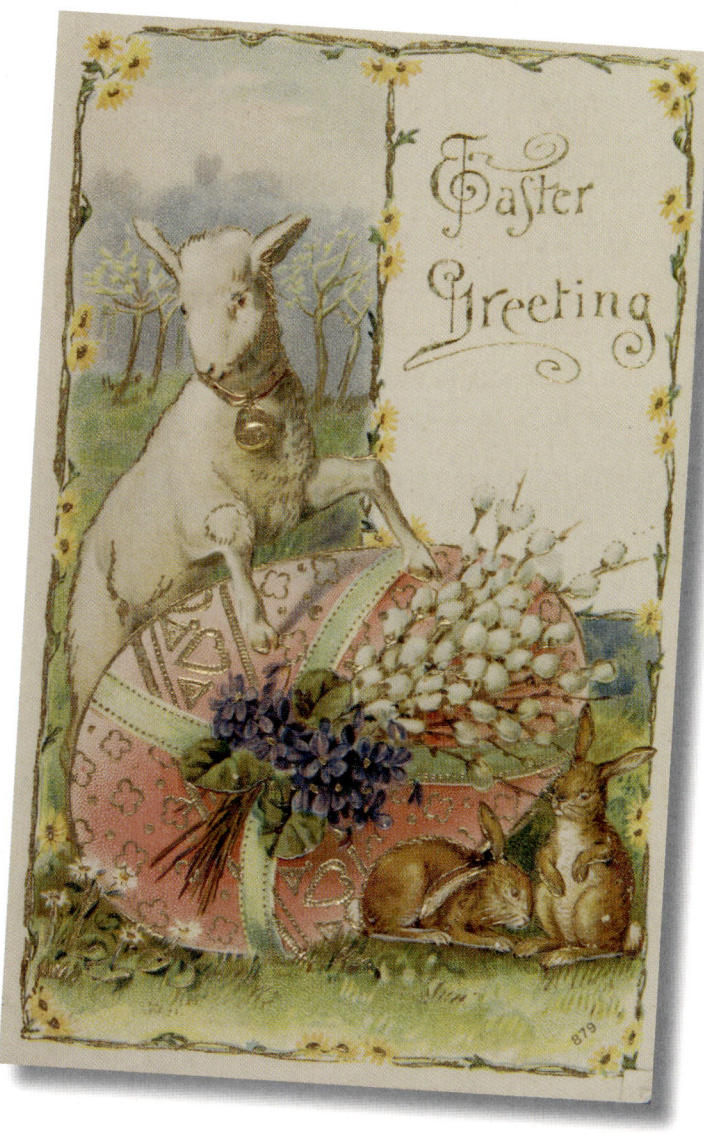

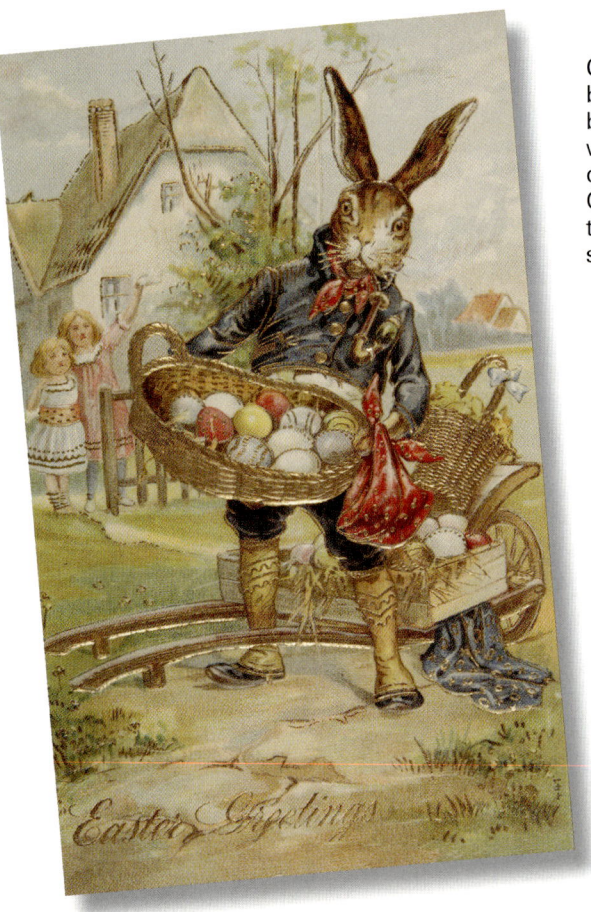

Colored eggs, originally dyed with vegetable dyestuffs, became more brilliant with the introduction of aniline dyes in the late 19th century. Rabbits are credited with either laying or delivering the eggs. In Germany it was believed that the Easter Bunny lays only red eggs on Maundy Thursday (the day before Good Friday) and other colored eggs on Easter eve. On our cards Mother and Father Bunnies deliver a large basket of eggs to a sweet little girl. A buck rabbit dressed as a middle-European country squire delivers his eggs in golden baskets and red sacks.

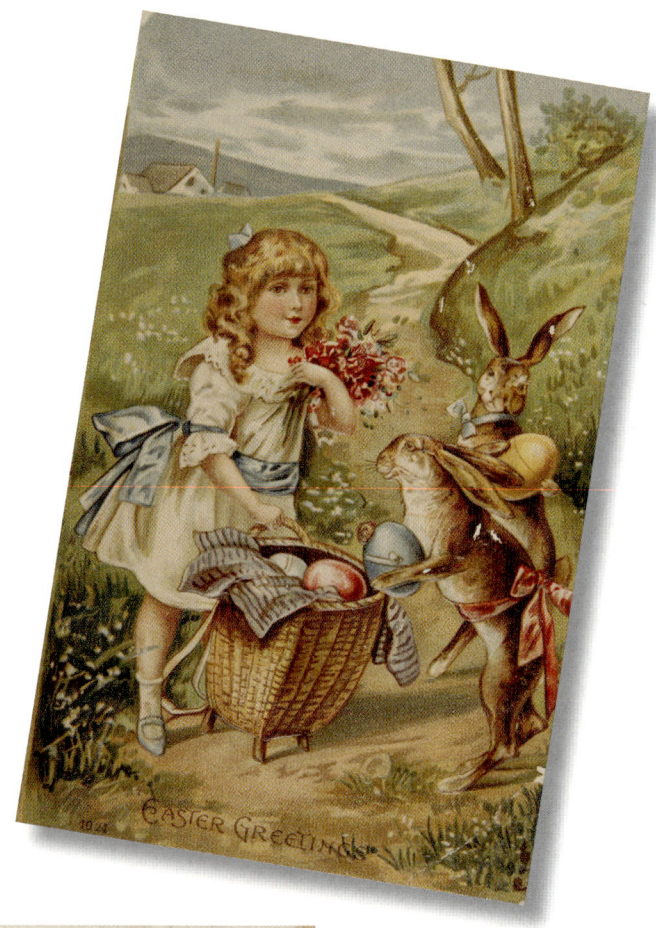

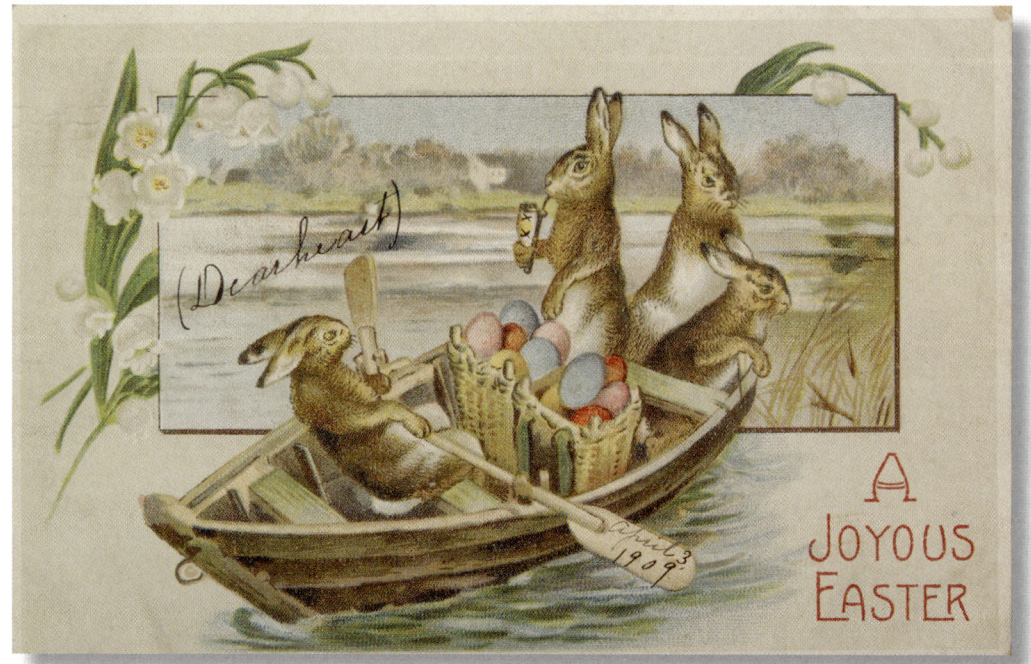

A family of rabbits, Mama, Papa (smoking a pipe), little daughter and young son (at the oars) are a rowing party set on delivering a hamper of eggs.

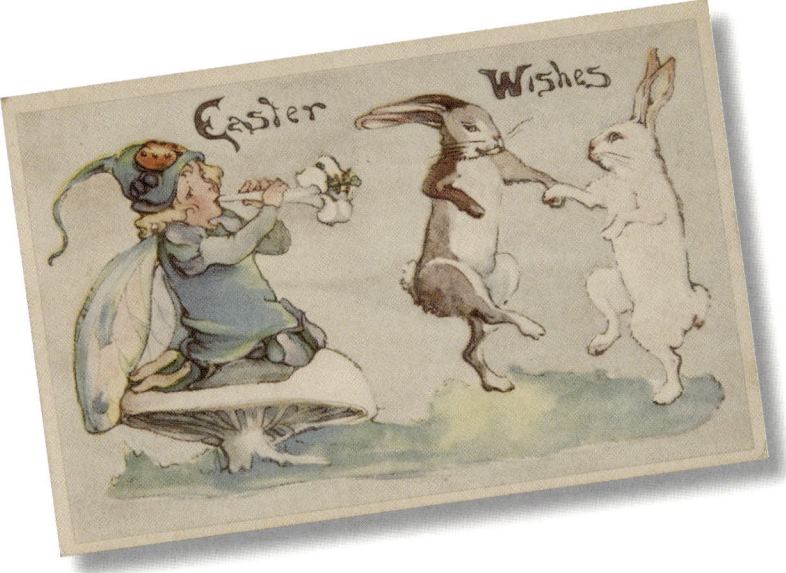

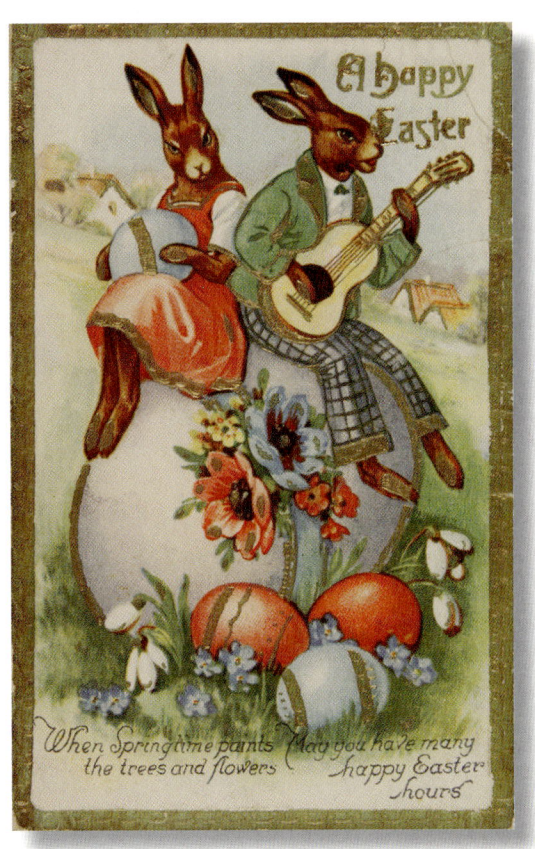

Rabbits enjoy music as players and dancers. Rabbits dance to the music of a winged elf kneeling on a mushroom. His instrument is an Easter lily. Dark hued-minstrel rabbits perform on a giant egg.

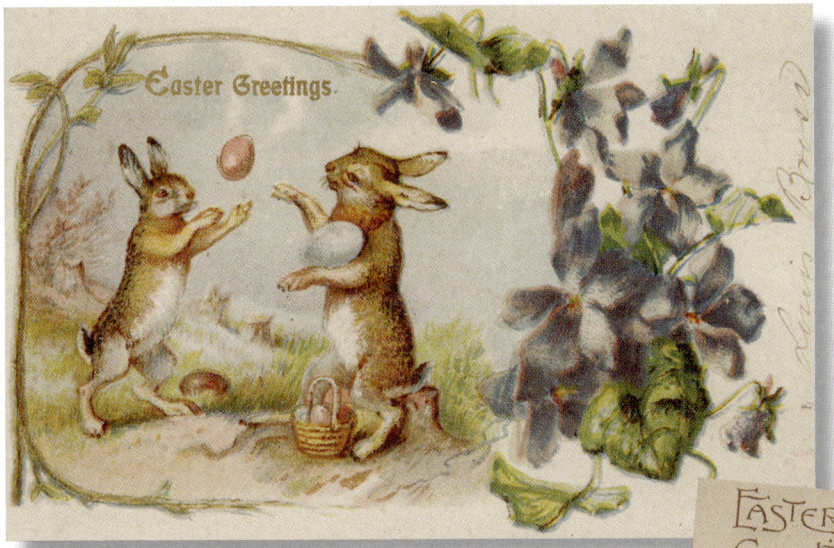

Games with Easter eggs are played wherever colored eggs are commonly used. Most feature rolling the eggs or some kind of cracking contest, whereby eggs are pitted against one another. The hardest shell wins. Egg tosses are rare, except in Bunnyland. The kid in the red cap holds the egg like a football. Who will go for the field goal?

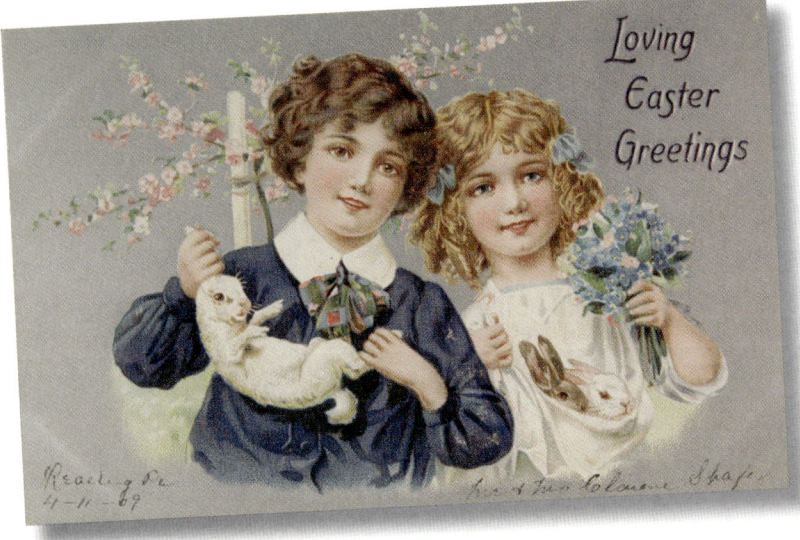

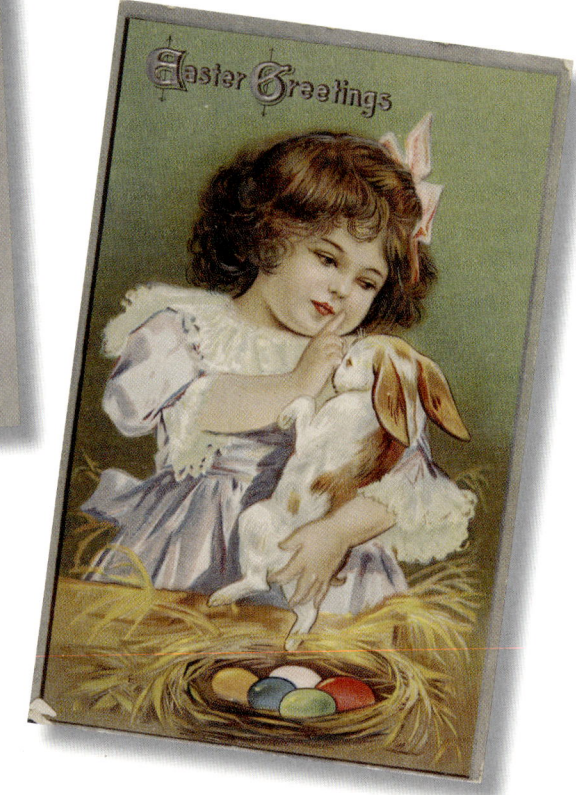

Kids and cuddly animals are a natural sentimental pairing. While the girls cuddle the rabbits, the boy holds an uncomfortable animal by his ears and feet. Did the little girl with the pink bow in her hair just catch her bunny at the nest? Is she admonishing him or promising "Mum's the word"?

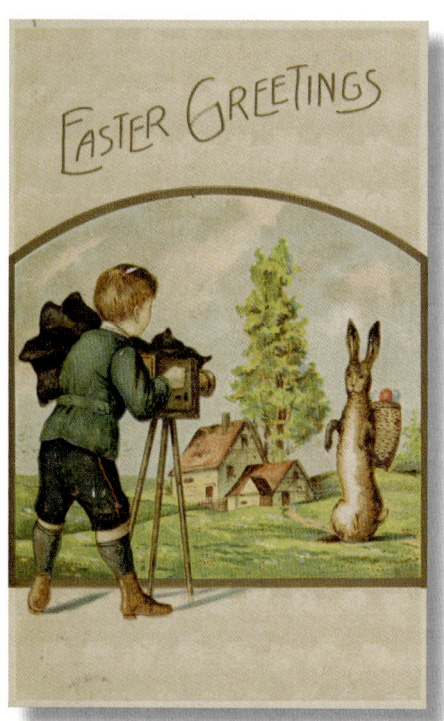

If "A picture is worth ten thousand words," what would photographic proof of the Easter Bunny caught in the act be valued at?

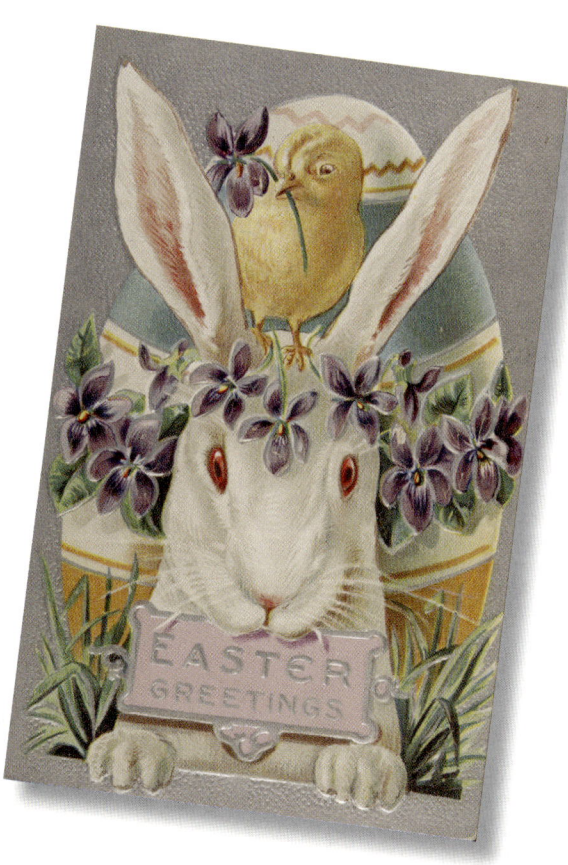

Many devotedly religious people actively dislike the Easter Bunny. Their reasons are twofold: he is pagan in origin and, most importantly for many, the rabbit appears to replace Christ as the central focus of the holiday. What, however, can give a better warm-and-fuzzy feeling than a cute bunny haloed in violets and topped with a chick bearing "Easter Greetings."

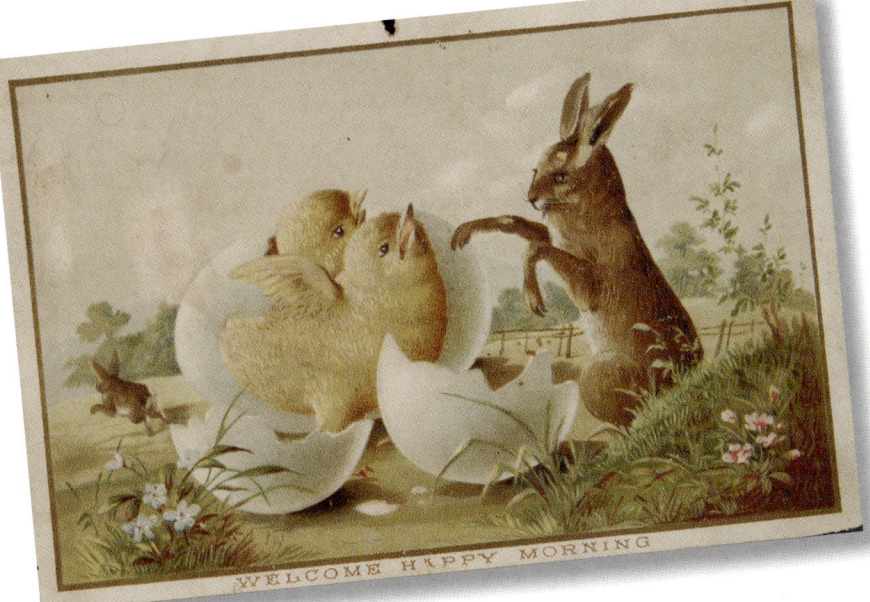

The Easter Bunny is often believed to lay Easter eggs. No one has ever answered the question, "Why?" Perhaps it is because little bunnies, like chicks, hatch from eggs.

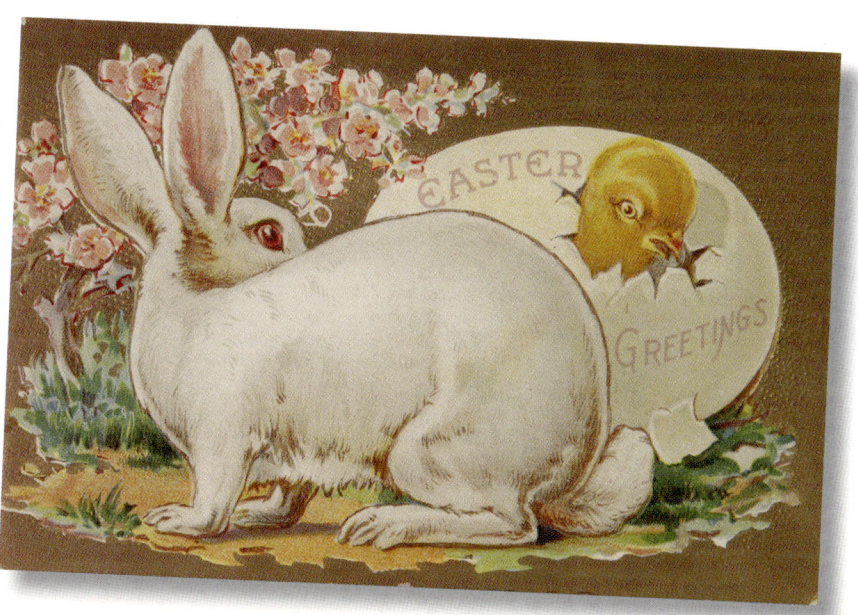

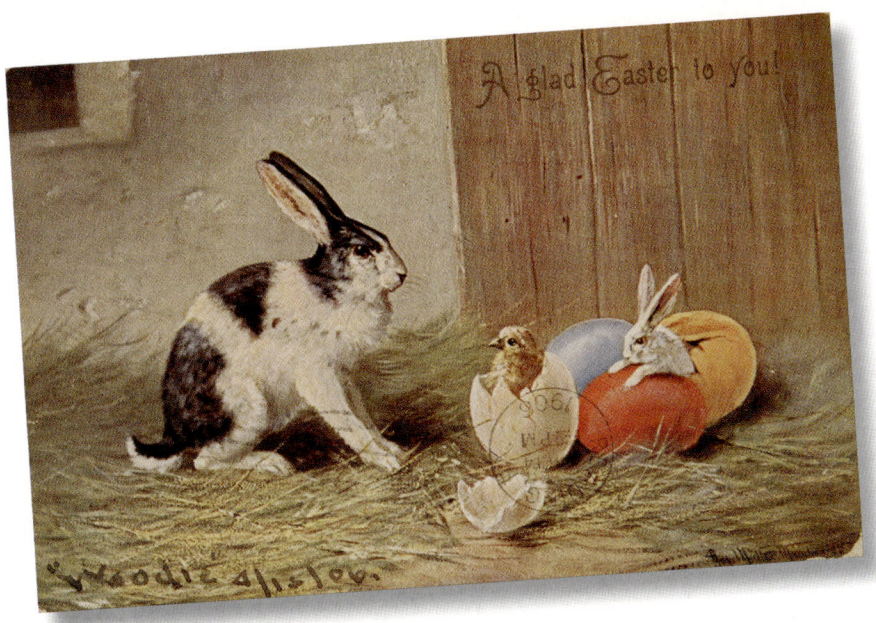

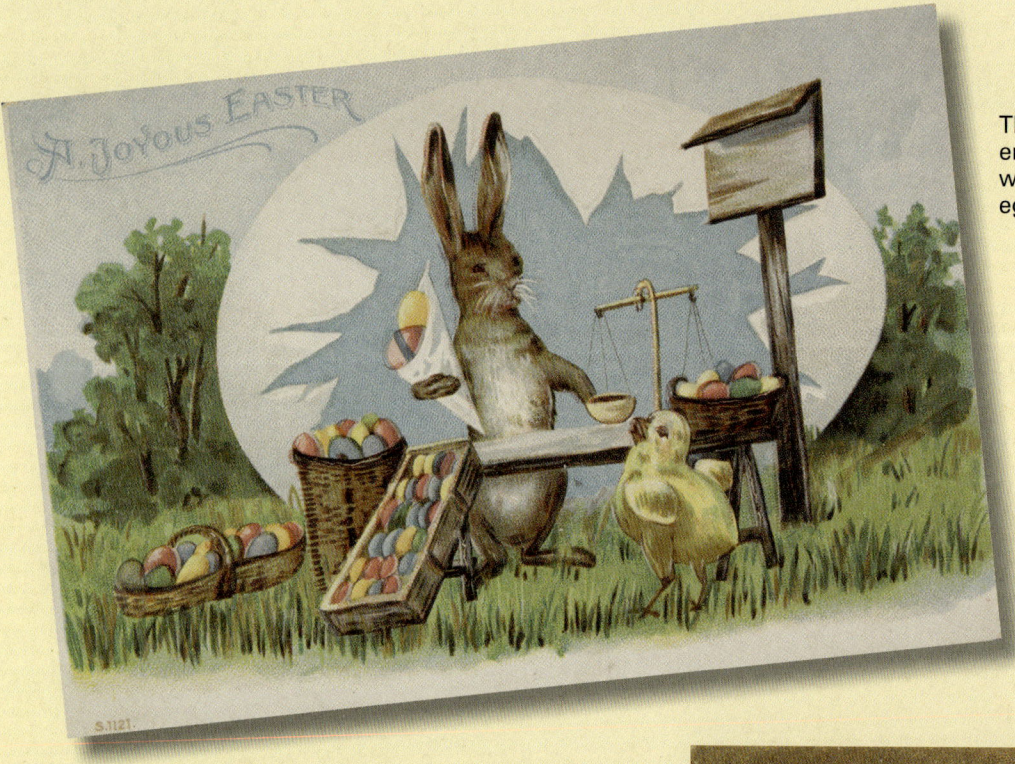

The Easter Bunny is a very talented soul. An artist, he paints with great skill. His canvas is an egg, naturally, or weirdly.

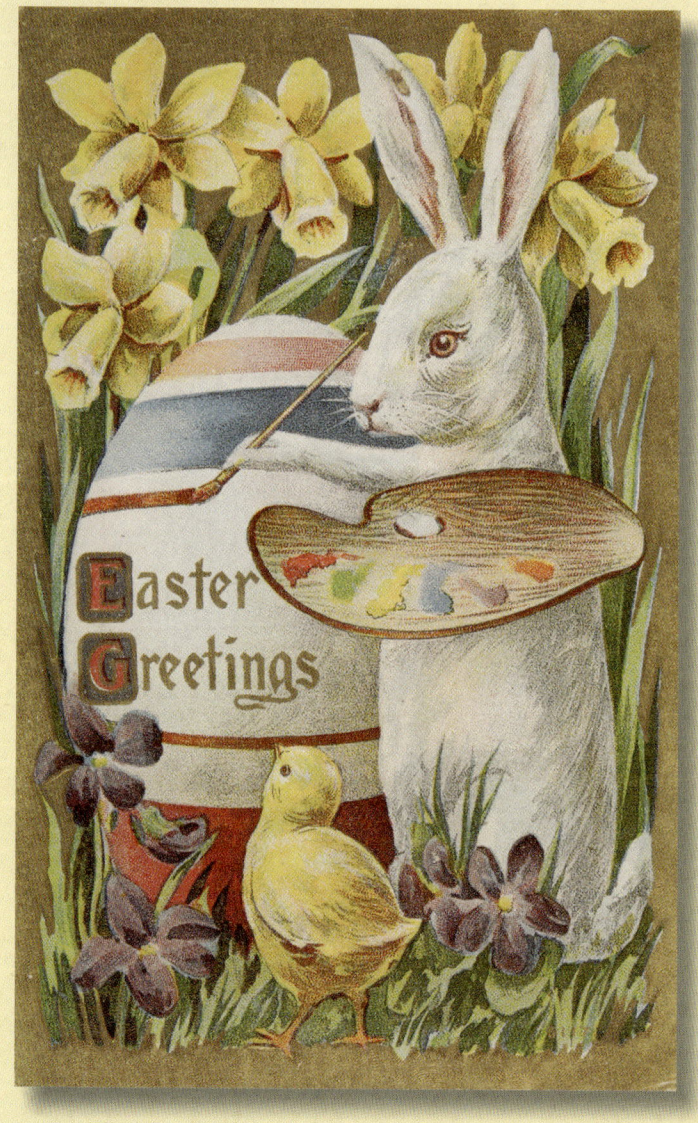

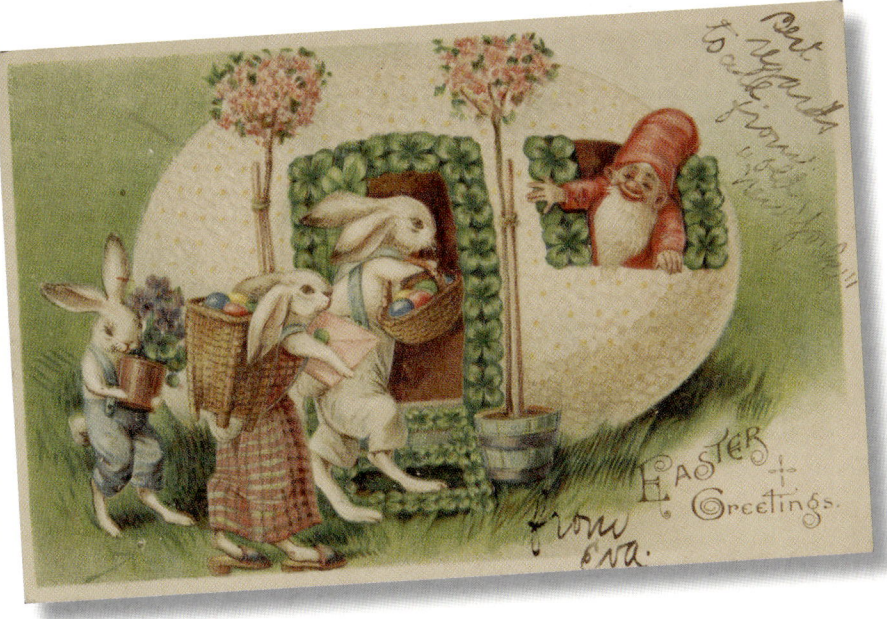

In "Easter Land," rabbits inhabit dwelling adapted from giant eggs. Two of a series of cards also include a Santa Elf thrown in for good measure. The most impressive of the egg dwellings even sports a stovepipe chimney.

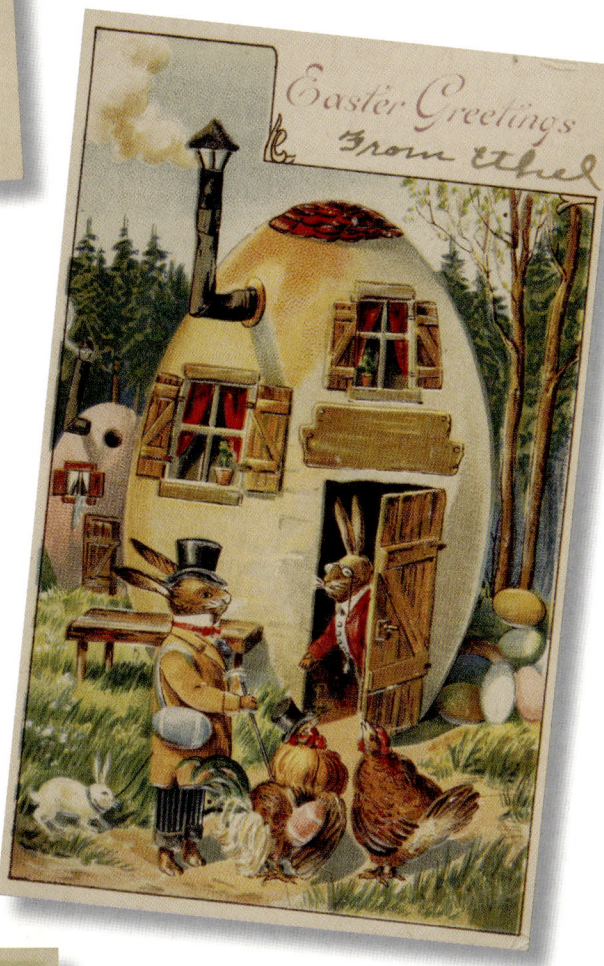

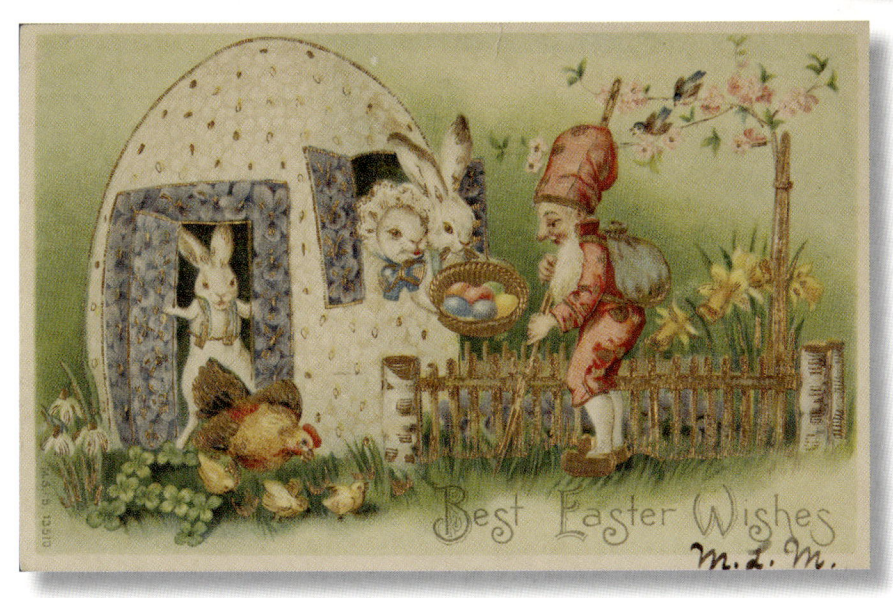

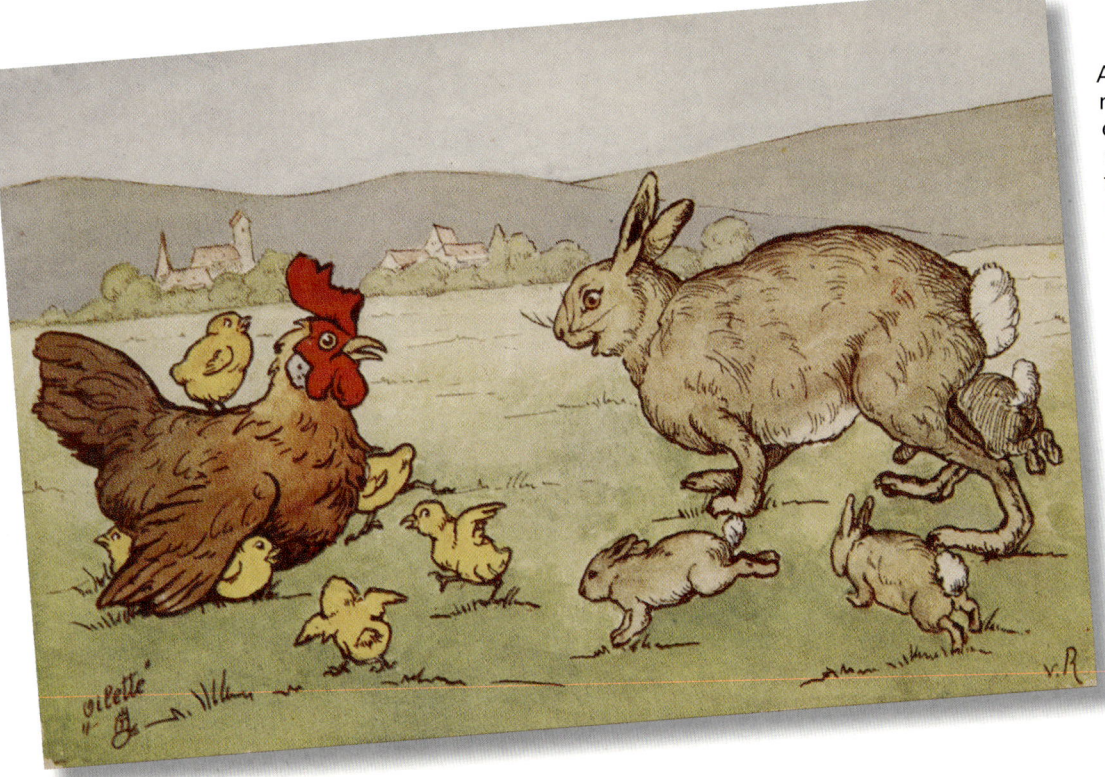

A bunny family and a rooster with his flock meet on a card dated 1914. The message on the reverse of the card is imprinted, "A Happy Easter to you" to which "Aunt Luella" added, "Dear Uncle Bright! – I'm sending this for spite. This pictures original maker Was an awful nature Faker." Luella was a cynic!

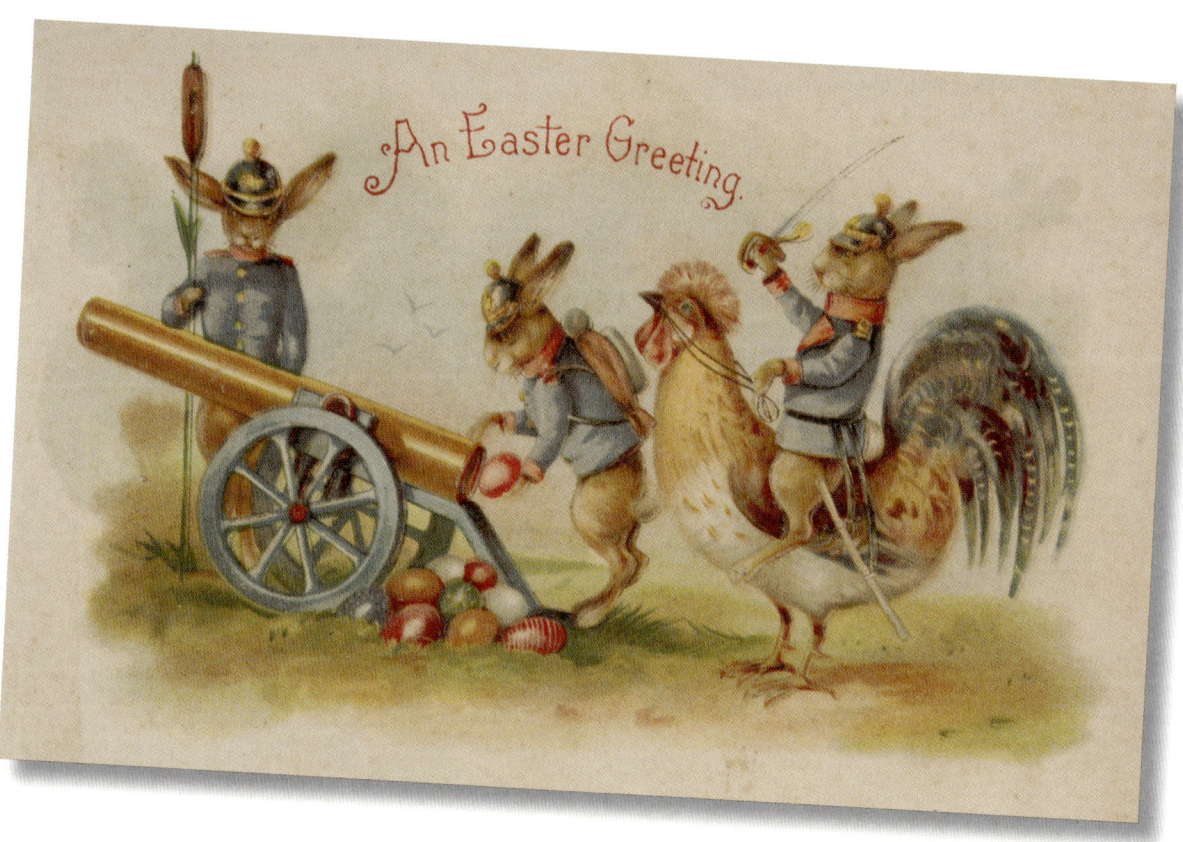

Can anyone top this printed-in-Germany card for inappropriateness in its glorification of militarism? The Prussian officer, saber in hand, rides a sturdy cock while his troops load a cannon with colored eggs, in lieu of cannon balls. The assistant's plunger is a giant cattail. This certainly celebrates Easter with a bang. "Peace and Joy to All Mankind." Indeed! *Collection of Mr. and Mrs. Michael Emery.*

5
St. Patrick's Day
We All Turn Green

There are twenty Saint's days or festivals commonly celebrated in America, ranging from the Feast of St. Anthony of Padua to St. Urho's Day; all but one of them remain sspecifically ethnic, regional, or parochial. Only St. Patrick's Day has become a national observance. It is widely asserted that, "Everyone is Irish on St. Patrick's Day." Nobody makes this all-encompassing claim about any other Saint's day. We are not all Welsh on St. David's Day (March 1), or English on St. George's Day (April 23), or Finnish on St. Urho's Day (March 16). But many Americans, of whatever descent, "wear the green" on March 17.

St. Patrick's Day has even displaced the observance of other Saint's days. Prior to the great Irish emigration to America in the 1840s and 1850s, the Pennsylvania Dutch had a tradition of planting peas on St. Gertrude's Day (March 17), but by the end of the 19th century everyone was planting peas on St. Patrick's Day.

While St. Patrick is the patron saint of Ireland and his day has always been celebrated with merriment and drinking, it is a much more festive occasion in the United States than in Ireland. [Indeed, now there are more Americans of Irish descent than there are Irish in Ireland.] The Irish certainly have shamrocks around but they don't wear green-dyed carnations, drink green-colored beer, nor do they have St. Patrick's Day parades… largely an American construct.

The first St. Patrick's Day parade was held in New York City in 1760 and, while similar events are now held in at least 30 states, New York's is still pre-eminent. New York's parade is occasionally controversial, as in the question of whether or not gay and lesbian units should be allowed to parade, a complex concern considering that the official reviewing stand is in front of St. Patrick's Cathedral and is presided over by the Archbishop of New York, who is often also a Cardinal of the Church.

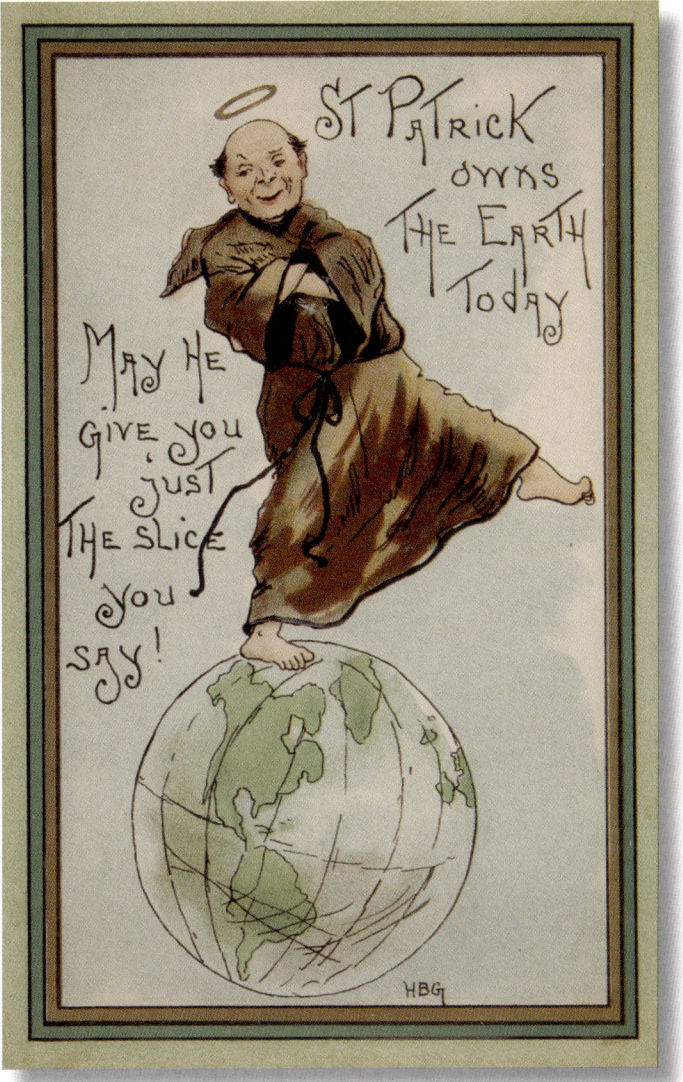

St. Patrick, the patron saint of Ireland, was actually born in Roman Britain (probably modern Scotland) around 385 A.D. Captured at age 16 by Irish raiders, he was enslaved for six years before escaping to the Continent where he wandered, or studied, for several years before a vision from God told him to return to Ireland and convert its pagan people to Christianity. Around 432 he landed south of present Dublin and began his work, which ended with his death in 464. All of Ireland mourned. He is, perhaps, best known for having banished snakes from Ireland. The spirit of St. Patrick would go wherever the Irish would travel.

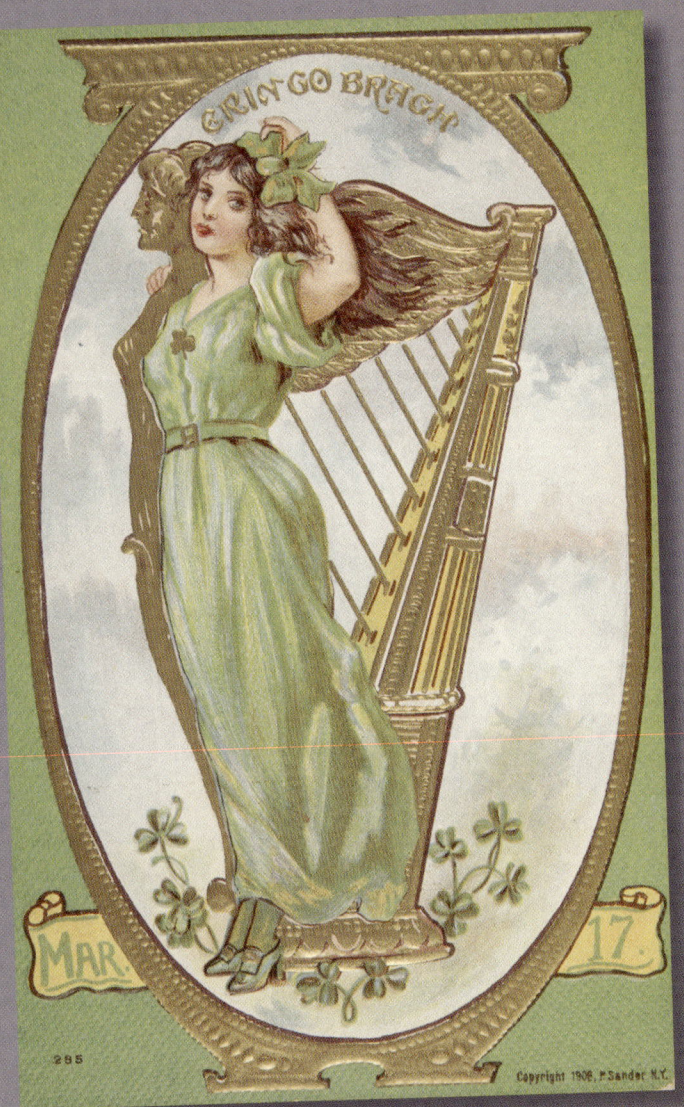

The harp is both the symbol of St. Patrick and of Ireland and is found on its presidential flag. The oldest form of the Irish Harp, the *clàrsach*, is small and usually carved from a single block of wood. The finest are often embellished with stylized female forms. On one card the ideal colleen is the model for the carving on a harp; on the other a green-clad lass displays a banner with a harp motif. *Harp flag: Collection of Mr. and Mrs. Michael Emery.*

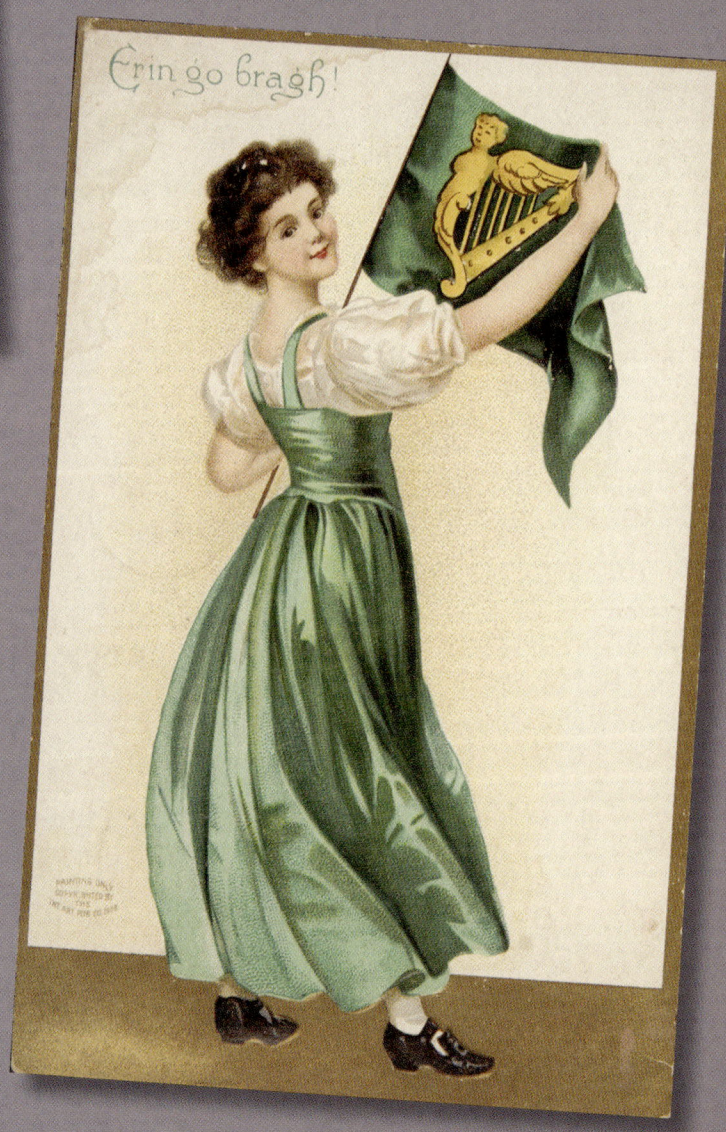

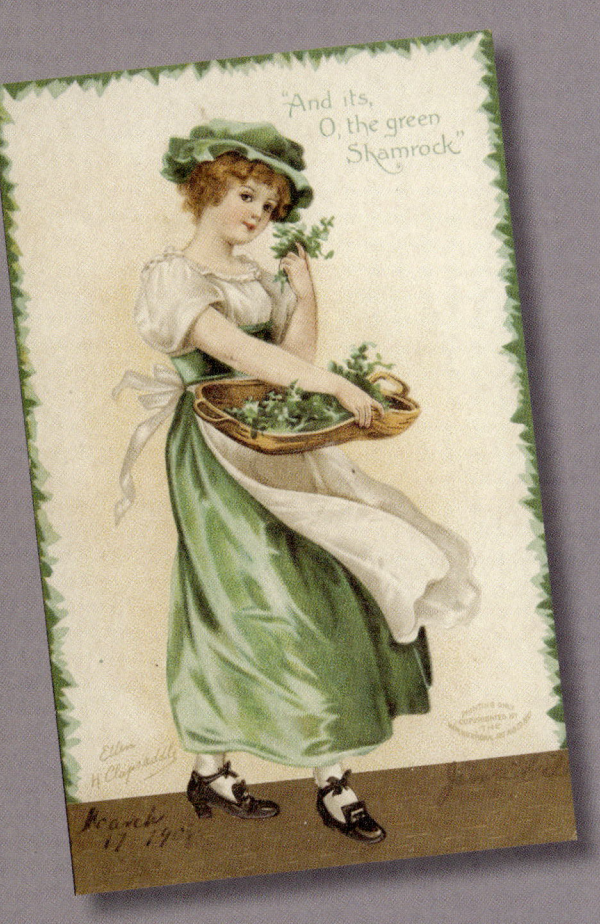
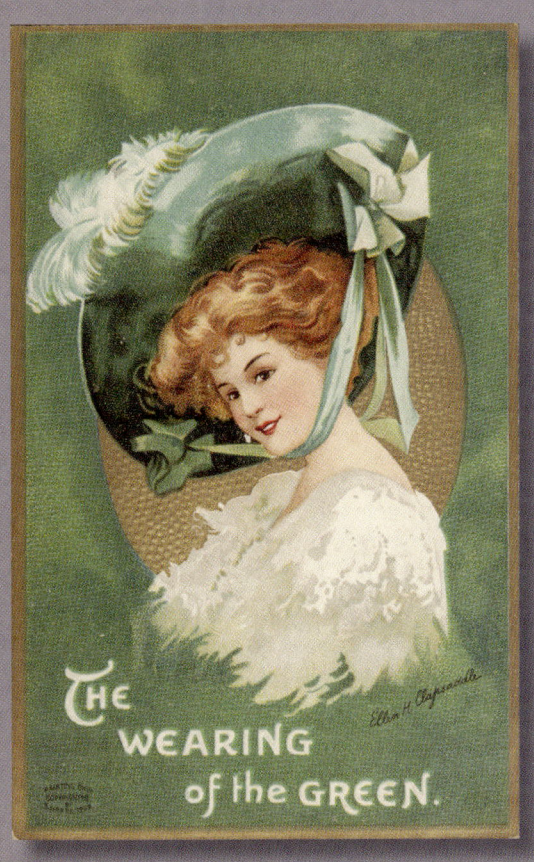

Ireland is the Emerald Isle so "What Color should be seen, Where our father's homes have been, But our immortal Green". Except for the lovely lady in the large hat, the other cards were designed by Ellen H. Clapsaddle (1863-1934), the most prolific woman graphic artist of her time, who created many hundreds of cards.

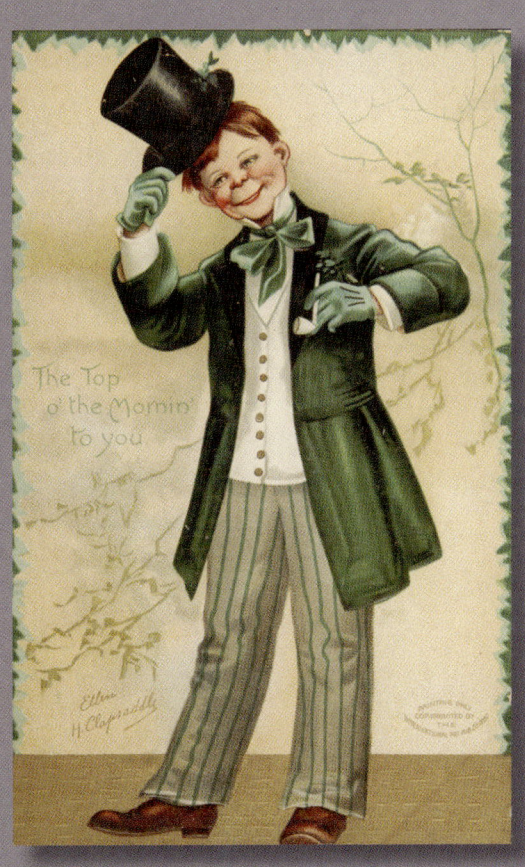
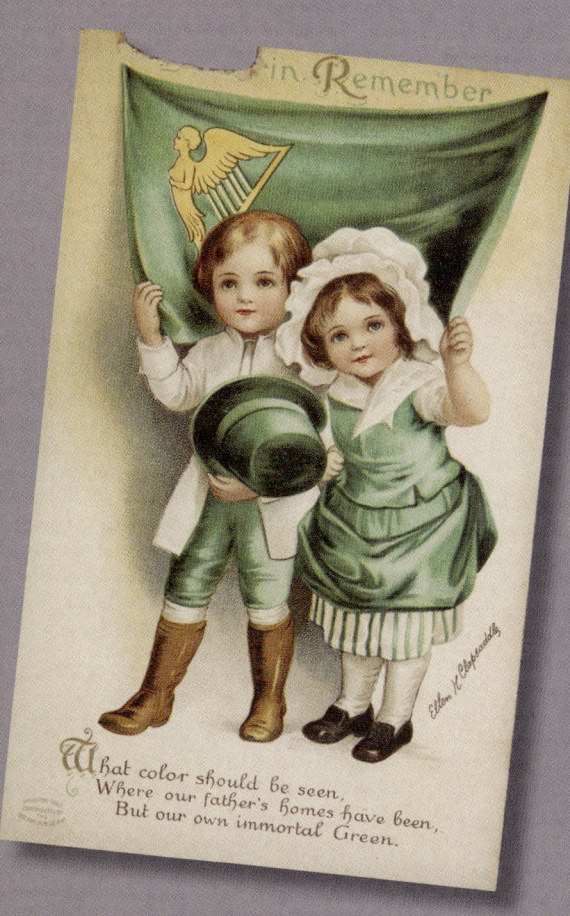

The modern miss uses the telephone to send her holiday greetings at a time when home telephones were a rarity.

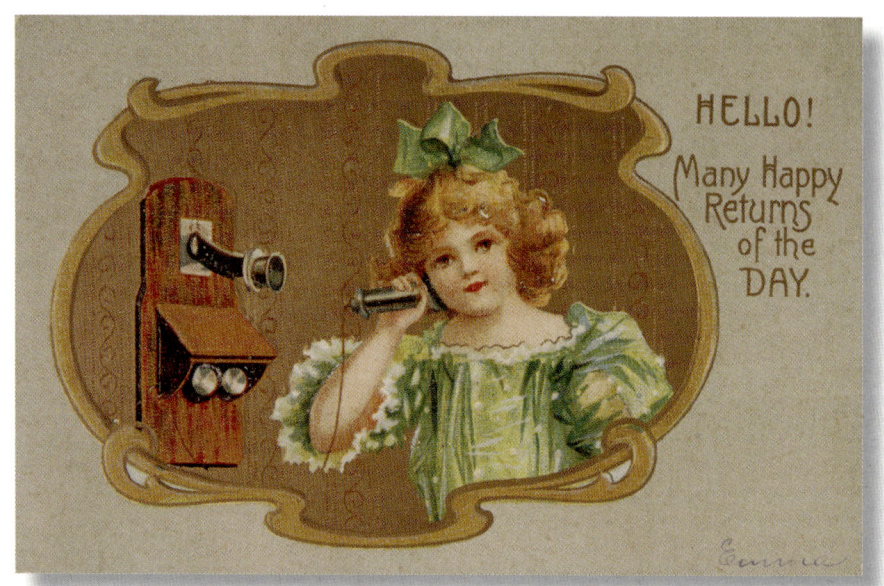

"Irish as Shaugnessy's pig," was a common expression. The artist who created the pig and the shamrock didn't realize that the shamrock has only three leaves. The man holds a shillelagh in his other hand.

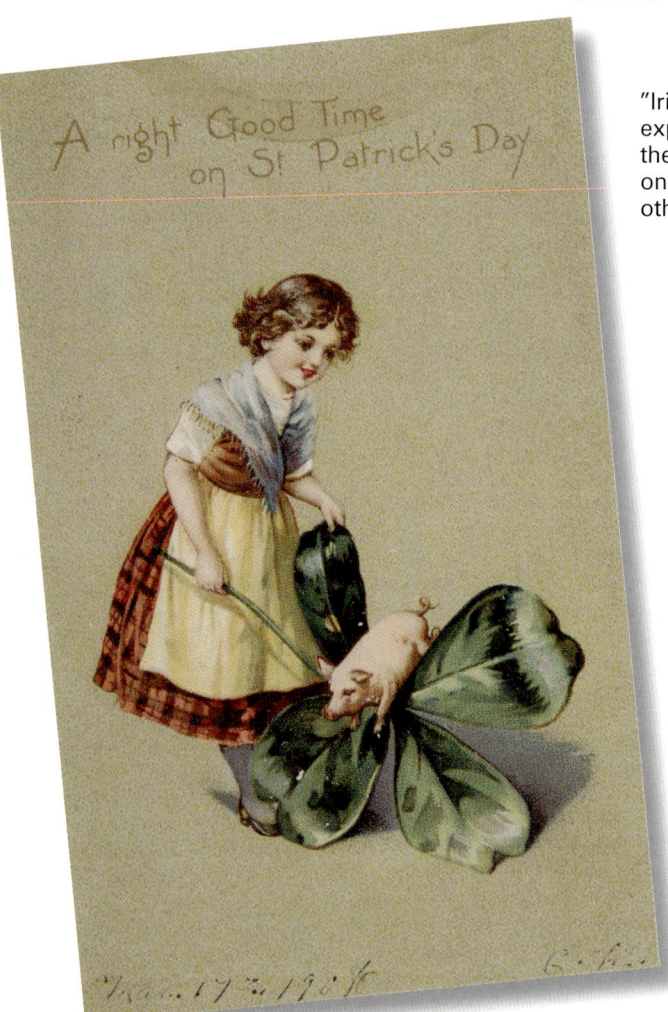

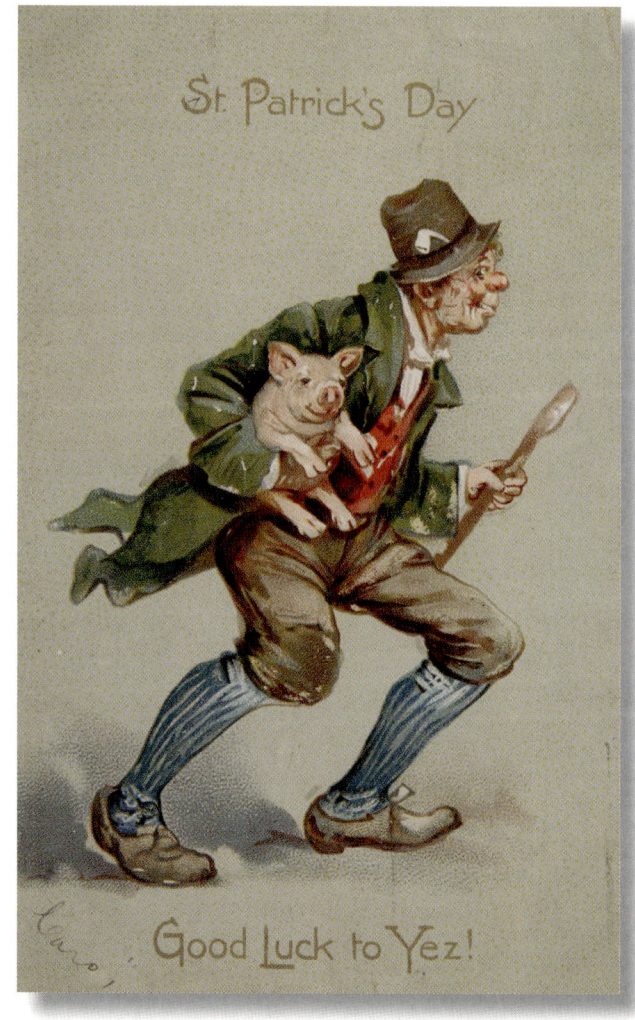

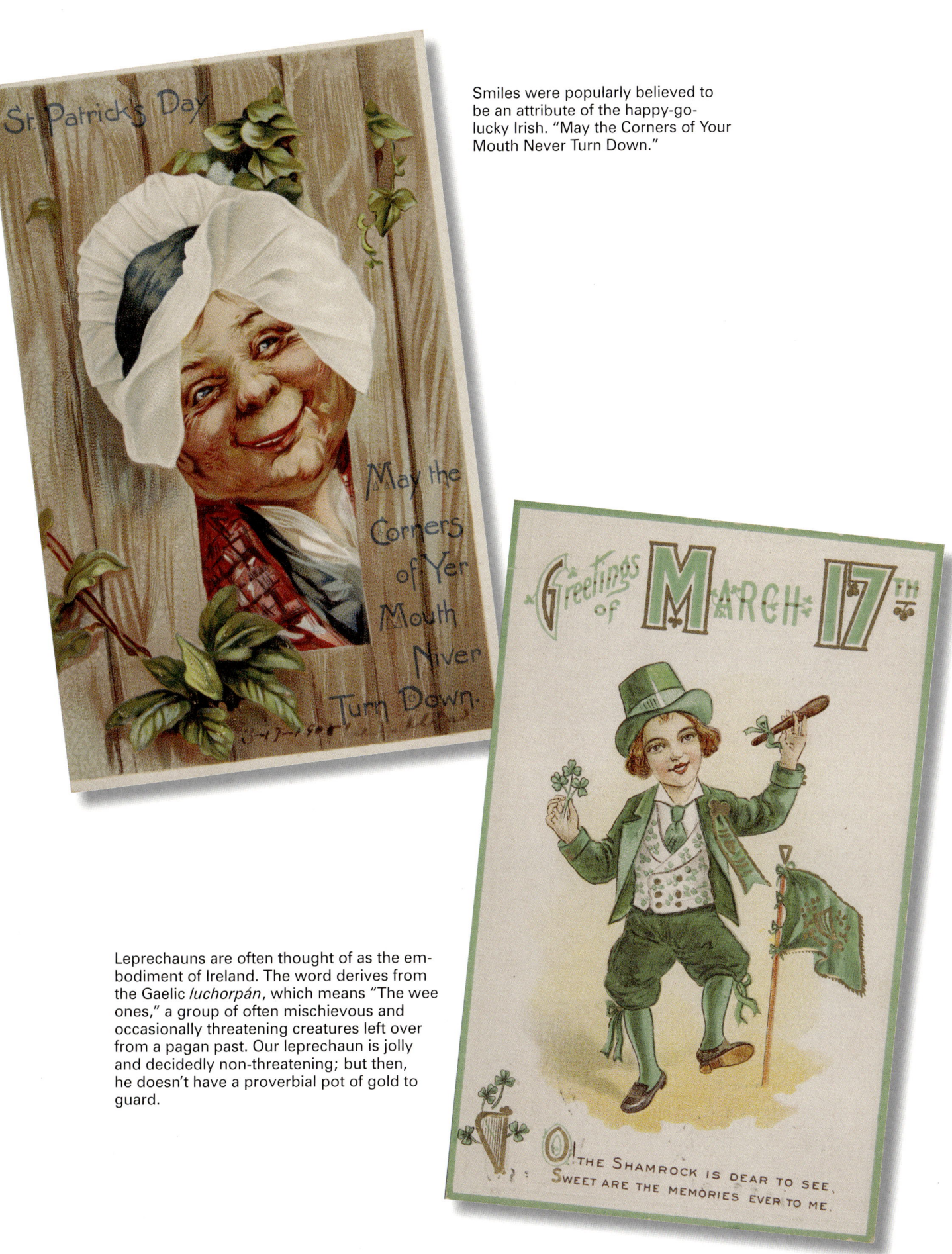

Smiles were popularly believed to be an attribute of the happy-go-lucky Irish. "May the Corners of Your Mouth Never Turn Down."

Leprechauns are often thought of as the embodiment of Ireland. The word derives from the Gaelic *luchorpán*, which means "The wee ones," a group of often mischievous and occasionally threatening creatures left over from a pagan past. Our leprechaun is jolly and decidedly non-threatening; but then, he doesn't have a proverbial pot of gold to guard.

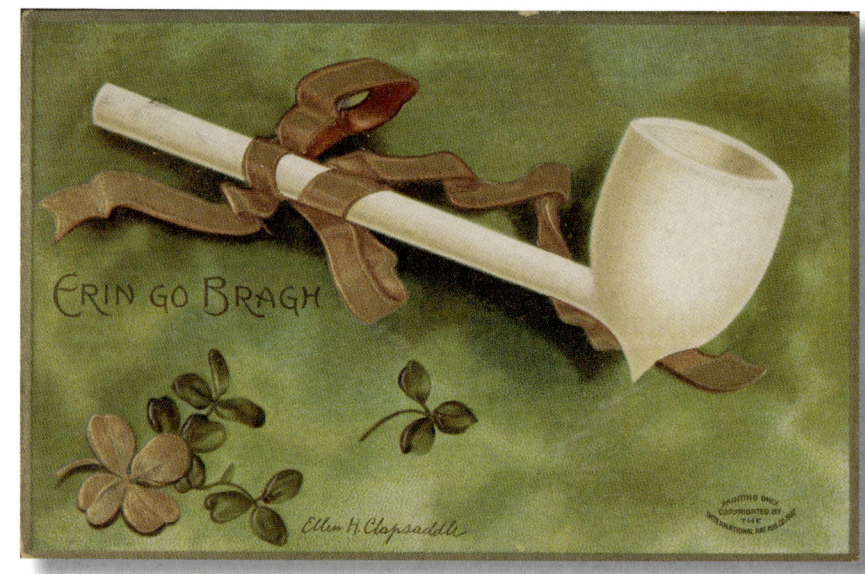

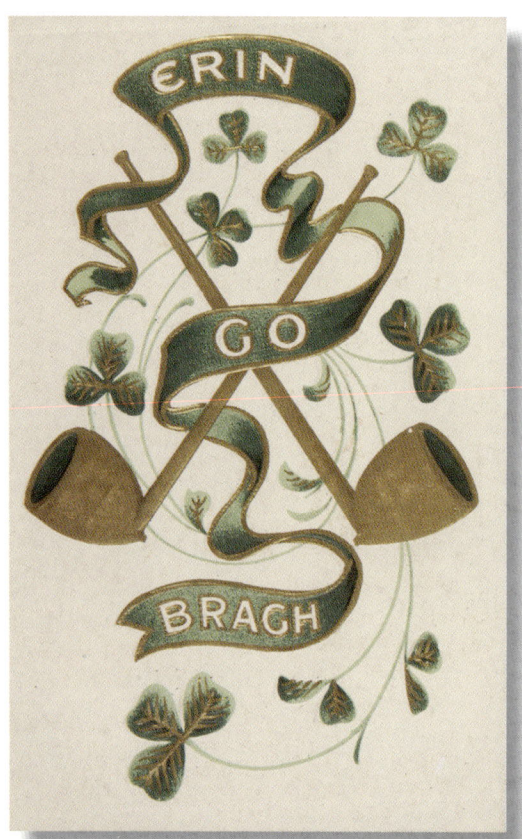

Old fashioned pipes are a reminder of home, but the shamrock is the most enduring talisman of Ireland. In the 19th and 20th centuries it also became a symbol of Irish rebellion and national pride. Botanically, there are three plants called "Irish Shamrock" that grow freely in the mild Irish climate: *Oxalis Acetosella*, *Trifolium procumbens*, and *Trifolium repens Forma minus*; all have three leaves and look like the common clover. Shamrock is the anglicized version of *seamróg*, the diminutive of Gaelic word for clover, *seamair*. The Druids associated *seamróg* with spring and the rebirth of the world at the Vernal Equinox. In Ireland today a custom remains to plant something new in your garden in "Patrick's Week," the period after March 17. Legend holds that St. Patrick used the shamrock to explain the Doctrine of the Trinity to those he wished to convert.

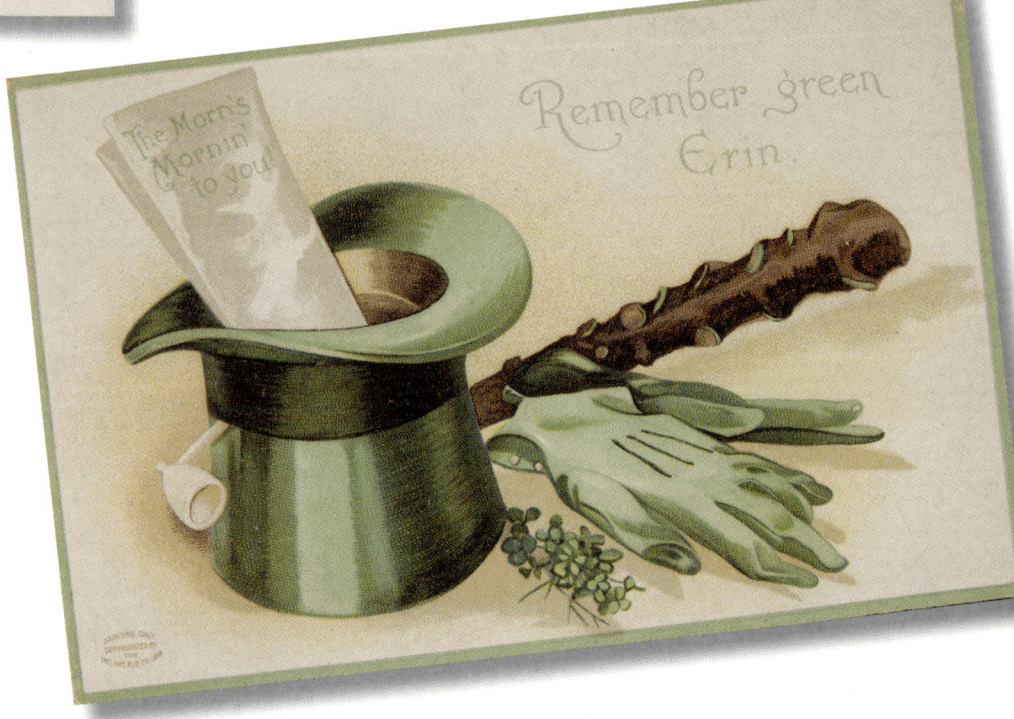

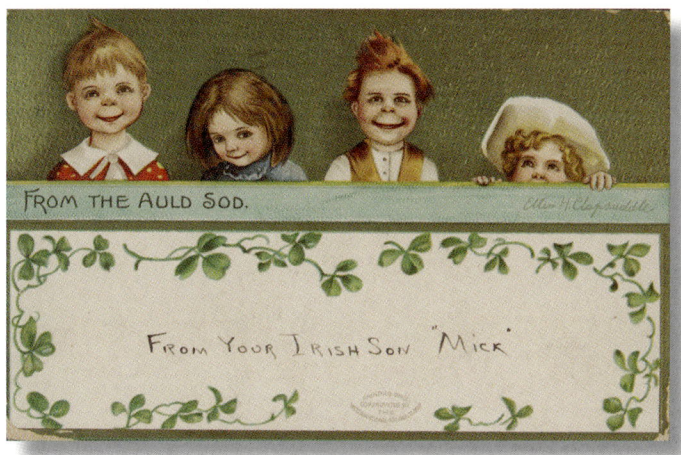

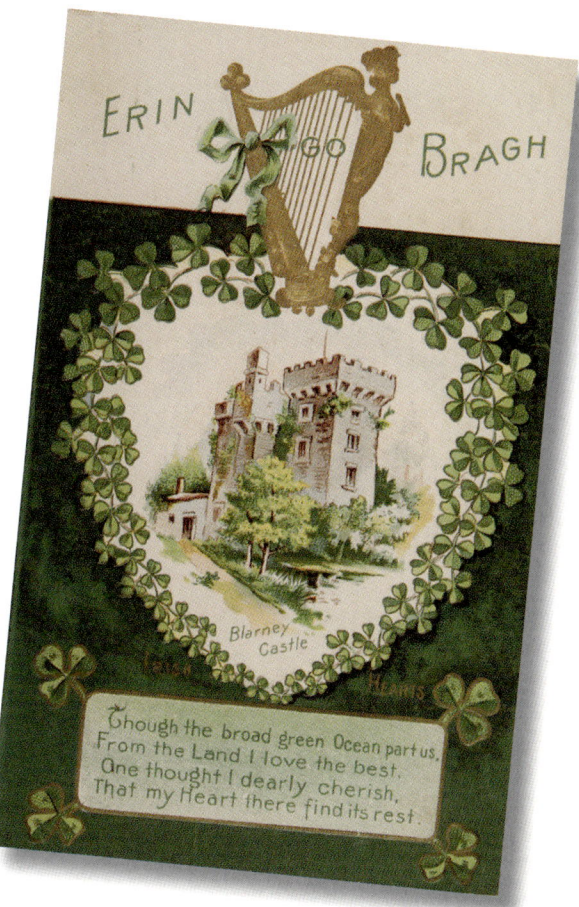

Sentiment and nostalgia for Ireland permiates many cards, presumably sent by first- and second-generation Irish Americans. Remembrances of the "Auld Sod" might simply recall smiling children and shamrocks or Blarney Castle framed in a heart-shaped shamrock wreath, or a pathetic moment recalling the sorrow of separation from old Ireland.

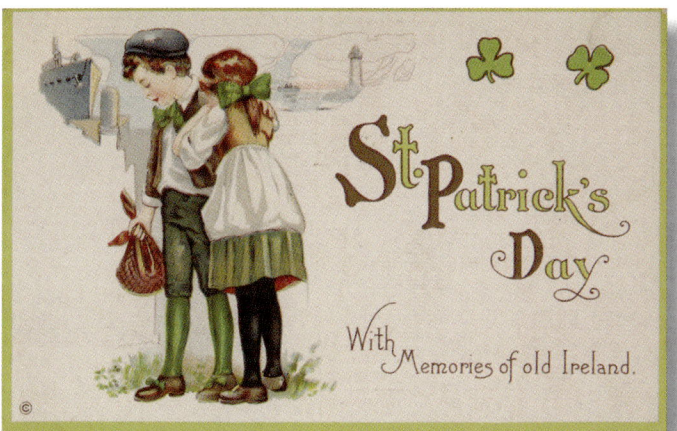

As the Irish became comfortable in their new country they proudly embraced their Americanism. Irish-American politicians became important leaders in many American cities. Penniless immigrant Thomas Kennedy arrived in Boston and subsequently became a partner in a thriving grocery business/tavern. He and his immigrant wife produced twenty children; one, John Francis Fitzgerald, "Honey Fitz," would become Mayor of Boston. Tom's great-grandson, John Fitzgerald Kennedy, would become President of the United States. In postcards we witness this transformation. Uncle Sam holds American and Irish flags in one hand and a shillelagh in the other. He wears a shamrock on his lapel. A young boy in an Uncle Sam suit holds an Irish banner, his green-clad, shamrock-decorated girlfriend holds an American Flag. They wish you, "A Jolly St. Patrick's Day," "A Friendly Celebration."

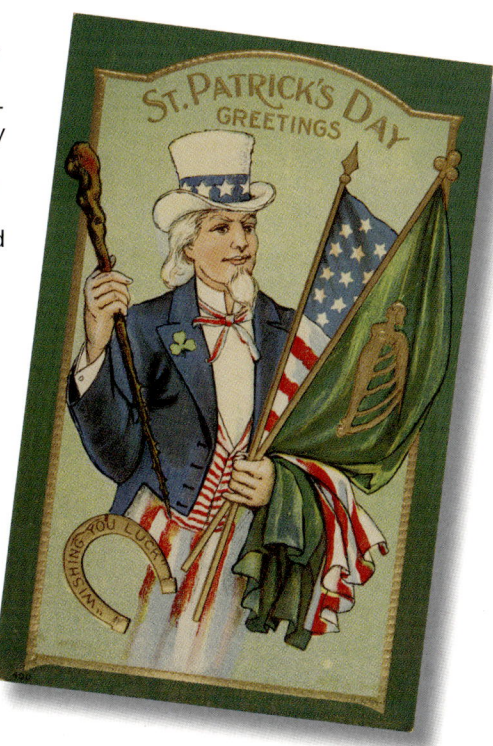

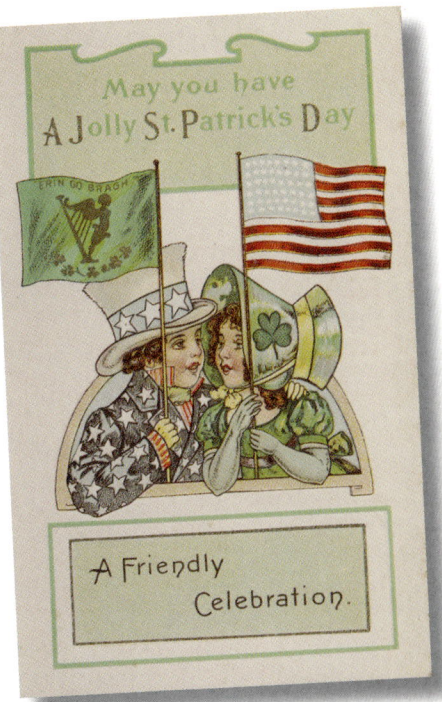

6
Patriotism

Celebrations & Memorials

Patriotic holidays never generated the volume of cards that Easter, Christmas, or St. Valentine's Day did but, in aggregate, they are interesting reflections of American culture. Almost universally celebrated is the Fourth of July, or Independence Day, marking the birthday of the United States. Interestingly, however, it did not become an official national holiday until 1941. John Adams, displaying uncommon prescience, wrote to his wife Abigail that the adoption of the Declaration of Independence… "ought to be solemnized with pomp and parade, with show, games, sports, guns, bonfires and illuminations from one end of this continent to the other." All he missed were picnics.

In our complex society the holiday can have alternative meanings. Native Americans often observe the day as one of respect to their ancestors, rather than honoring the founding fathers. Some African-Americans prefer to celebrate Juneteenth, June 19, the day in 1865 when the news of the Emancipation Proclamation finally reached Galveston, Texas.

Independence Day was first celebrated in Philadelphia on July 4, 1788, when warships docked on the Delaware River fired a thirteen-gun salute in honor of the thirteen states. This type of celebration morphed into the widespread use of firecrackers and "rockets," or fireworks. The first Fourth of July Parade took place in Washington D. C., having been organized by President John Quincy Adams. However, from the beginning feasting was an important part of July Fourth festivities; at first there were banquets, then there were picnics, which, by the 20th century, were featuring newly discovered "Patriotic foods including hot dogs and hamburgers," both of which are German in origin.

Closely allied to the Fourth is *Flag Day*, whose roots extend back to 1861. Officially, however, Flag Day is a much younger holiday. First recognized by a proclamation issued by President Woodrow Wilson in 1916, it didn't become a legal holiday until the administration of Harry Truman in 1949.

Memorial Day has the most complex history of any of our patriotic holidays deriving from the post-Civil War era. Also known as Decoration Day, it evolved in both the South and the North. A Confederate Memorial Day is still celebrated, officially and otherwise, in parts of the South. There are multiple claimants for the recognition of who first celebrated Memorial Day in the North. Many credit Henry C. Welles, a Waterloo, New York, pharmacist, with the honor. Welles suggested to veterans organizations that on May 5, 1866, they should decorate the graves of their fallen comrades with flowers. The first nationwide Decoration Day was held on May 30, 1868, organized by the premier Civil War veterans group—the Grand Army of the Republic, the G. A. R.

The holiday has expanded from its original purpose to include church services and patriotic parades. Over the years the holiday's scope has been broadened to memorialize soldiers of all of our wars. Because it has become the unofficial start of the summer holiday season for many Americans, its observation was moved from May 30 to the last Monday in May, clearing the way for a guaranteed three-day weekend.

Two other patriotic holidays no longer officially exist, *Washington's Birthday* (February 22) and *Lincoln's Birthday* (February 12) having been melded into *Presidents' Day*, celebrated on the Third Monday in February. George Washington was actually born on February 11, 1732, which was officially changed to February 22 several years after the adoption of the New Style or Gregorian calendar.

Richmond, Virginia, was the first town to officially celebrate the great man's birthday in 1782, while he was still very much alive. It was after his death, in 1799, that Congress passed a resolution calling for the country to observe February 22, 1800, as a day dedicated to his memory; but it wasn't until 1832 on the centennial of his birth, that widespread commemoration of his birth became popular.

Lincoln's Birthday, February 12, was never as widely celebrated as was Washington's. Southern states resisted. Today, in its stead, many churches celebrate Race Relations Sunday on the Sunday nearest February 12, in memory of Lincoln's role in Emancipation. Some hardcore southerners, however, continue to celebrate Robert E. Lee's birthday as an alternative. Both holidays, like the new Presidents' Day, had devolved to become days devoted to sales and other forms of merchandizing. Washington chops down prices, Lincoln gets thrifty deals.

Fireworks, originally called "rockets," have been used to celebrate the Fourth of July since 1777. Firecrackers appeared in the 1820s and sparklers in the 1880s. By the 1870s American companies were marketing fireworks for home use with such enticing names as Cherry Bombs, Roman Candles, and Flying Dragons. In the early years of the 20th Century all were freely available and no laws regulated their use. The young lad wrapped in a flag holds a firecracker that looks like a stick of dynamite. He proclaims, "Hurrah a Bully Fourth." "Bully" was a favorite expression of Theodore Roosevelt, who was President when the card was mailed. A courtly Uncle Sam gallantly kisses the hand of Lady Liberty or Columbia.

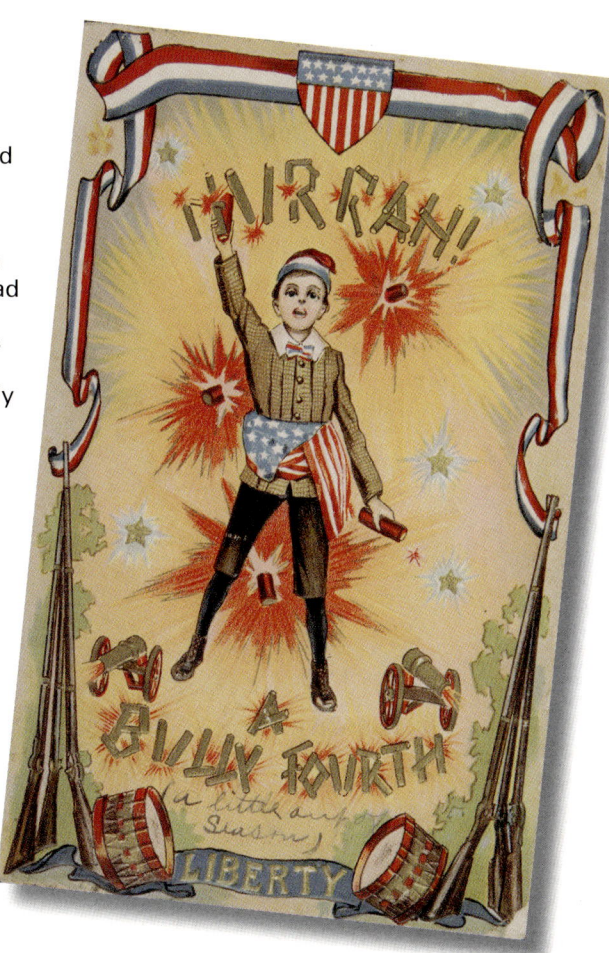

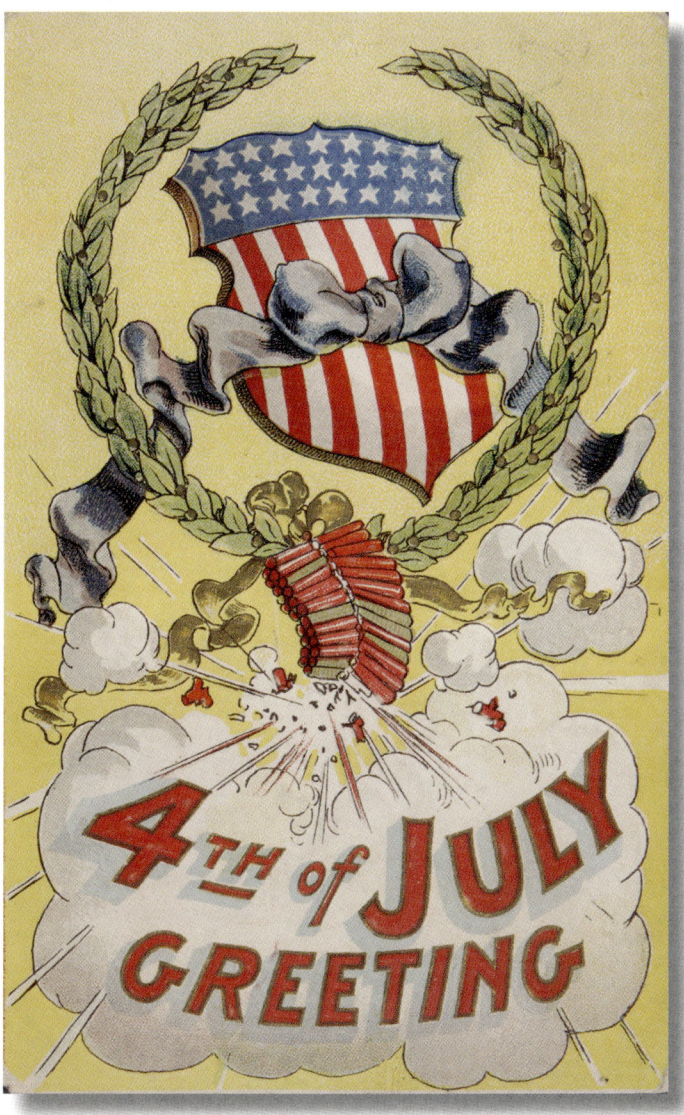

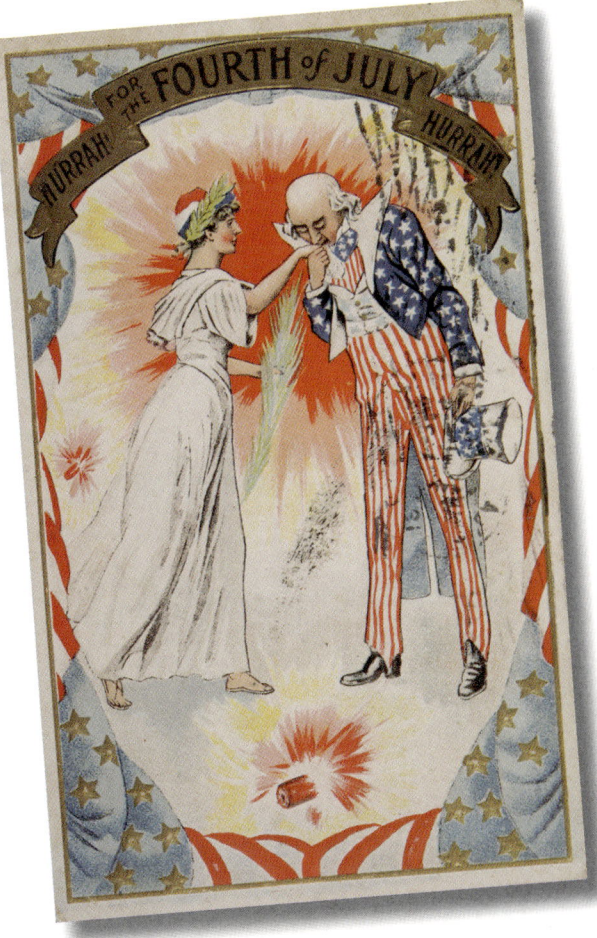

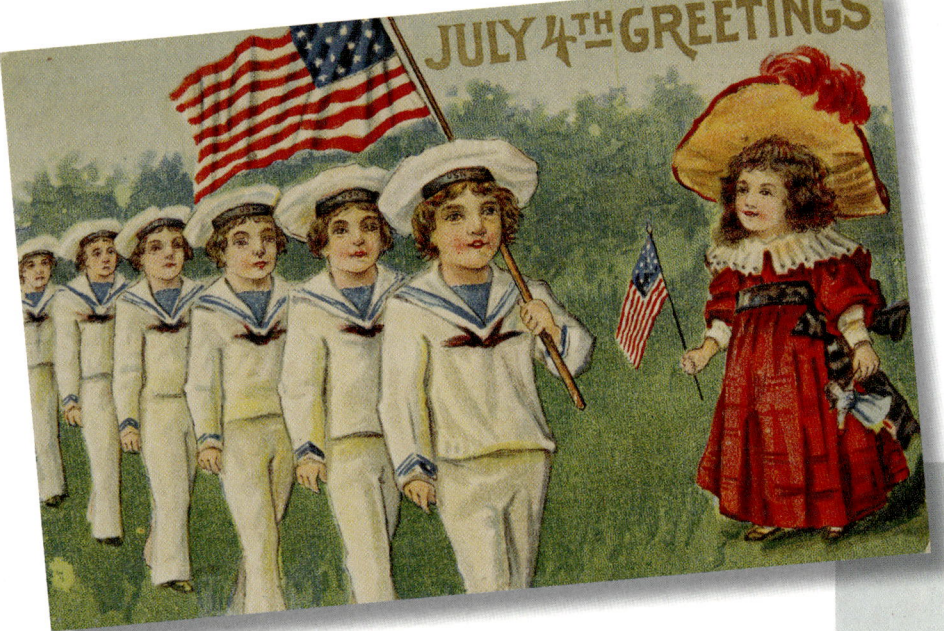

A regiment of clean-cut lads, dressed in fashionable sailor suits, parades before a doll-holding girl wearing an impossibly adult hat. *Collection: Mr. & Mrs. Michael Emery*

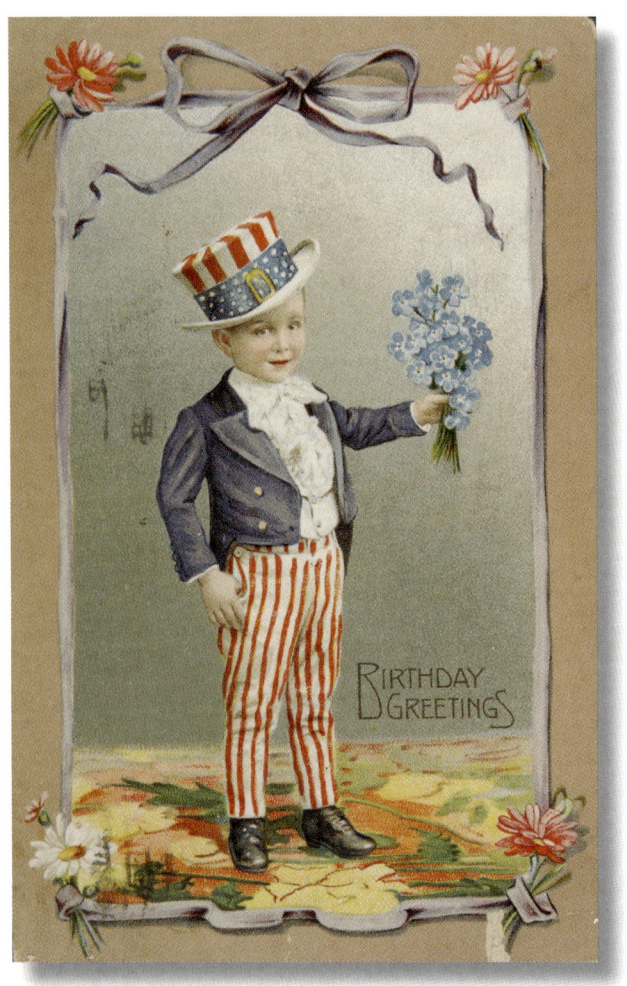

The character of Uncle Sam is based on a real man, Sam Wilson of Arlington, Massachusetts. Born in 1766, he ran away from home at 14 to serve in the Revolutionary Army. Later he went into the meatpacking business and became an important supplier of provisions to the U. S. Army during the War of 1812. All his barrels of meat were marked "US." People started calling them "Uncle Sam's meats" as they were known for their high quality. After the war "Uncle Sam," as a patriotic figure, began appearing in political cartoons: first as a young man with stars and stripes on his shirt. Uncle Sam's characteristic costume is derived from two earlier symbolic characters often seen in parades, "Brother Jonathan" and "Yankee Doodle," perhaps with a final polish added by a minstrel show clown named Dan Rice in the 1840s. The Uncle Sam we all know is the creation of Thomas Nast, a famed cartoonist who, in the 1870s, gave Uncle Sam his chin whiskers. The little kid bearing the bouquet is, in the words of George M. Cohan's popular song, "A real live nephew of his Uncle Sam Born on the Fourth of July." *Uncle Sam: Collection Dr. Russell Eaton*

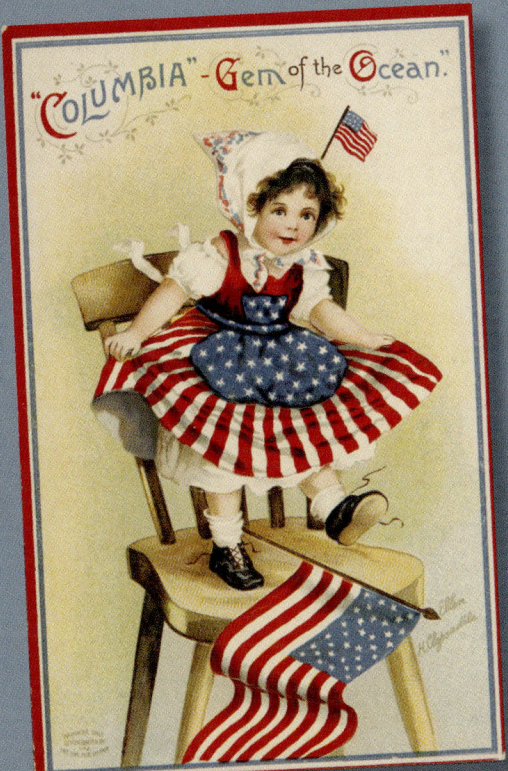

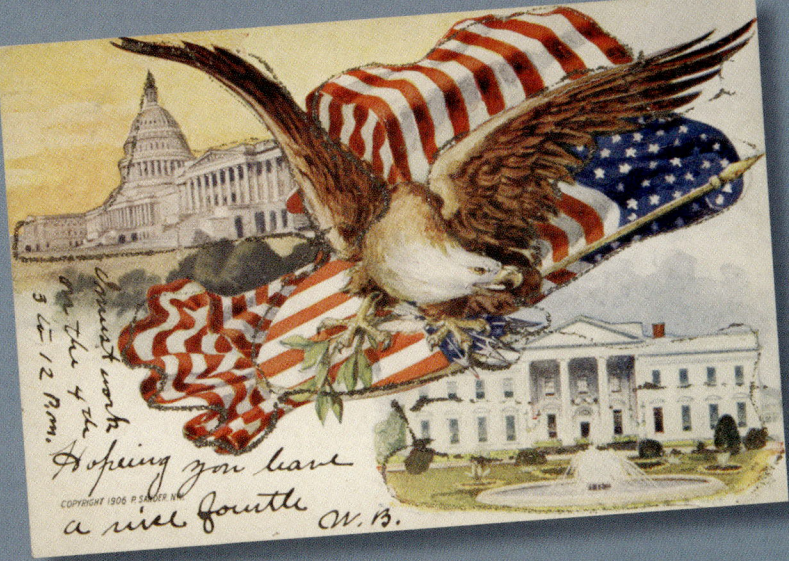

A banner-bearing Eagle soars over the Nation's Capitol and the White House. The message on the front reads, "I must work on the 4th 3 to 12 p.m. Hoping you have a nice Fourth W.B." It was mailed on July 4, 1907 to "Miss Adda Little of Strasburg Penna."

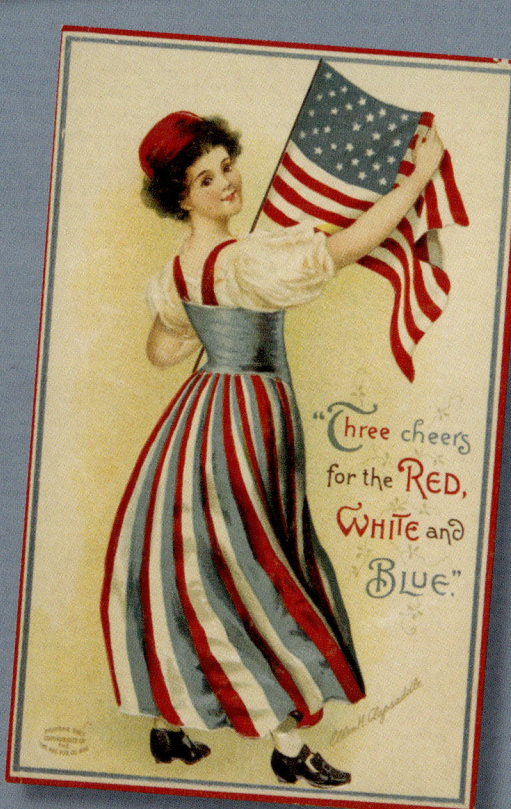

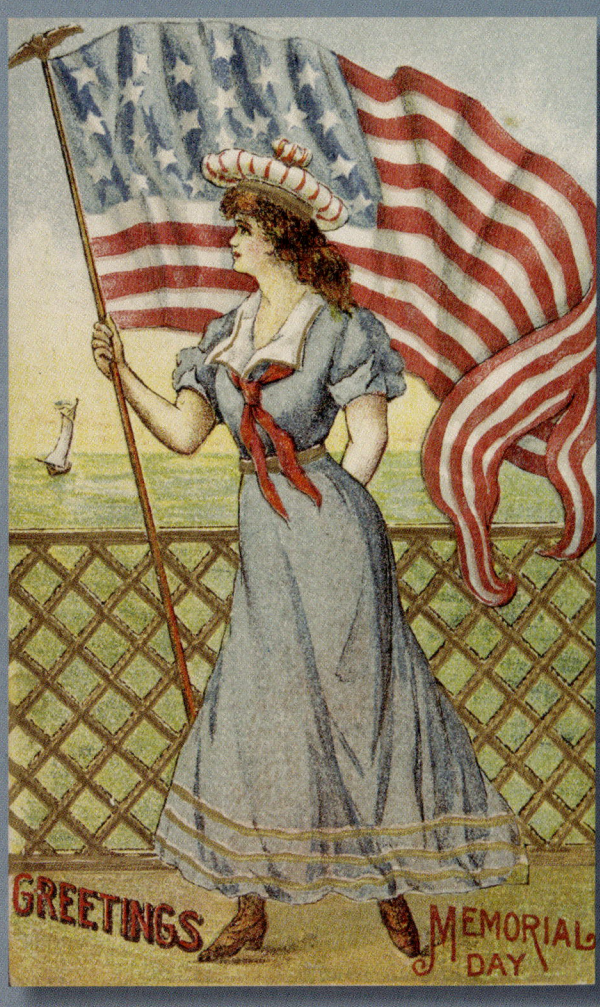

"Columbia is the female counterpart of Uncle Sam. She is often shown as a little girl or, in the case of artist Ellen H. Clappsaddle's rendition, she is a comely young lass, the same one Clappsaddle used as the spirit of Ireland in the previous chapter. Only the colors and the flag have changed. *Both cards, Collection: Dr. Russell Eaton*

The patriotic and solemn nature of Memorial Day is evident from this *c.* 1910 card. *Collection: Mr. and Mrs. Michael Emery*

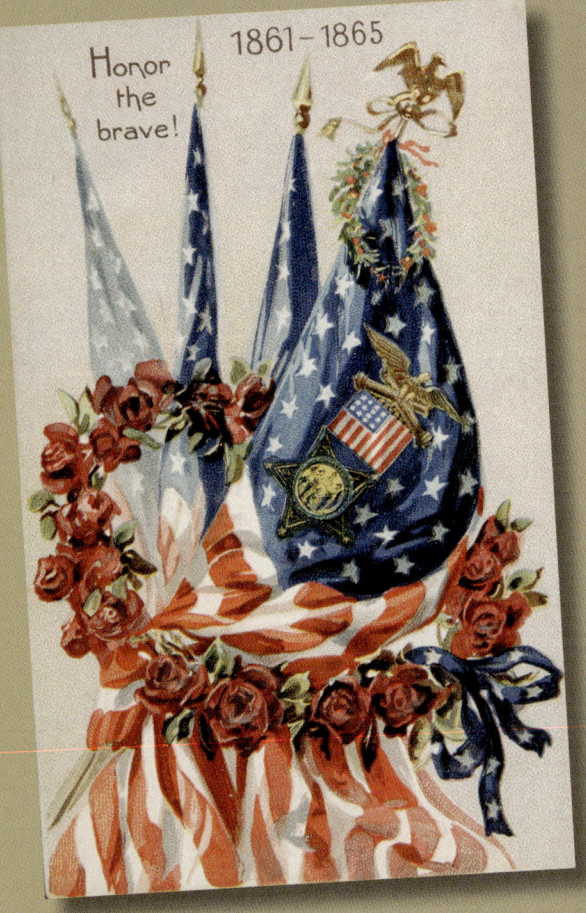

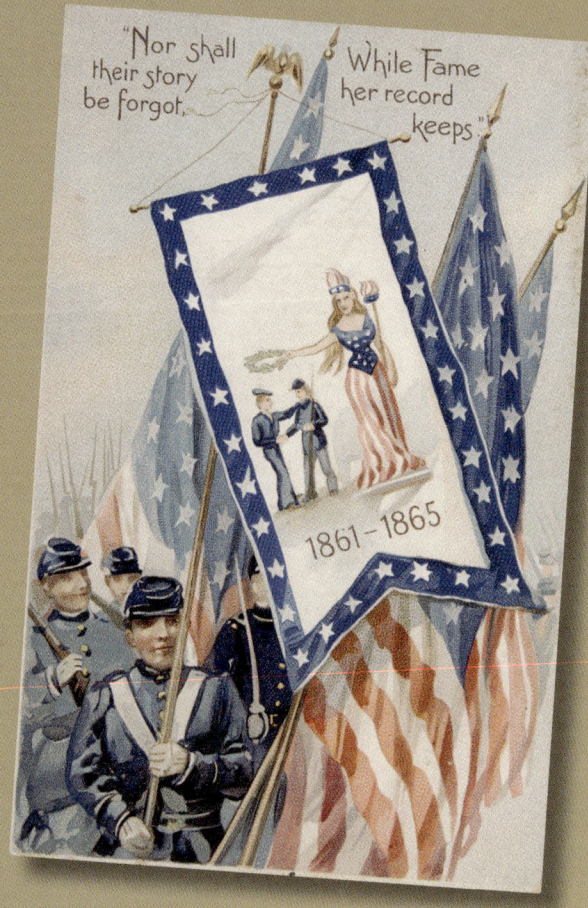

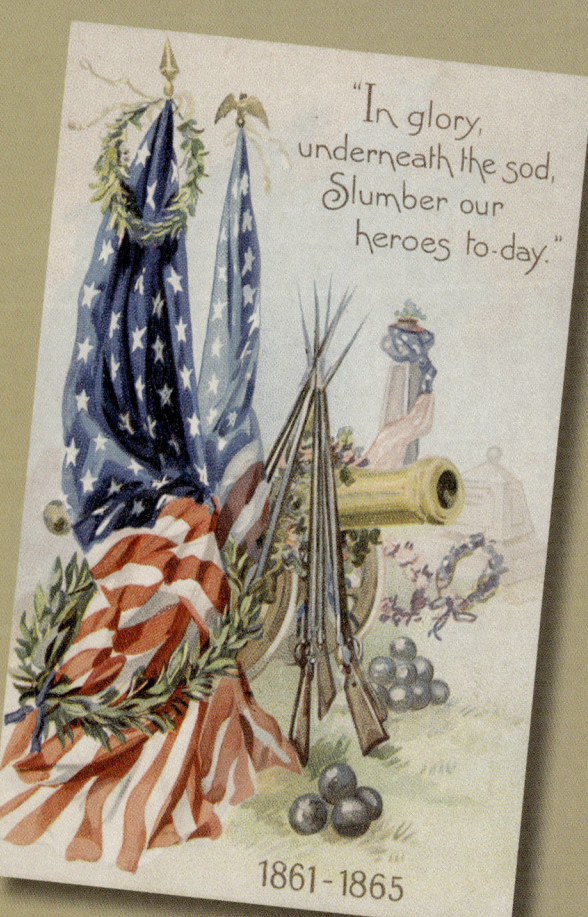

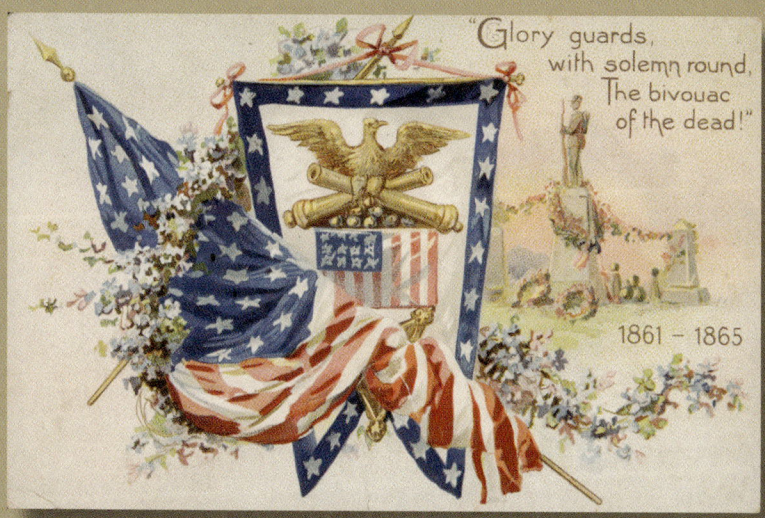

Memories of the Civil War were vivid when these cards were created, between 1905 and 1910. Civil War veterans were everywhere and most Americans had a relative who had served in the military. Note that all the cards commemorate the Northern Side and the Men in Blue. Only one card, "Glory guards. …," has a message on the back, but this doesn't relate to Memorial Day at all. Stella writes to Sue," Thank you ever so much for you[r] postal. It certainly is good. How did you get home from [the] love feast[?]"

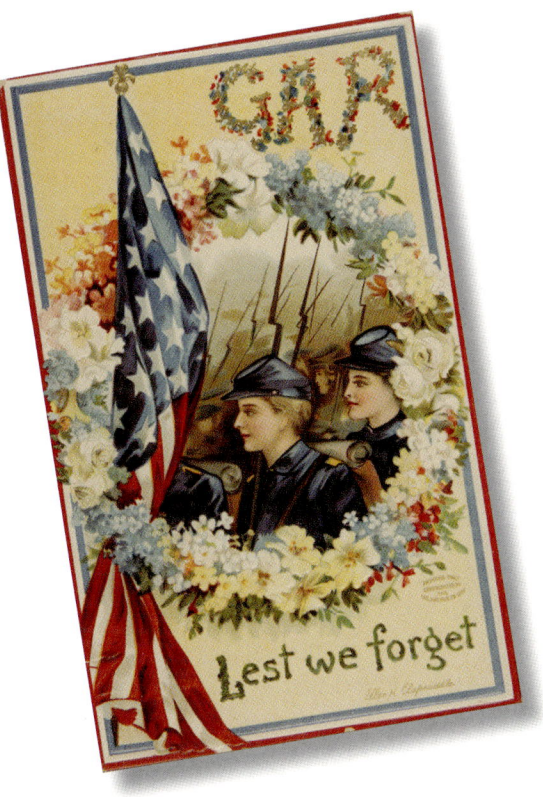
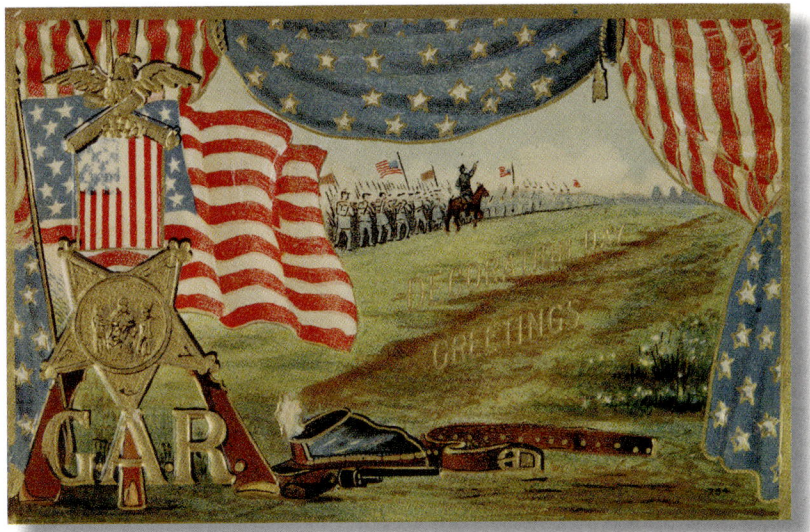

The GAR, the Grand Army of the Republic, was the premier veteran's organization created after the Civil War. The GAR was the prime instigator in making Memorial Day a legal holiday, to memorialize not only the Northern dead, but the Union's victory as well. In most places in the North the GAR ran or, at least, controlled local Memorial Day observations and, in the immediate post-war years, was closely allied with the Radical Republicans, who were bent on punishing the South. At Arlington National Cemetery, the local GAR post even sent guards to prevent the decoration of the graves of Confederate dead. The GAR's five-pointed star insignia was widely respected in the North. By the turn of the 20th century, however, a strong note of conciliation emerged within the organization, but it wasn't reflected in these cards. *"GAR, Lest we forget," DECORATION DAY GREETINGS" and "Memorial Day Greetings."* Collection Dr. Russell Eaton.

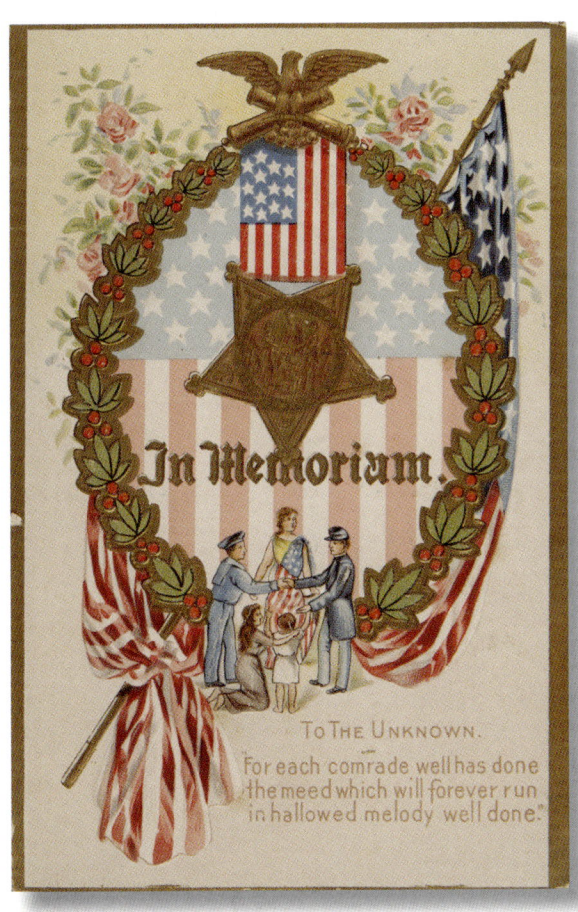
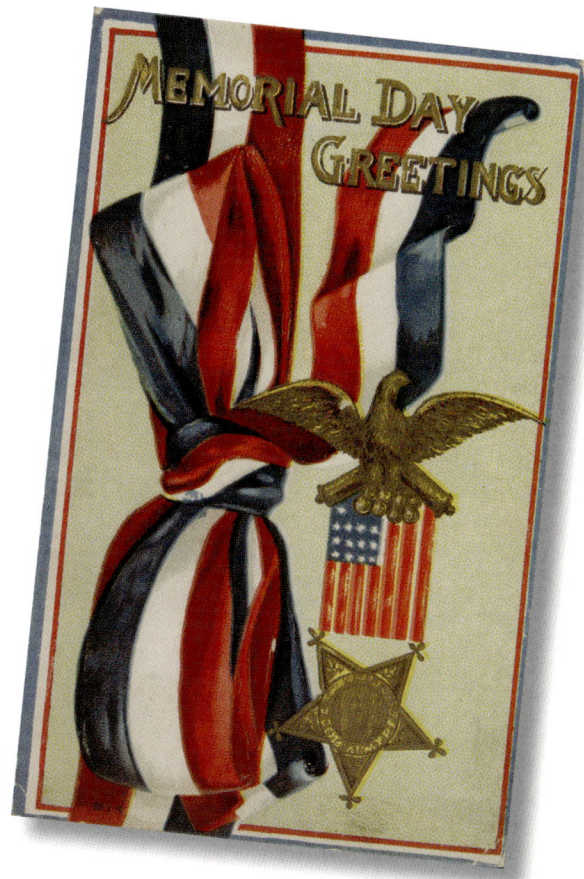

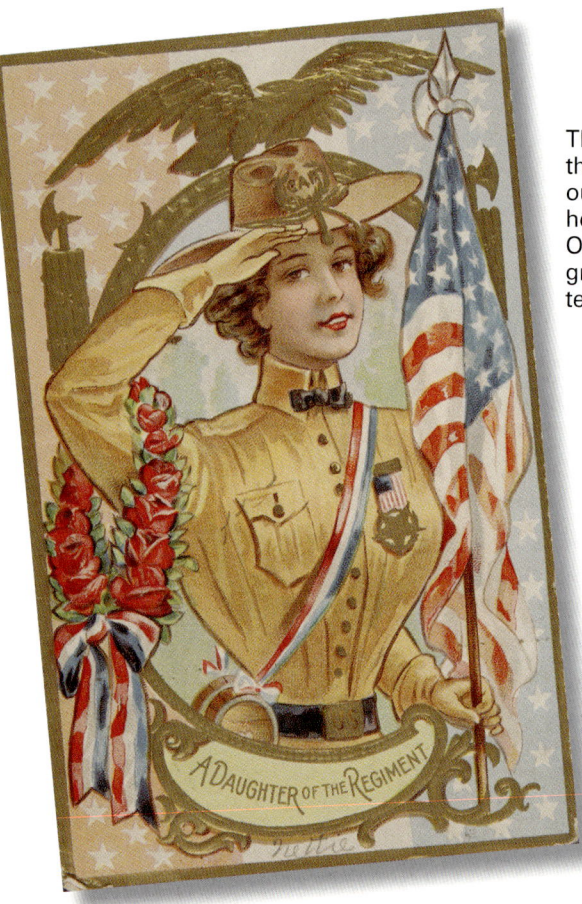

The typical ladies auxiliary member of the GAR certainly didn't look as glamorous as this. "Nettie" uses the card to tell her grandmother "Mrs. J. Hammond, Oxford … Pa" that, "You have another grand-daughter from your grand-daughter." *Collection: Dr. Russell Eaton*

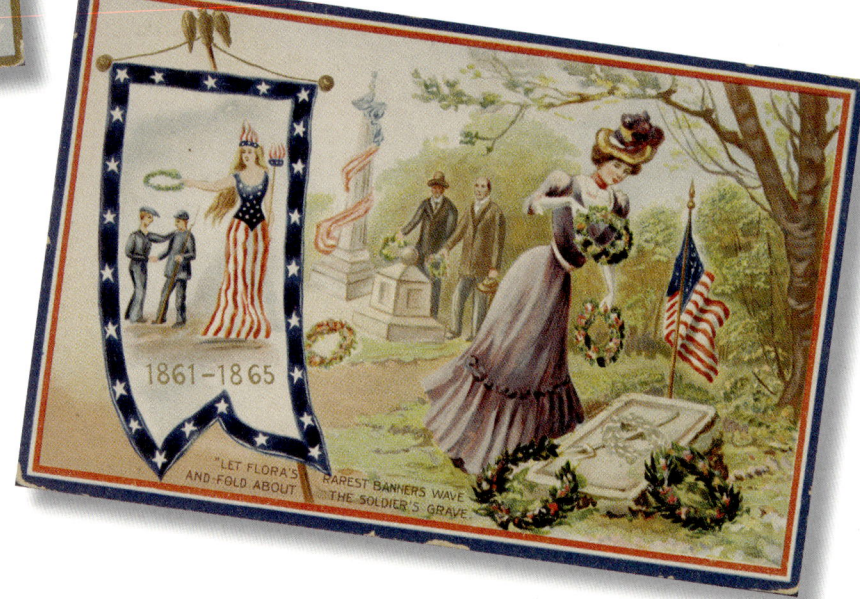

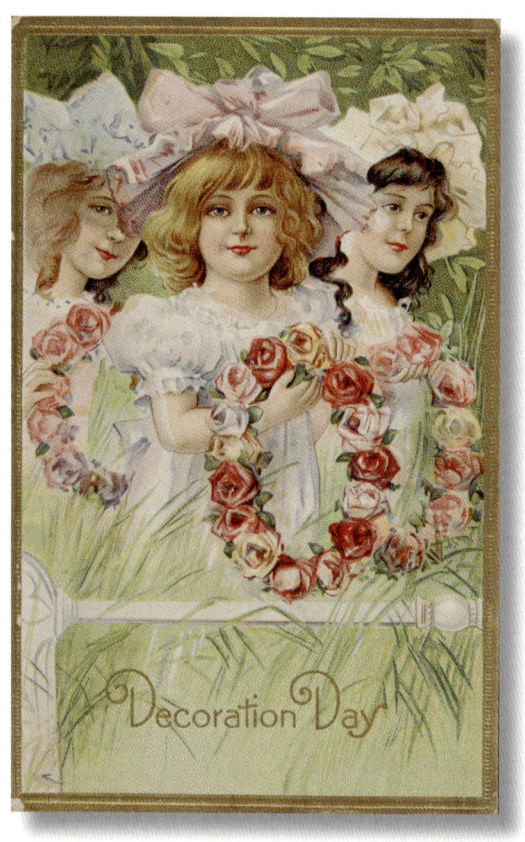

Call it Memorial Day or Decoration, the holiday was often seen as one where women would play an important part. They were to be the principle decorators of graves. Some observers, such as Senator Chauncey Depew from New York, expected that the key role females played in Memorial Day would lead to a healing of North-South animosities and it was hoped that women of both regions would decorate all soldiers' graves. After all, this would only be natural because women "… exemplified that maternal affection … is grander and more lasting than patriotism." *Card with banner. Collection: Dr. Russell Eaton*

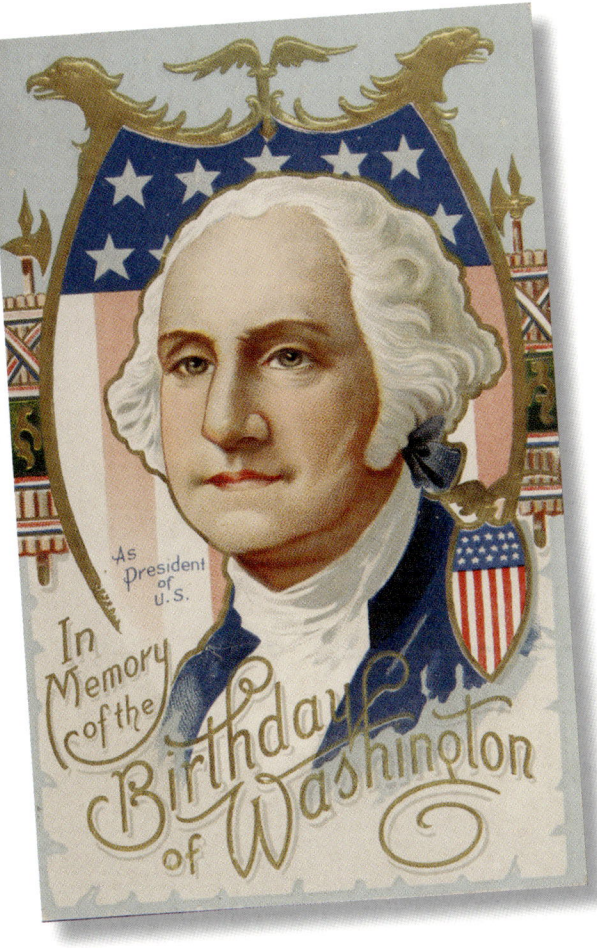

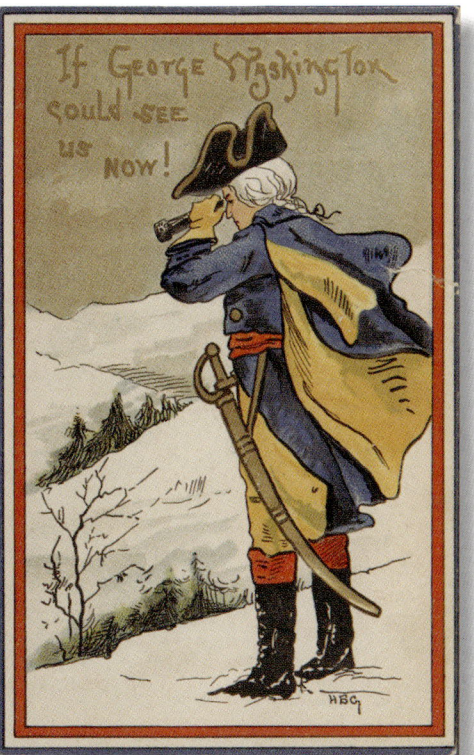

George Washington was the American hero *par excellance* and was widely celebrated throughout America. A Virginian by birth and residence, he was an emblematic being whom both Northerners and Southerners could venerate. "What would Washington have done?" was a question seriously asked.

Stories about George Washington's youth and adolescence were mostly invented by his 19th century biographers and have no, or little, basis in fact. The most popular of these is the tale of him chopping down his father's cherry tree and then fessing up. "Father, I can not tell a lie." This myth introduced by Parson Mason Locke Weems (1759-1825) in the 1806 edition of his *The Life and Memorable Actions of George Washington*, would come to provide the holiday with its most enduring symbols. Toy hatchets and candy-covered cherries became epidemic around February 22. "Washington First in Peace..." Collection: Dr. Russell Eaton

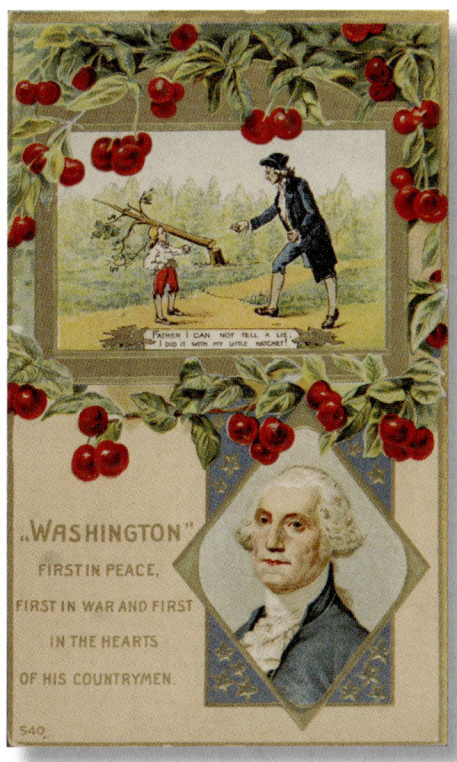

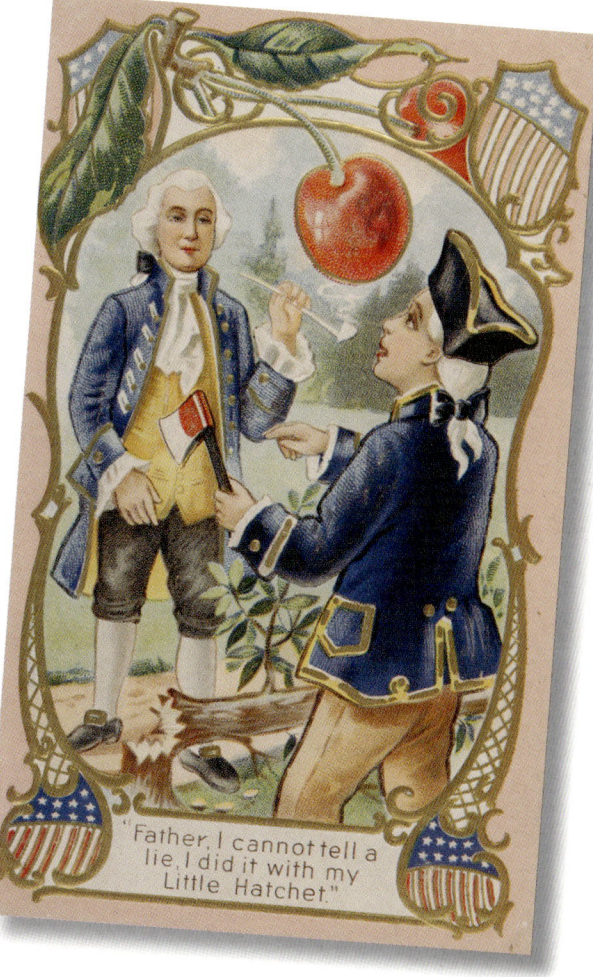

73

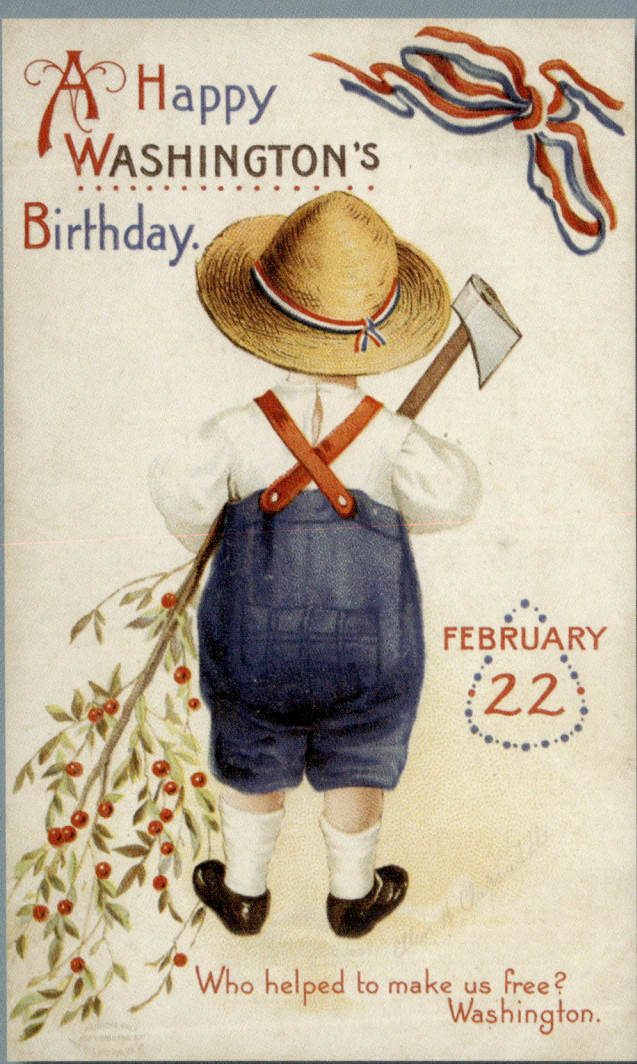
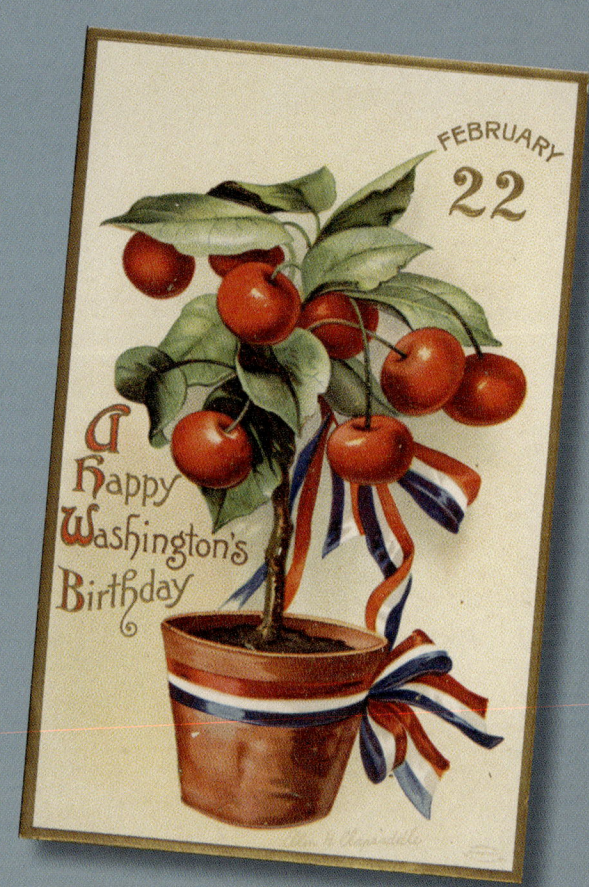
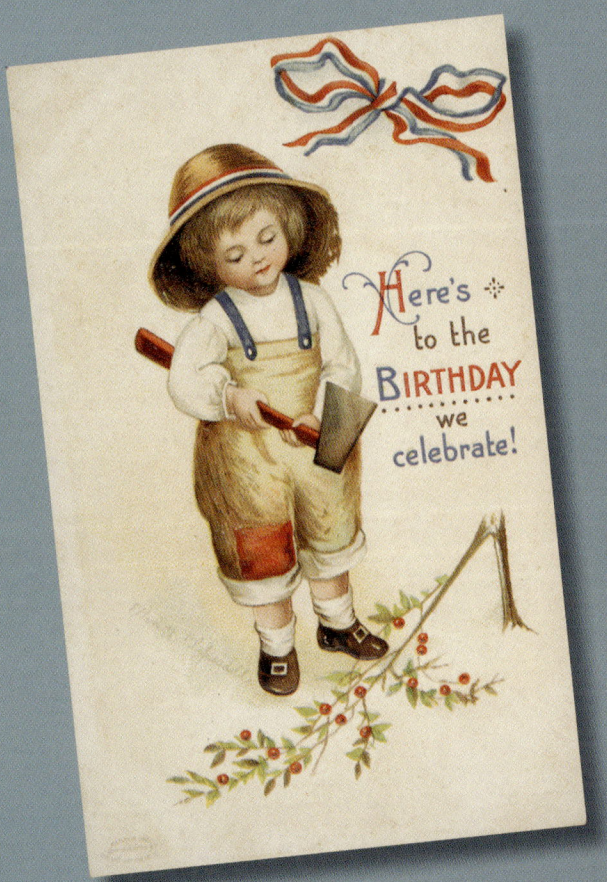

Ellen H. Clappsaddle put her hand to designing Washington's Birthday cards and gave us a botanically improbable cherry tree and two images of an impossibly cute little George Washington. *Cherry Tree. Collection: Mr. and Mrs. Michael Emery.*

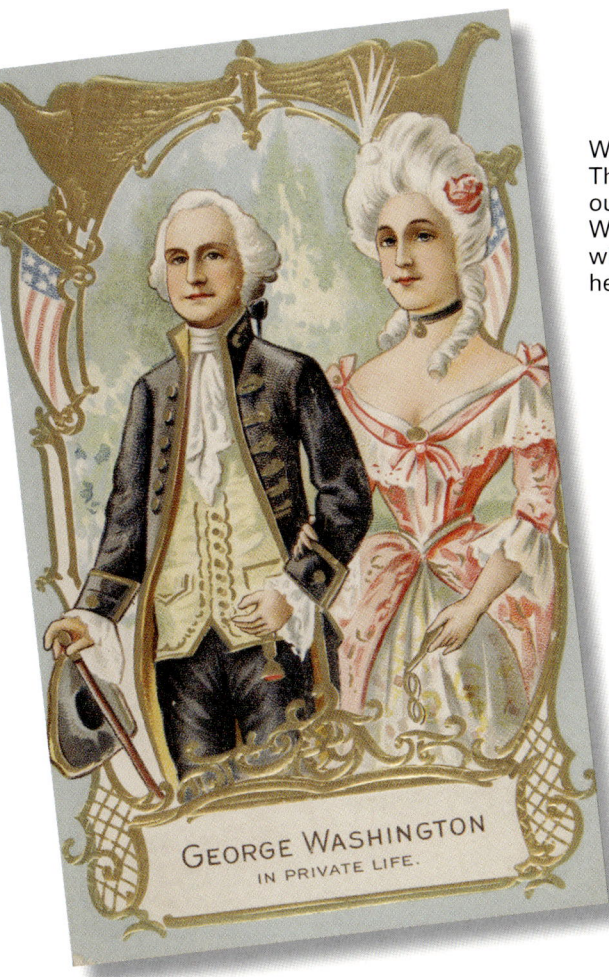

Was George Washington a swinger? The artist who designed this card obviously didn't know that, while George Washington was over six feet tall, his wife, Martha, was barely five feet in height.

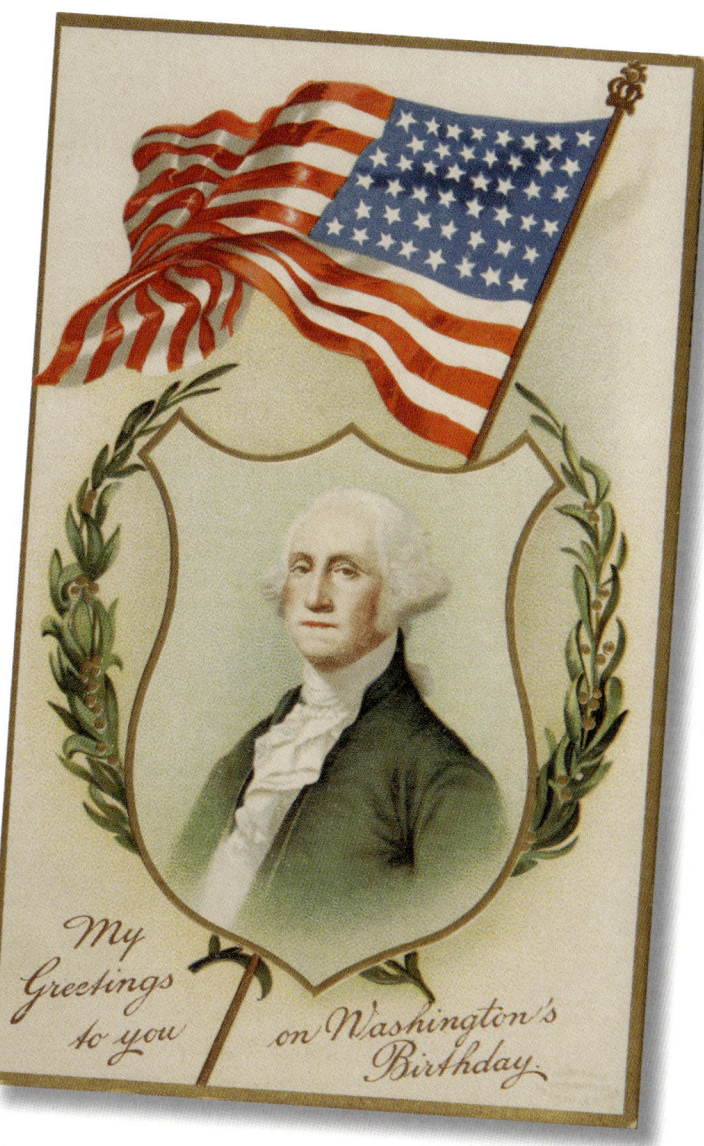

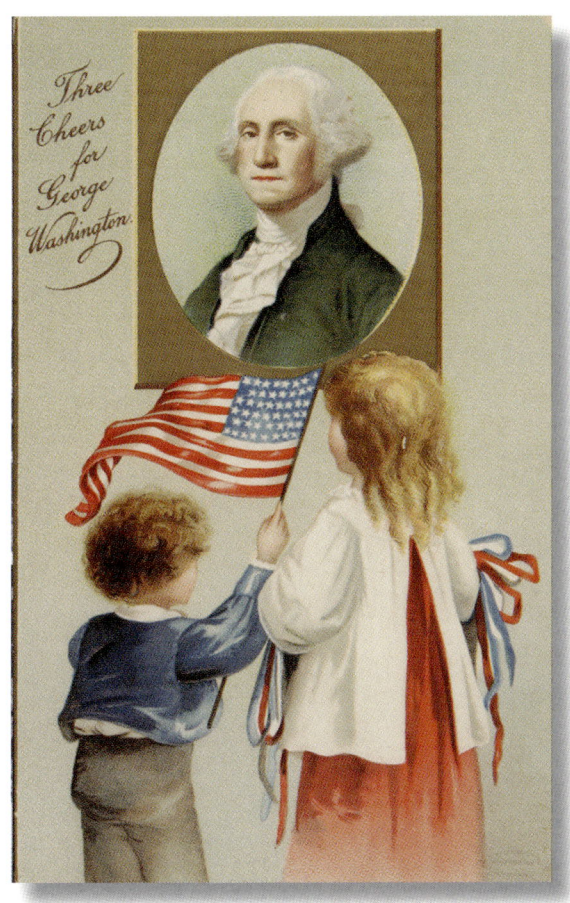

Generations of American school children grew up in schoolrooms decorated with images of George Washington derived from artist Gilbert Stuart's famed portraits. In the upheavals of the 1960s and 1970s the patriotic images fell by the wayside. A new foundation associated with Mount Vernon, Washington's home, is spearheading a 21st century campaign to return Washington to schools.

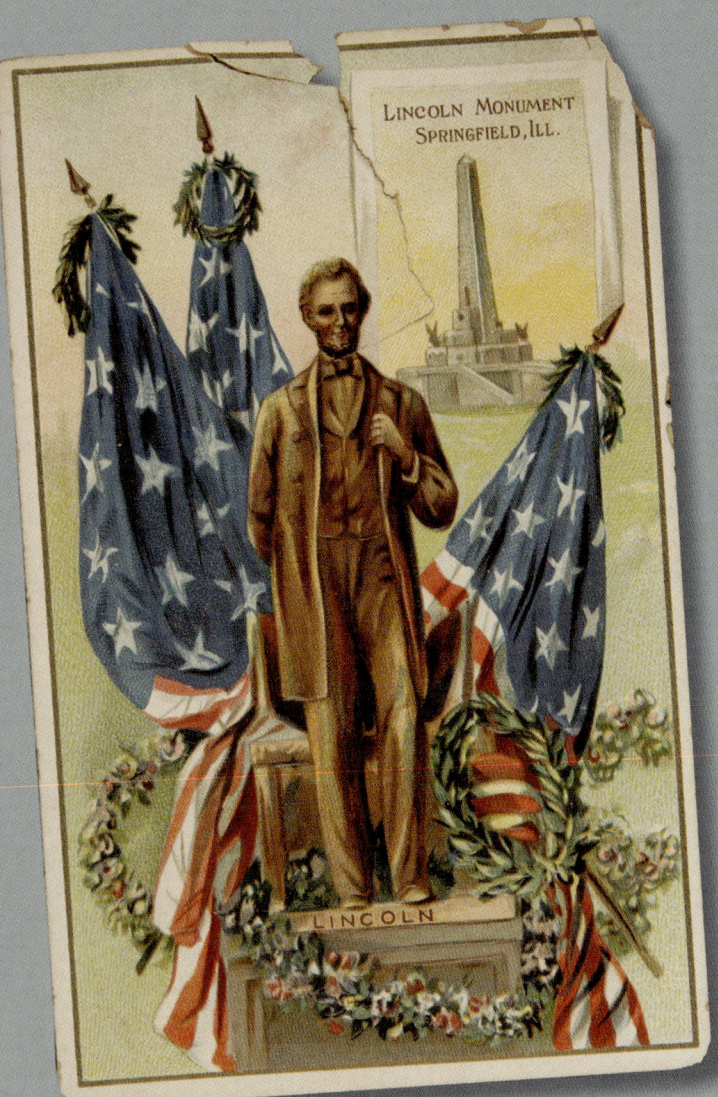

Abraham Lincoln, "The Martyred President," had a holiday, but it never generated the volume of postcards as did George Washington's holiday. It is interesting to note that by the year of the Centennial of Lincoln's birth, 1909, two additional Preaidents, James A. Garfield and William McKinley, had been assassinated, but only Lincoln was looked upon as a martyr: he died to protect the Union. A toy invented by a son of famed architect Frank Lloyd Wright, "Lincoln Logs" continues to be popular with children and commemorates "Honest Abe's" humble origins. *Lincoln Centennial cards. Collection: Mr. & Mrs. Michael Emery*

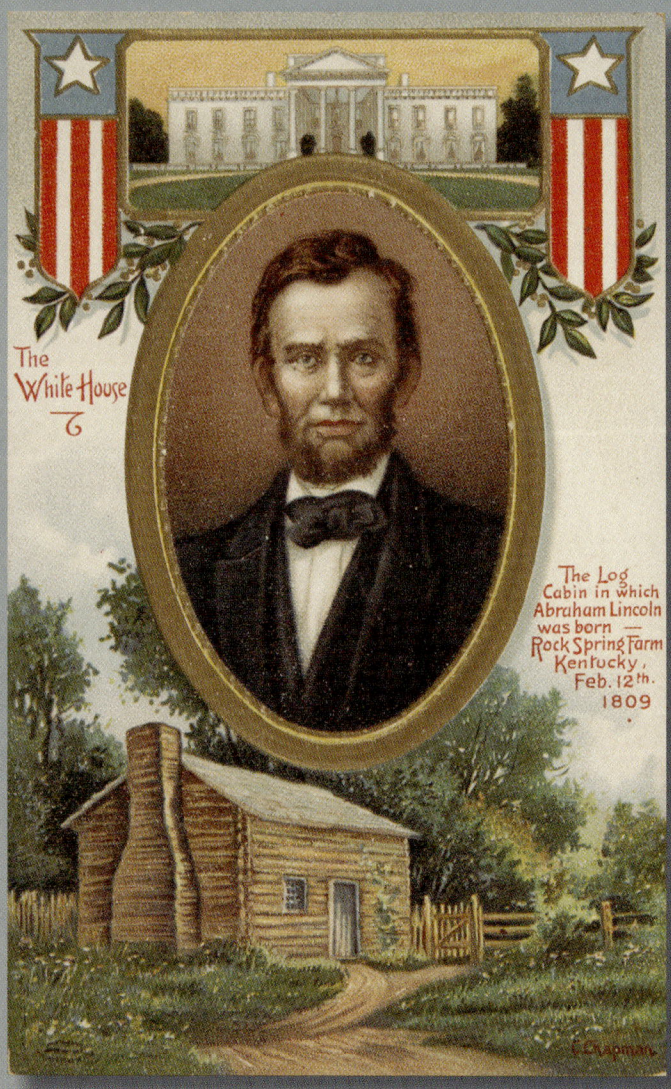

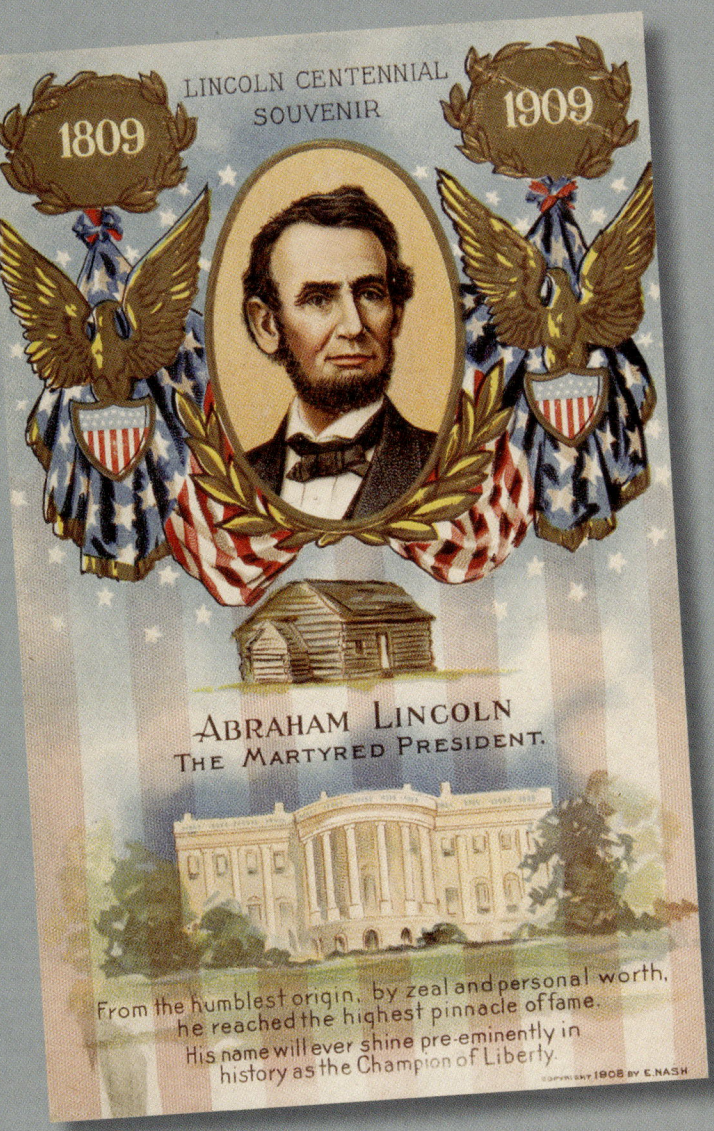
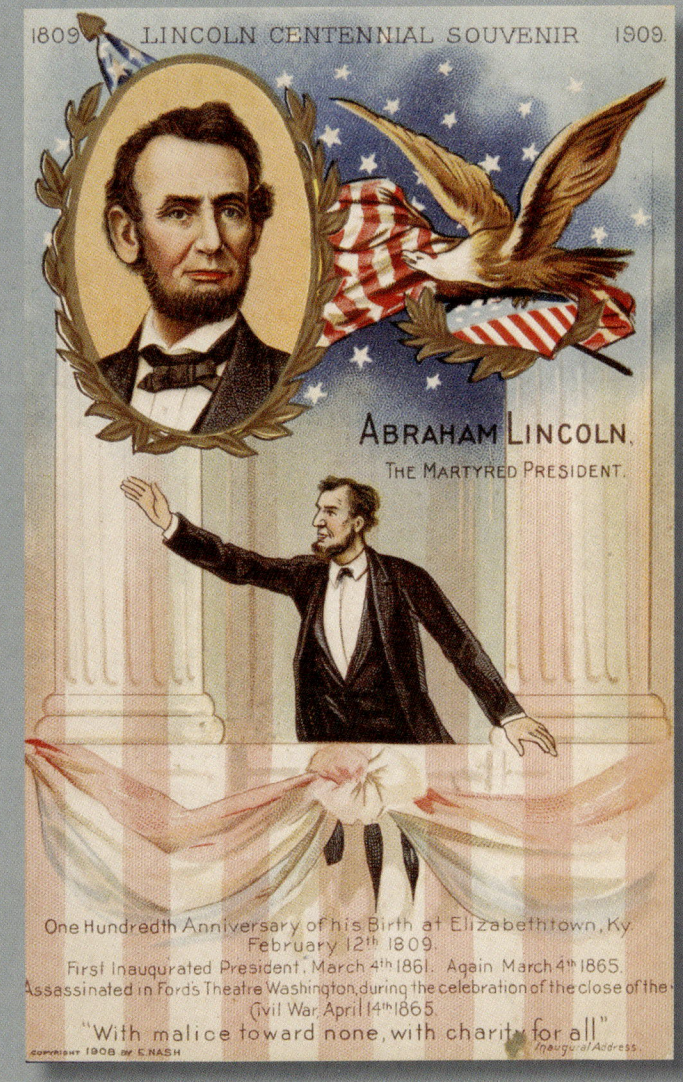

Lincoln's portrait, derived from a photograph, graced Northern schoolrooms in tandem with George Washington's well into the 20th century. The "Great Emancipator's" Gettysburg Address was memorized by generations of school children.

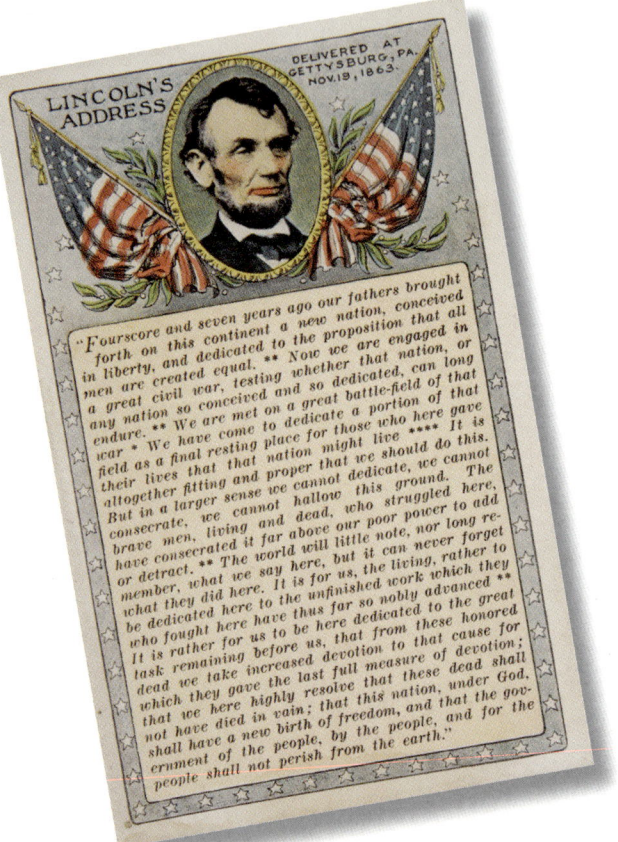

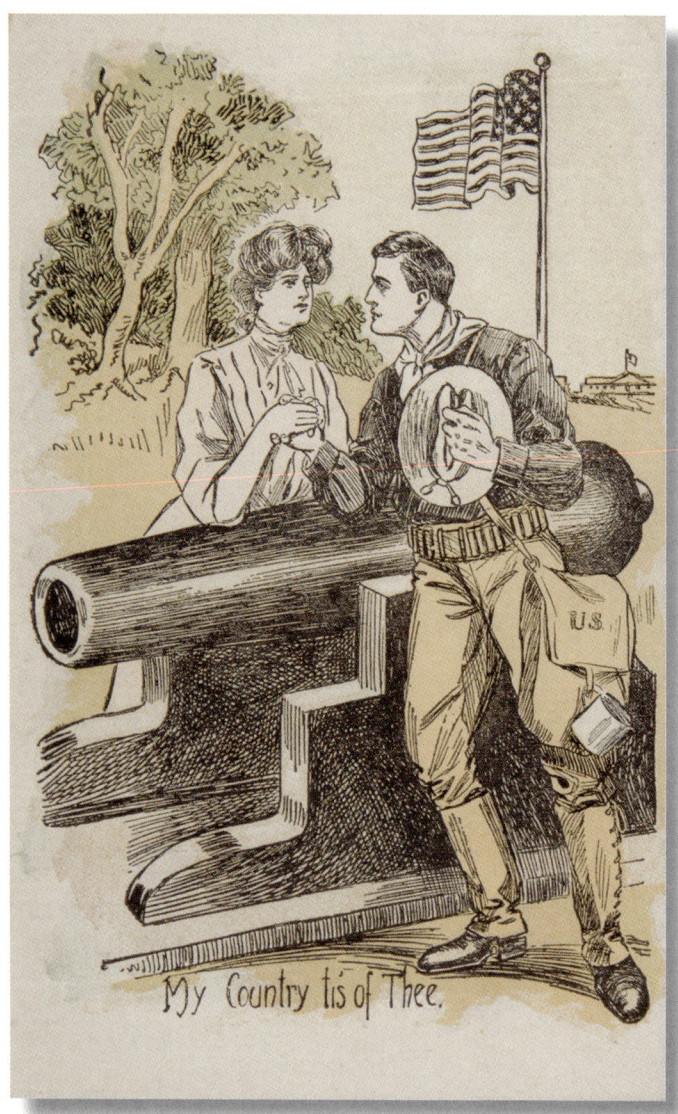

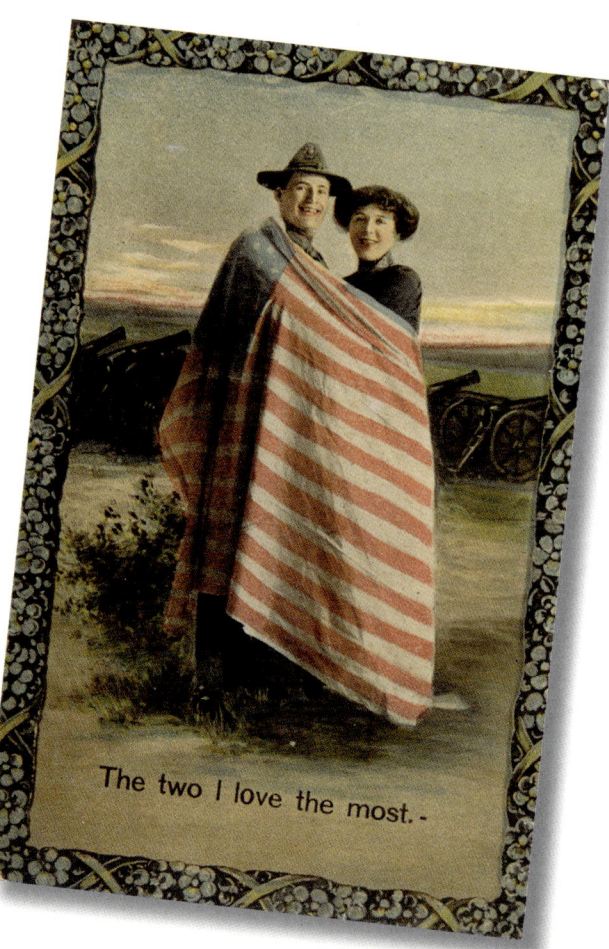

The flag, patriotism, and romance are a heady mix. A handsome couple, he in the uniform of a Rough Rider of the Spanish-American War, meet over a cannon while Old Glory waves in the distance. A World War I "Doughboy" and his love are literally wrapped in the flag. After World War I ended with an armistice, the joyous Allied Powers – England, France, the United States along with Canada – would celebrate November 11 as Armistice Day. After World War II and the Korean War, veterans groups urged that the date be set aside to commemorate veterans of all wars. Accordingly, in 1954 President Dwight D. Eisenhower signed a bill which specified that "… Armistice Day would thereafter be commemorated as Veterans' Day." *Collection: Dr. Russell Eaton.*

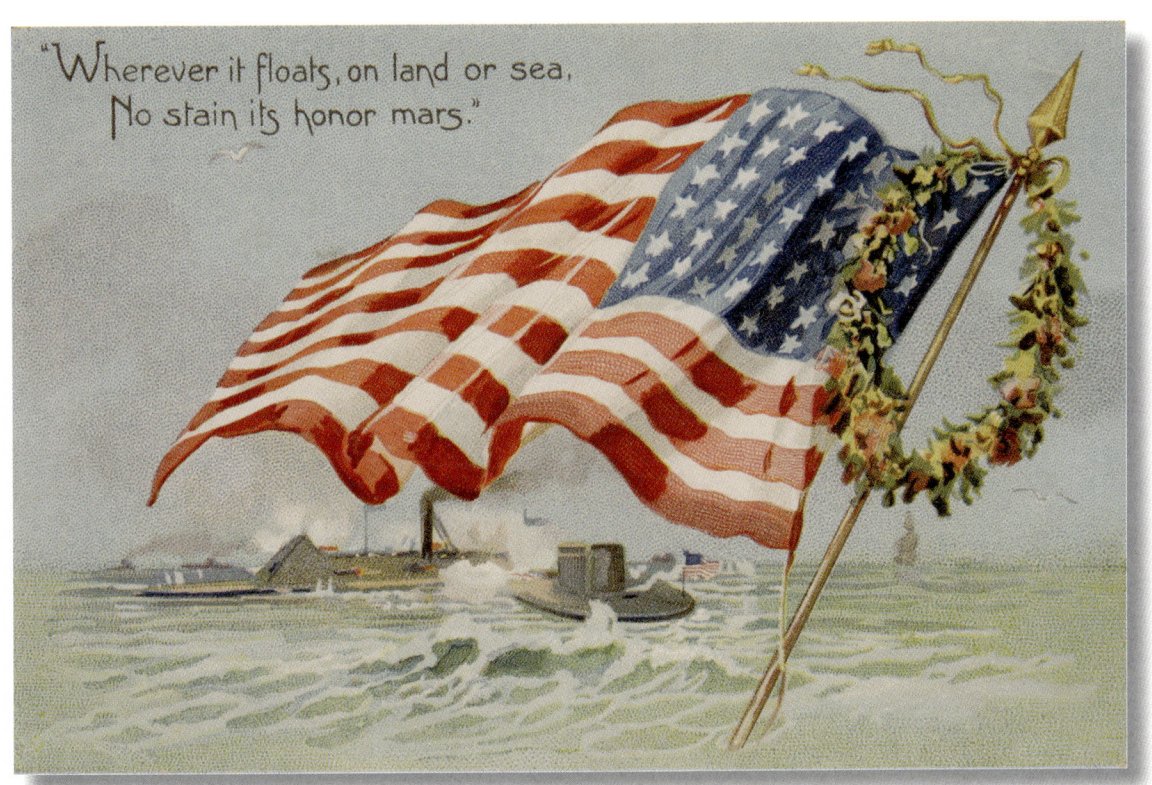

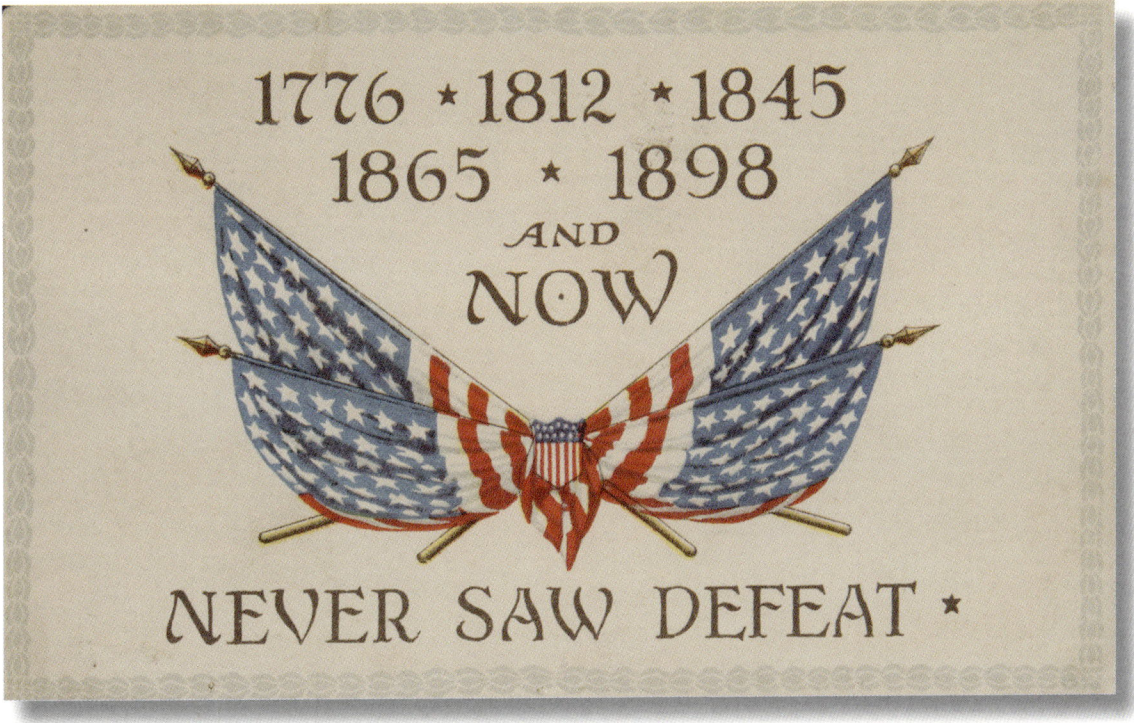

The American flag is the ultimate symbol of the United States. Beneath the motto, "Wherever it floats on land or sea, No stain its honor mars," is a vignette depicting a Spanish American War scene. The World War I era card commemorating American victories in the Revolution, War of 1812, Mexican War, Civil War, and the Spanish-American War was mailed by a soldier stationed at Camp Devens near Fitchburg, Massachusetts on October 8, 1918 to his Mother, "Mrs. Mattie Cook, Atlanta Indiana." The message reads, "I am O.K. and hope this finds you folk all O.K. It has been pretty cold here for several days [and] we had a big frost last night. I suppose it frosted back there and killed everything long before now. We are still under quarantine yet. I do not know when we will get out…." During World War I when epidemics of serious ailments, such as measles or diphtheria, broke out Army camps were often placed under quarantine. *Card with message. Collection: Dr. Russell Eaton*

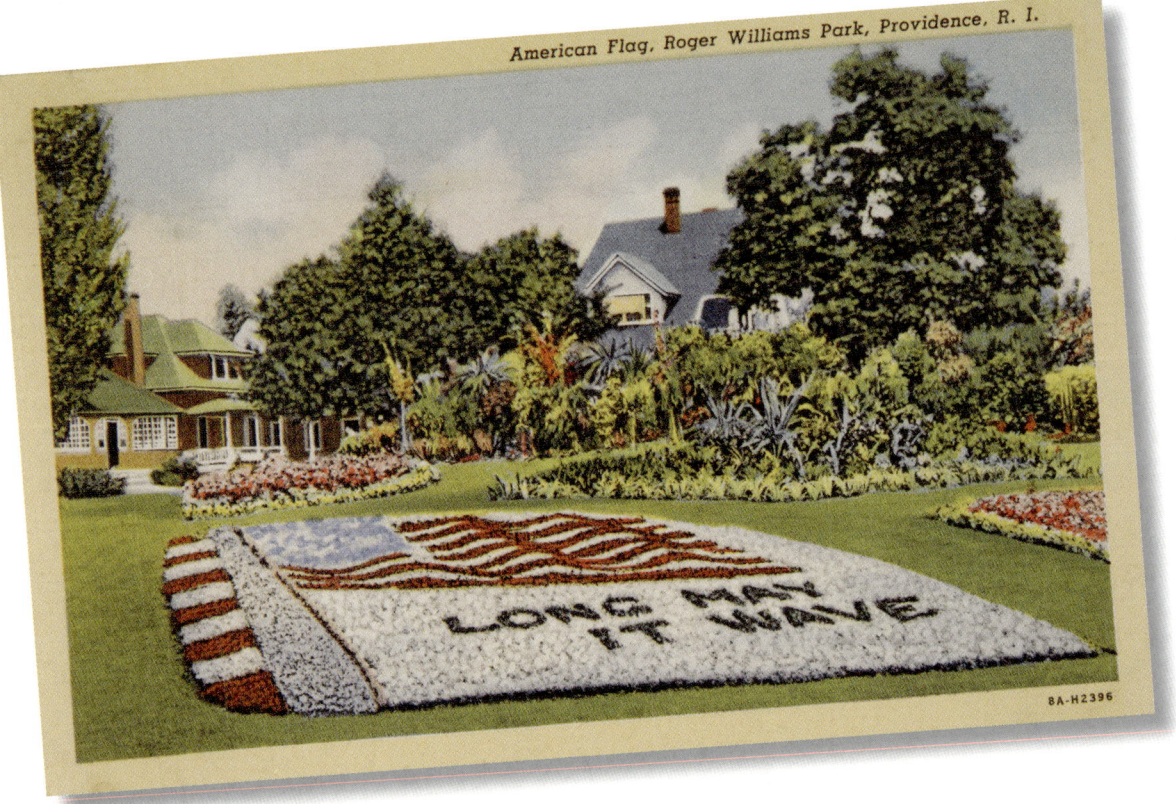

During World War I, floral displays glorifying the flag became all the rage in America. This carpet bed of annuals, possibly sweet alyssum (white), wax begonias (red) and ageratum (blue), was an ornament of Roger Williams Park in Providence, Rhode Island, well into the 20th century. In 1916 before the United States had entered World War I, President Woodrow Wilson first issued a proclamation establishing June 14 as Flag Day in commemoration of June 14, 1777 when the Continental Congress replaced the British banner with the Grand Union flag (which may or may not have been sewn by Betsy Ross) featuring 13 white stars in a circle on a blue field and 13 white and red stripes. June 14 didn't become an official holiday until signed into law by President Harry S. Truman in 1949.

How much more patriotic can one get than to have 3600 children create a living flag? In 1908, 43 years after the Civil War ended, the GAR (The Grand Army of the Republic) was still going strong and could turn out large crowds for its annual Encampments. While the GAR has faded, the Flag as symbol endures.

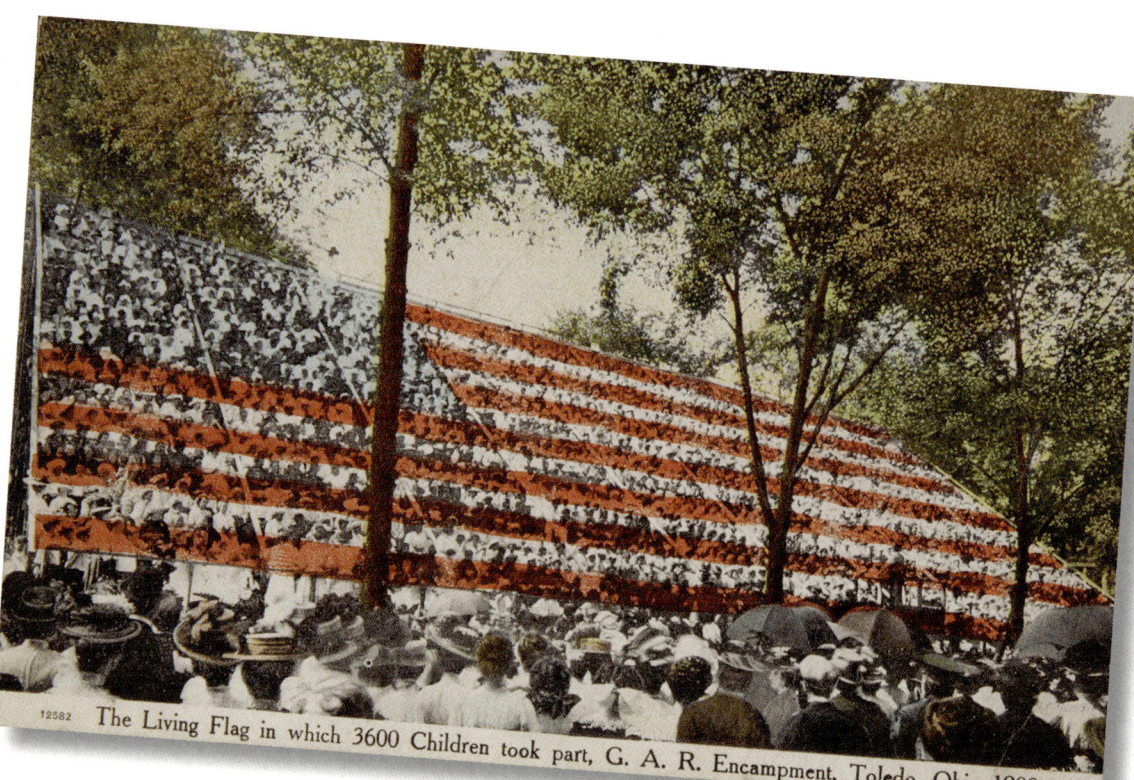

7
Halloween

Talking Pumpkins & Witches

Halloween has been the quintessential children's holiday. In the late 20th century it was adopted by the gay community as a major party time, and since then many other adults have also become very Halloween-oriented. Today Halloween is second only to Christmas in the sale of candies, ornaments, and other holiday paraphernalia. It is unique in the widespread sale and rental of costumes.

Like many holidays, Halloween can be traced back to the pagan past, in this case to a Celtic harvest festival, *Samhain* observed on November 1, which honored the Lord of the Dead. The Celts also believed that *Samhain* (meaning summer's end and pronounced "sarwin") was a time of transition when all the souls of the departed during the previous year would gather to travel together to the land of the dead. Many times the living would wear masks and/or costumes so the restless spirits would not recognize them.

When, during the fourth century, the Christian church sought to abolish all pagan festivals, including *Samhain*, there was great resistance. Accordingly, the church Christianized the holiday by denominating November 1 as All Saints Day. October 31, All Hallows' Eve, evolved into Halloween.

Over the years the harvest festival aspects of Halloween diminished and it became the children's holiday we recall, celebrated by youngsters dressing up, often as ghosts and goblins—the very spirits their ancestors feared. The colors of Halloween are orange, associated with fall and the harvest, and black, the symbol of death.

Orange is especially associated with a Jack-O-Lantern, the grotesque carved pumpkins we all know. In England and Ireland, people often saw pale, strange lights moving over bogs and marshland, probably caused by the spontaneous combustion of methane (also called "marsh gas") given off by decaying organic matter, and popularly believed to be lanterns held in spectral hands by the souls of sinners condemned to walk the earth. One especial sinner was Jack, an evil blacksmith – hence the Jack-O-Lantern. Jack-O-Lanterns were carved from turnips in Scotland, potatoes in Ireland, and mangels (field beets) in England. The carved pumpkin is an American tradition.

Black is popular for three beings: bats, cats, and witches. Bats, being creatures of the night, are symbols of evil and are associated with the most recognizable Halloween symbol, the witch. The witch is, in turn, often seen with her companion, a black cat who, with its mistress, is believed to have evil powers or the ability to assist the witch in performing her evil. When *Samhain* was celebrated, cats, especially black ones, were thrown into bonfires to ward-off evil in the coming year. Bonfires, not a part of the American Halloween tradition, with or without feline fuel, remain popular in Ireland.

Skeletons and tombstones are rare on traditional cards. That today they are popular Halloween motifs perhaps reflects the influence of the Mexican celebration of the Day of the Dead, with its emphasis on the macabre and funereal. Similarly, mummies and grisly remains are, no doubt, 20th century borrowings from popular culture, especially horror movies.

"Give me a treat or I'll play a trick on you," is an old custom probably dating from *Samhain,* when spirits of the dead could appear at the doorways of the living to demand food. Later at Halloween, in the British Islands, the poor would go door-to-door begging for food. The phrase "Trick or Treat" is American in origin and dates from the 1930s. It combines elements from the Old World begging tradition with "supernatural" occurrences happening to the perceived guilty, such as a toppled outhouse or a piece of farm equipment unaccountably appearing on a barn roof.

Today tricks are rare, but treats are common where many homes, especially in suburbia, distribute many pounds of treats. A favorite American confection is "candy corn" or "chicken feed," a sugar-laden treat that recalls the harvest origins of the holiday.

A highly destructive form of Halloween emerged in the late 20th century in decaying American cities, especially Detroit. "Devil's Night" evolved, in which marauding bands set fire to abandoned buildings, occasionally creating urban infernos. Evangelical Christians are especially critical of the pagan roots of Halloween and, as the holiday has become increasingly popular, paradoxically its observation has been banned from many schools. For most Americans, however, it is a day for the kids to "Trick or Treat" and for the adults to party.

In America Halloween was mostly a children's holiday, a day on which children could dress up and play, be frightened by a ghost story or, perhaps, even hitch a ride on a witch's broom.

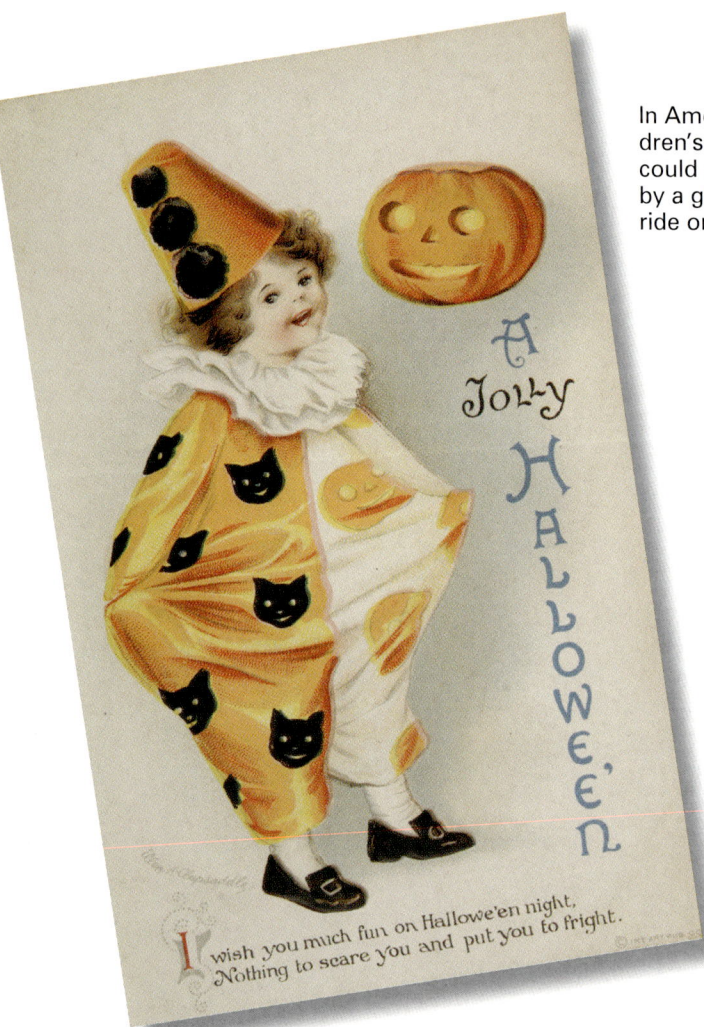

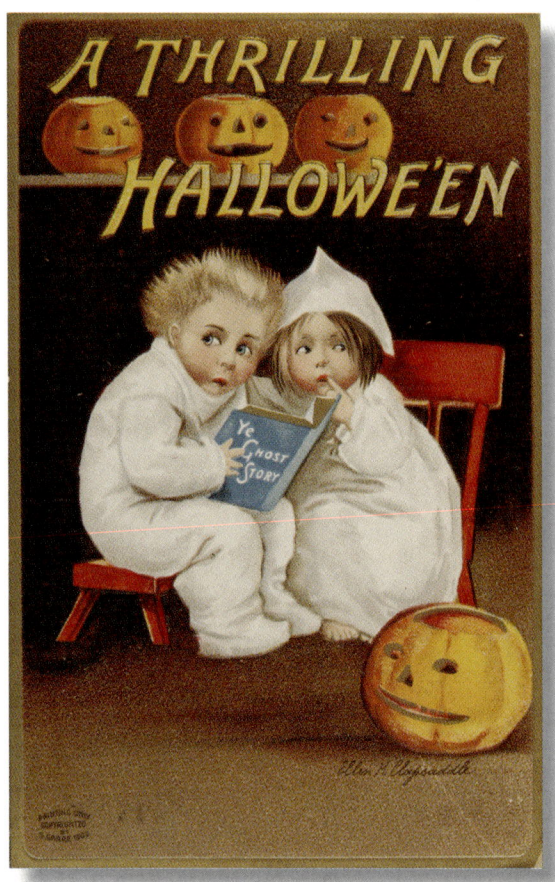

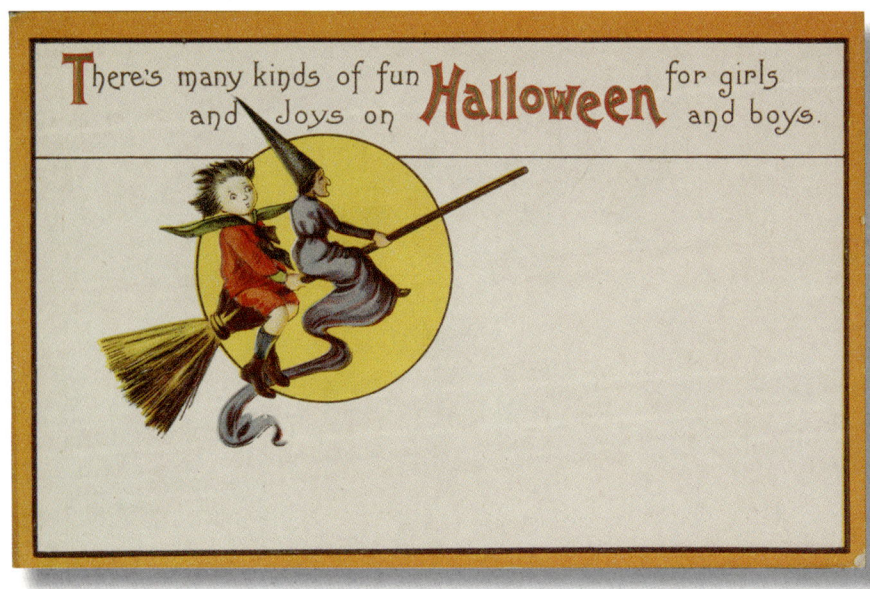

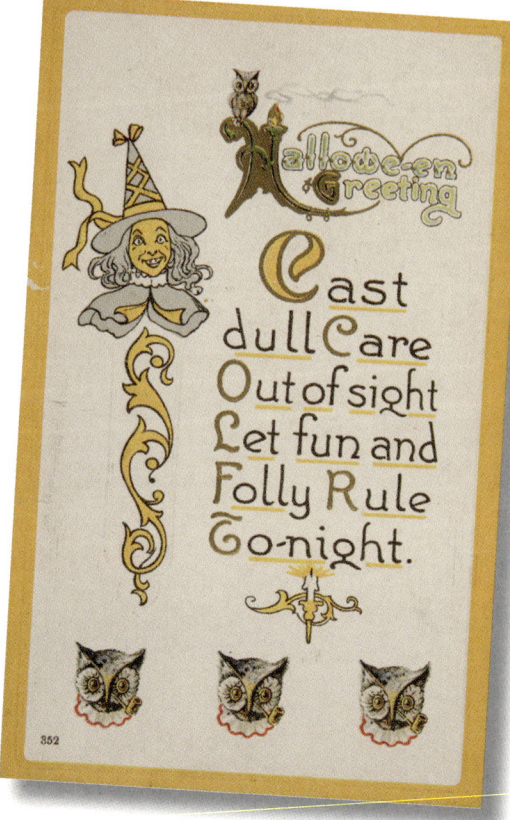

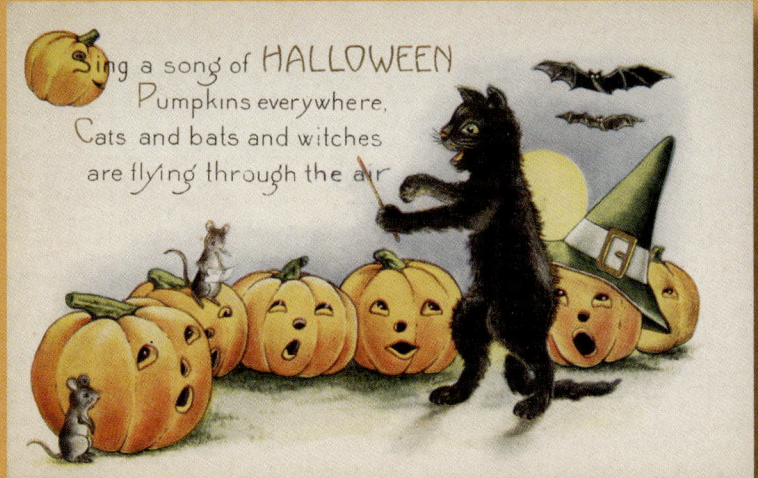

Along with expressive Jack-O-Lanterns, occasionally substituting for a head, Halloween cards often feature black cats, bats, and crows. On this eve strange things can happen: mice dress up and a feline conductor leads a pumpkin choir.

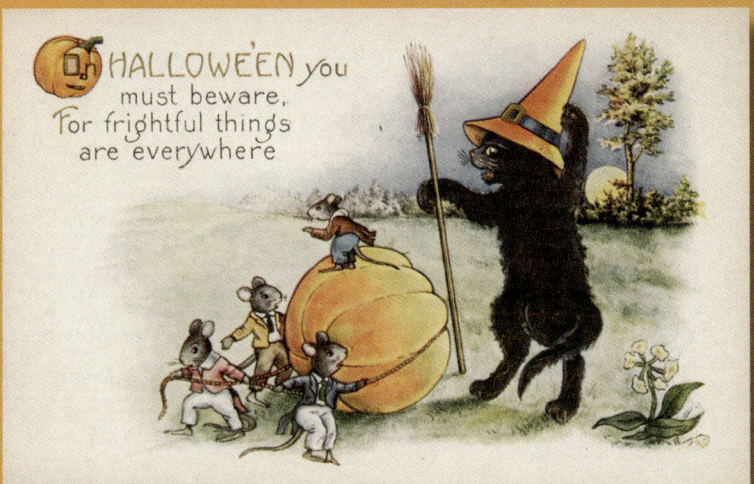

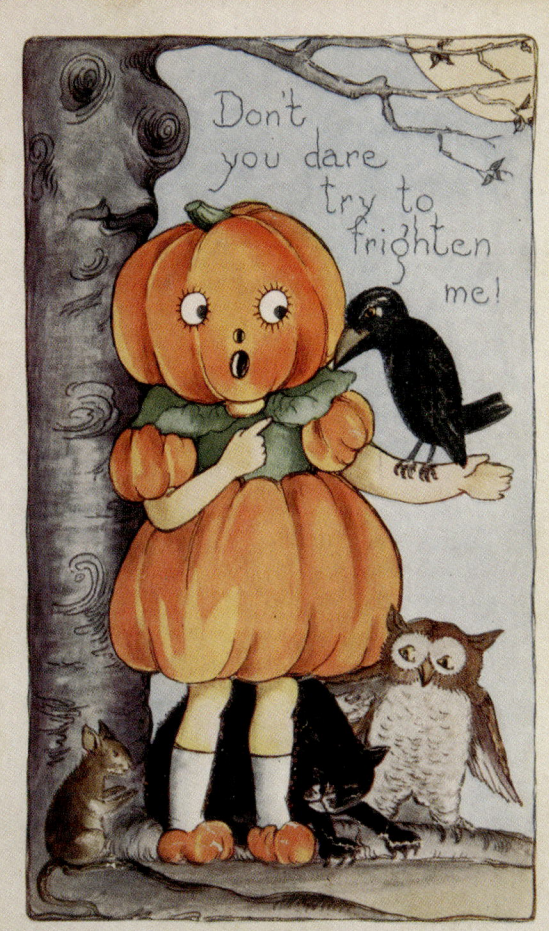

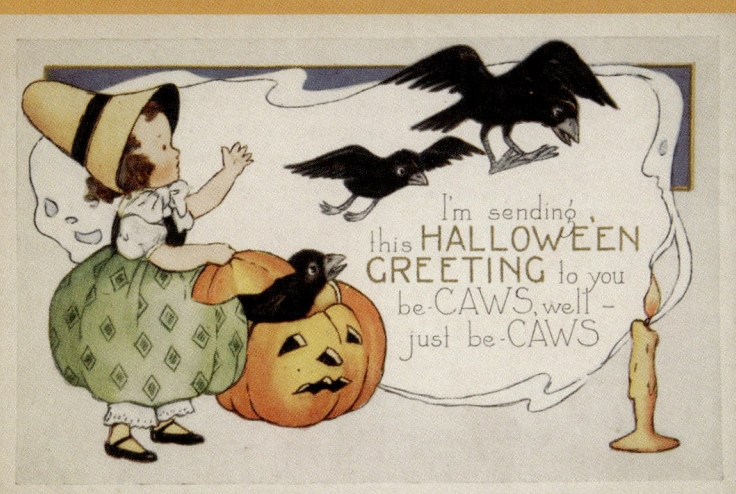

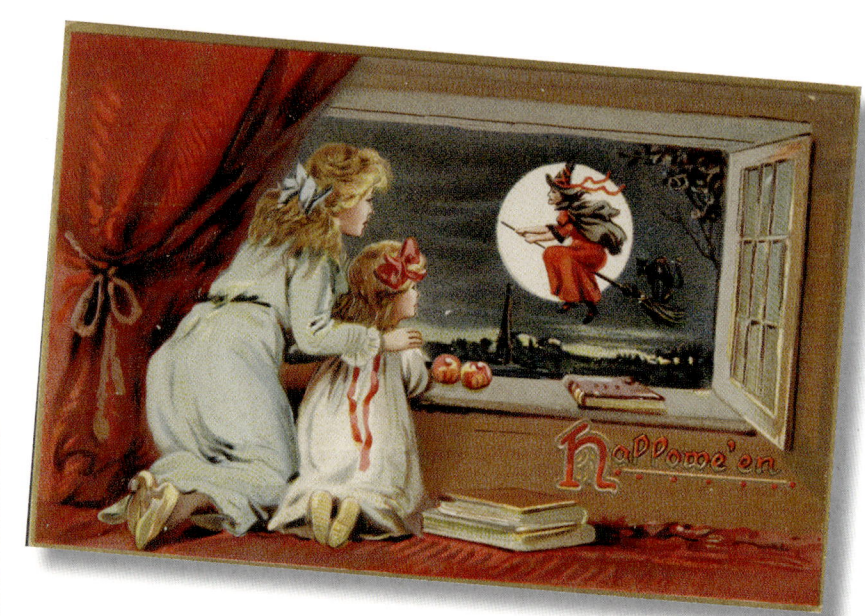

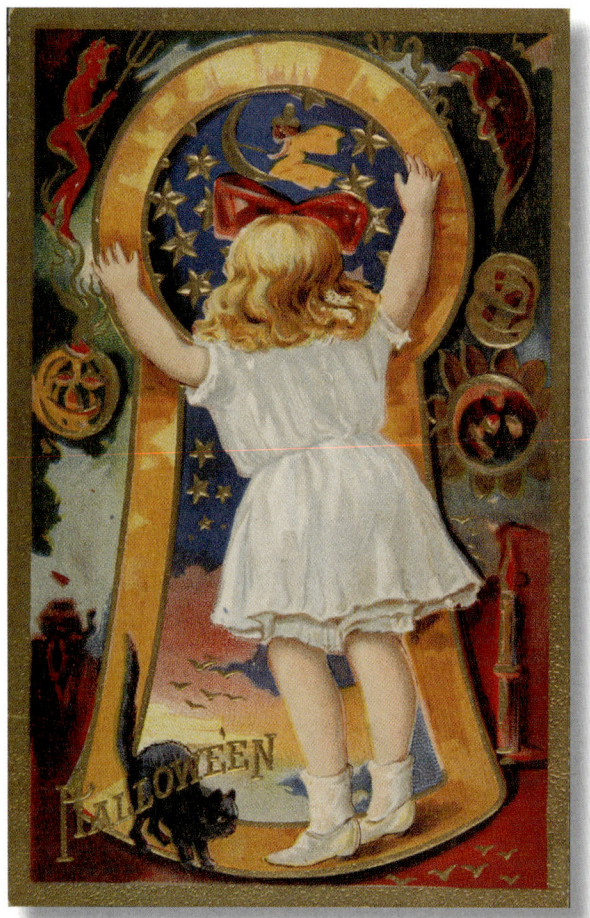

On the magical night anything was possible. Angelic sisters witness a witch flying on a broom in front of a full moon. Another innocent stands in a keyhole observing a broom-riding witch, a crescent moon and a plethora of stars. A holiday cake, perhaps in part left over from St. Valentine's Day, erupts with witches and demons while an amazed family watches.

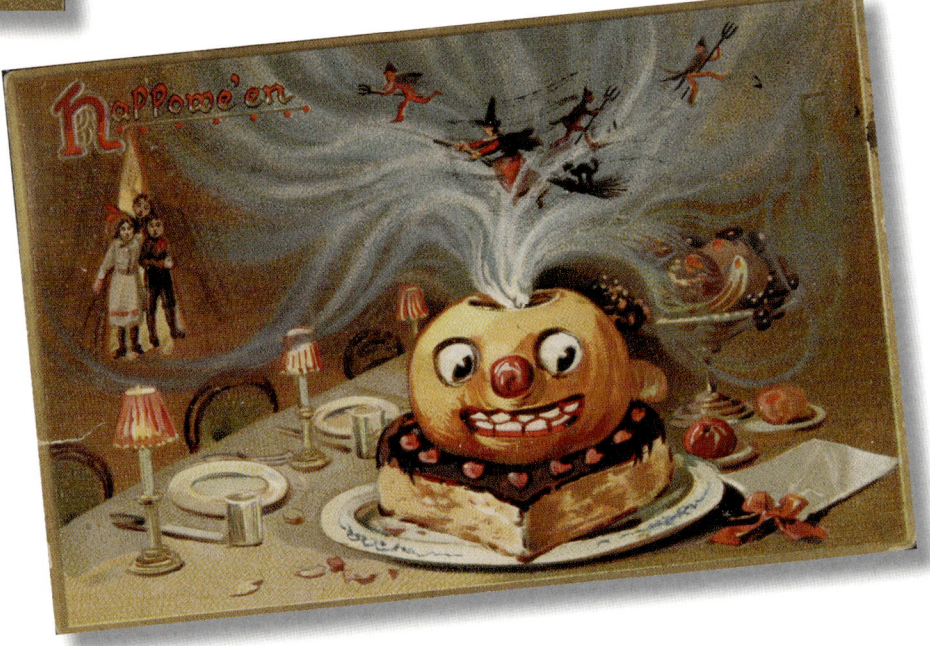

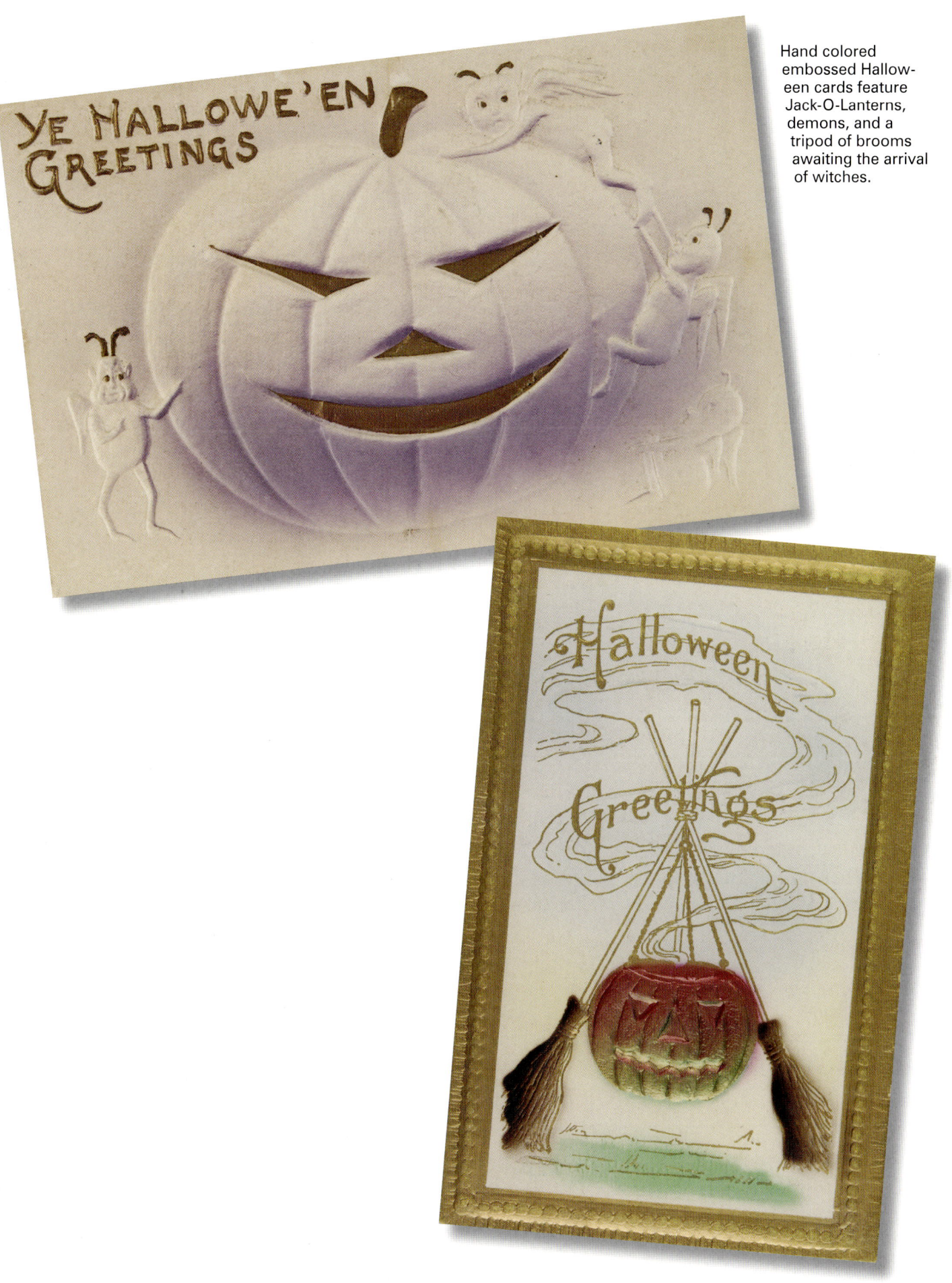

Hand colored embossed Halloween cards feature Jack-O-Lanterns, demons, and a tripod of brooms awaiting the arrival of witches.

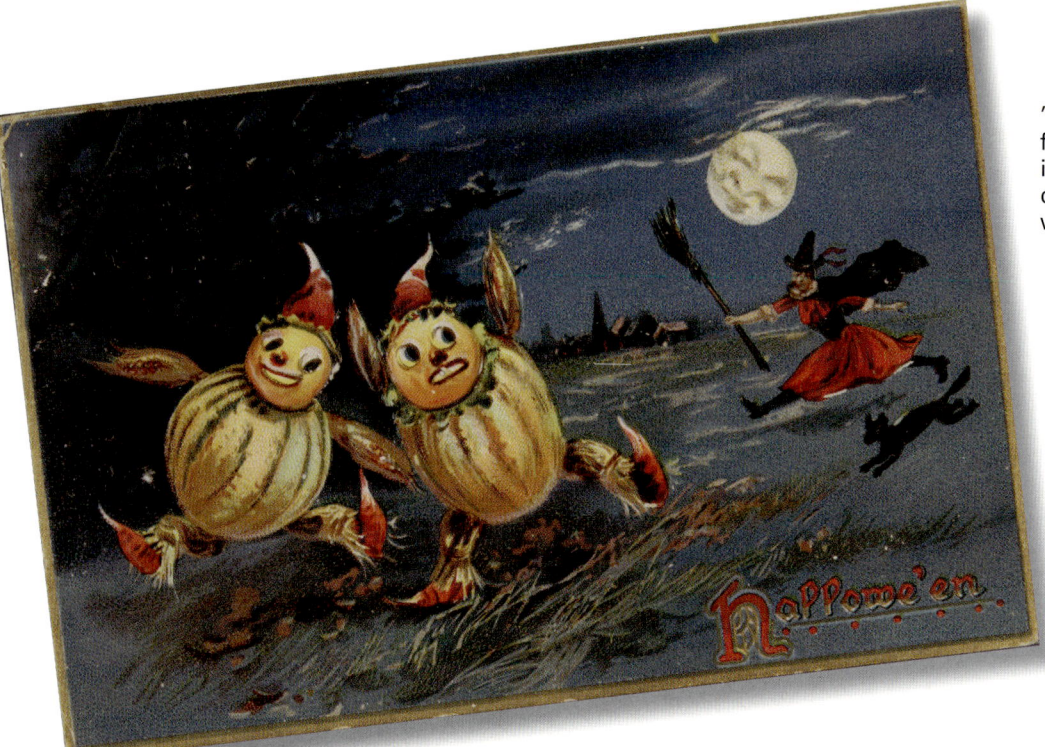

"Gourd Men," impish creatures, flee a pursuing witch, broom in hand, and her black cat. A disapproving Man-in-the-Moon watches.

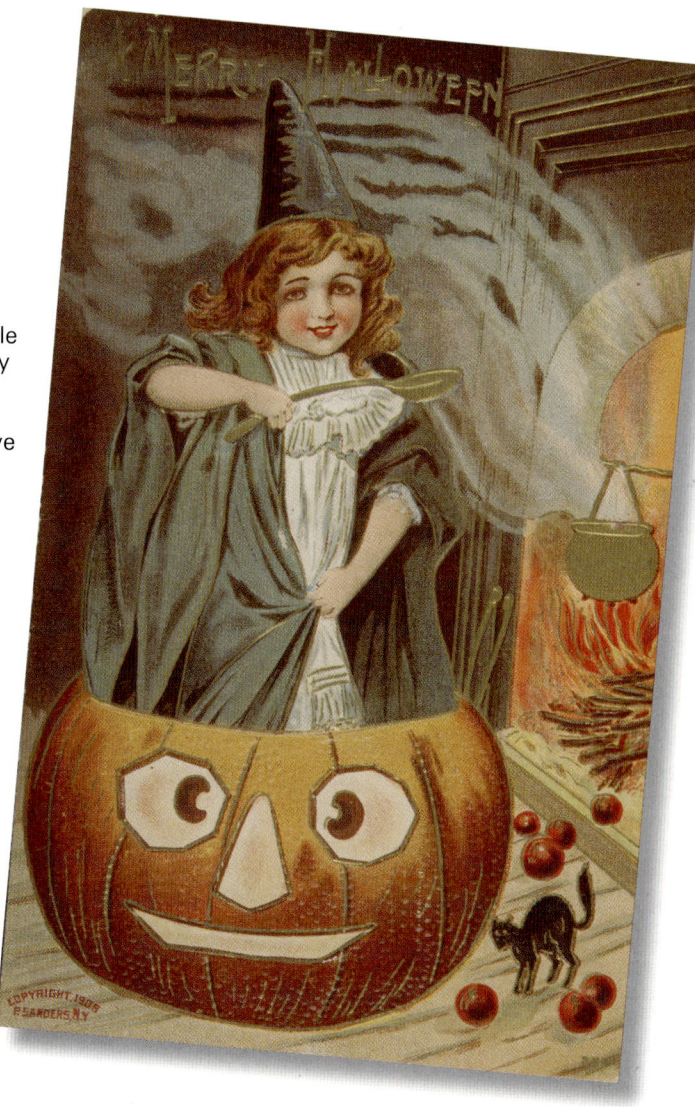

"A Merry Halloween" is an unusual greeting card salutation, but the little girl in the witch costume is certainly surrounded by the paraphernalia of the day – black cat and bubbling cauldron, as she stands in a massive Jack-O-Lantern.

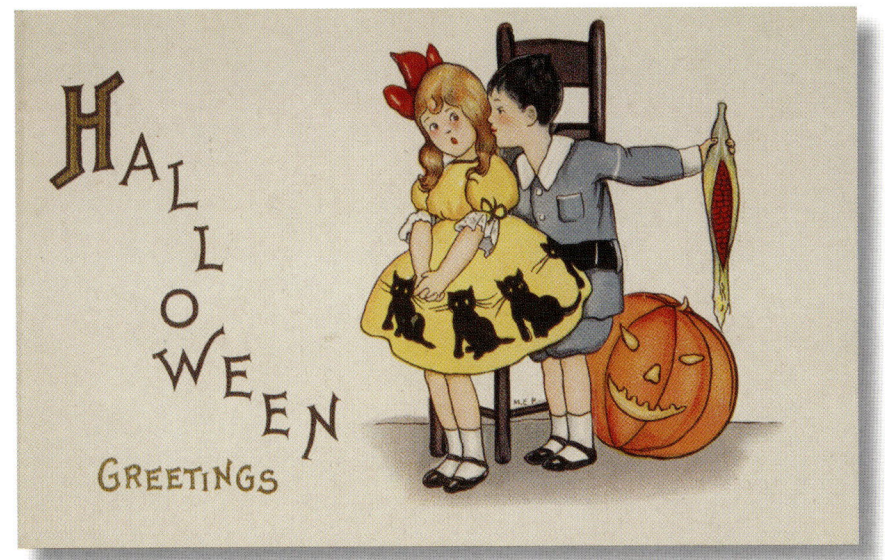

There were at least five cards in this *circa* 1910 series of "HALLOWEEN GREETINGS." In card 400A the young boy, corn ear in hand, attempts to kiss the young miss. Suddenly shy in card 400C, he hides behind a Jack-O-Lantern. Finally, on card 400E she serves him a plate of doughnuts. Note the ornamentation on her skirt and the tablecloth. The series was drawn by an artist identified as "M.E.P."

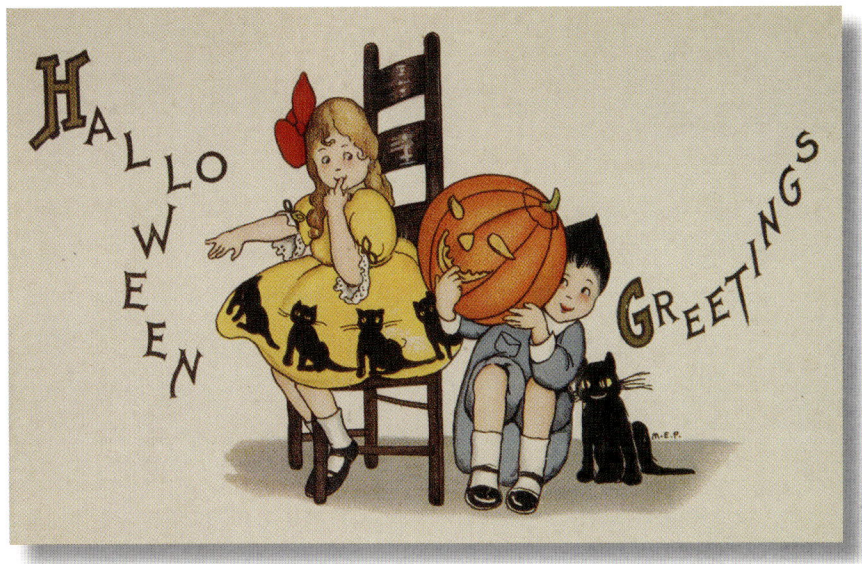

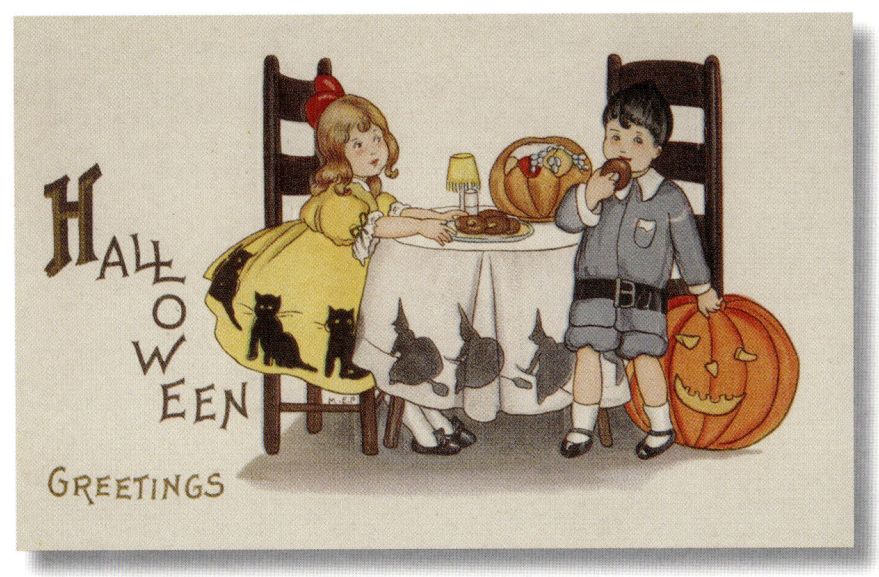

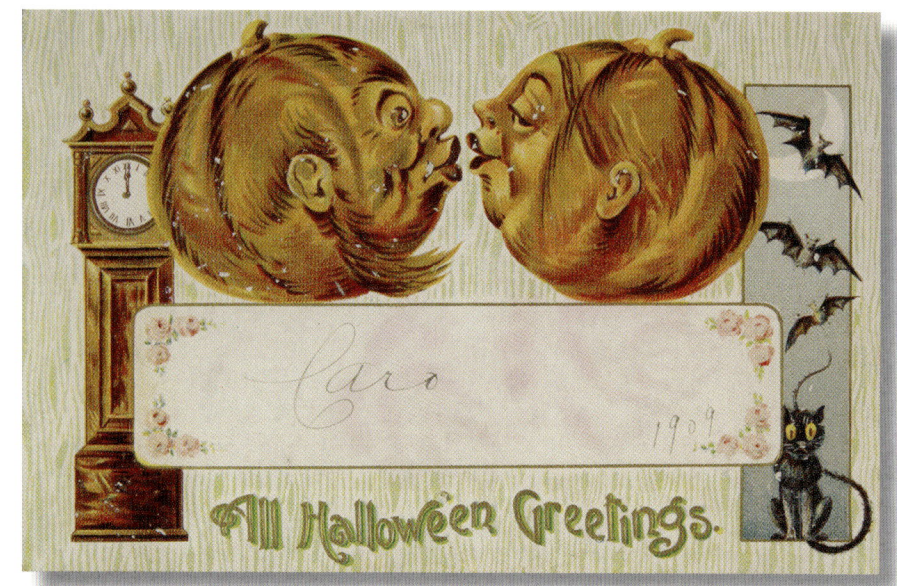

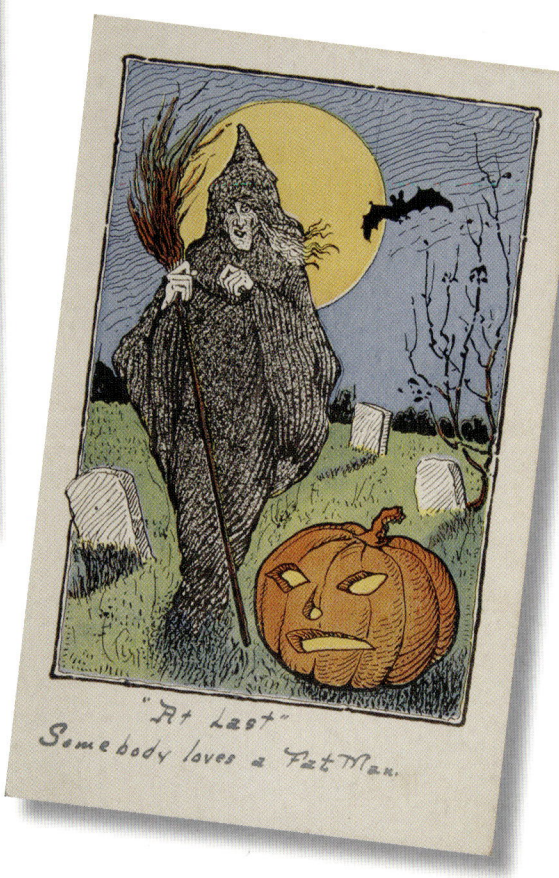

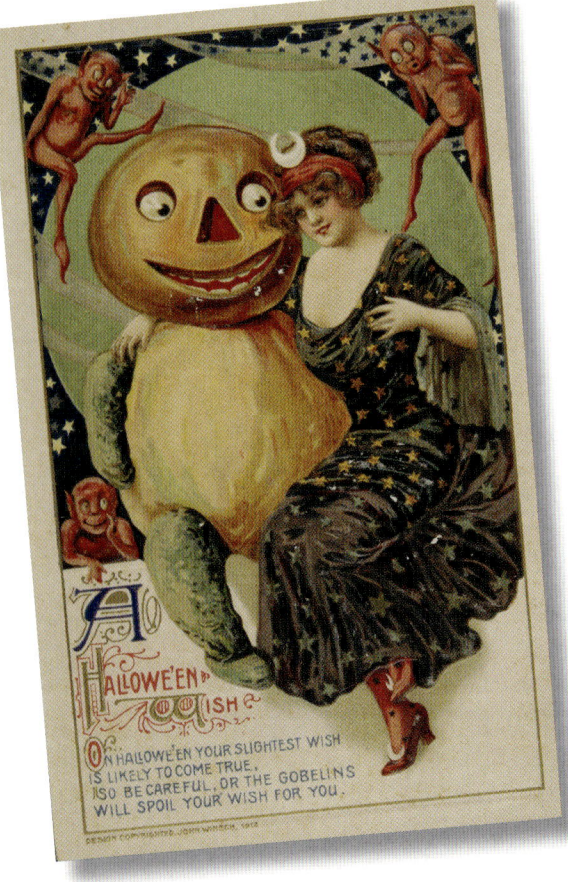

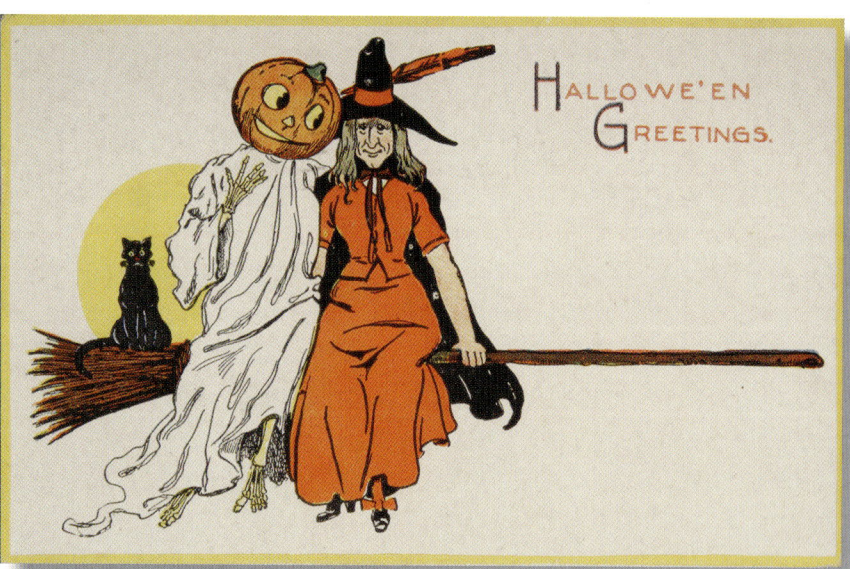

Halloween makes for strange romances. Aged anthropomorphic pumpkins kiss as the clock strikes twelve and a witch and a Jack-O-Lantern-headed ghost court sitting on her broom. A very attractive young woman wearing a star-spangled dress with a crescent moon in her hair finds a surprising romance. Perhaps she kissed a toad hoping for a prince! And a wry Jack-O-Lantern observes, "'At Last' Somebody loves at Fat Man."

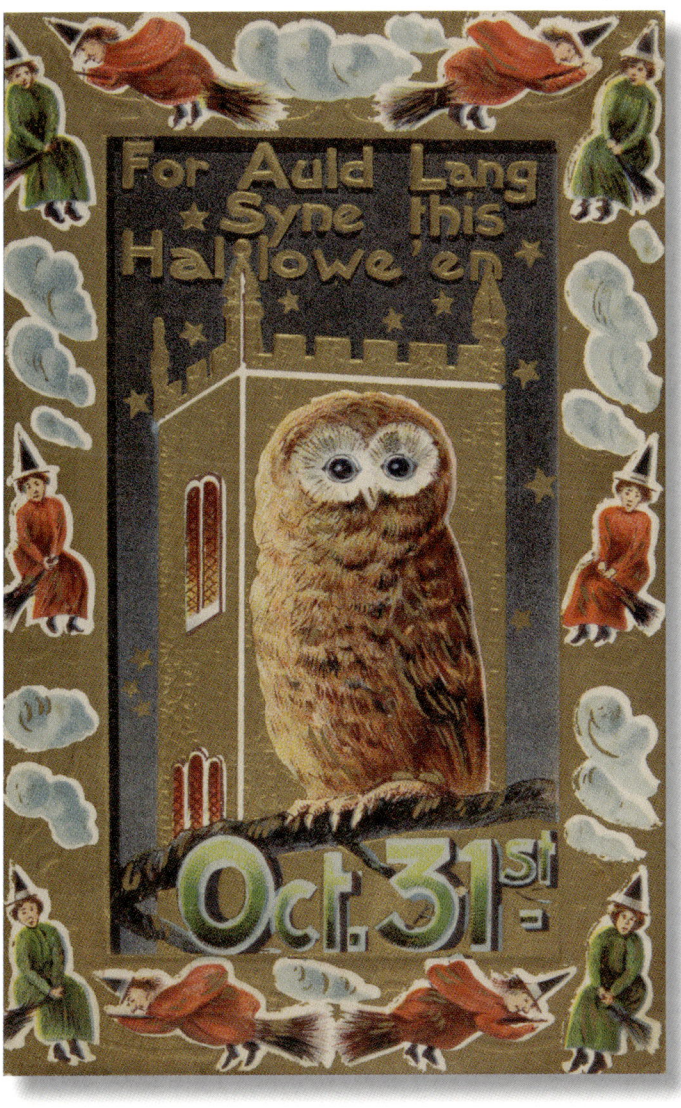

A combination of New Year and Halloween symbolism makes for an unusual card. The message on the reverse sent to Miss Sara Reed of New Castle, Pennsylvania, is equally unusual. "Dear Girlie [sic] In memory of the night X left New Castle seven years ago, bidding G. good-bye only to face these unhappy years"

An especially malevolent wizard (notice the absence of hair) is framed by demons and accompanied by a vicious-looking cat as he extends "Halloween Greetings."

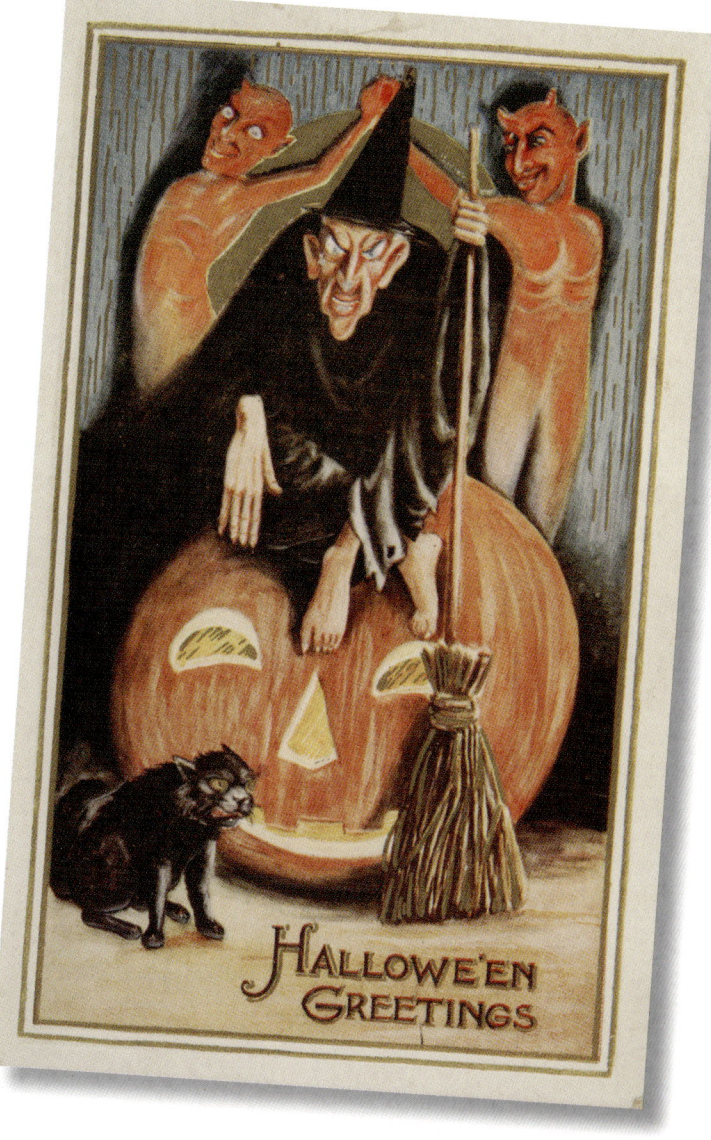

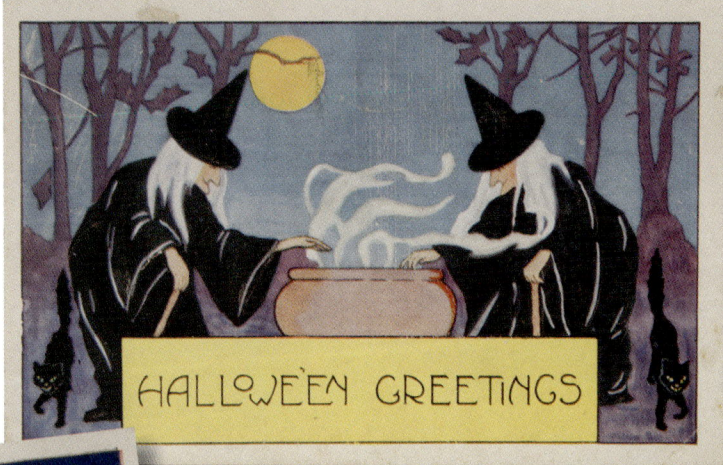

The witch is the most common image of Halloween and is symbolic of evil spirits that traditional folks believed to be roaming the world on All Hallows' Eve. The witch is, of course, pagan in origin and to be accused of practicing witchcraft was very serious. In 17th century Salem, Massachusetts, a number of women and one man convicted of being witches were put to death.
By the early 20th century most people, especially the educated, mostly gave up on believing in witches and these supernatural beings became caricatures associated with pointed hats, bony fingers, big noses, unkempt long black hair, and often black garments. They are usually accompanied by black cats, broomsticks, bats, owls, and cauldrons. And, of course, they ofttimes cavort in the presence of all manner of demons and magical creatures – usually by moonlight.

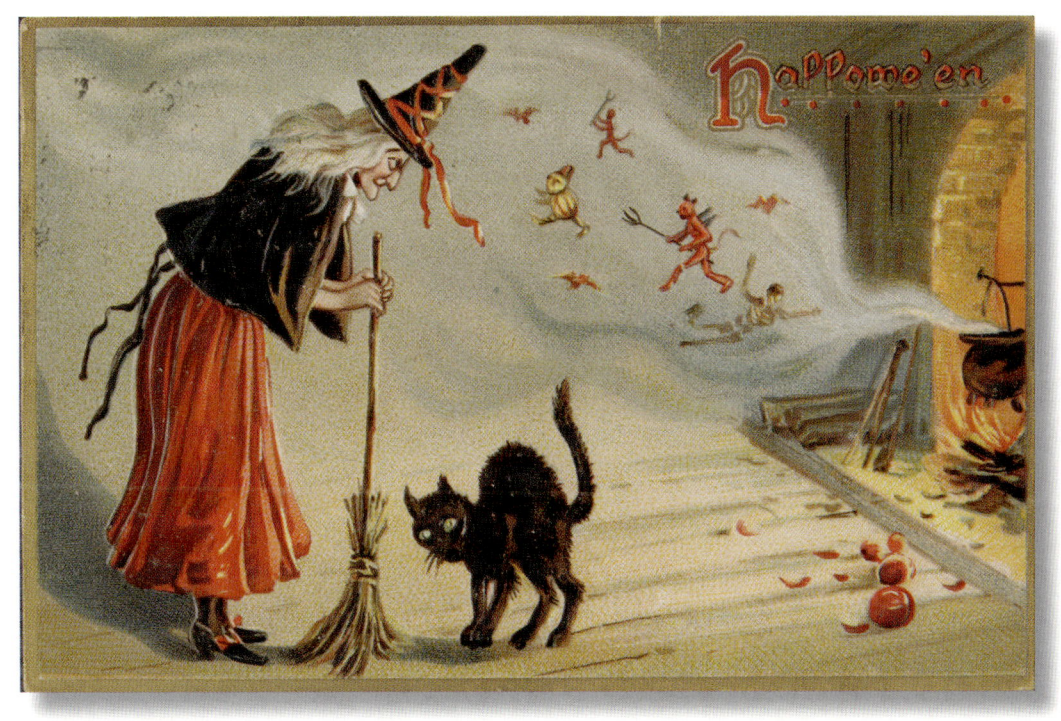

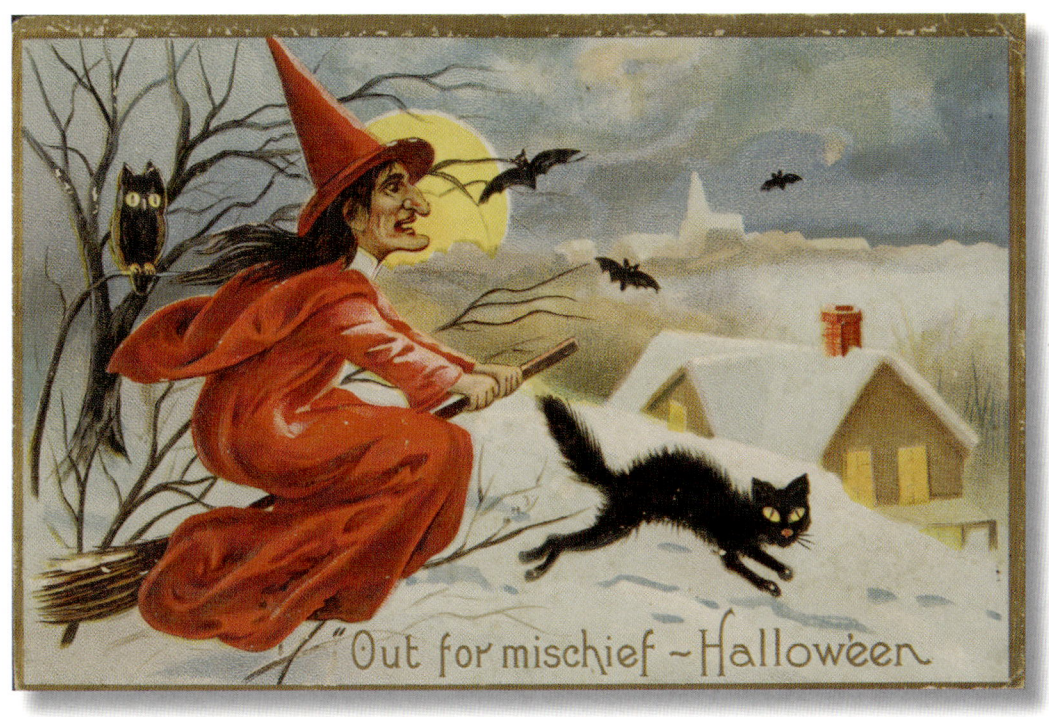

For those who prefer "Witch Lite" there are many old cards that present us with pleasant or juvenile beings. Artist: Frances Brundage (1841-1937) created these non-threatening images. Take note that one black cat even has a cute red bow at its neck.

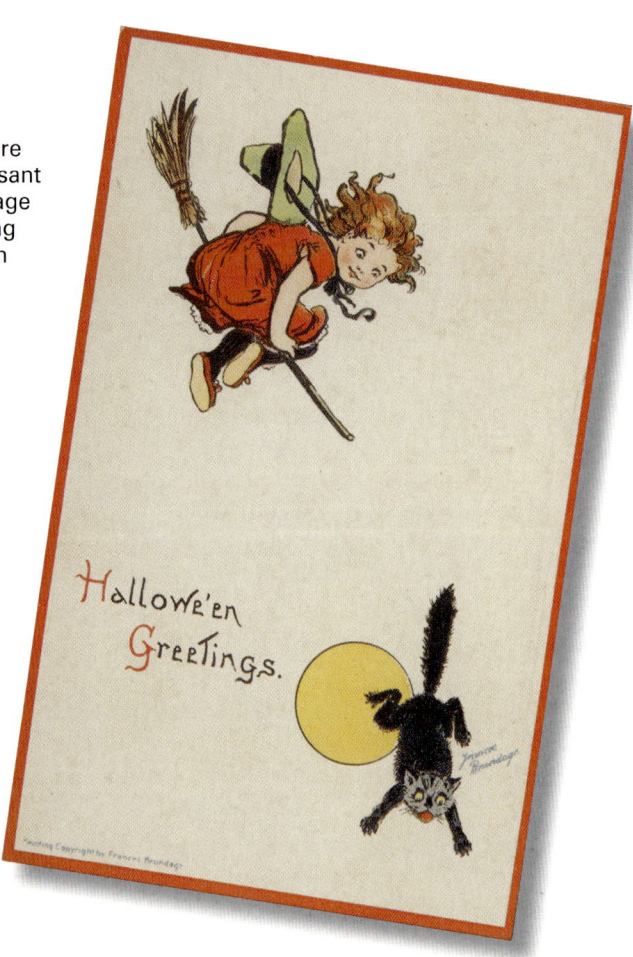

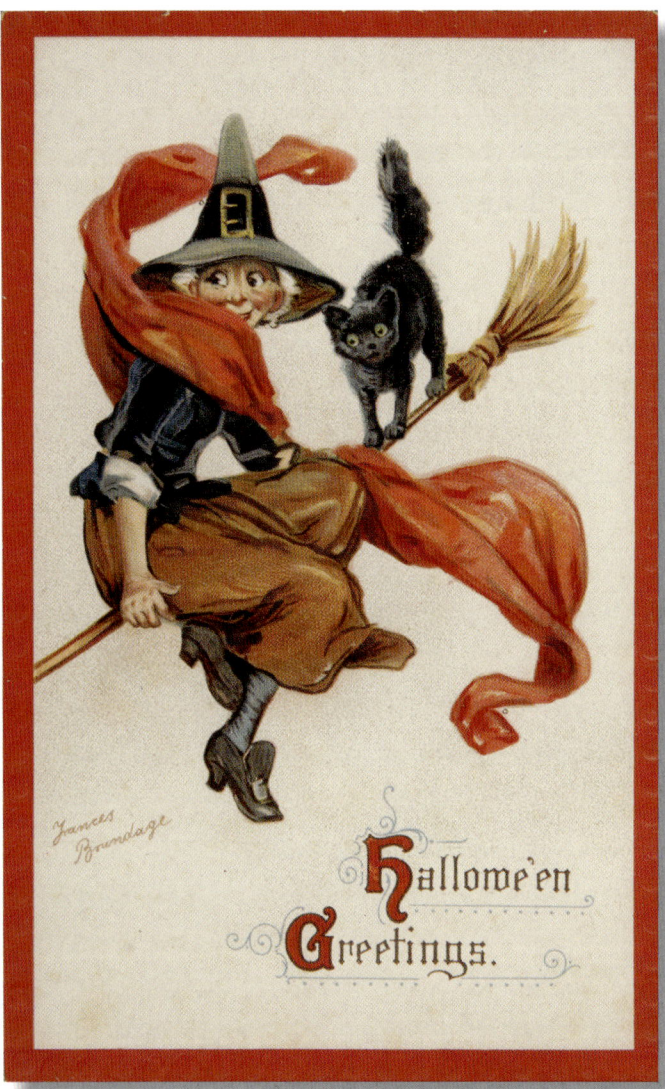

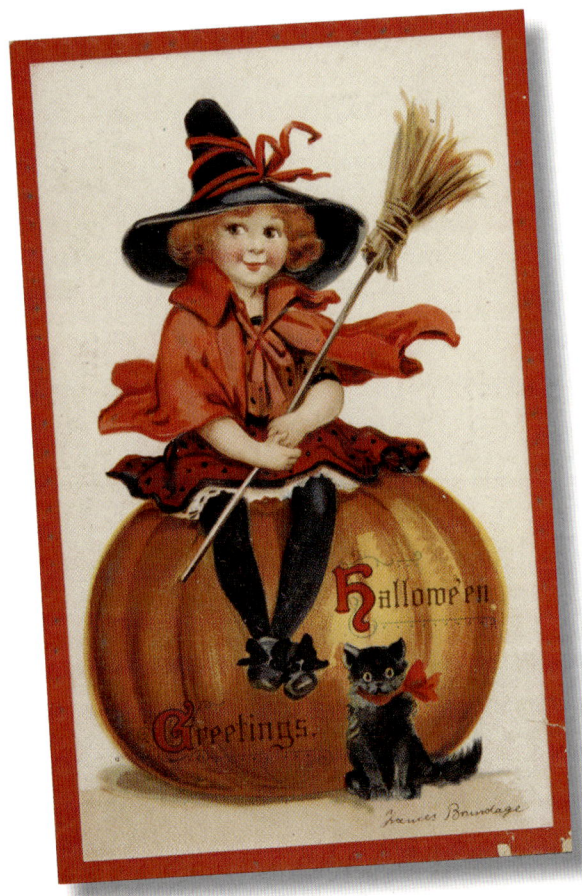

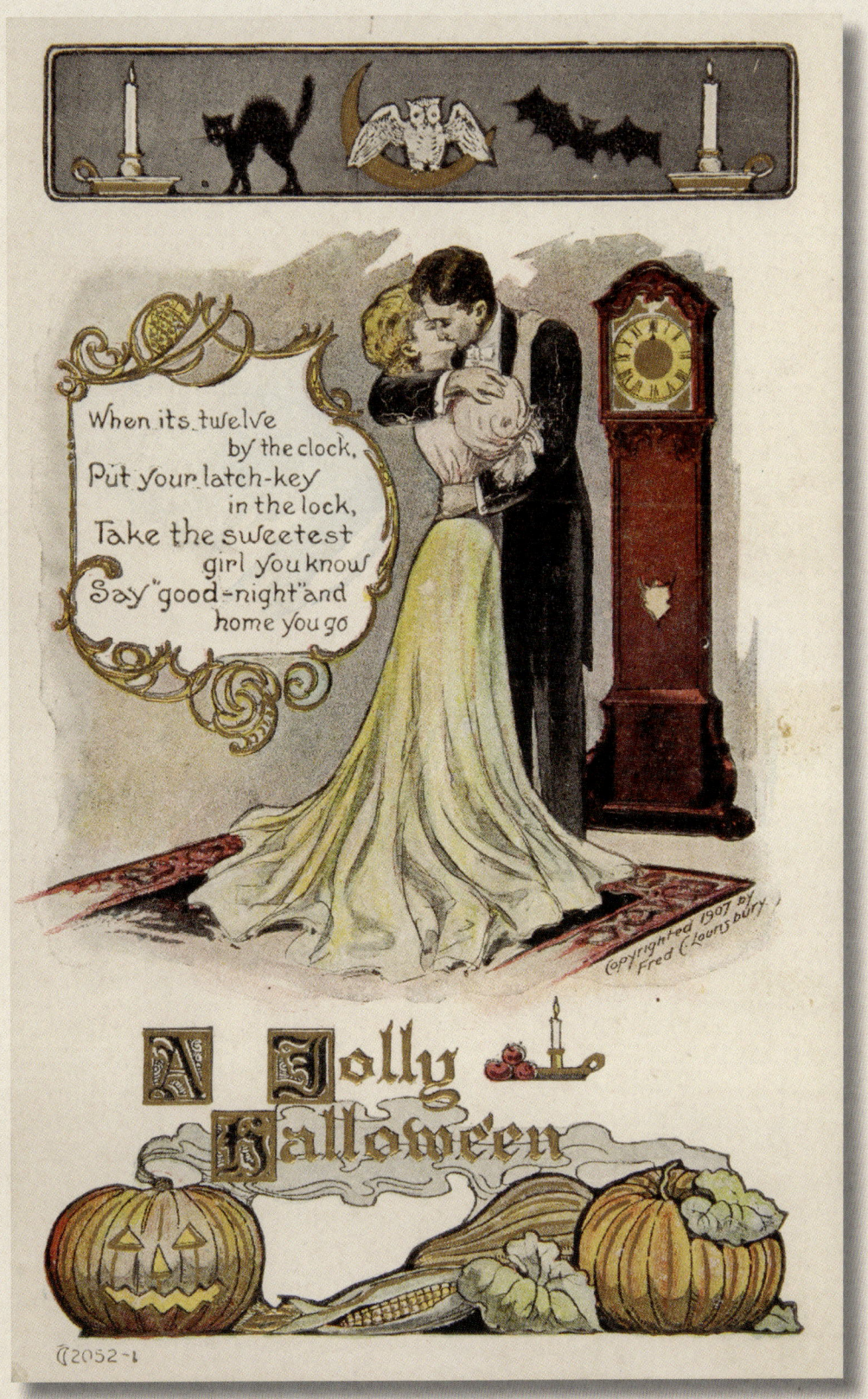

Romance and Halloween are no longer paired in common imagination, but they once were. Midnight was an especially auspicious time.

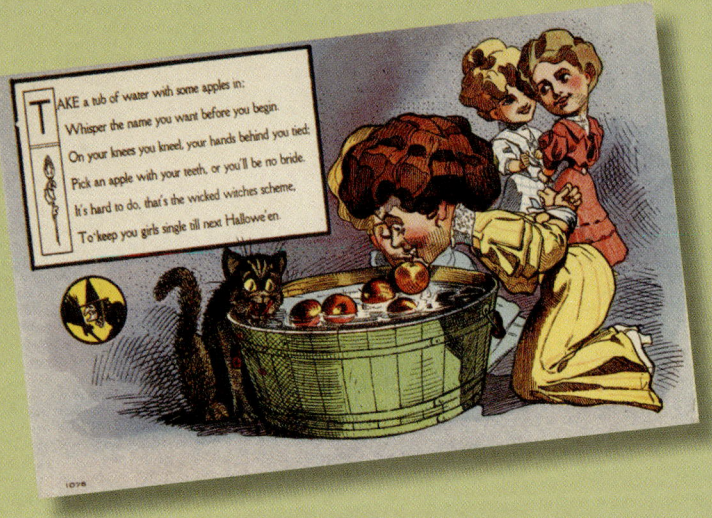
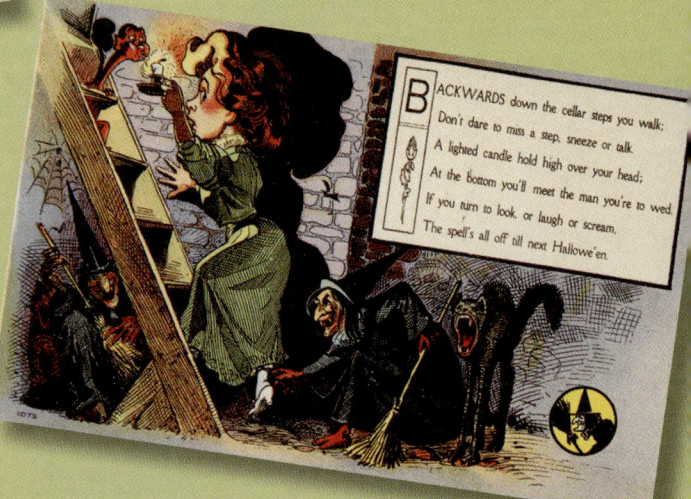
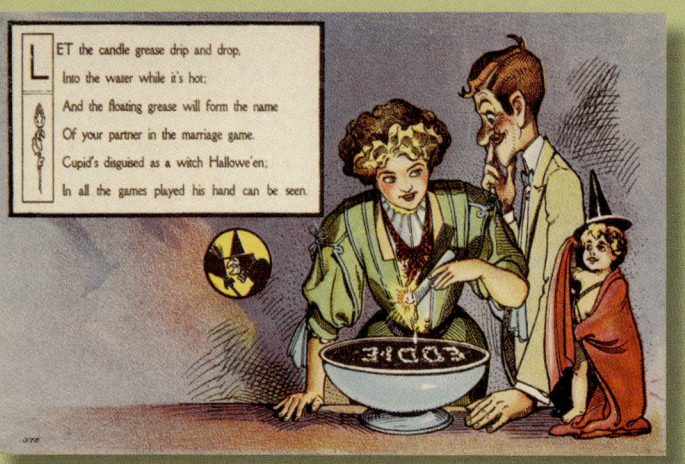
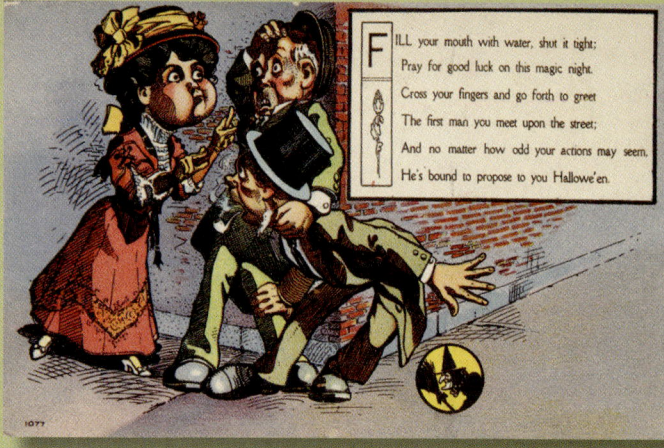
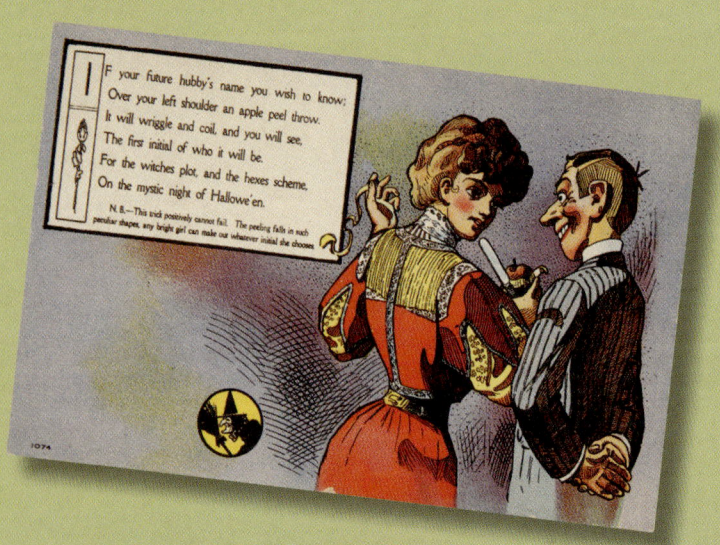

An entire alphabet of devices and techniques can divine who your true love will be. Just follow the advice given on these five representative cards from "Halloween Series No 1"

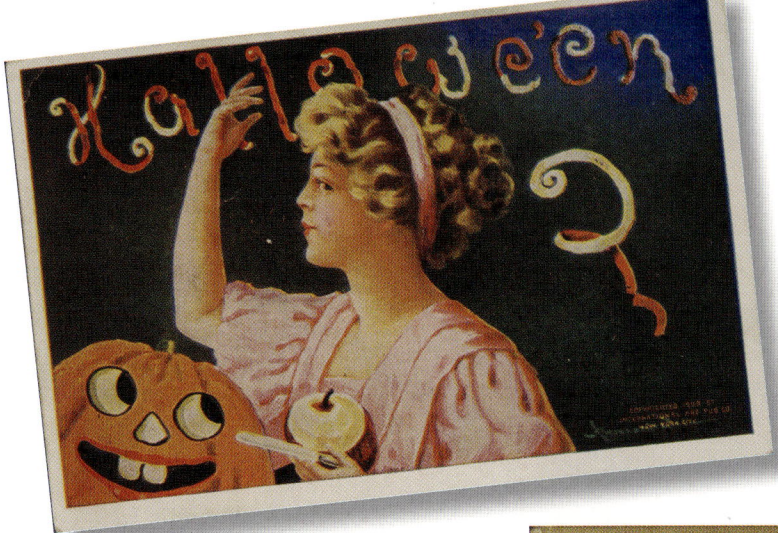

This young lady tosses her long, unbroken apple peel over her left shoulder, secure in the knowledge that the initial it forms will be that of her future husband. This technique, needless to say, only works on Halloween.

Impish apples get ready, in a washtub of water, to help prophesize future mates. A mischievous, steaming Jack-O-Lantern looks on.

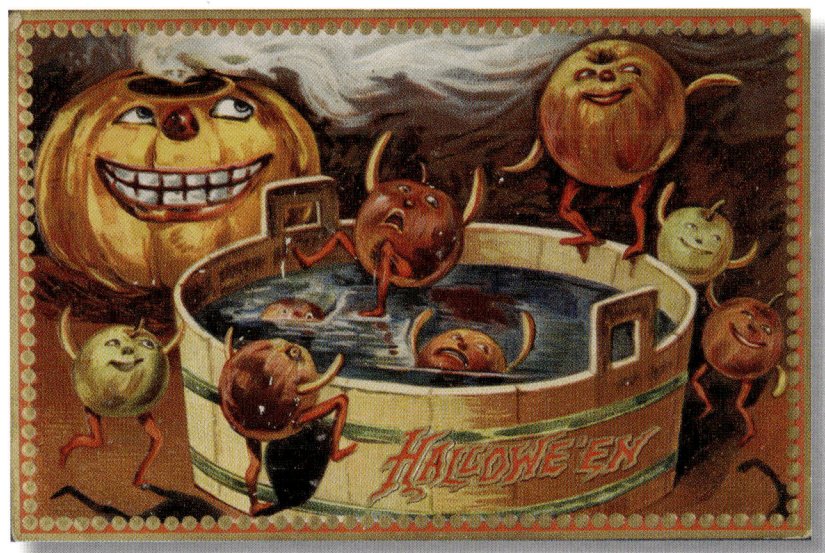

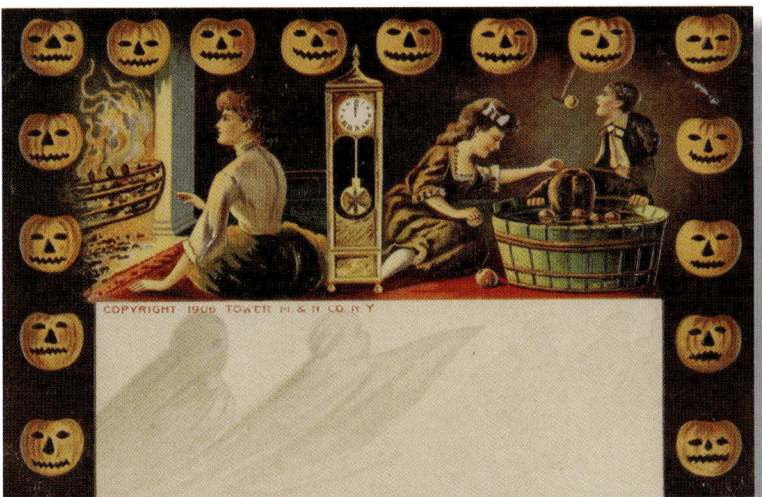

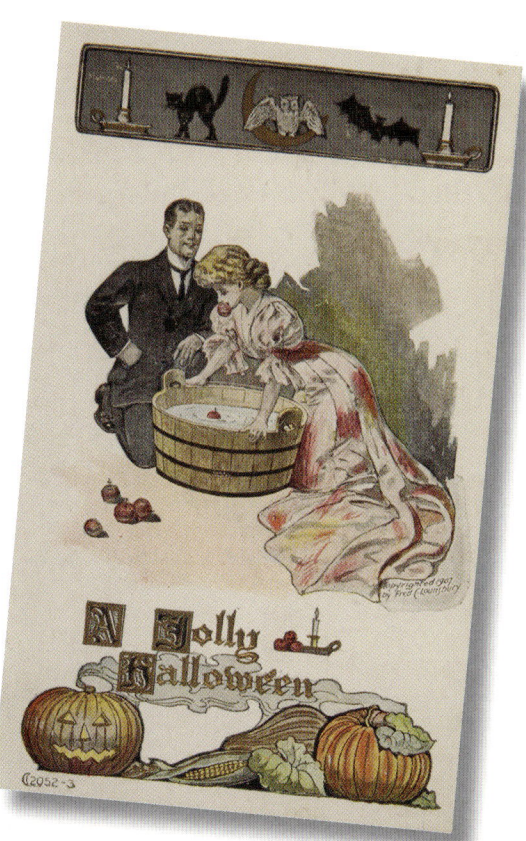

Both boys and girls, men and women could bob for apples or attempt to bite an apple on a string. If the boy caught an apple in his mouth, the girl nearest to him would be his girlfriend. The first boy to bite the apple on the string would be the first of his friends to get married. The elegantly dressed young lady has assured her relationship with the man kneeling beside her.

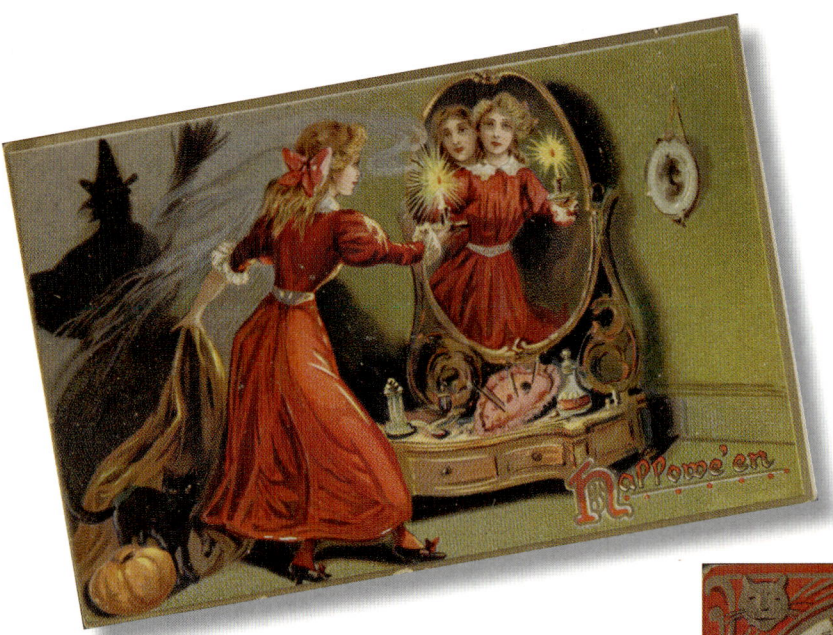

The simplest of all ways to discover who your future mate would be was to look into your mirror by candlelight on "HALLOWE'EN" (which seemed so much more unusual than Halloween.) The message on the back of the man reflected in the mirror card reads, "Mary, this picture looks so familiar to me I thought I would have to send it to you. I will write later. Edna"

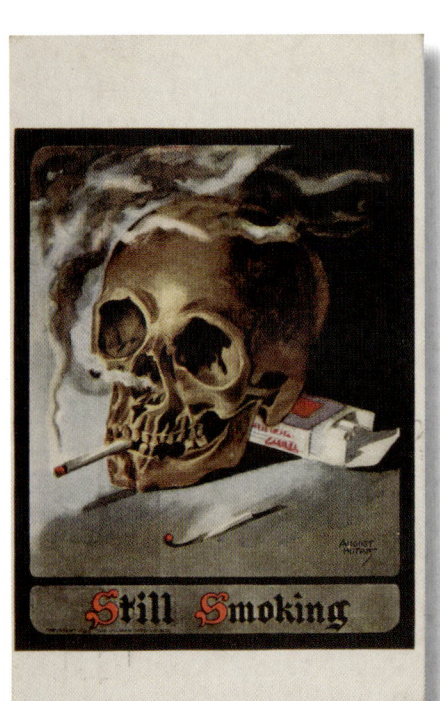

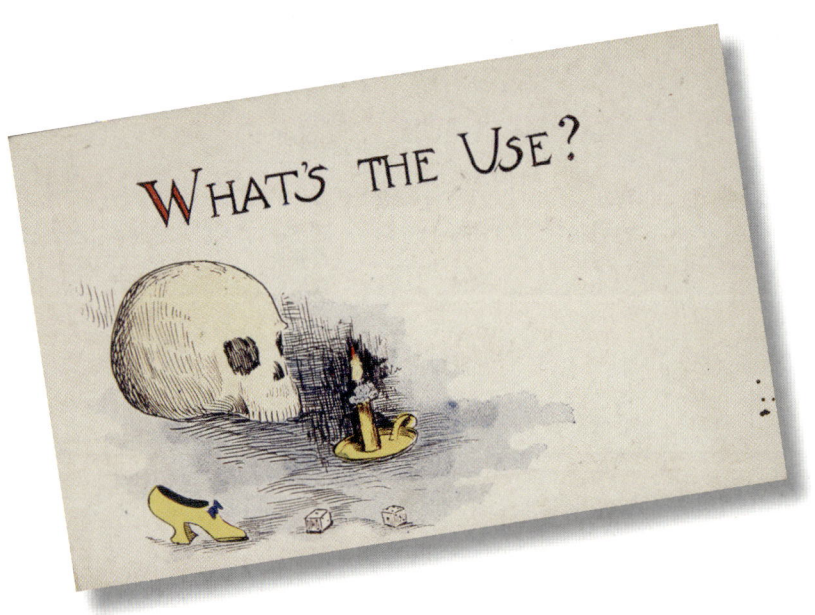

Skeletons and skulls were not common Halloween symbols in the early 20th century – they only become popular thanks to the influence of the "Day of the Dead" culture of Mexico. Both of these cards date from the first decade of that century. "What's the Use?" references women and fate. "Still Smoking," sent to Mr. Charles Palmer of Lancaster Pennsylvania, "From a Friend" is a statement of early anti-tobacco sentiment.

8
Thanksgiving

Pilgrims & Prescient Turkeys

Harvest festivals are ancient in origin and almost universal. The Jews since ancient times have observed *Sukkoth*, the Feast of the Tabernacles, as a celebration of the earth's plenty. The ancient Greeks honored Demeter, the goddess of grain, with an annual festival *Thesmorphoria* held in October. The Romans, who adopted so much from the Greeks, held their *Cerealia* in honor of their grain goddess, Ceres, whose name has been given to the popular breakfast food, cereal. Harvest festivals are found elsewhere in Europe and in the British Isles.

Traditionally at "Harvest Home" in England, the last of the grain harvest (or 'corn' as it was called) would be paraded in carts decorated with flowers, branches, and ribbons, sometimes driven by a "Lord" and "Lady" of the harvest. Christianized, the celebration was moved into the church on a Harvest Home Sunday, with the altar being decorated with seasonal produce. This later custom was popular among the Pennsylvania Germans, as well, and, interestingly, today it is being revived in suburban churches with congregants bringing items grown in their gardens to be used first as altar decorations then to be donated to food banks.

The Harvest Home Festival and the Dutch feasting customs that the Pilgrims assimilated during their ten-year stay in Holland are the basis of the American Thanksgiving.

There were at least two Thanksgiving celebrations held in America before the famed one celebrated by the Pilgrims at Plymouth in 1621. One was held in 1607 when an independent group of English settlers led by one Captain George Popham feasted with a group of Indians near the mouth of the Kennebec River. More officially, on December 14, 1619, a group of about forty colonists under the leadership of Captain John Woodleaf celebrated a day of Thanksgiving at Berkeley Hundred near present Williamsburg, Virginia.

In the ensuing years many thanksgiving observances were held in the thirteen colonies and the ensuing states. They were harvest-related and mostly without an Indian presence. The modern holiday of Thanksgiving can be credited to a campaign mounted by Sarah J. Hale (1788-1879), the editor of an important woman's magazine, *Godey's Lady's Book*. On October 3, 1863, after the pivotal Northern Civil War victories at Gettysburg and Vicksburg, President Lincoln proclaimed the fourth Thursday of November as Thanksgiving Day. As our modern Christmas became more and more important economically, the day after Thanksgiving Day (not often called "Black Friday") became the unofficial start of the Christmas holiday shopping season. In an attempt to stimulate the Depression Era economy, President Franklin Delano Roosevelt moved the holiday back to the third Thursday in November to allow for a longer shopping season, but an uproar ensued. In 1941 Congress passed legislation, signed by the President, making Thanksgiving a legal holiday.

The symbols of Thanksgiving are familiar: Indian corn and other fruits of the autumn harvest, Pilgrims, and, of course, the turkey—the center of our major civic feast day. Thanksgiving, generating a four-day weekend, has become the most heavily traveled holiday in America. In many homes today the holiday itself has become a tripartite event, as Thanksgiving has shed its religious significance for most. In the morning one attends a parade or, at least, watches one on television; then feasts and, lastly, watches football games – also on TV.

The Thanksgiving parade is the ultimate fusing of festival and commerce, usually sponsored by local merchants and ending with the arrival of Santa Claus at a prominent retail venue. The first major Thanksgiving Day parade was sponsored by Gimbel Brothers Department Store in Philadelphia in 1920. Four years later, Macy's store picked up the custom in New York City. Today Macy's Thanksgiving Day Parade is an event attended by over a million people annually and is televised to a vast national audience.

Thanksgiving is rich with the imagery of autumn, redolent with elements of religion and touched with hedonism.

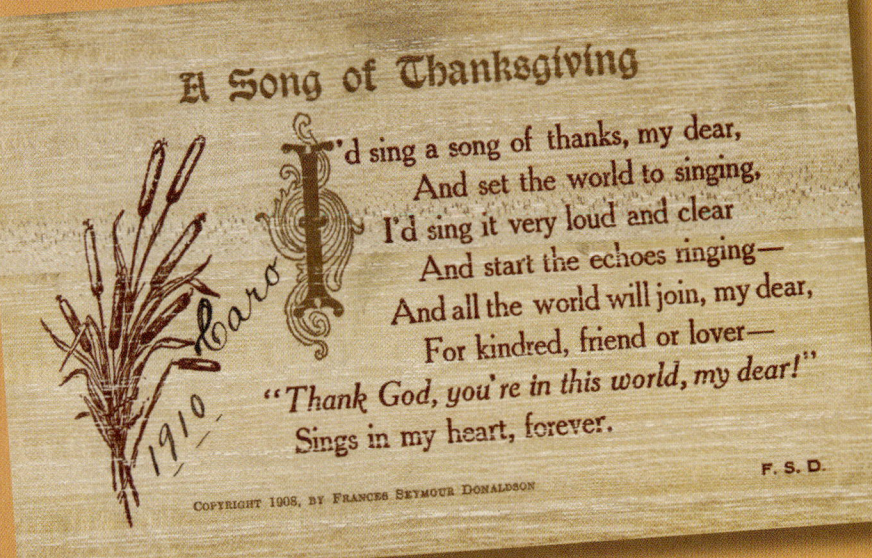

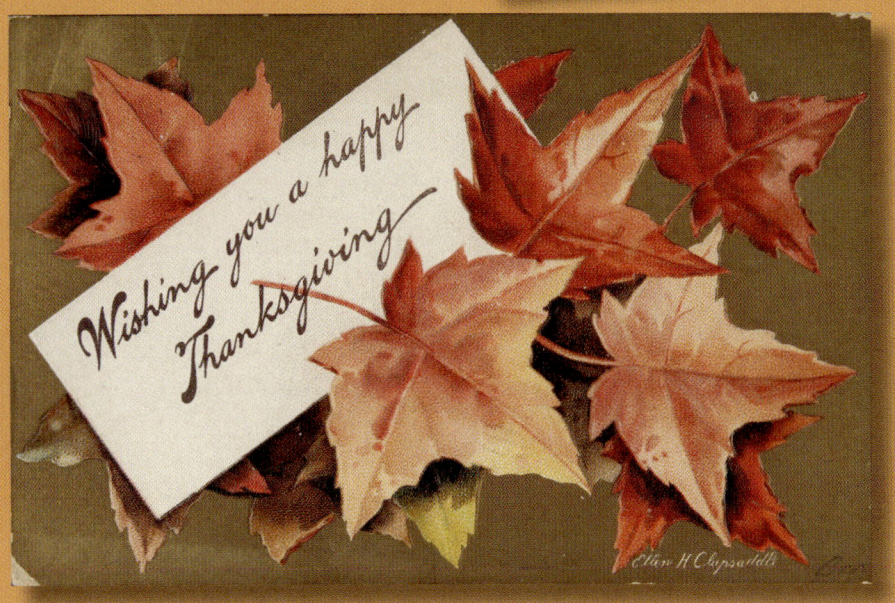

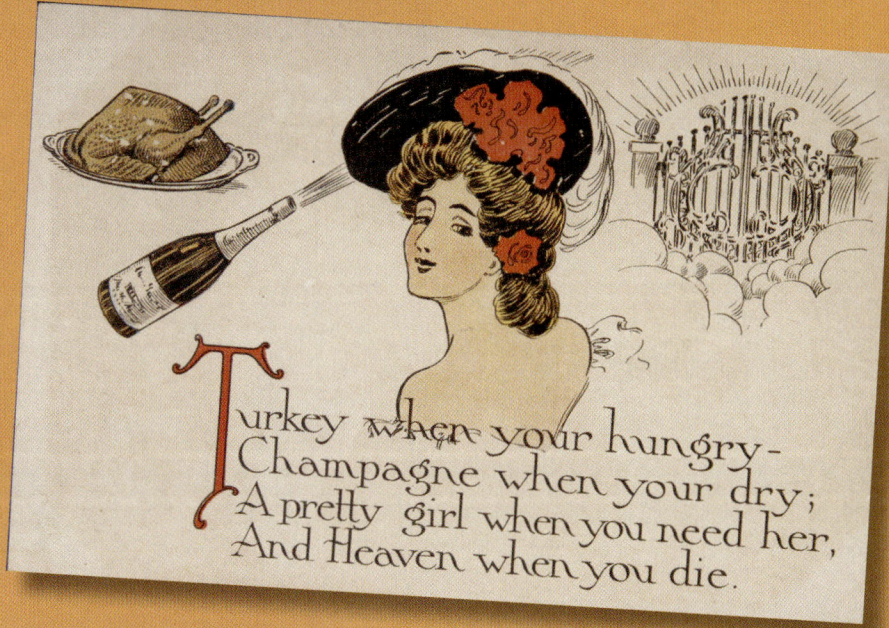

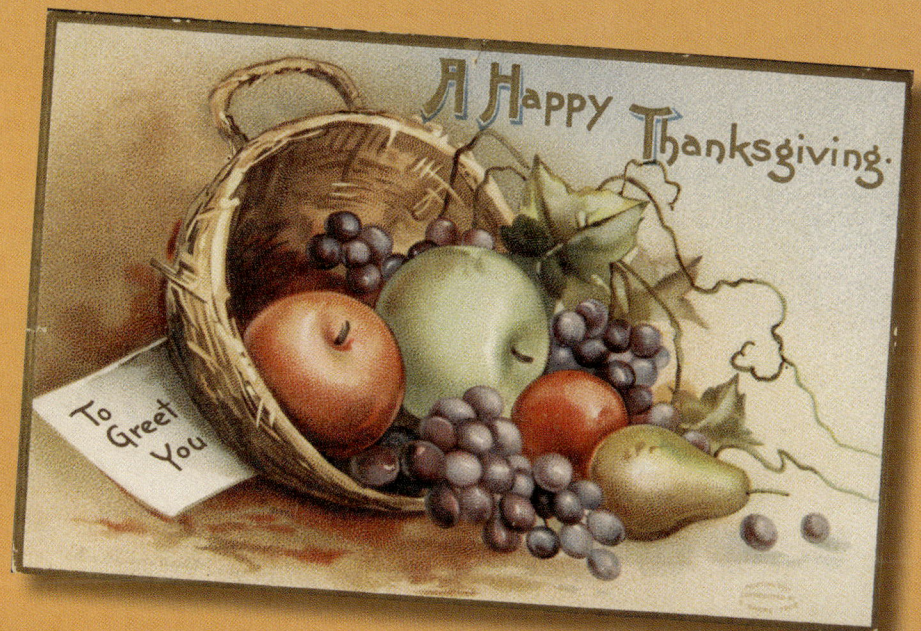

The Earth's Bounty is very important to Thanksgiving with fruits, pumpkins, corn and other grains being featured prominently.

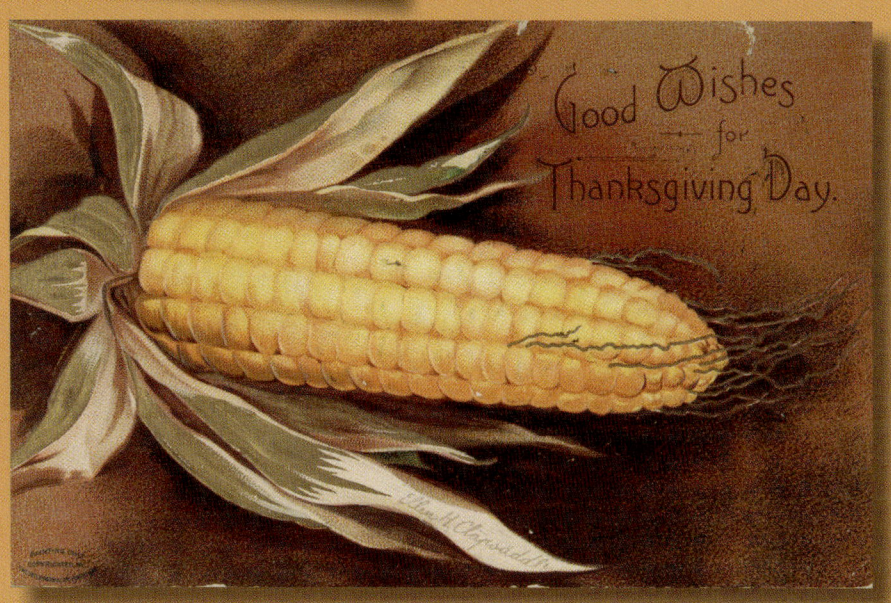

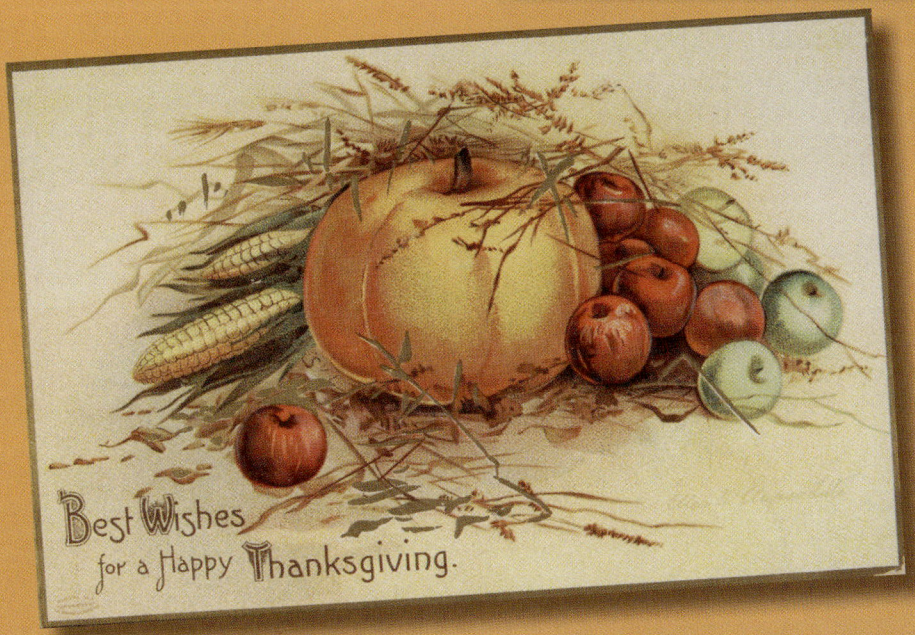

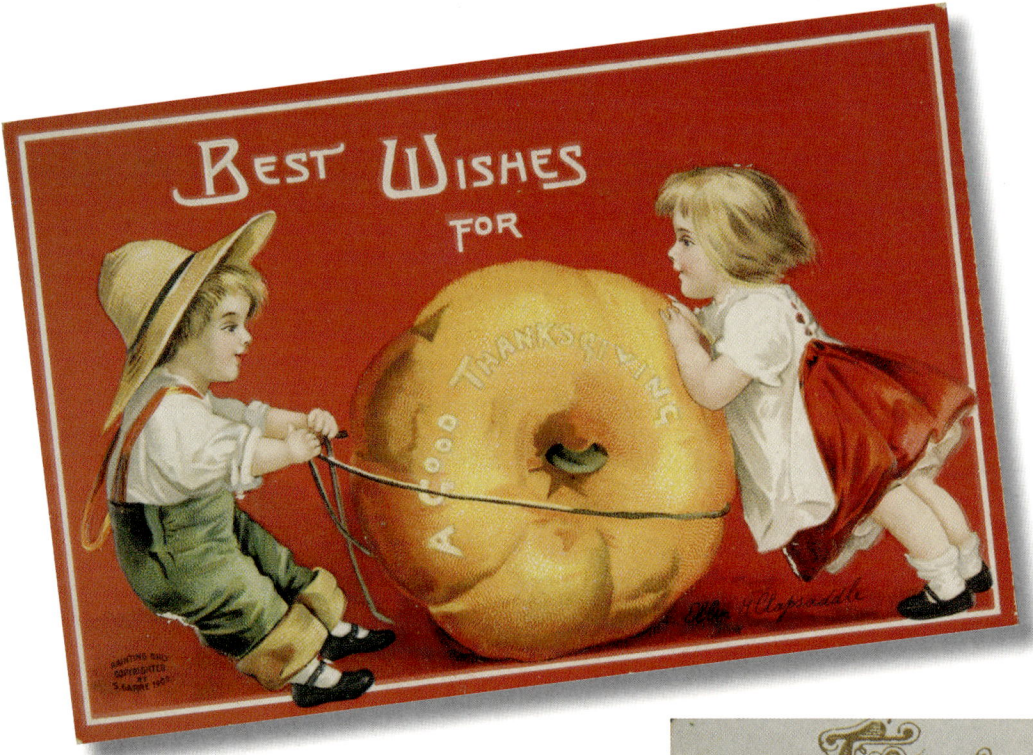

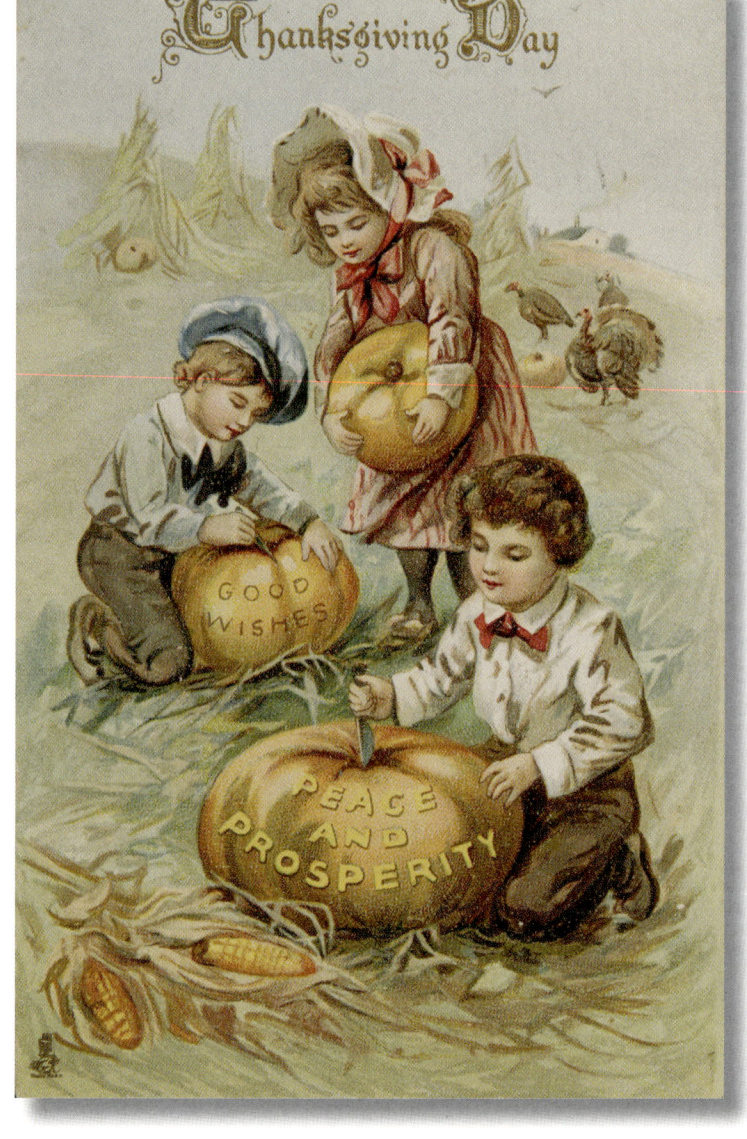

The pumpkin, in its natural uncut form, is an important Thanksgiving image, especially when it is paired with children. Three fashionably dressed tots select pumpkins in a field also inhabited by corn shocks and turkeys. Two children play with a huge pumpkin in an image copyrighted in 1908 by artist "S. Garre."

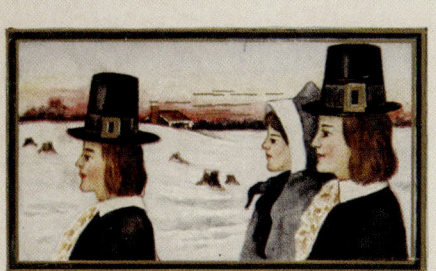

Pilgrims are an important part of our Thanksgiving mythology. In actuality their popular image is a mixture of two groups: the Pilgrims, who landed here in 1620 and celebrated their first Thanksgiving the following year, and a much larger group of English settlers, the Puritans, who arrived in Massachusetts Bay beginning in 1630. The familiar black and gray clad figures are Puritans. The Pilgrims favored bright colors. On many cards we see male and female couples – symbolically the parents of an American people. Parenthetically, the buckles often seen on Puritan men's hats, were unknown before the end of the 17th century.

HEAP high the board with
plenteous cheer
and gather to the feast,
And toast that sturdy Pilgrim band
whose courage never ceased.
Give praise to that All-Gracious One
by whom their steps were led,
And thanks unto the harvest's Lord
who sends our "daily bread."

ALICE WILLIAMS BROTHERTON

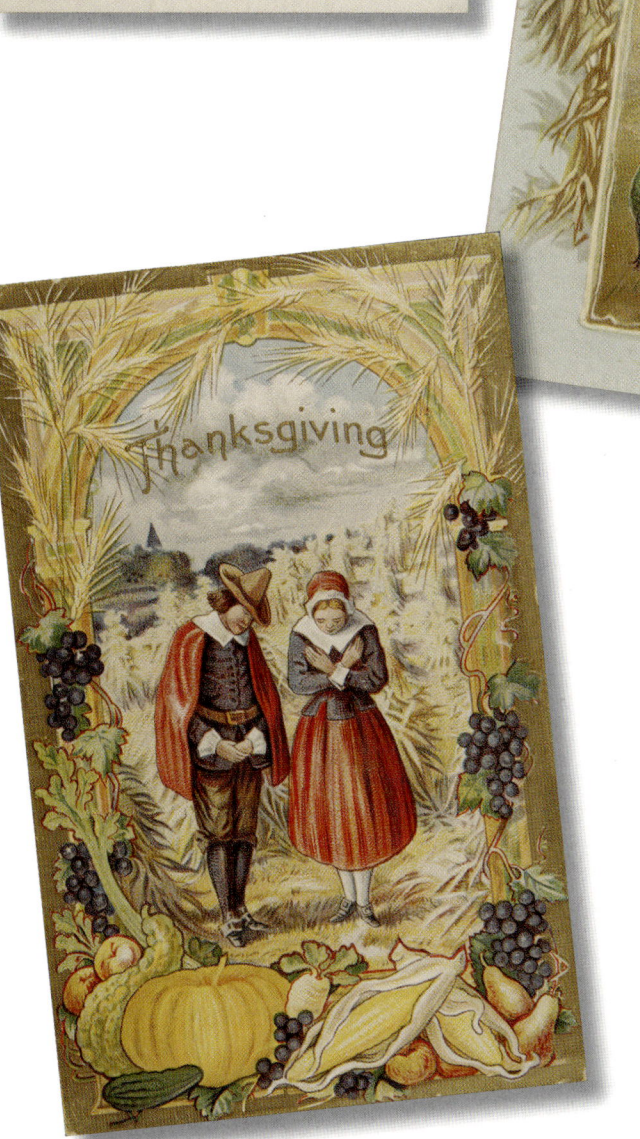

A white-clad Pilgrim boy leads a turkey to the slaughter by a rose leash. One wonders if the artist knew the pagan origins of floral garlands. At any rate, it is incongruous with the standard imagery.

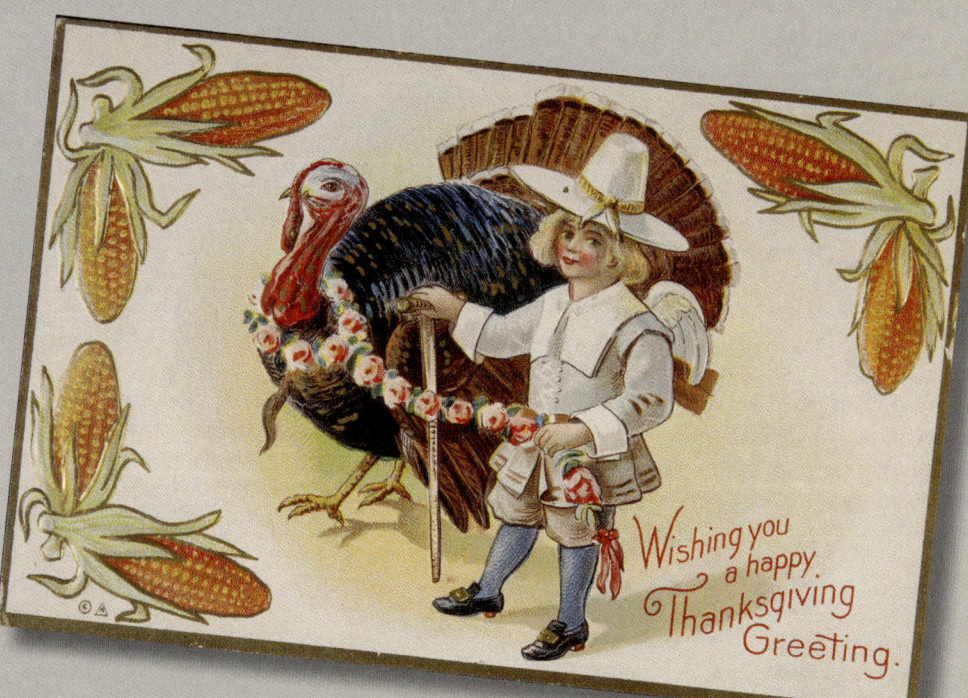

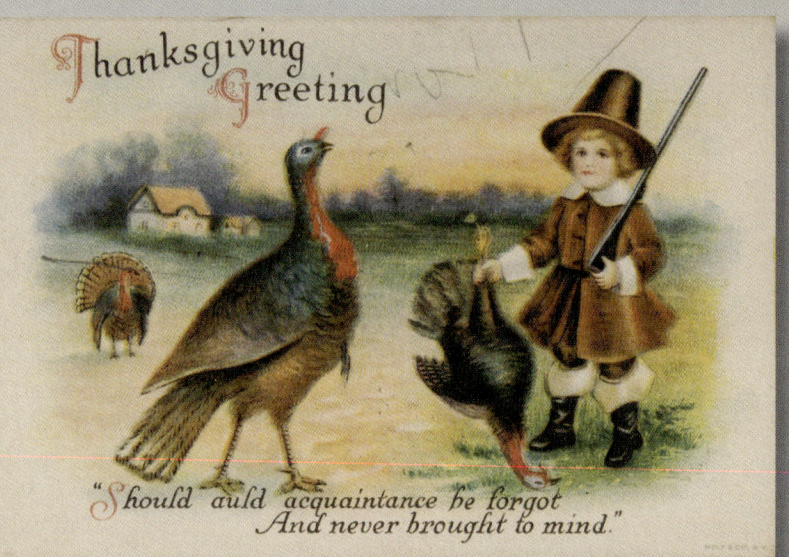

While no one knows what birds, if any, were eaten at the first Thanksgiving, by the late 19th century the turkey and Thanksgiving had become inseparable. Hunting the bird was, of course, was man's or boy's work.

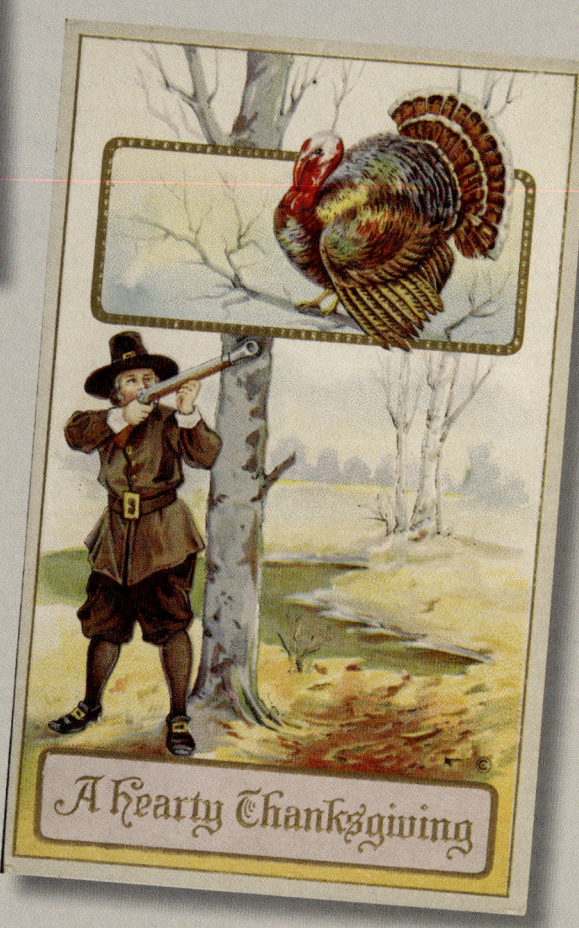

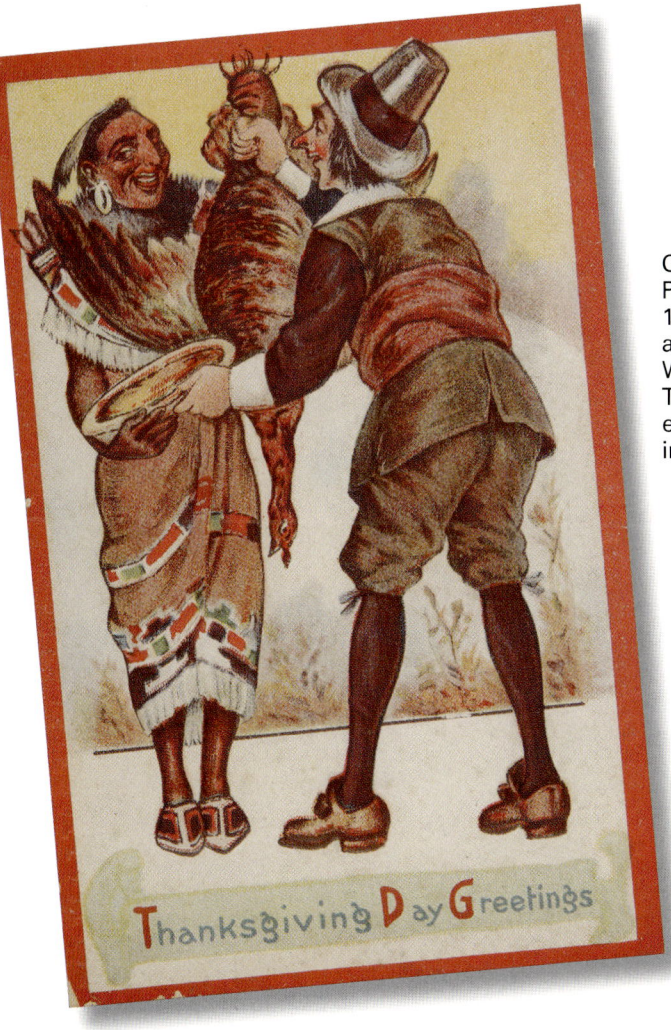

On the legendary first Thanksgiving, the Pilgrims (about 50 survivors of the original 100 settlers) held a three-day harvest feast also attended by about 90 members of the Wampanoag tribe let by their Chief, Massasoit. The Indians, keen hunters, traditionally provided game. Legend assures us that turkeys were included.

Preparing the Thanksgiving feast was woman's work and began with plucking the bird. Interest in colonial kitchens became intense when America approached its Centennial in 1876. For many years following, images of women in colonial garb in antique settings became very common. These were popularized through the very many hand-tinted staged photographs sold in the early 20th century by Wallace Nutting (1861-1941) and his followers.

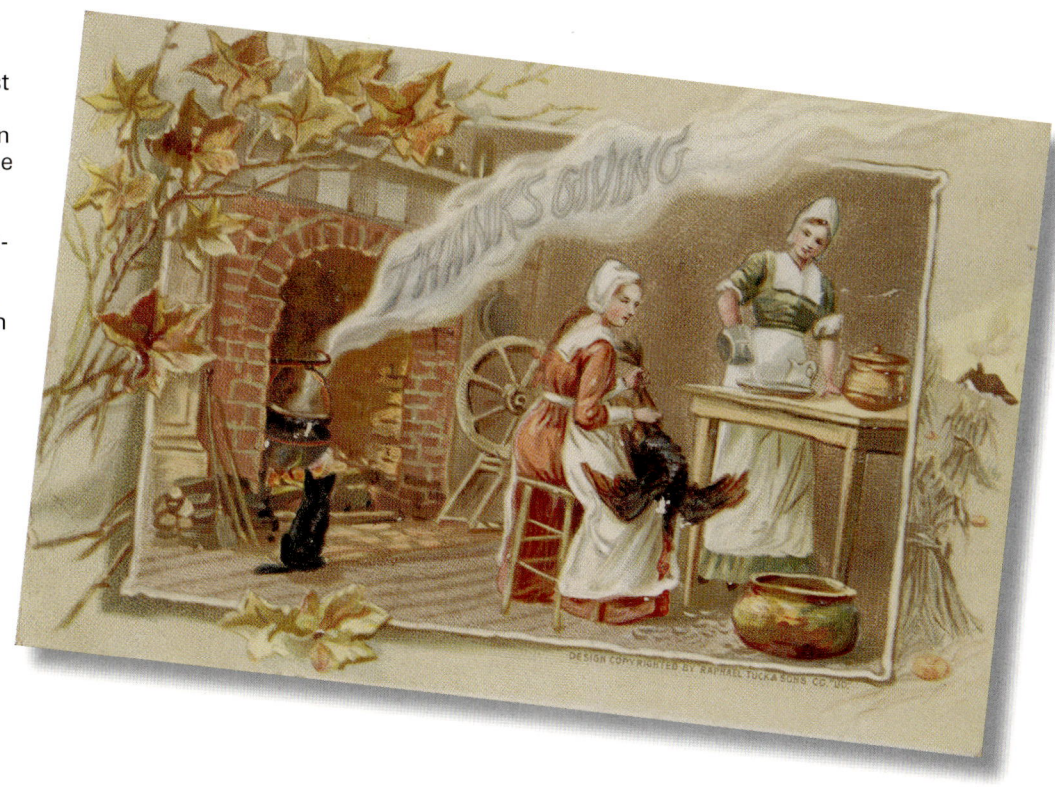

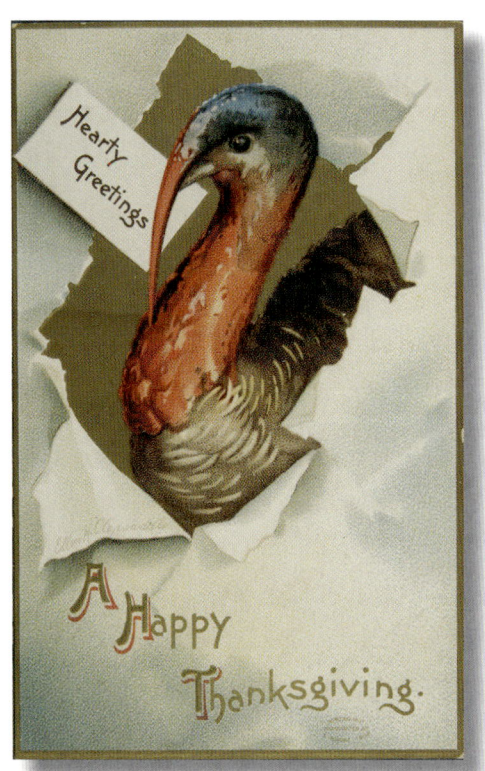
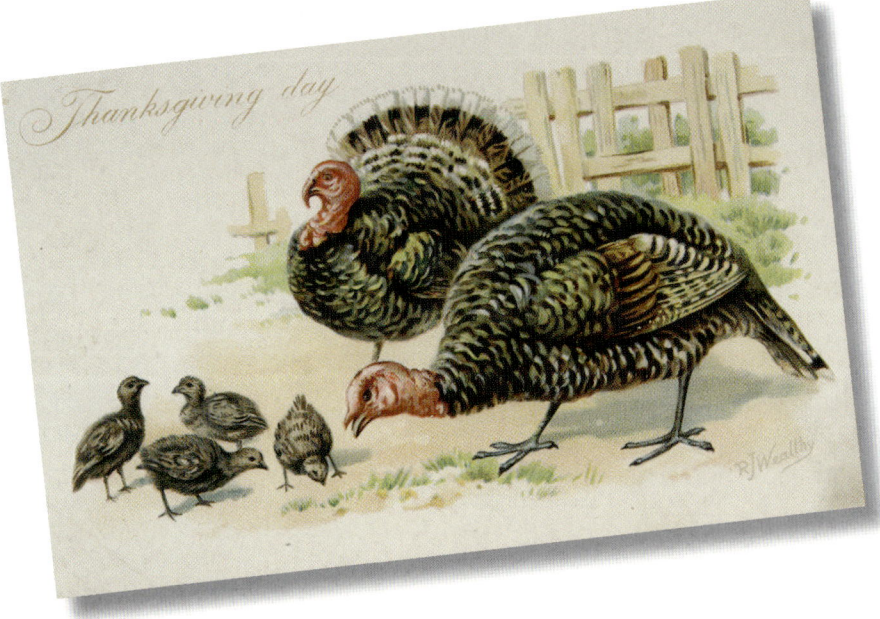
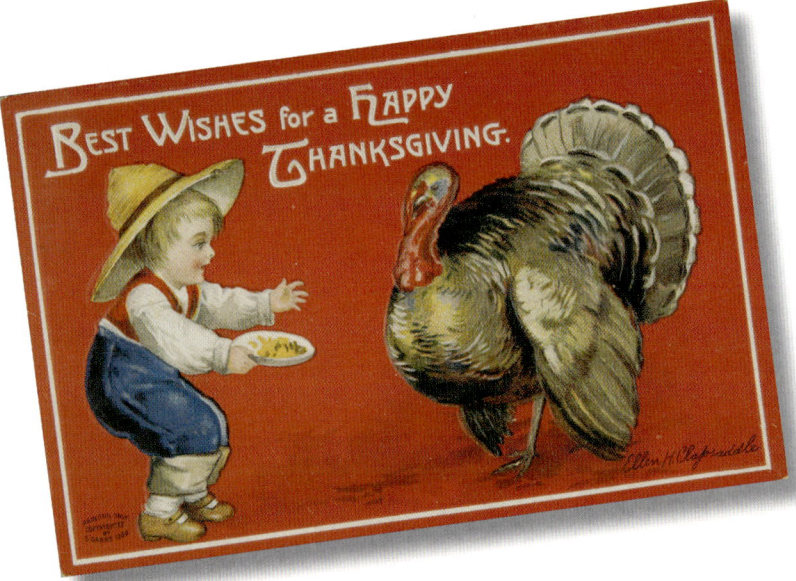
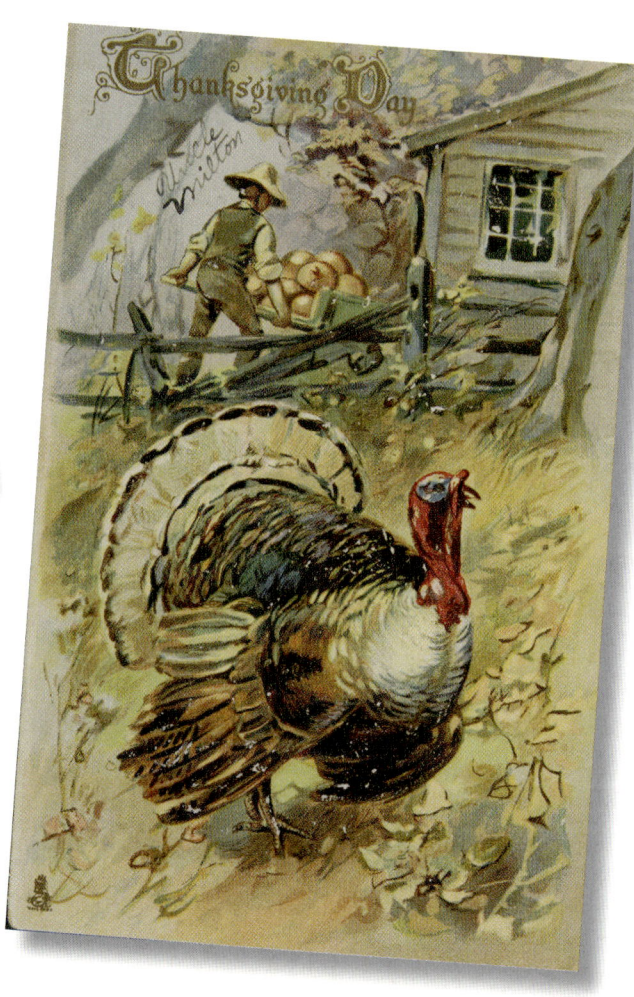

Why is the turkey called a turkey? The bird is an American native, but there is a supposition that early explorers confused it with a different bird, the European turkey cock. A more colorful explanation is that the doctor on Columbus's ship, the Santa Maris, shouted "*tukki,*" the Hebrew word for "big bird" when he first sighted one. Although turkeys are not native to the Caribbean, the story is a good one. Peaceful turkeys enjoy a placid life in and around an old fashioned farm. The little boy with the dish of corn might have questionable motives.

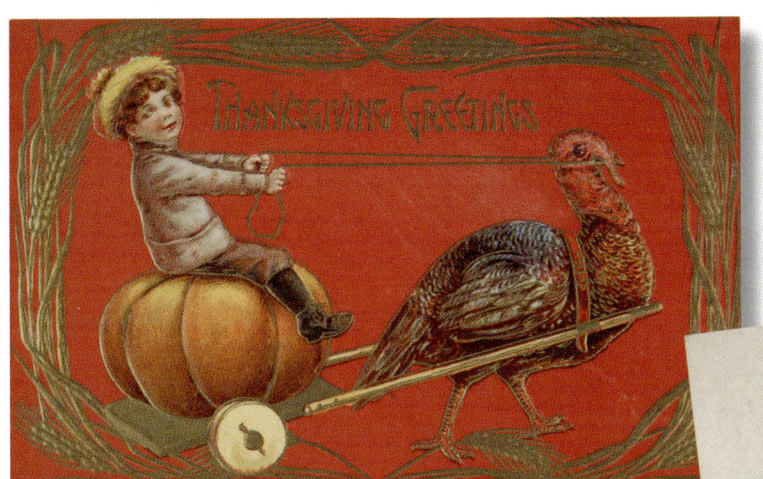

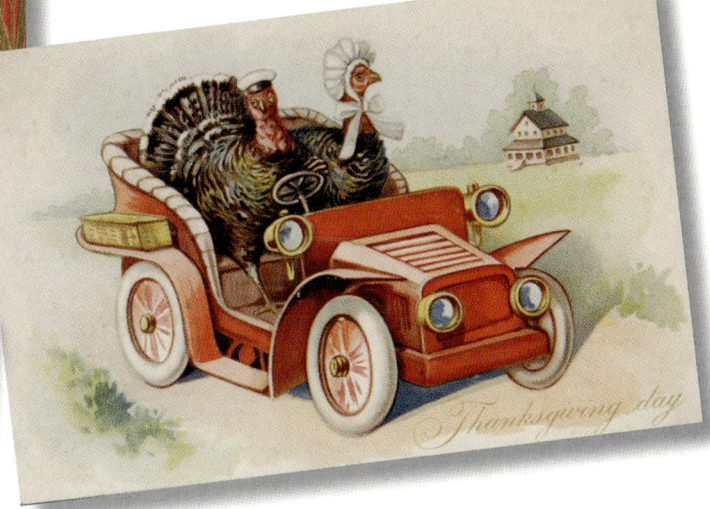

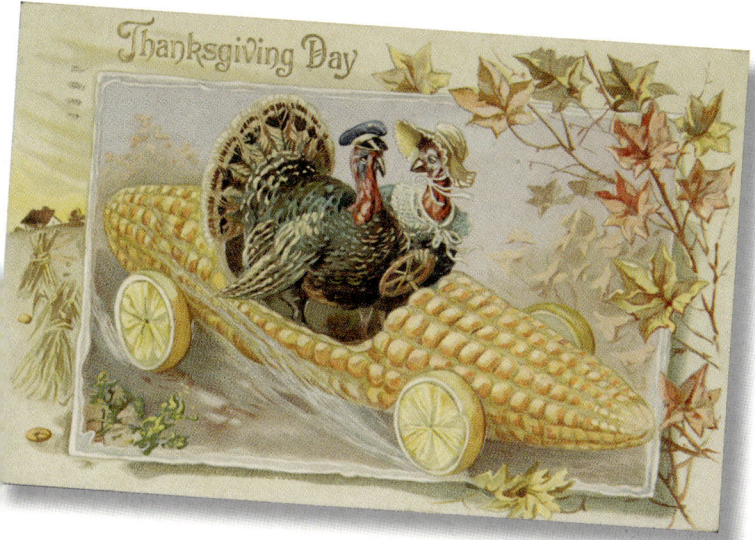

Like chicks and Easter bunnies, turkeys are often shown in strange positions. A large tom turkey pulls a pumpkin vehicle while other toms and hens tool around in the latest automobiles. The corn vehicle is certainly organic and puts mere ethanol to shame!

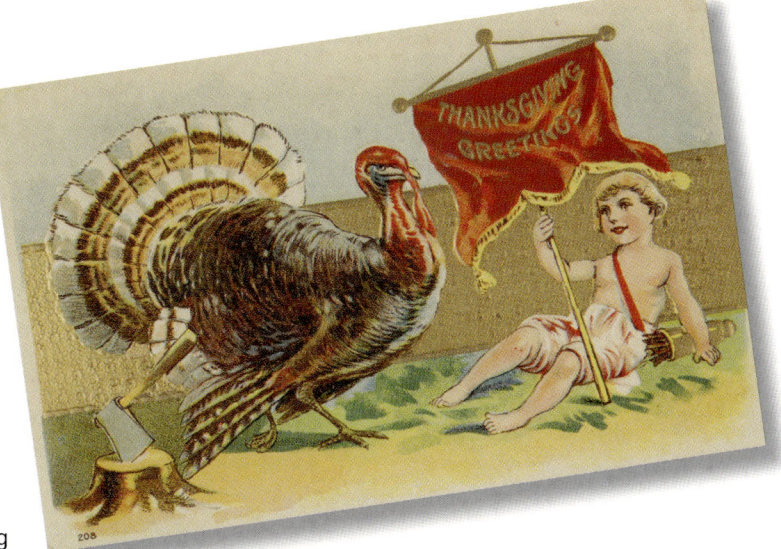

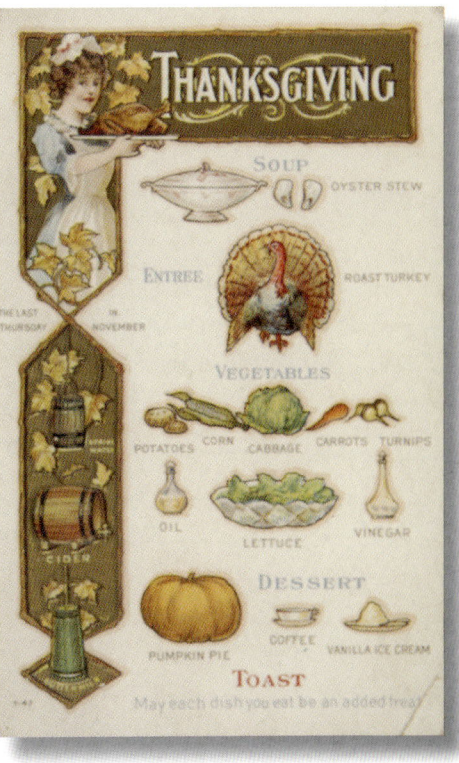

In a strange mixture of symbols, Cupid (note his quiver of arrows) has been misplaced from a Valentine. He holds a Thanksgiving banner near a grand Tom. The hatchet in the stump is a portent of a coming event.

The classic Thanksgiving menu is shown on a card mailed in 1916.

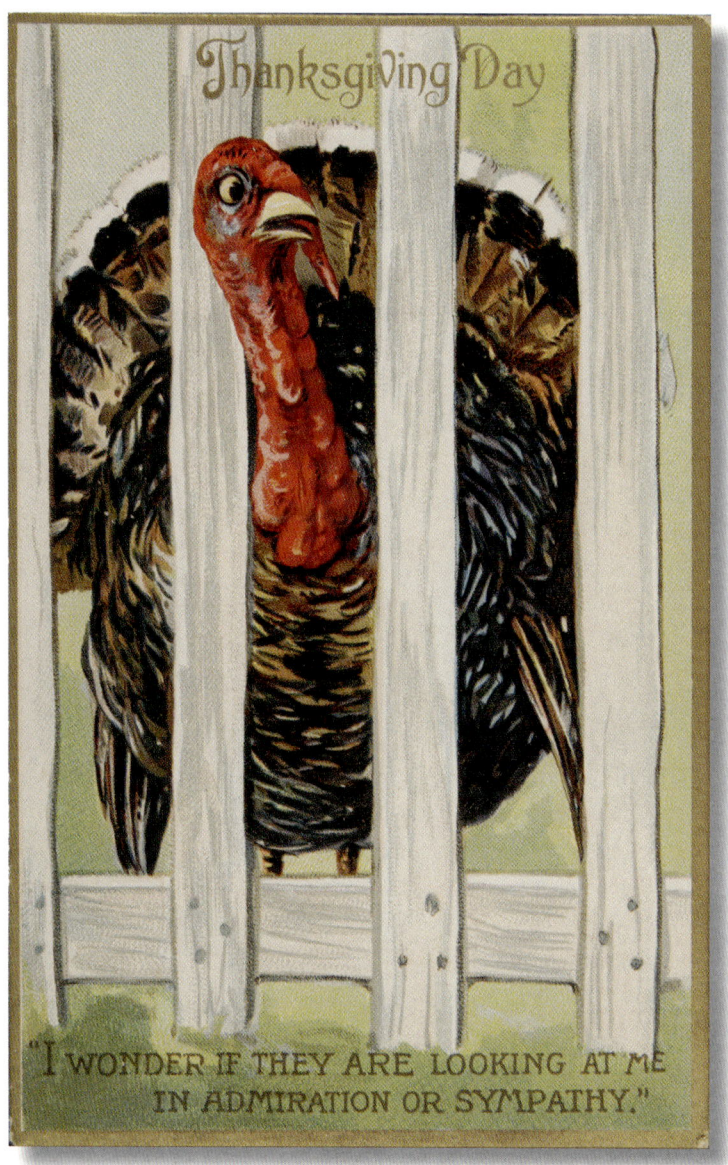

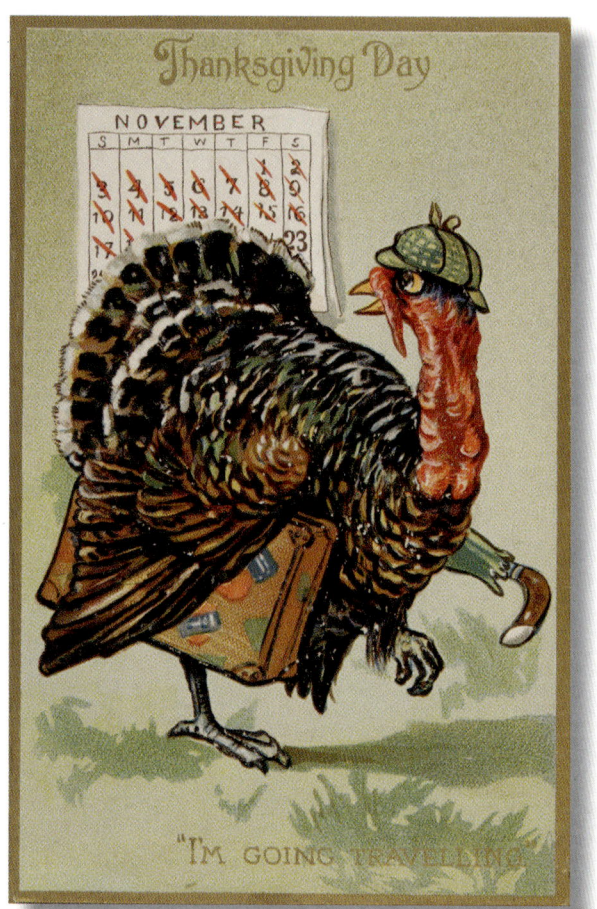

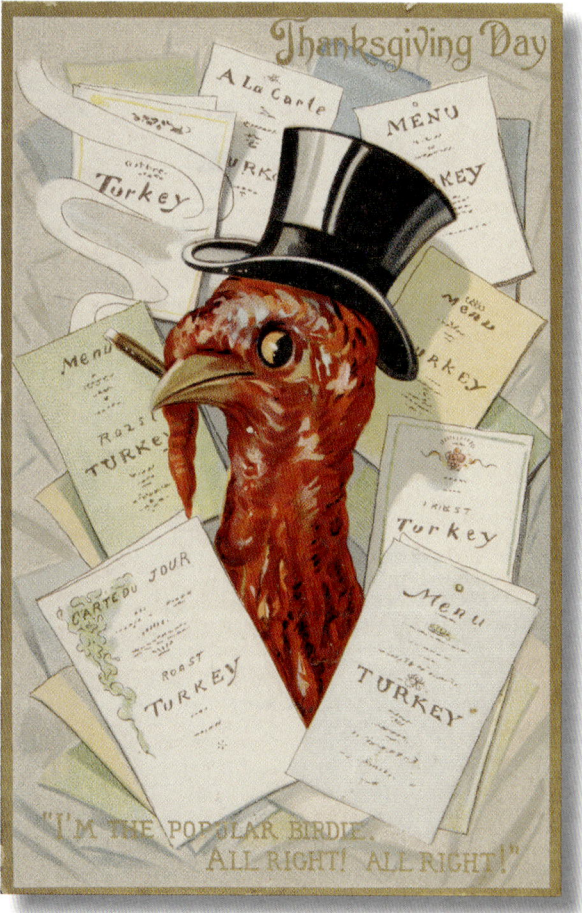

The prescient turkey knows what's coming – and, unsurprisingly, it is not a pleasant prospect for him.

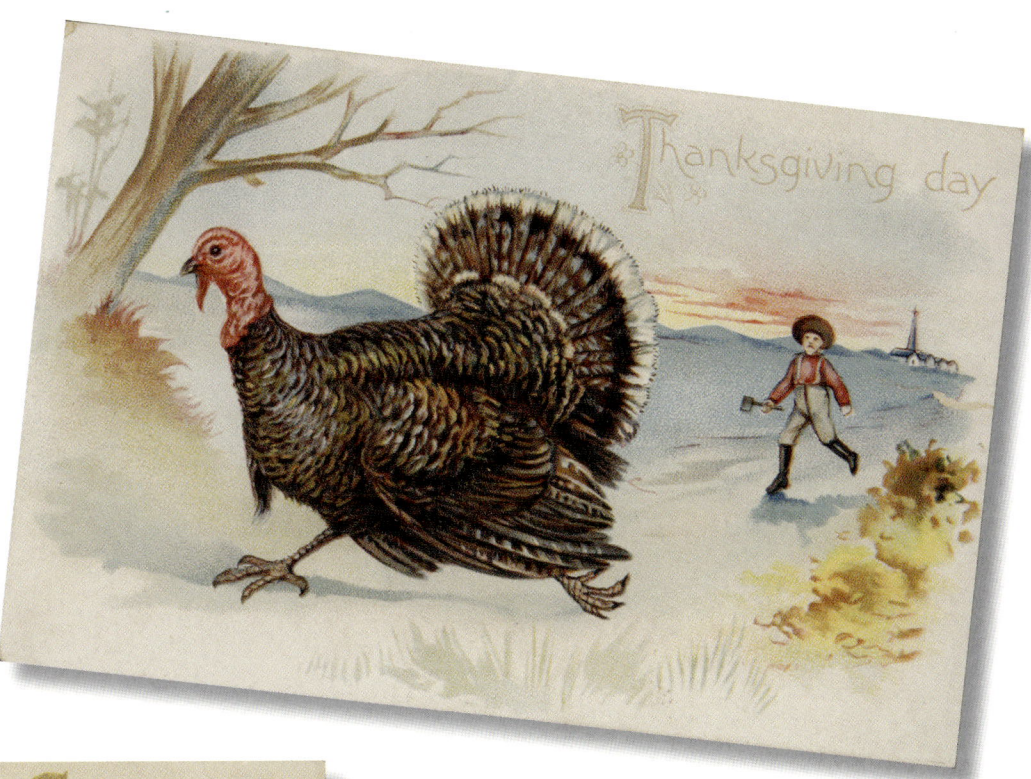

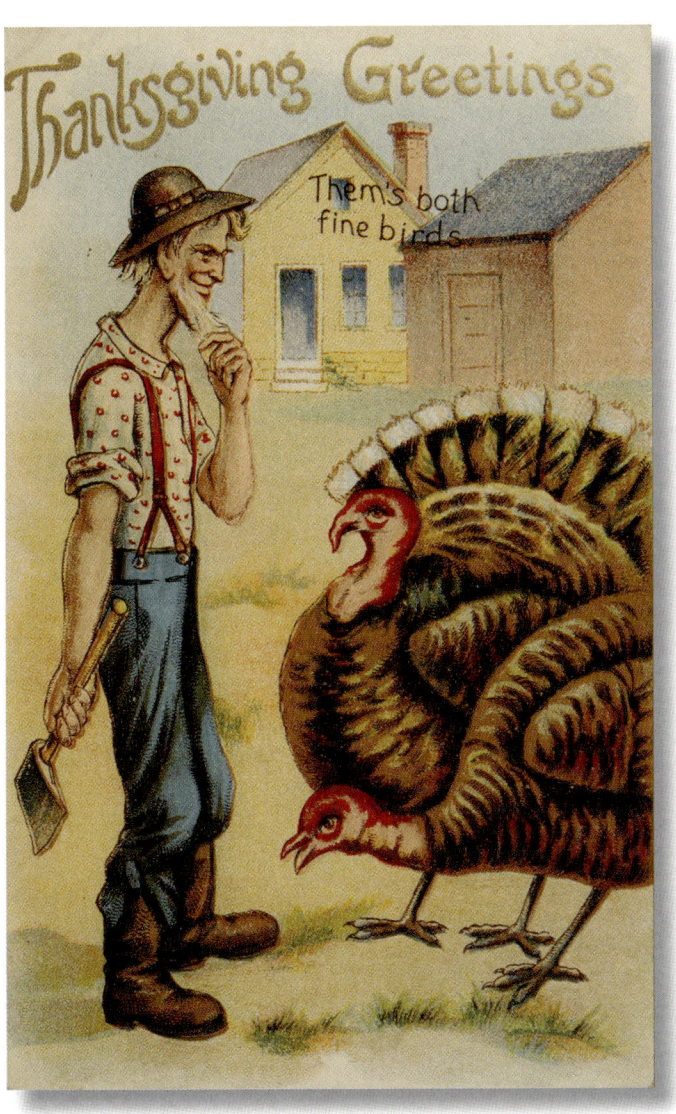

The traditional turkey met his end, not in a packing plant, but often with a farmer and his hatchet. One wonders if the man approaching a wild bird actually expected to close in for the kill with his hatchet in hand. The farmer has a decision. "Them's both fine birds," he observes. Over-hunting decimated wild stock. In recent years, thanks to conservation efforts, wild birds are now, once again, common in much of its traditional range.

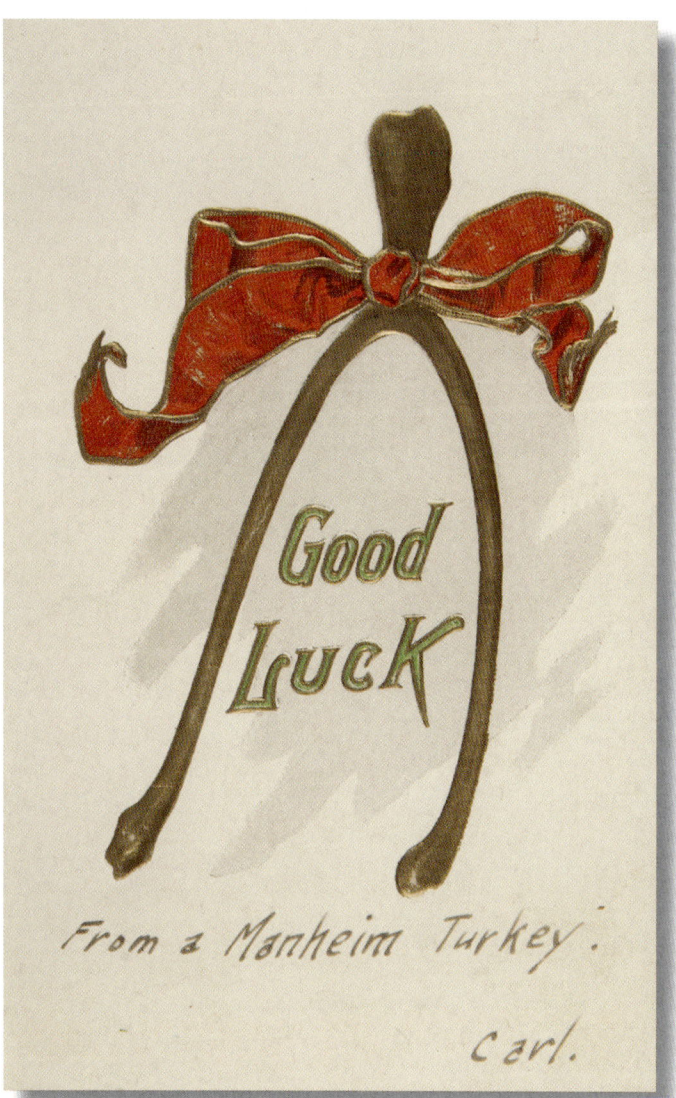

Snapping a bird's wishbone is ancient; most probably going back to the Romans. It was well established in medieval England and, no doubt, was brought over by the Pilgrims. Philologists believe that bone breaking contests gave rise to the expression, "getting a lucky break." Not so lucky for the turkey!

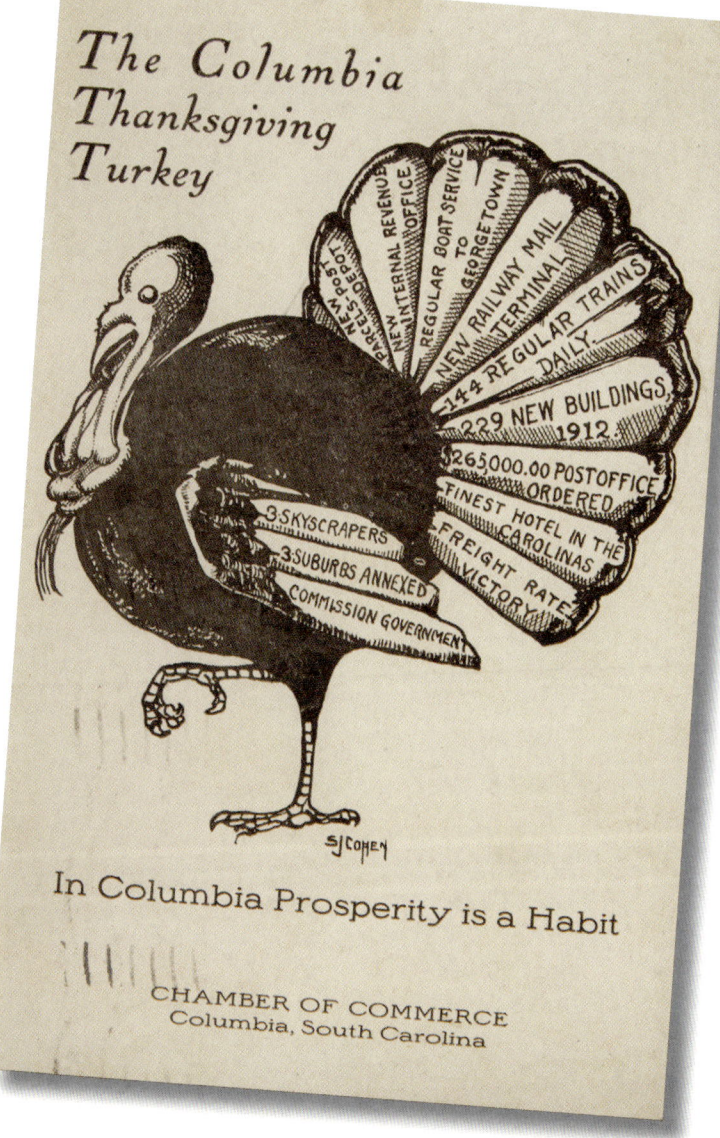

The turkey, traditionally the most extravagant item on the Thanksgiving table, became a symbol of affluence as explored in a card touting the prosperity of Columbia, South Carolina. On the reverse "A.N." notes, "the only trouble is the turkey hasn't room for more feathers." It was mailed in 1913 to a man in New Bern, North Carolina.

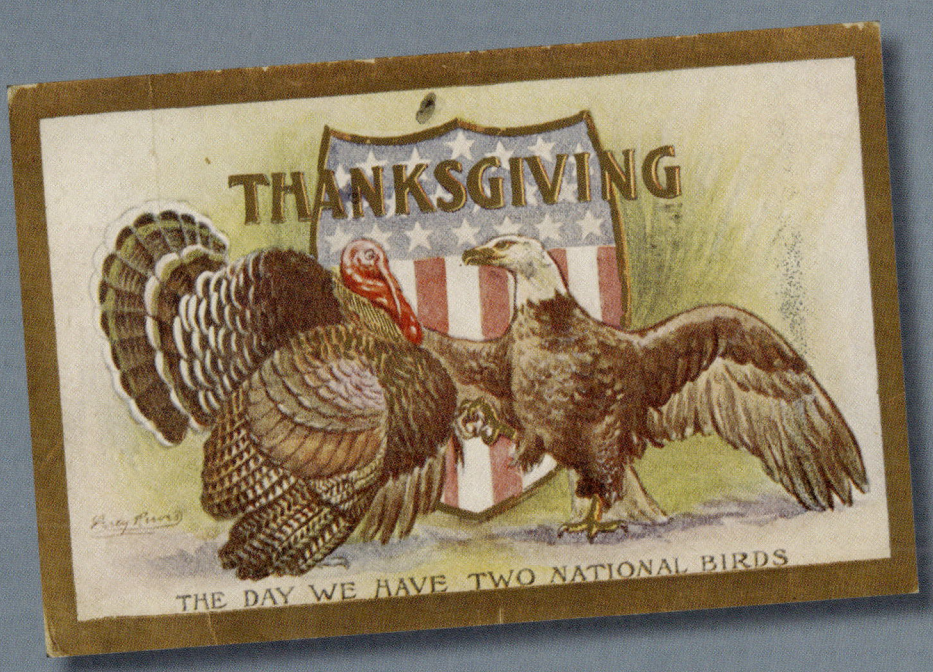
THE DAY WE HAVE TWO NATIONAL BIRDS

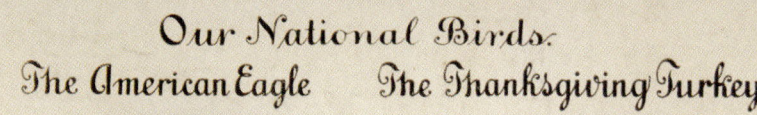
Our National Birds.
The American Eagle   The Thanksgiving Turkey
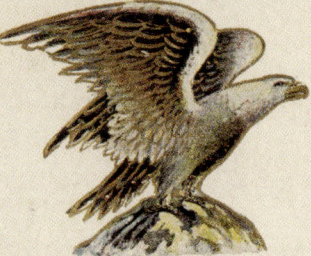 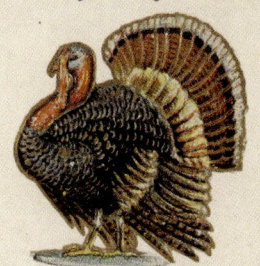
"May one give us peace in all our states.
The other a piece for all our plates."

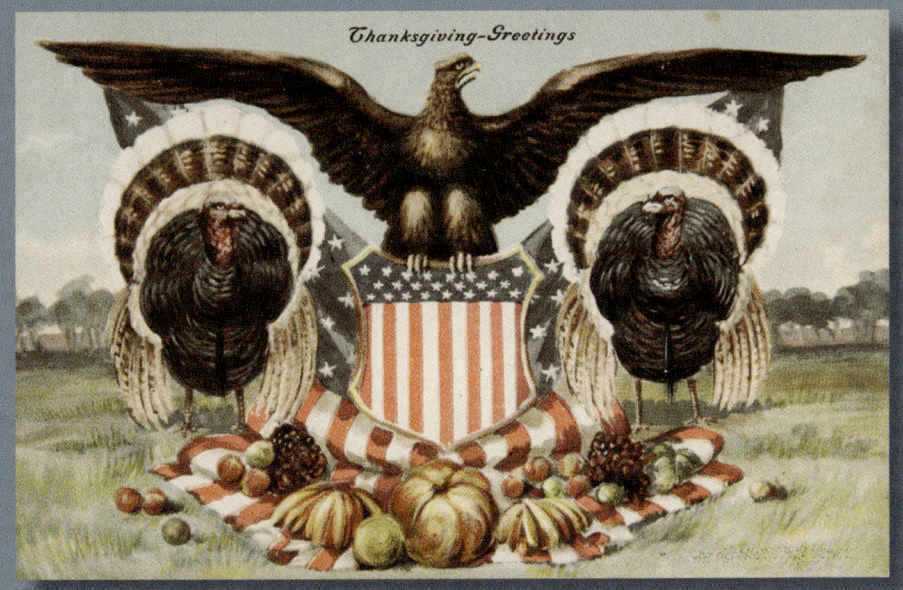

After Independence, Congress actually debated what our national bird should be. The majestic bald eagle was the clear choice but Benjamin Franklin, often the contrarian, thought that despite the eagle's grand appearance, as a raptor it had "a bad moral character." Eagles, albeit not bald headed ones, were common in European mythology. They were a symbol of Rome's might and a double-headed eagle was symbolic of the Hapsburg family and the Holy Roman Empire. Franklin preferred a unique American bird – one without a European precedent. A "true, original Native of North America" – the turkey. What would we eat at Thanksgiving if the turkey had become our national bird? Eagle is tough and gamey.

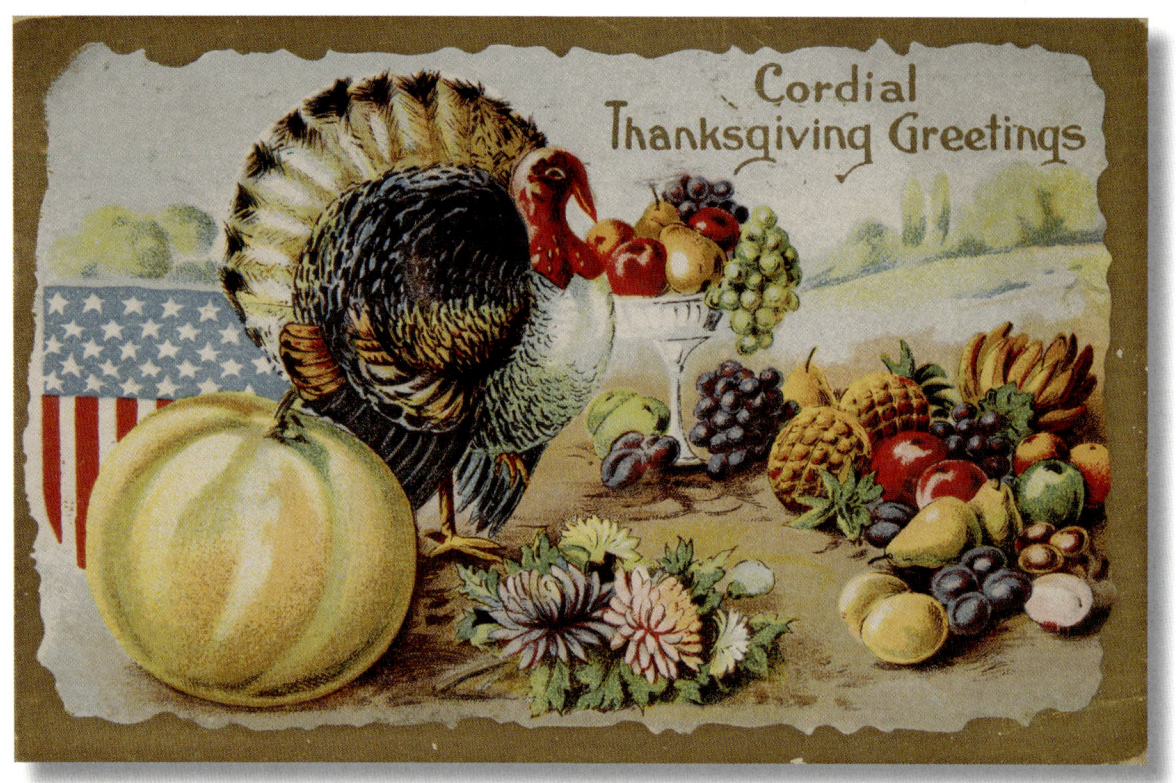

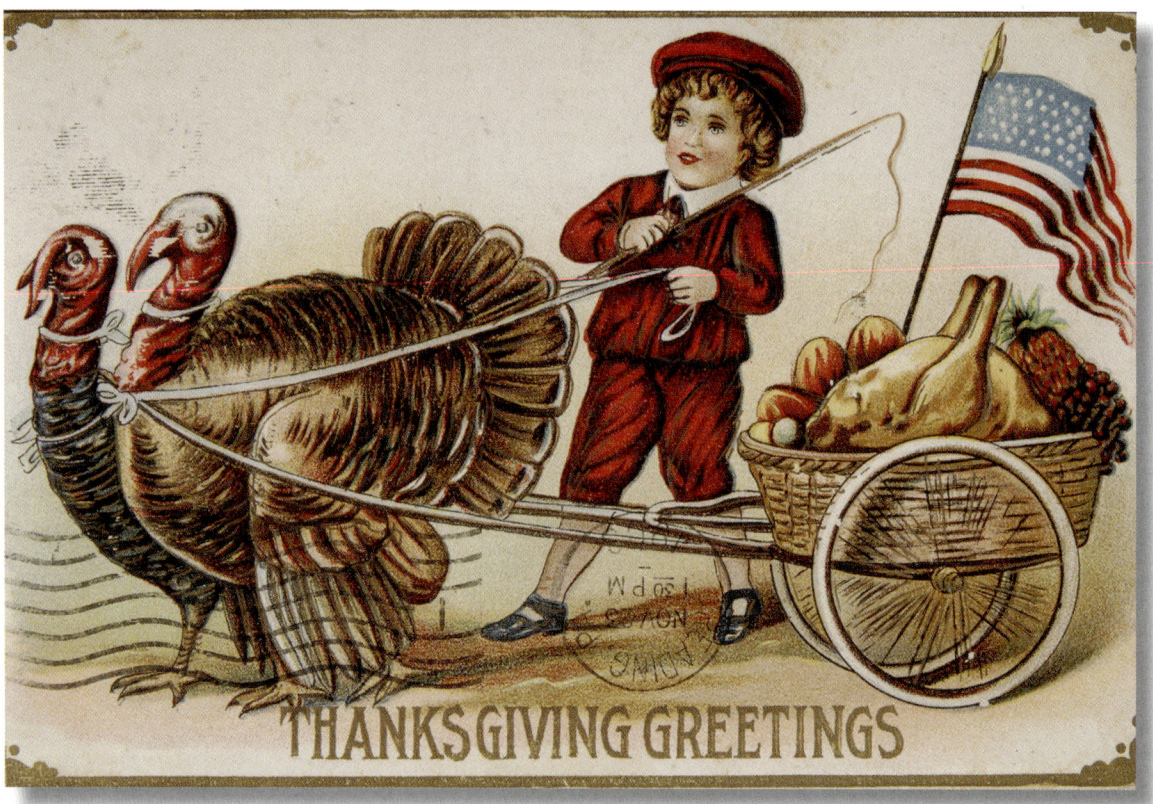

In the early 20th century, Thanksgiving was often thought of as a patriotic holiday and patriotic symbols abound. A star-spangled shield stands next to a turkey on a card expressing "Cordial Thanksgiving Greetings." A flag emblazons a cart, drawn by two Toms, which contains a roasted bird. More interesting yet is the red, white and blue imagery of the Pilgrim cards – foretelling an American future. The message on the back of the patriotic turkey-in-the-wishbone card mailed in 1909 is, "We are ready for the boys. Will cook them Thanksgiving Dinner …."

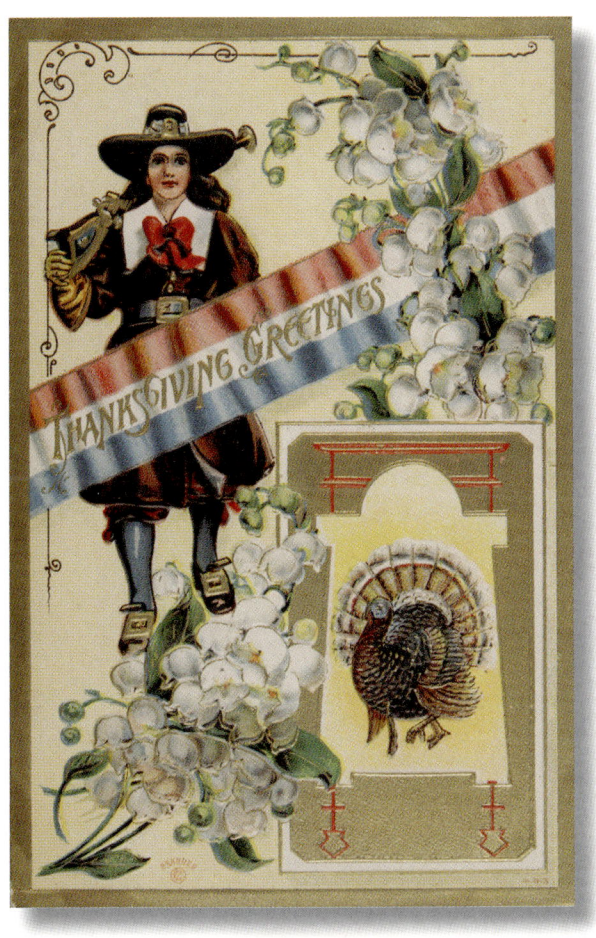
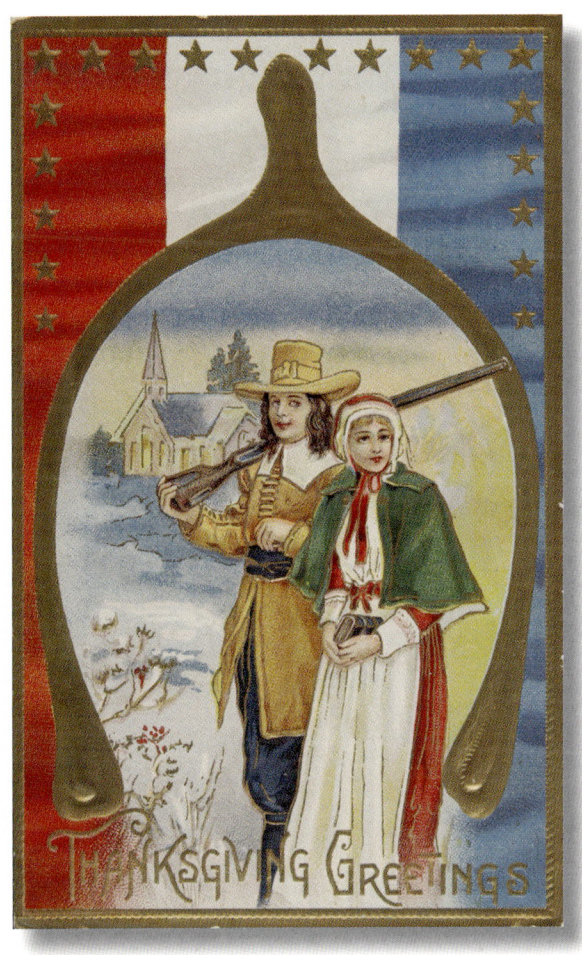
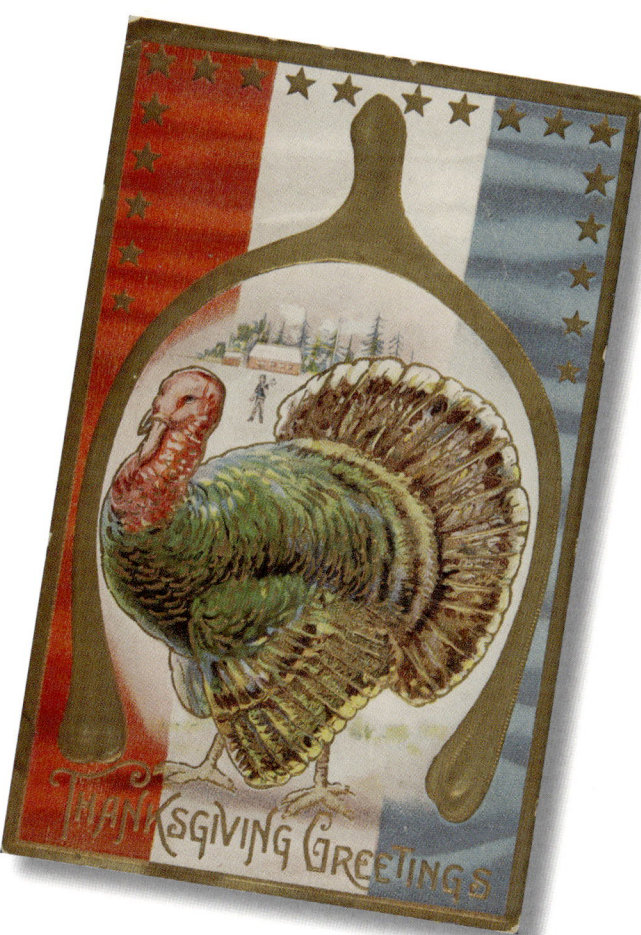

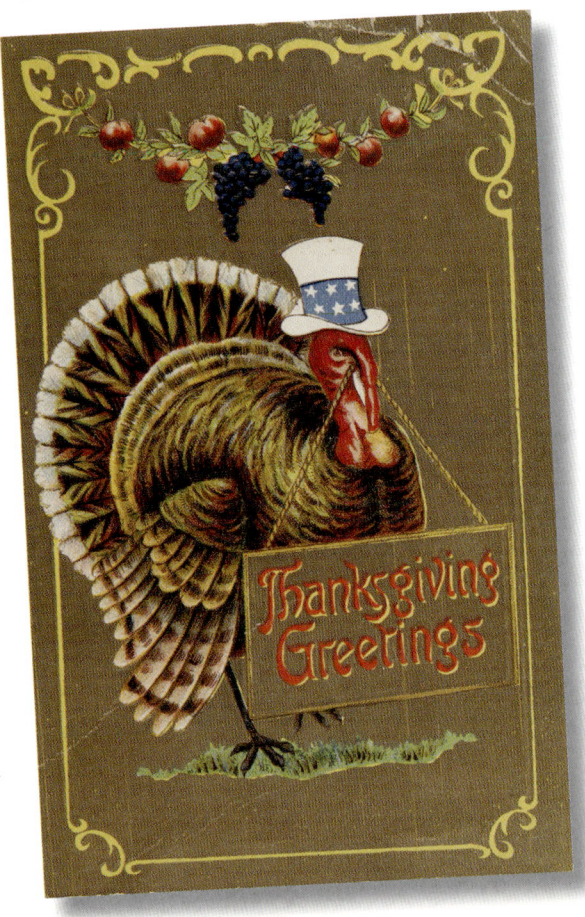
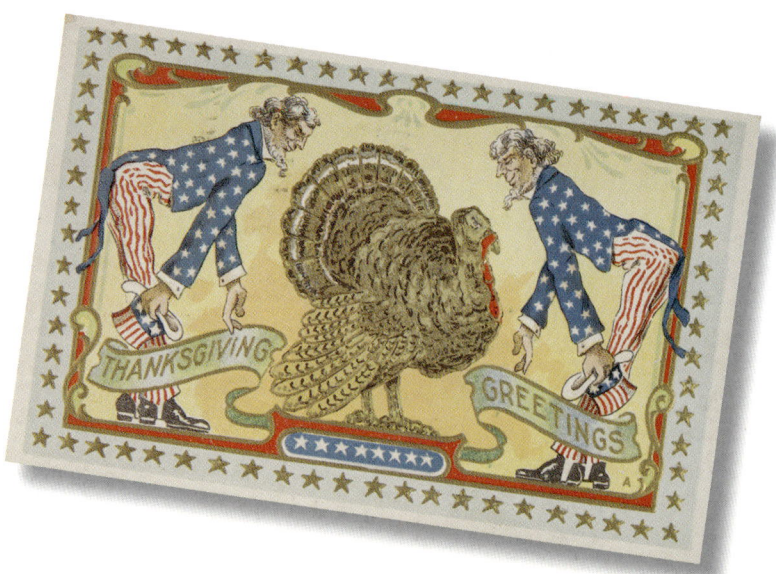
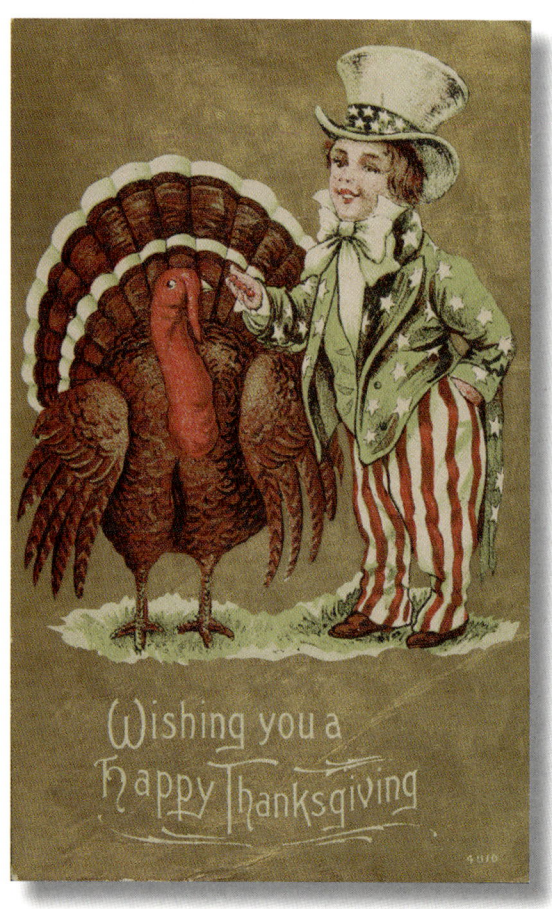
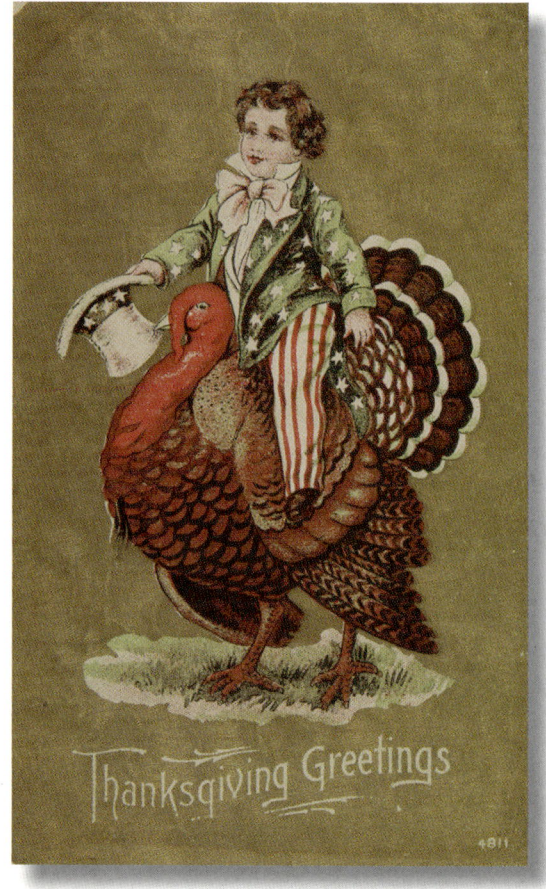

Uncle Sam, Junior and Senior, team up with turkeys and a glorious tom even wears one of Uncle's hats.

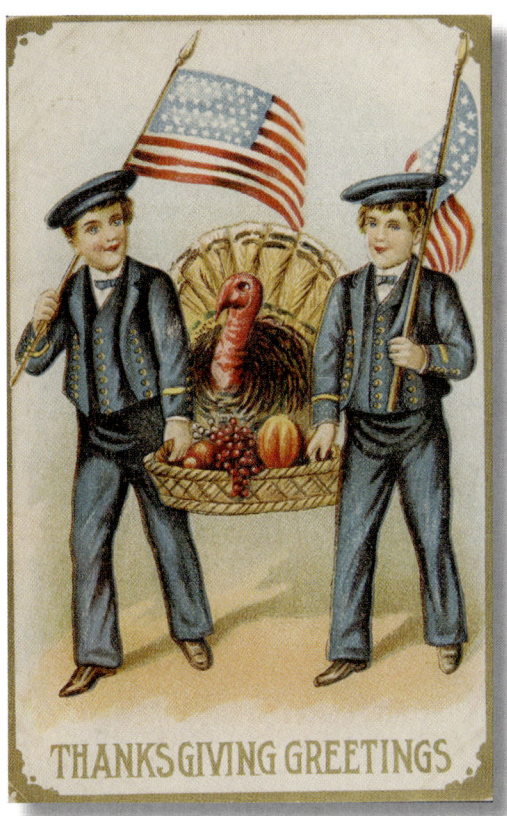

An honor guard brings in the fixings for a Thanksgiving feast. The turkey always seen on cards is an older variety close to the wild bird. After World War II most commercially raised birds are of a white-feathered strain with an enormous breast. In today's world "heirloom" or "heritage" turkeys bring a premium on the market. *Collection: Dr. Russell Eaton*

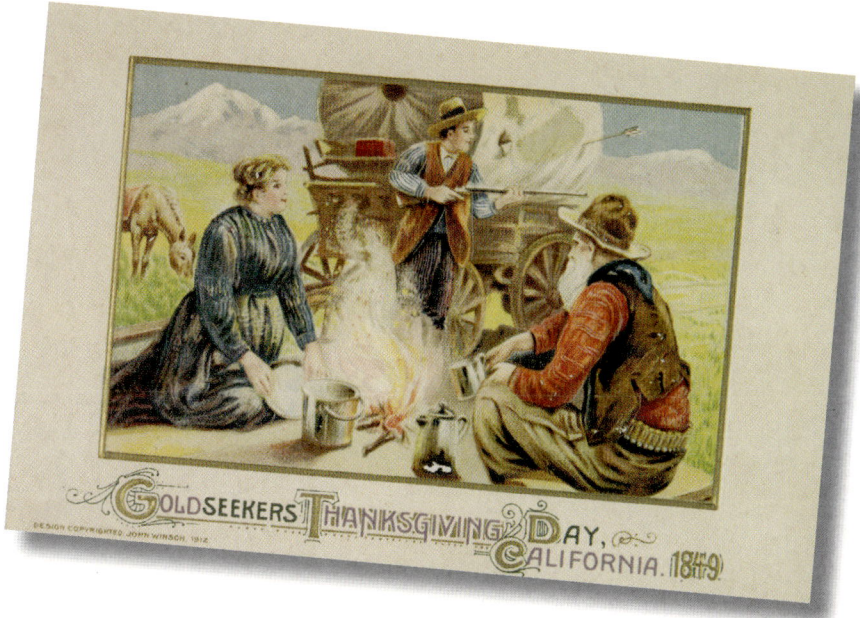

The Pilgrims have been replaced by the "Forty-Niners" on a Thanksgiving card published *circa* 1910. Rather than being mailed, this card was awarded to "Henry Moyer" as an "Attendance card for the second month of school term of 1912-1913" by "Miss Weik [,] Teacher"

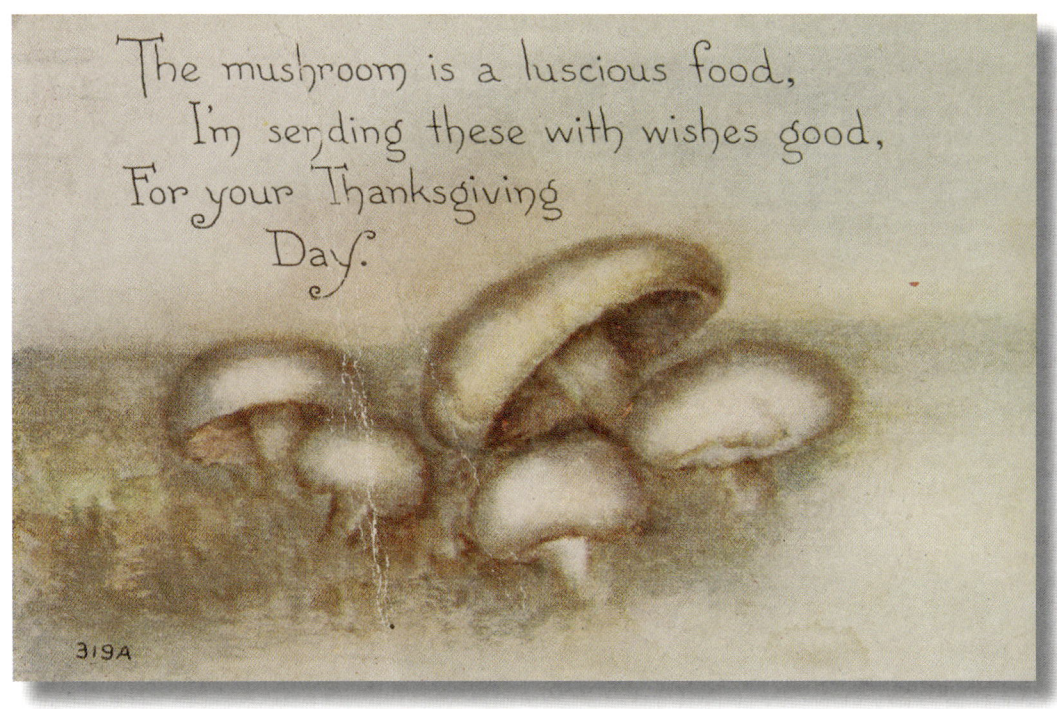

Is there any Thanksgiving food-oriented card that is more bizarre than this one featuring mushrooms? Published by F.A. Owen of Danville, New York, it was sent by Harry on November 23, 1917 and simply reads, "I am fine. Love to mother & Jennie." Harry was in the military and the card bears a stamp "PASSED BY CENSOR".

9
Christmas

More Religion & A Strange Man in the House

The date for the celebration of Christmas, and many of its associated customs, is firmly rooted in the pre-Christian past. When Christ was born is not precisely known, but likely it occurred in winter. The first celebration of the Nativity on December 25 was held in Rome, sometime in the 4th century, a date probably chosen to reconcile the Christian and pagan calendars. The Romans' major winter festival, the *Saturnalia*, was held from December 17th to 23rd, followed in short order by *Brumalia*, on December 25, celebrating the "Birthday of the Unconquered Sun." This, in turn, occurs soon after the Winter Solstice that marks the point after which days become longer. This is approximately the same time as the Jewish Festival of Lights, *Hanukkah*.

The period from December 25 through January 6, when the Orthodox Churches celebrate Christmas, has been a celebratory period at least from Roman times. In England and, to a lesser extent, in America, these days are observed as "the Twelve Days of Christmas," celebrated in the carol that begins, "On the First Day of Christmas my true love gave to me a partridge in a pear tree." Using some of this same period of time, Dr. Maulana Karenga, a UCLA professor from Nigeria, invented the holiday "Kwanza," so that African-Americans would draw away from the 'white' holidays of Christmas and New Year.

Giving gifts during this special time of the year is an ancient tradition that can be traced to Egypt in the time of the Pharaohs, as well as later in the Roman Empire. The bestowing of gifts was believed to promise good luck during the coming year. Christians continued and expanded on the custom commemorating the gifts that the Three Wise Men brought to the Christ Child in the manger. The legendary fourth century bishop of Myra (in present-day Turkey), St. Nicholas, is credited with being a progenitor of the modern Santa Claus. A wealthy but modest man, Nicholas anonymously helped needy people by leaving gold coins or a filled purse for them. In some countries today, gifts are still exchanged on the Feast of St. Nicholas, December 6, rather than on December 25.

Christmas Eve in America is, for many, even more celebratory than Christmas Day. It is then that Santa Claus delivers his presents and, further, it commemorates the night sky in which the Star of Bethlehem led the Three Kings to the Christ Child's birthplace. Darkness is also a great opportunity for the use of fire and candles, thus following many ancient traditions. In Scandinavian countries it is believed that the spirits of the dead visit their former homes on Christmas Eve, so food is left out for them and lighted candles welcome them. Today children leave milk and cookies for Santa.

Bonfires, lamps, and candles celebrated Christ's triumph over the "darkness of paganism." Since the Middle Ages, churches light candles on Christmas Eve, and in the American southwest "luminaries," or bonfires, were an important aspect of Christmas Eve. Domesticated, these have become the familiar glowing paper bags filled with a layer of sand supporting lit candles. In Cajun country, in Louisiana, riverside bonfires remain a frequent component of Christmas celebrations.

Many people begin the celebration of Christmas weeks in advance, with the holy period of Advent, 22 to 28 days, and ending with Christmas Eve. The Advent calendar, a custom originating in Germany, spread throughout Europe, providing a way to both heighten religious awareness among children and to occupy the youngsters' attention during the long wait for Christmas. It is during this period, also, that people traditionally do their gift shopping and send their Christmas cards.

The earliest Christmas cards in America were handmade ones, perhaps exchanged by Moravians, a small German denomination which settled in Pennsylvania beginning in 1742. The first printed Christmas cards, however, were produced in England in 1843. Postcard-like, they were crafted by John Calcott Horsley and sold for a shilling, then a significant sum of money. The production of many of these cards shifted to Germany in subsequent years, and it was German-born Louis Prang (1824-1909) who, in 1875, printed the first American Christmas cards at his plant in Roxbury, Massachusetts. Today cards are sent by the hundreds of millions—many electronically by email.

A joyous aspect of the holiday is the singing of Christmas carols. While some are religious and solemn, such as "Silent Night," many others are playful or festive in style, like "God Rest Ye Merry Gentlemen." Indeed, many early carols were melodies that could be danced to as well as sung. In America Puritanism almost marked the death knell of the carol, but it persisted in rural areas and after 1800 it increased in popularity with community carol sings, then becoming popular throughout the country.

Christmas is sacred and profane. It is a world with Christian symbolism of crèche-centered nativity scenes and angels as well as a secular universe of Santas, wreaths, candy canes, holly sprigs, and decorated evergreens—and especially gifts—observed, celebrated, or tolerated by almost all Americans.

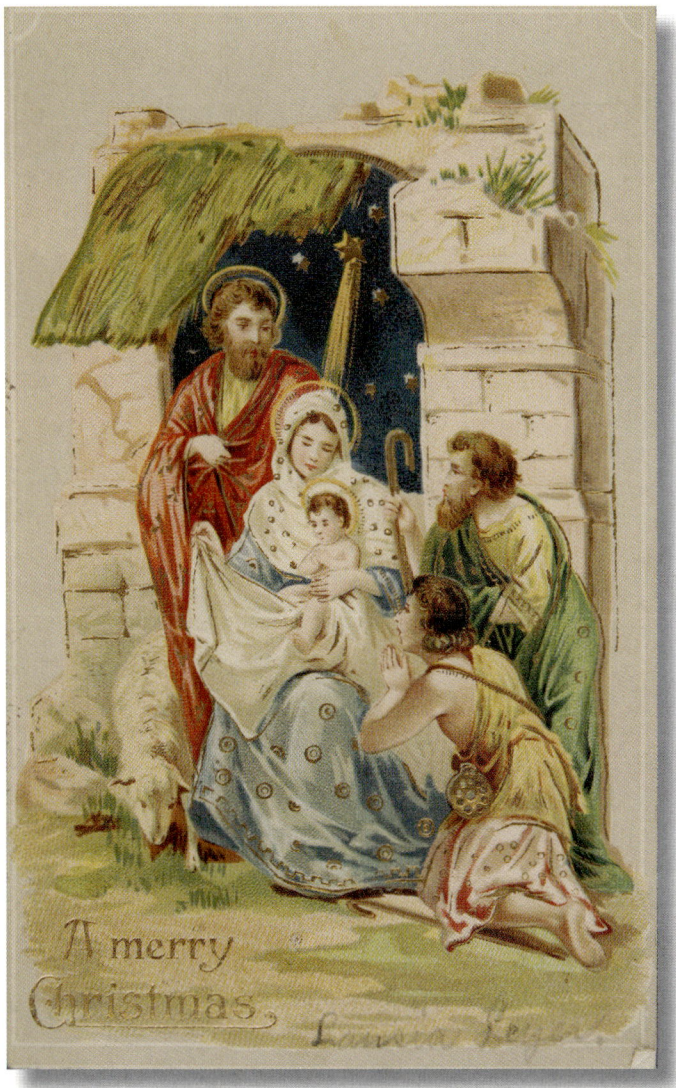

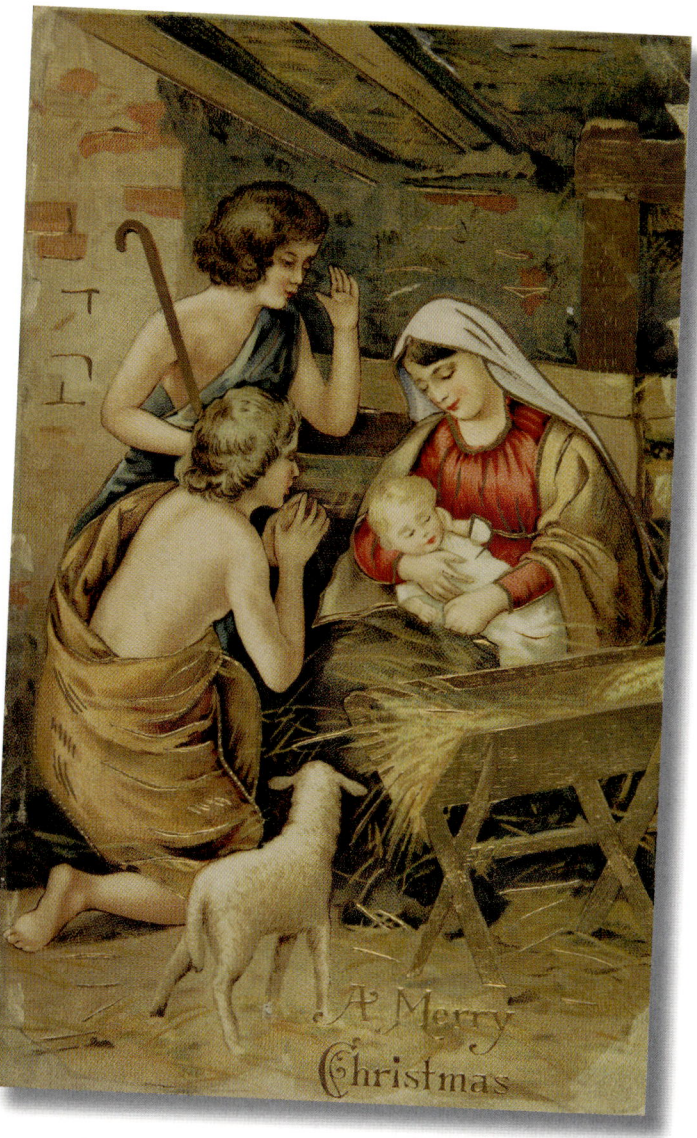

The birth of Christ and the associated miracles are central to the traditional Christmas Story. Manger scenes remain popular on contemporary cards.

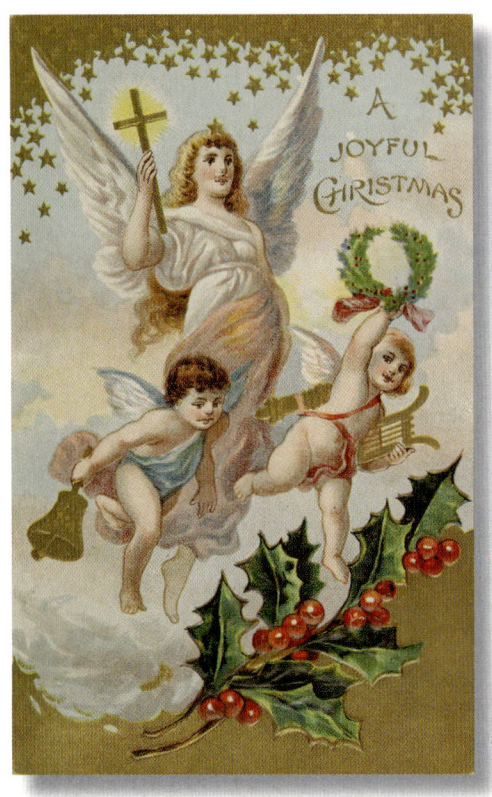

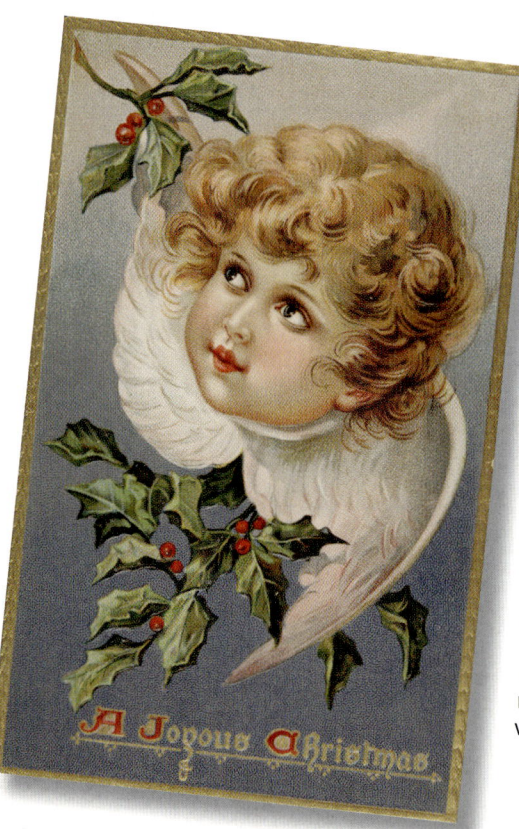

Angels, celestial beings, take their name from the Greek word *angelos*, which translates as "messenger" or "herald." It was an angel who appeared to the shepherds in the field. The harbinger was followed by a "multitude" of angelic beings singing in praise of God. Holly is another important Christmas symbol. Since it bears fruit into the winter it is considered a symbol of eternal life as well as a portent of what is to come. Holly, because its thorny leaves resemble the crown of thorns Christ wore at his crucifixion, is also a symbol of the passion. Legend also maintains that the true cross was made of holly wood.

The secular, the pagan, and the popular mix on many cards. Angels, Santas, holly, Christmas trees, and bells all appear in snowy landscapes. Ringing of church bells on Christmas dates to the Middle Ages. In English churches, especially, bell ringing on Christmas Eve is very important. Sleigh bells are a popular Christmas decoration and charities, like the Salvation Army, attract attention (and contributions) to their kettles by ringing yuletide hand bells.

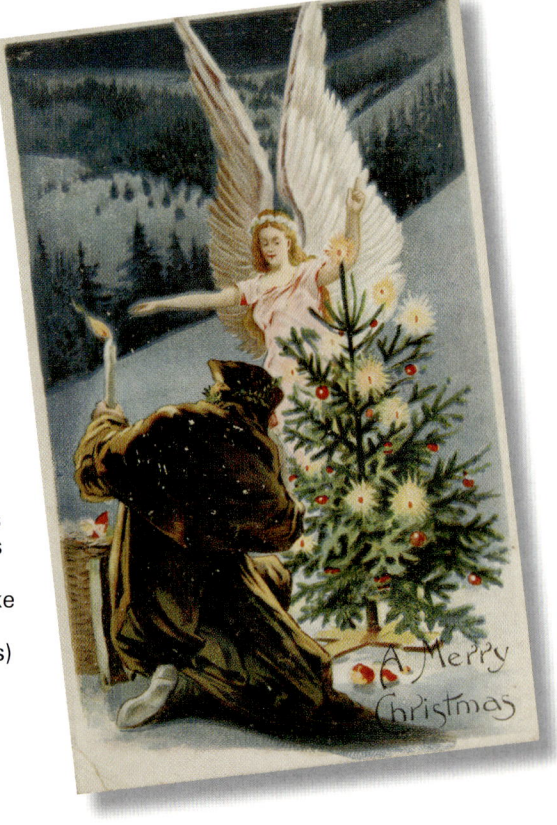

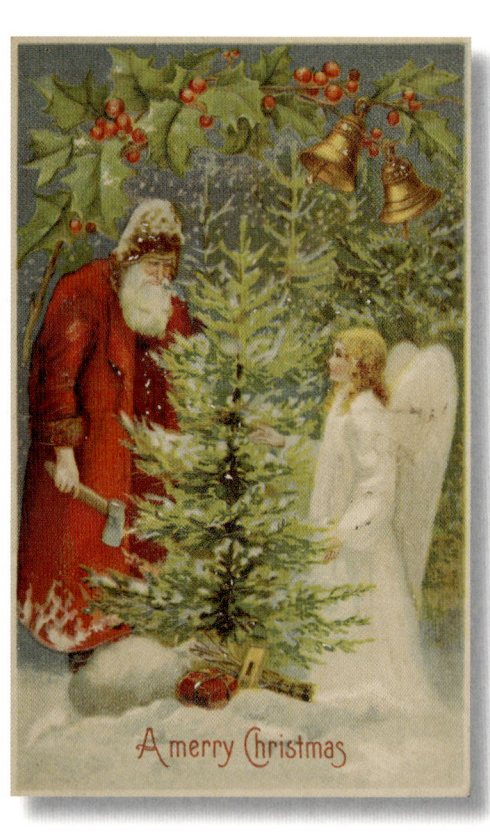

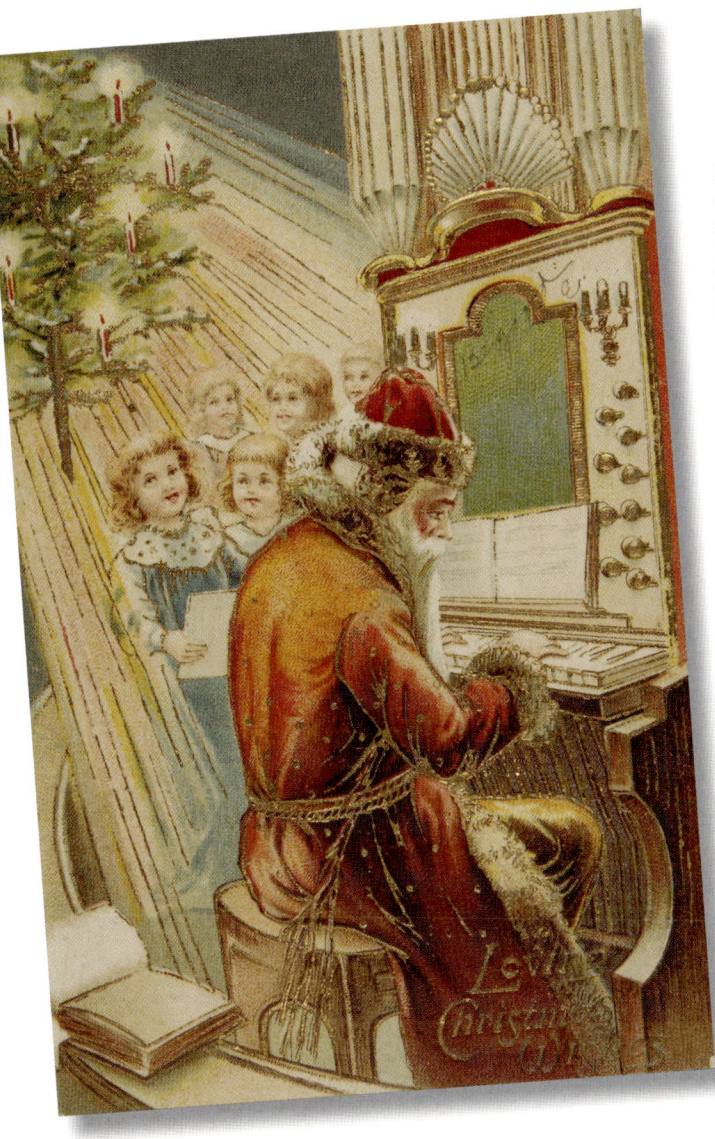

Santa as the organist provides music for a magical church worthy of a Harry Potter movie, complete with a floating Christmas Tree. In a more conventional interior, choir boys sing hymns while visions of Santa and his reindeer dance in their imaginations.

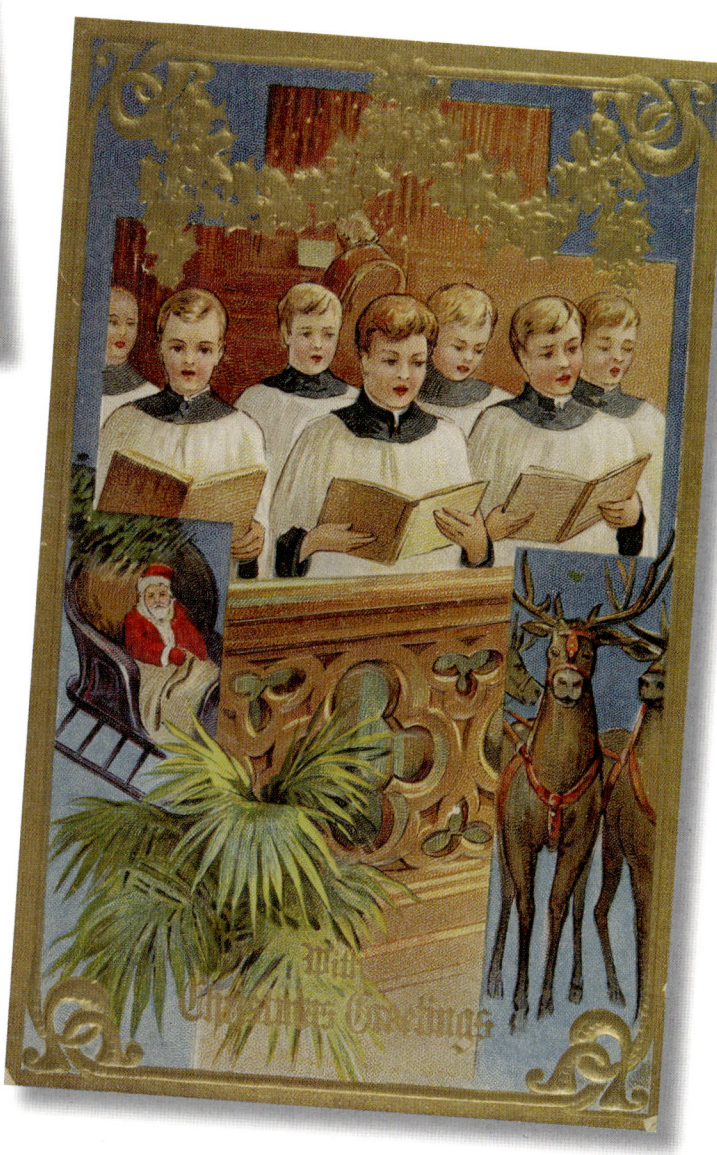

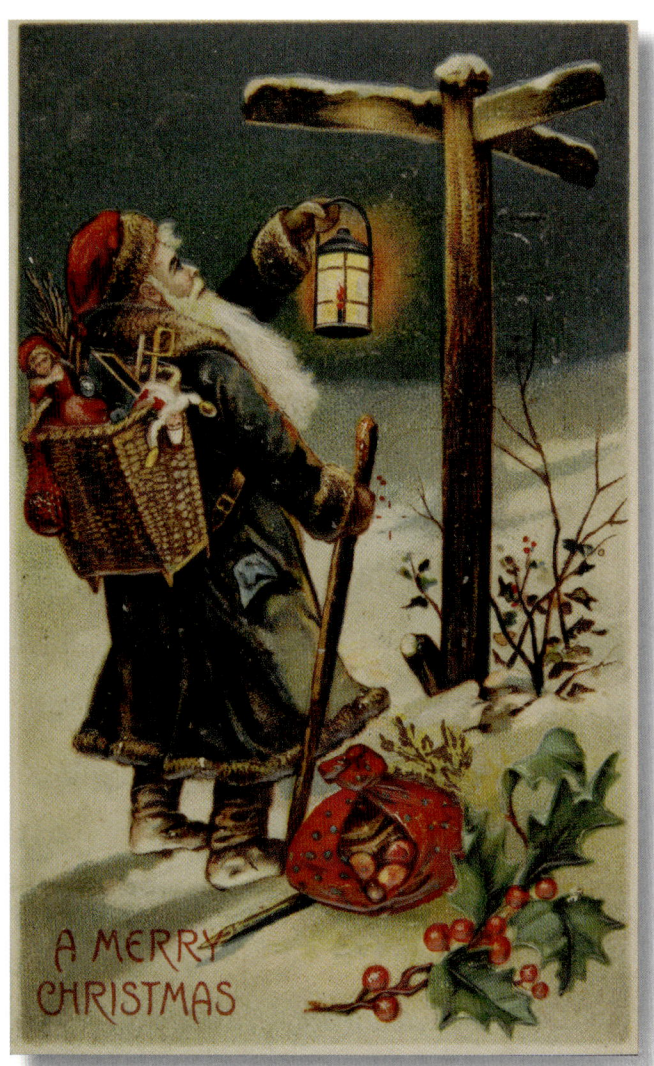

It took a long time for our modern popular image of Santa Claus to take form. Ultimately he is like America itself – an amalgamation of many forms and traditions. There are three major historical antecedents: English, German, and Dutch. The English provided Father Christmas, a figure shown wearing a crown of holly who, after the Reformation, replaced Saint Nicholas. The Germans brought St. Nicholas himself and the Dutch brought us *Sinter Klaas*, who wears bishop's robes and rides a white horse. All have origins in the pagan world with the St. Nicholas and *Sinter Klaas* forms deriving from the Germanic god Wotan. It took the 1823 poem attributed to Clement Clarke Moore," A Visit from Saint Nicholas", also known as "The Night Before Christmas," to transform Santa from a bishop to a portly figure in a fur suit. American literary giant Washington Irving (1783-1859) gave us the information about gifts being brought down the chimney. The same German-born caricaturist Thomas Nast (1840-1902) who gave us our Uncle Sam image helped to define our Santa. His cartoons created the rotund bearded being we all know. The final codification of Santa postdates the golden age of postcards and is thanks to images of Santa Claus created for the Coca Cola Company by Howard Chandler Christy (1873-1952). Think of it: white and red – Coca Cola and Santa Claus.

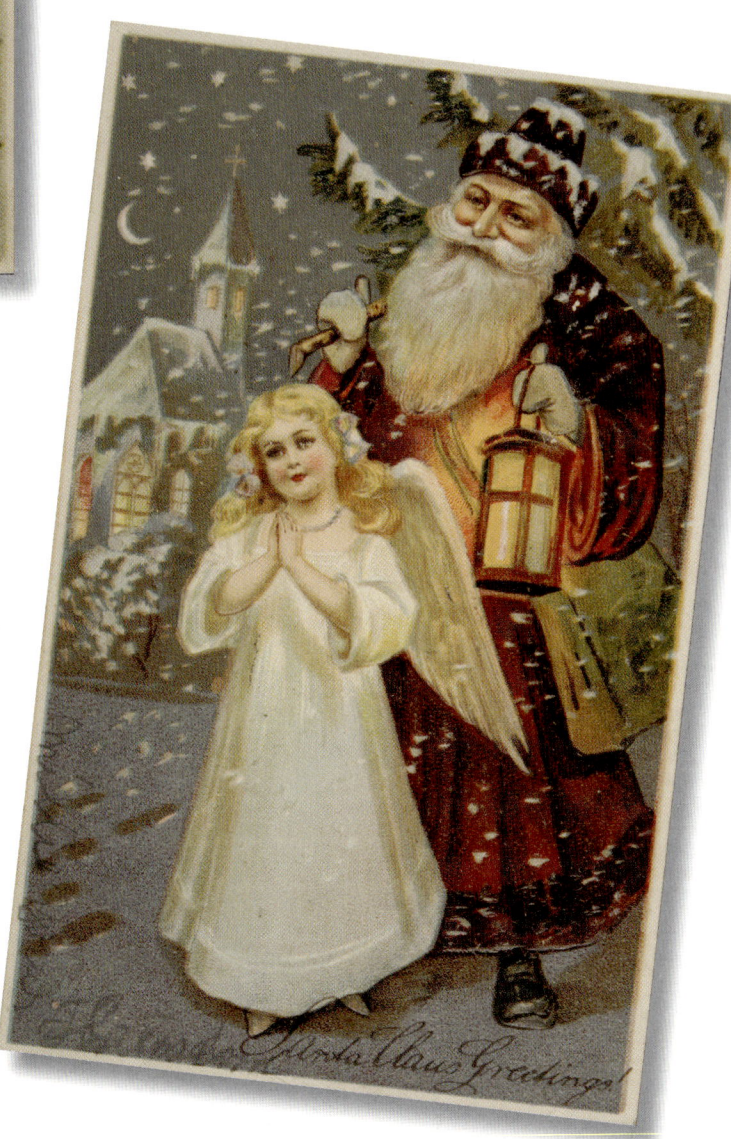

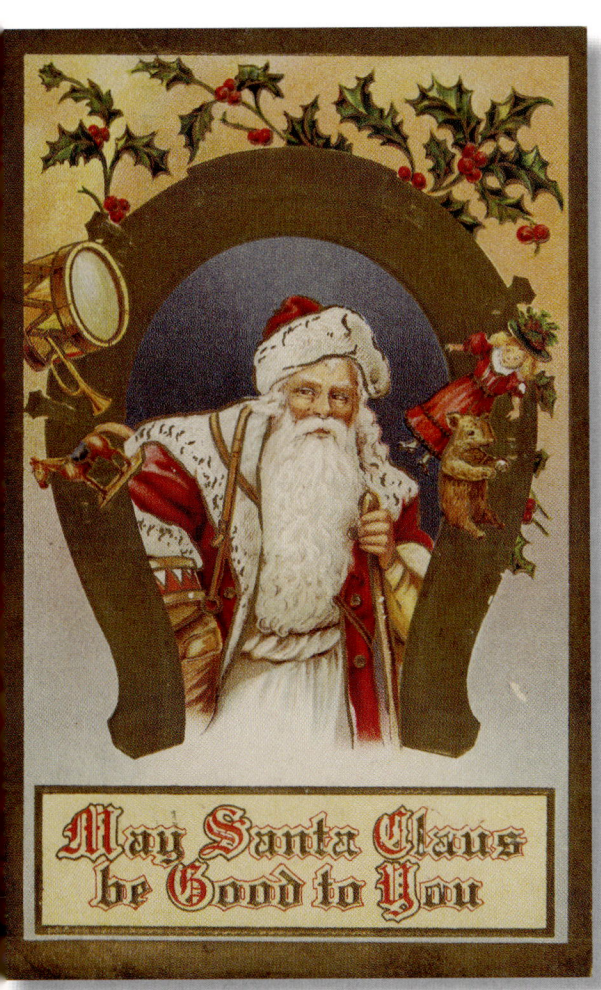
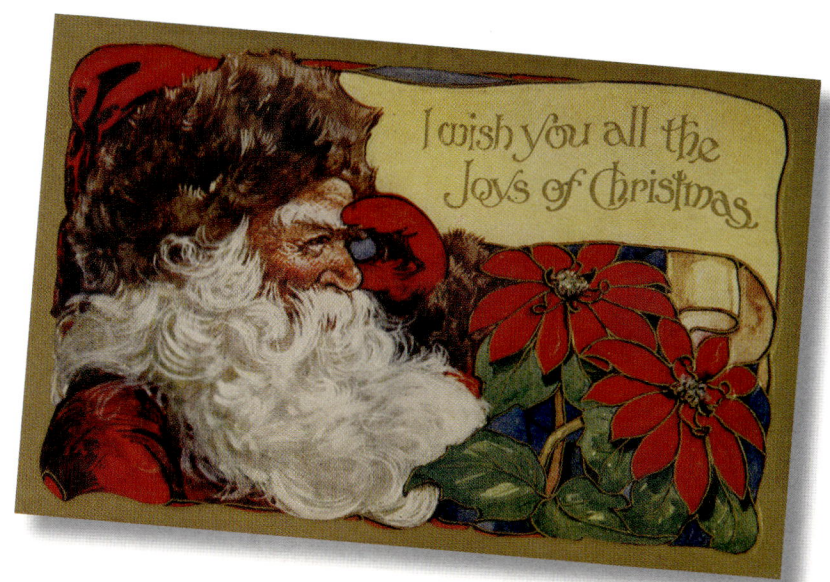
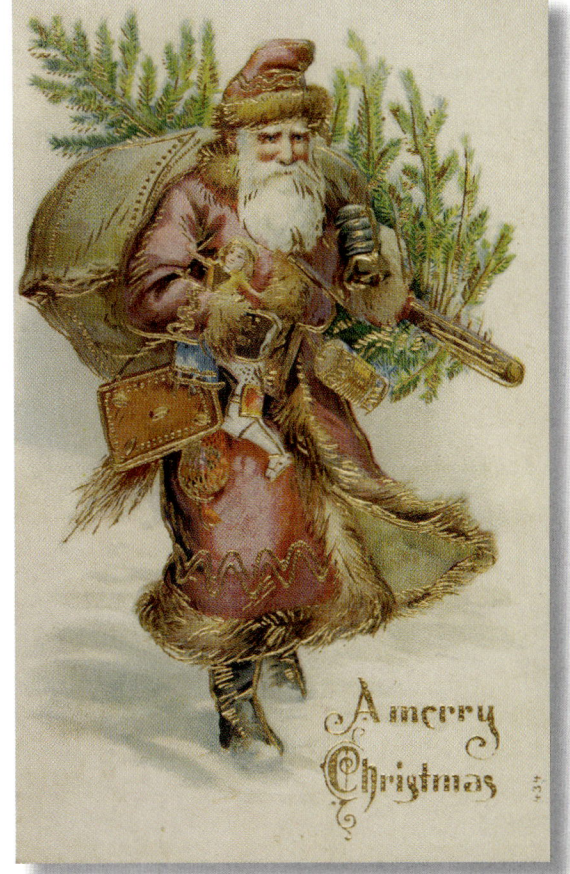
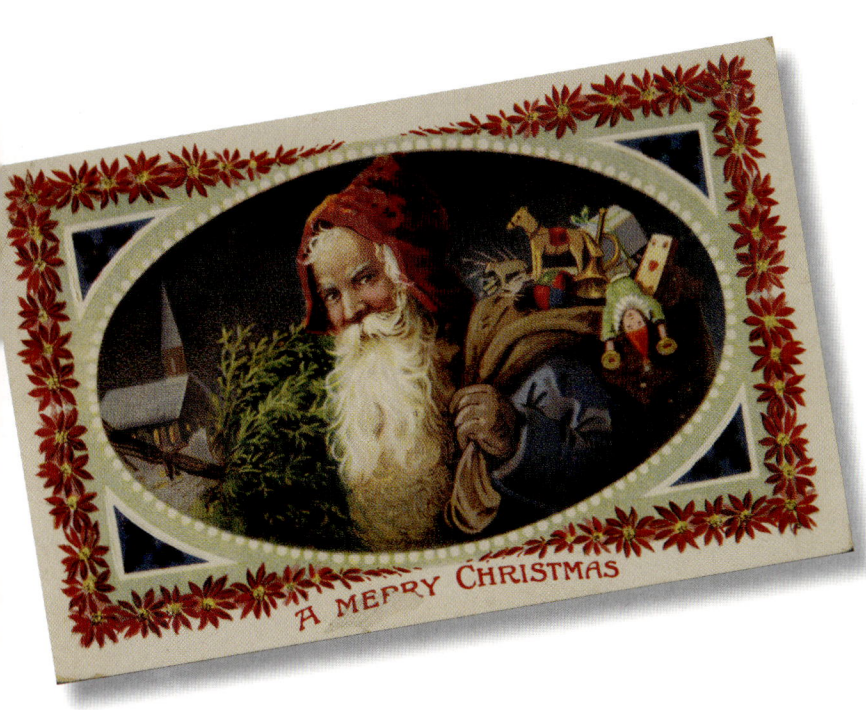

Santa sits atop the world and, hammer in hand, hangs a wreath, a symbol of eternity. Traditionally made of greens, the Christmas wreath celebrates life in the depth of winter.

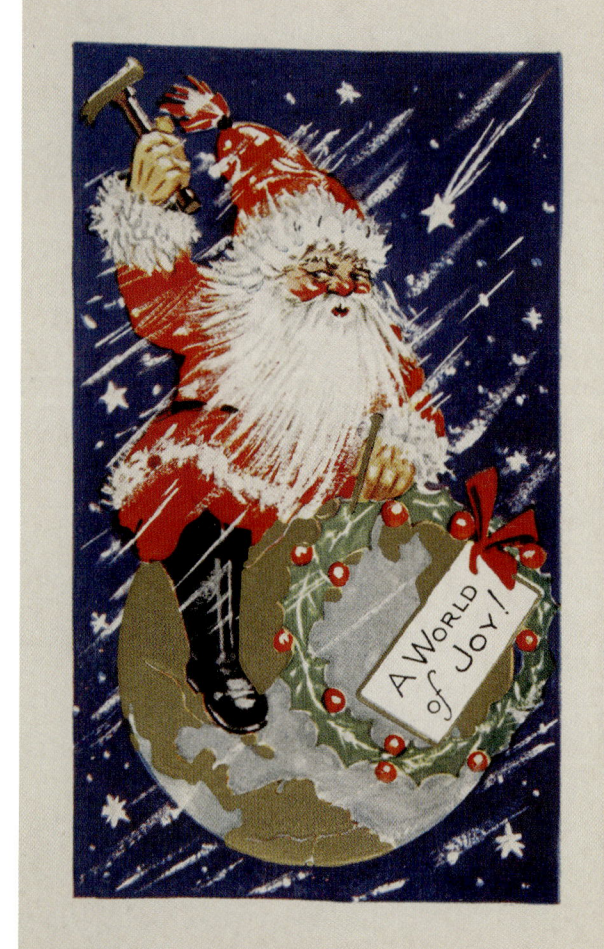

Santa is an American patriot. Note the American flags decorating his sleigh drawn by reindeer. Why airborne mammals? St. Nicholas eventually became the patron saint of Russia; from there his legend spread to Lapland, a culture in which reindeer figure prominently. This, and Lapland's remoteness, might explain why Santa lives at the North Pole and travels by a reindeer-drawn sleigh. Traditionally eight in number, they were named in, "A Visit from St. Nicholas,": "Now! Dasher, now! Dancer, now! Prancer, and Vixen, "On! Comet, on! Cupid, on! Dunder and Blixem;" The "most famous reindeer of all, Rudolph the Red-nosed Reindeer," emerged from a store souvenir given out by Montgomery Ward in 1939. In 1949 the song recorded by cowboy singer, Gene Autry, became a hit and "the rest," as they say, "is history."

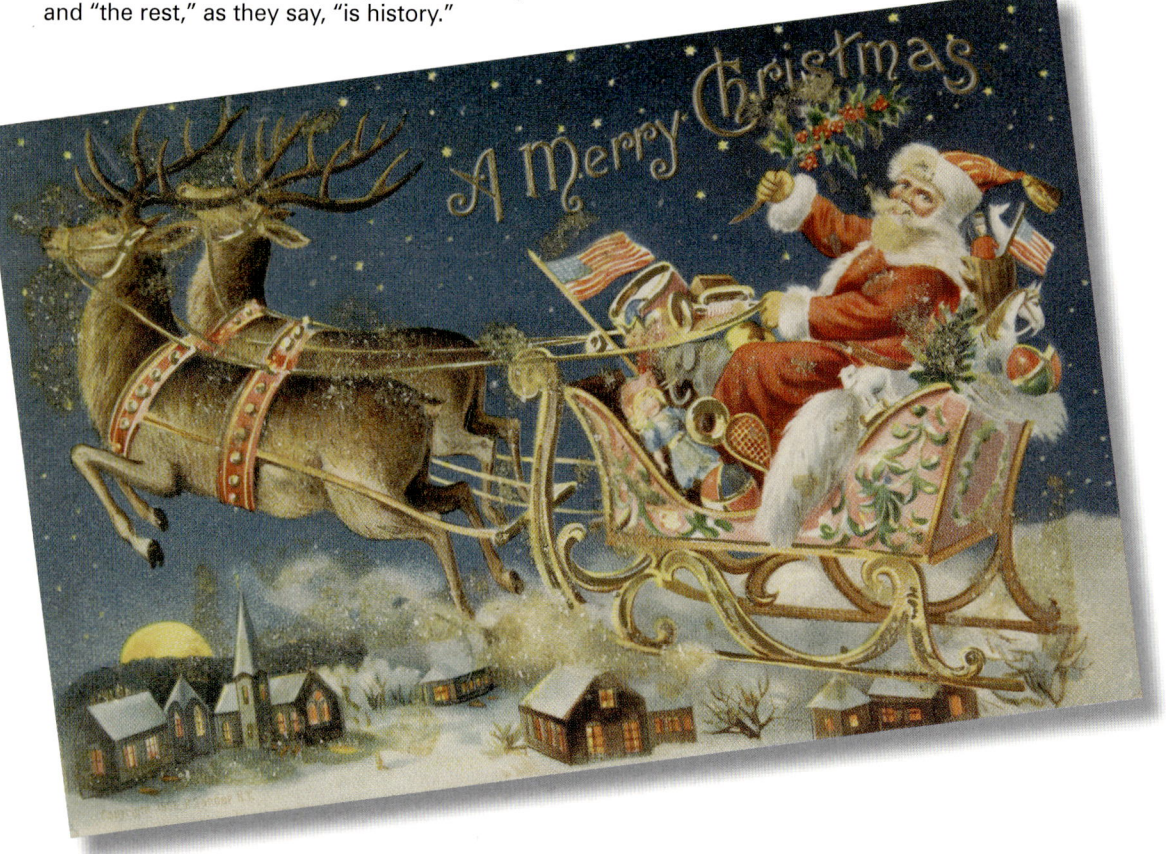

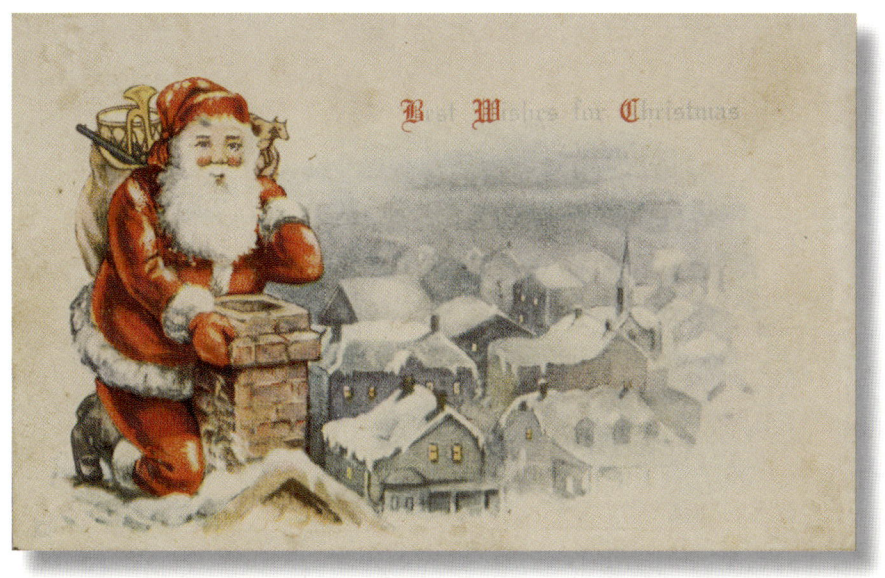

Santa's gift delivery system is varied. From the Dutch, with the wide chimneys of their houses, we acquired the image of him entering the home *via* the rooftop where, by the mid-19th century he was filling stockings. Occasionally, in a more innocent time, he entered the room of sleeping children.

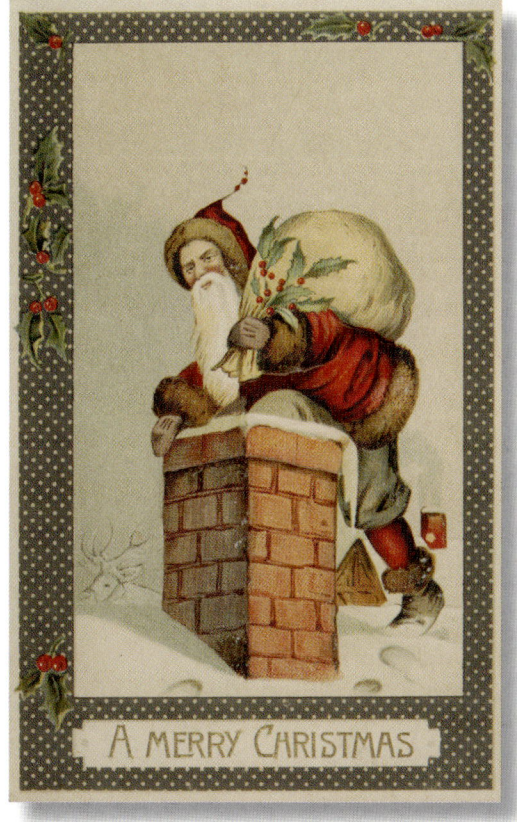

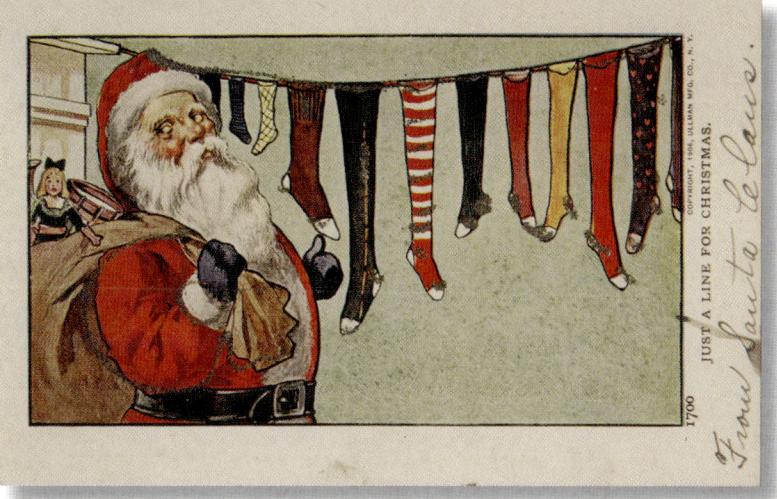

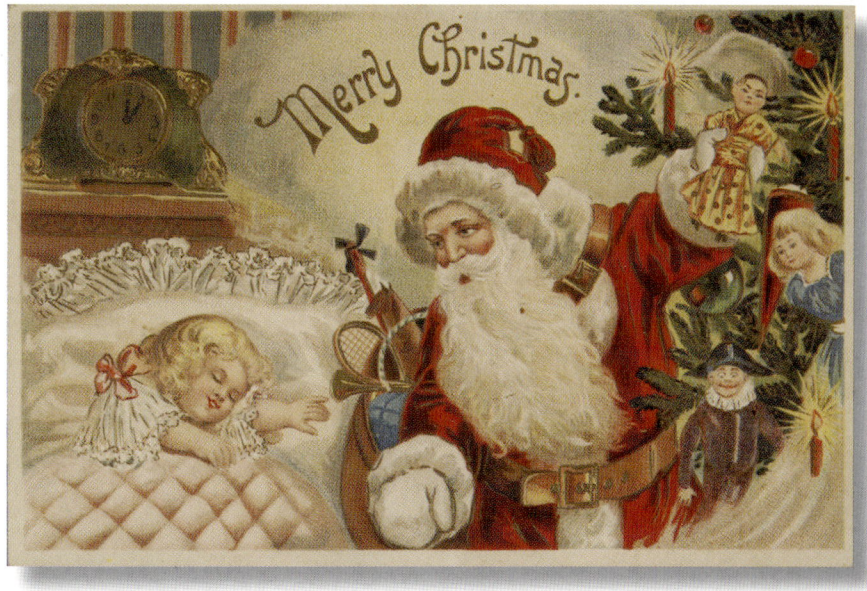

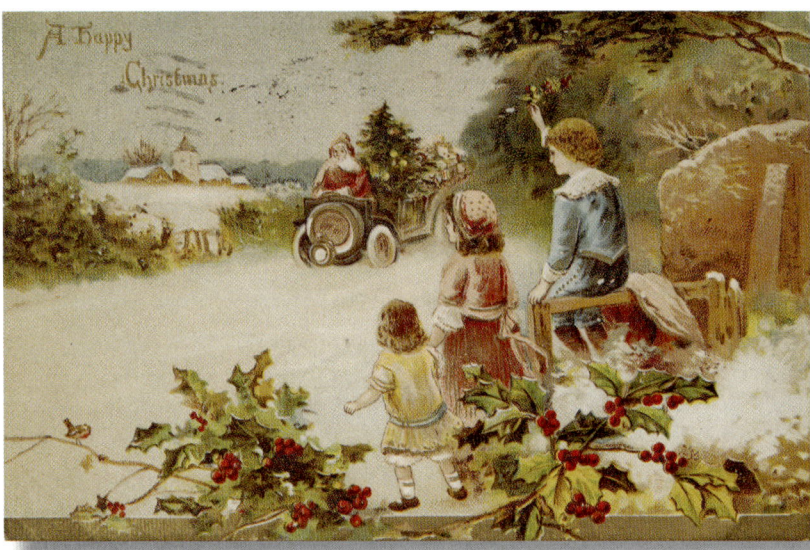

A modern-day Santa in 1909 arrives by auto. Mailed to Fred Kershner in Reading, Pennsylvania, the message reads, "Well Fred do you think Santy [sic] is going to be good to you this year. I am afraid he will not treat me as [in] other years." Poor "Sallie."

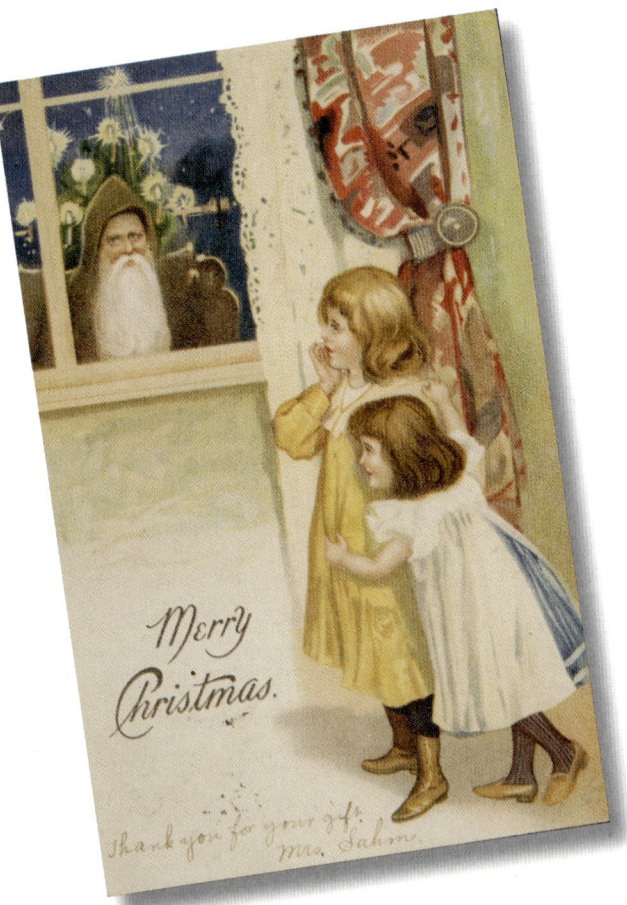

A rather medieval Santa arrives bearing a lighted Christmas tree. Little girls look on in wonder.

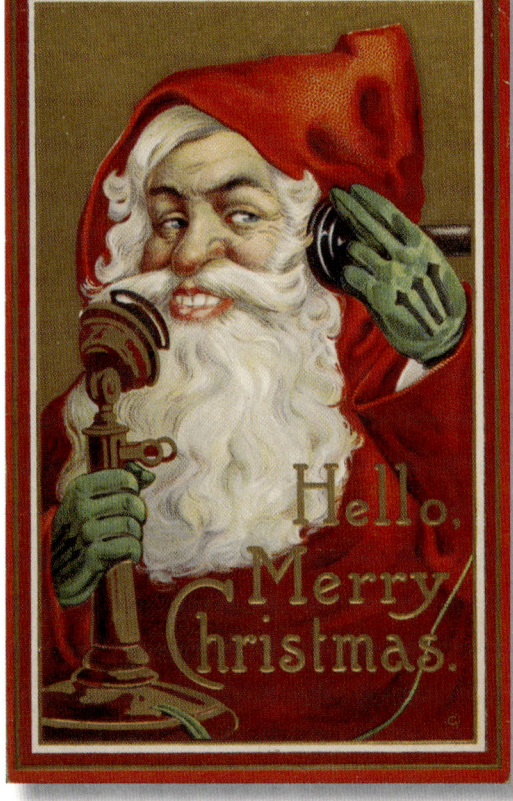

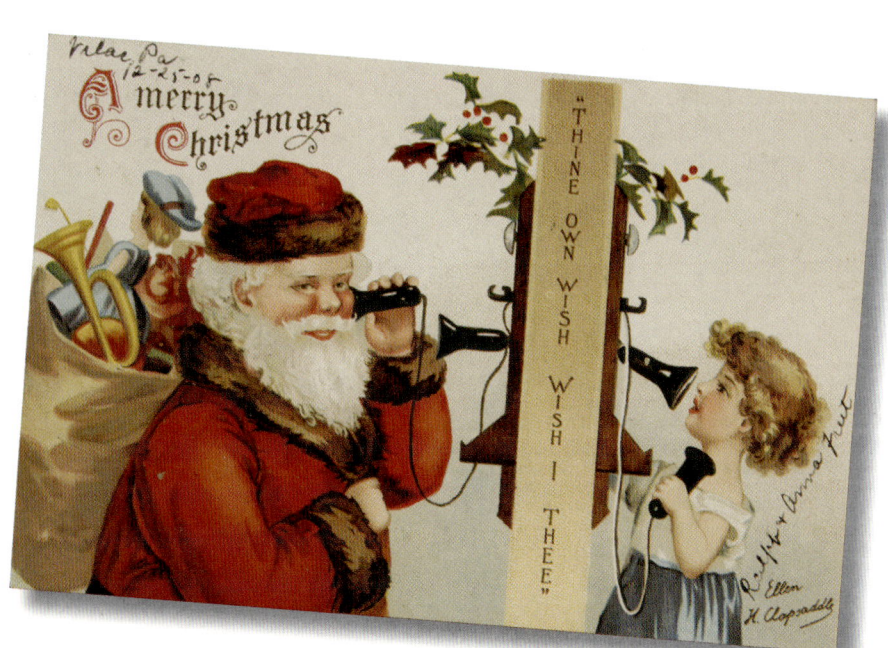

Modern Santas use the telephone. The very unusual green-gloved Santa was mailed in 1915.

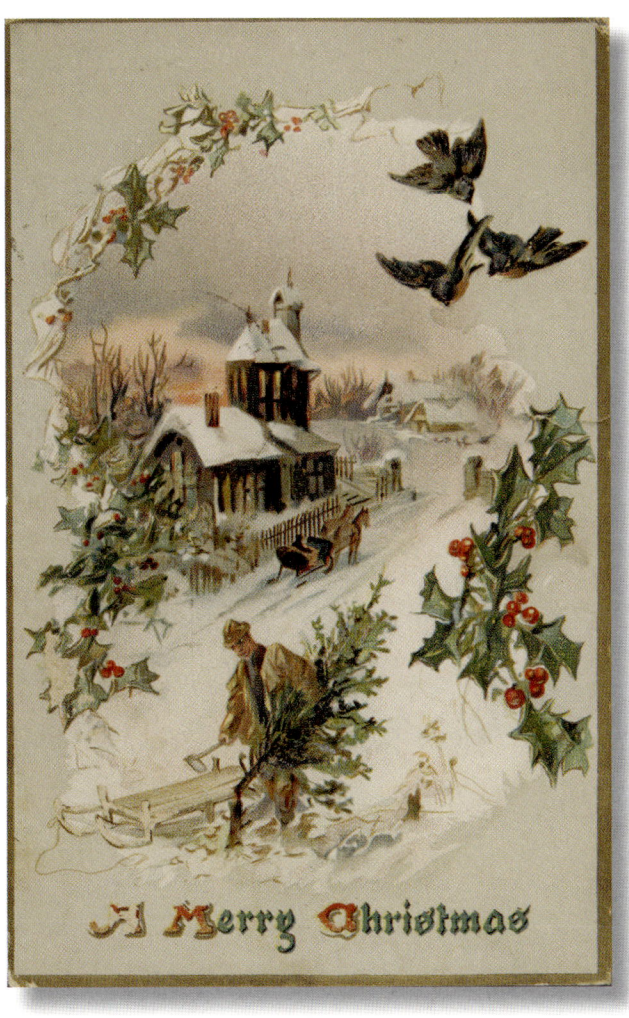

The Christmas tree was introduced to Americans by the Pennsylvania Germans and one of the earliest depictions is found in an illustration of an event that occurred in 1809 that was painted by Lewis Miller (1795-1882). The image of harvesting a tree is nostalgic. Most once-live trees actually come from tree farms.

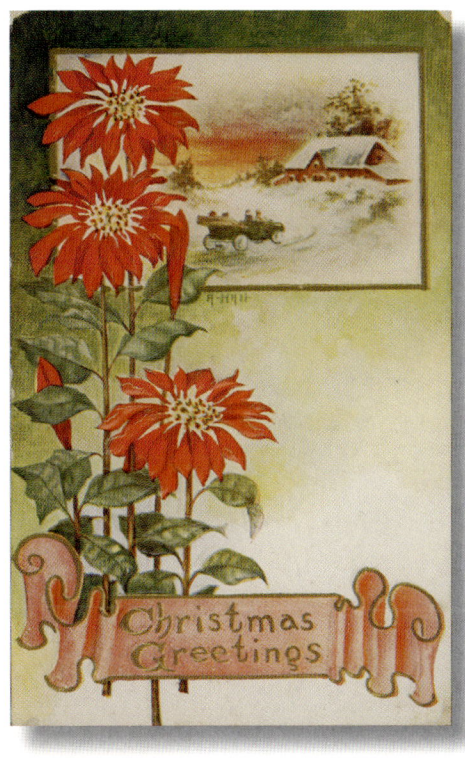

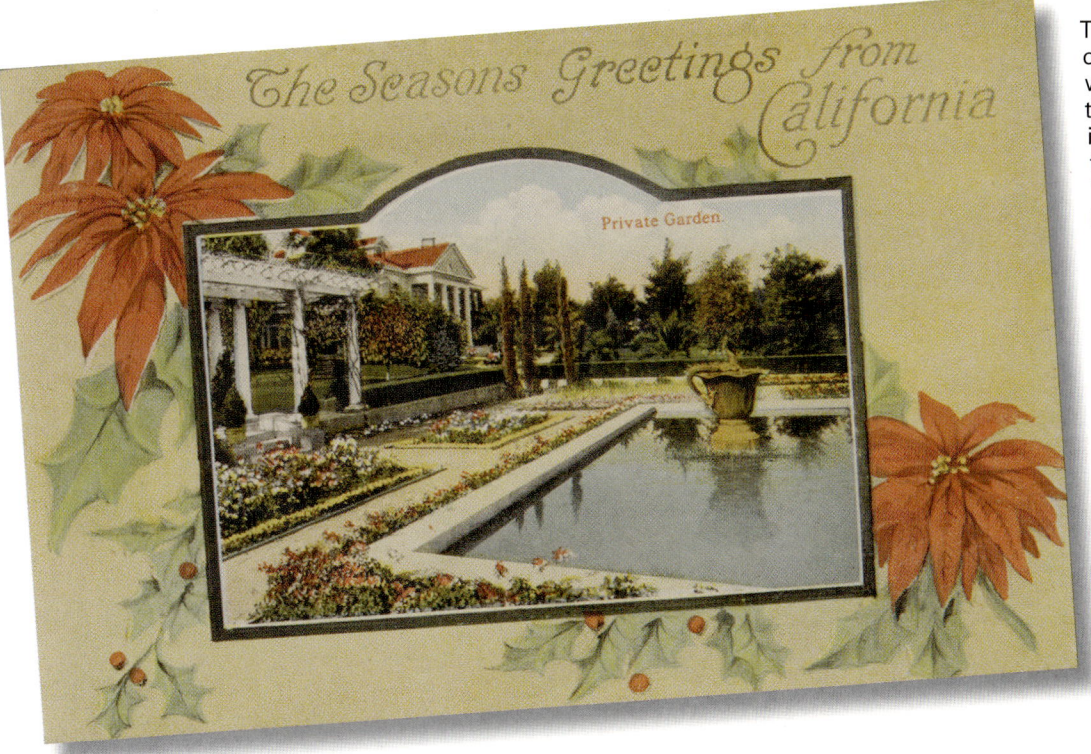

The poinsettia, a native of Central America, was introduced into the United States in the 1820s by the Brooklyn, New York-born American minister to Mexico, Joel Poinsett. Very adaptable to greenhouse culture, it early became a symbol of Christmas, with its bright red bracts being compared to the Star of Bethlehem. Modern hybridization has led to the development of hundreds of varieties of the plant in many hues and shapes.

Santa frolicking with kids is a popular theme. Note that the Santa in the brown fur-trimmed suit wears a crown of holly on his hat in the style of Father Christmas.

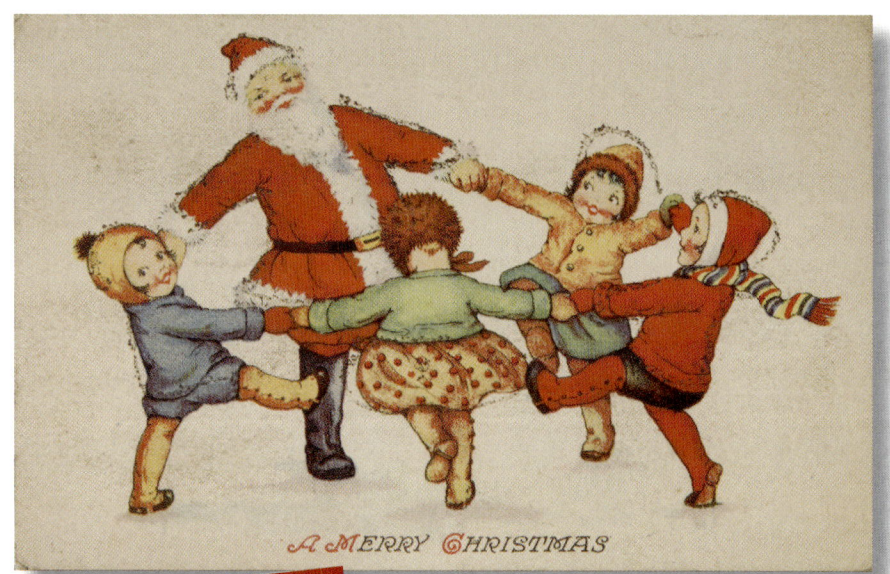

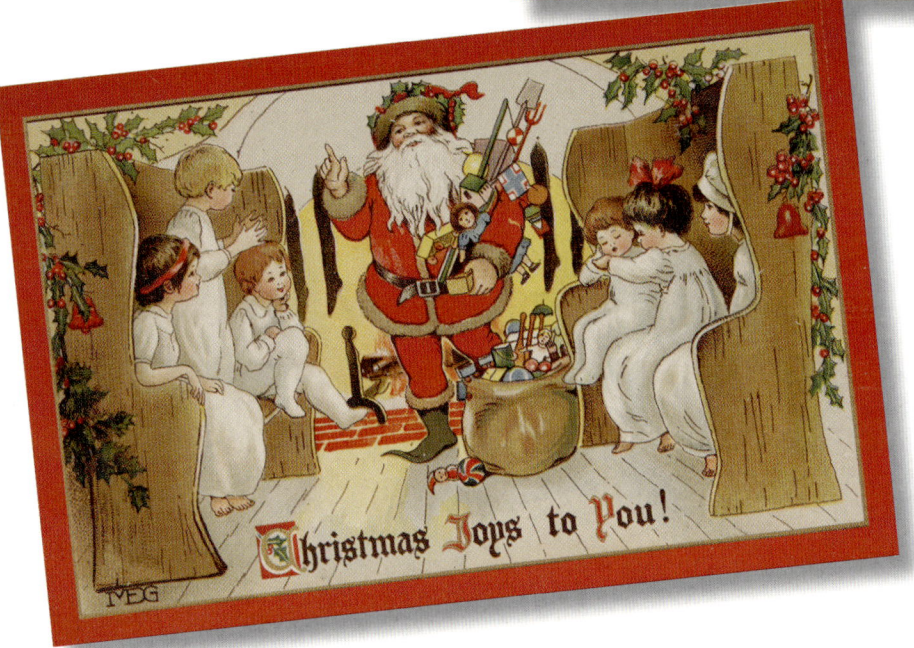

Belsnickle is a derivative of the German "Pelz-nickle", which means "Nicholas in Furs". *Belsnickle*-ing was introduced into America and took root in several areas, most famously in the Pennsylvania Dutch region. This extremely rare card shows this Christmas custom in Lee County, Texas, *circa* 1910. The *Belsnickle* wore a mask and costume and went from door to door carrying small gifts and a switch. Good children would be rewarded. Naughty ones would be punished. Collection: Oscar D. Beisert, Jr.

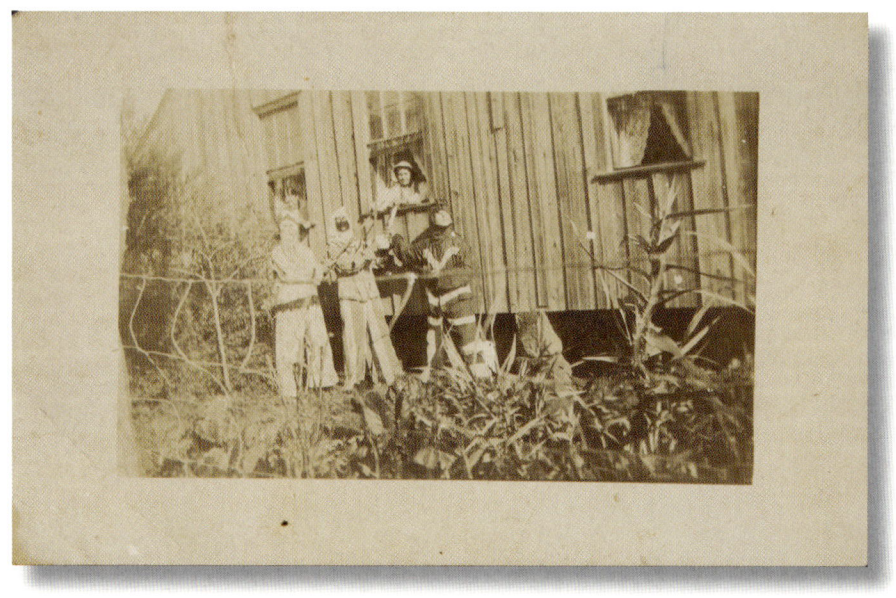

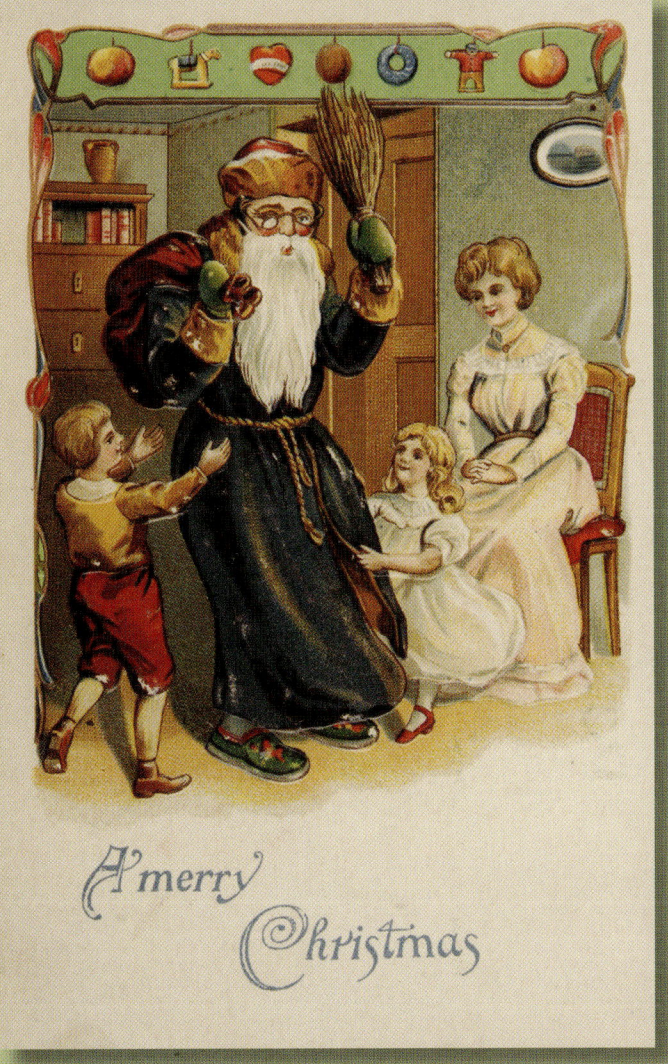

The English Father Christmas, along with the German *Belsnickle*, rewarded the good and punished the naughty. Both are often portrayed with gifts and switches. These Father Christmas figures perform their expected duties.

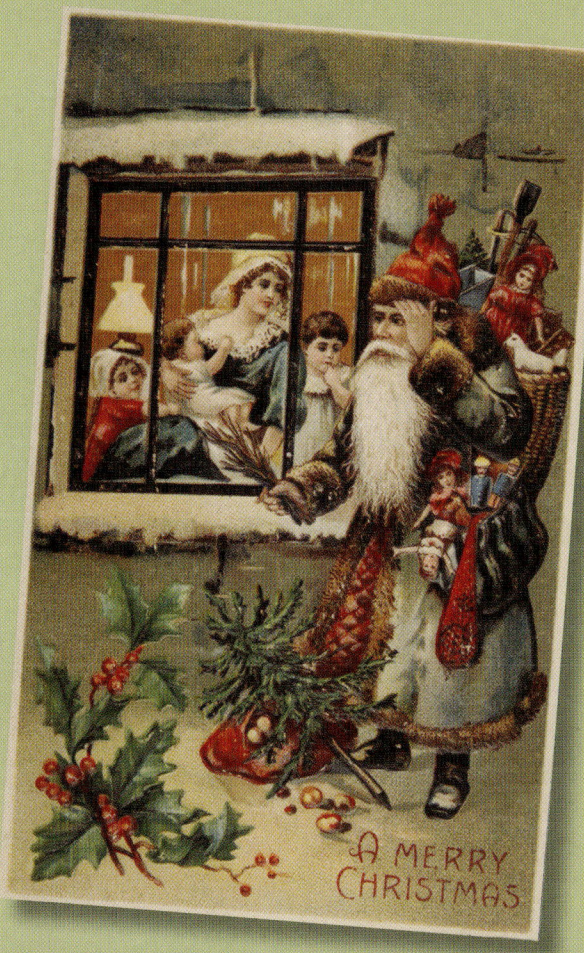

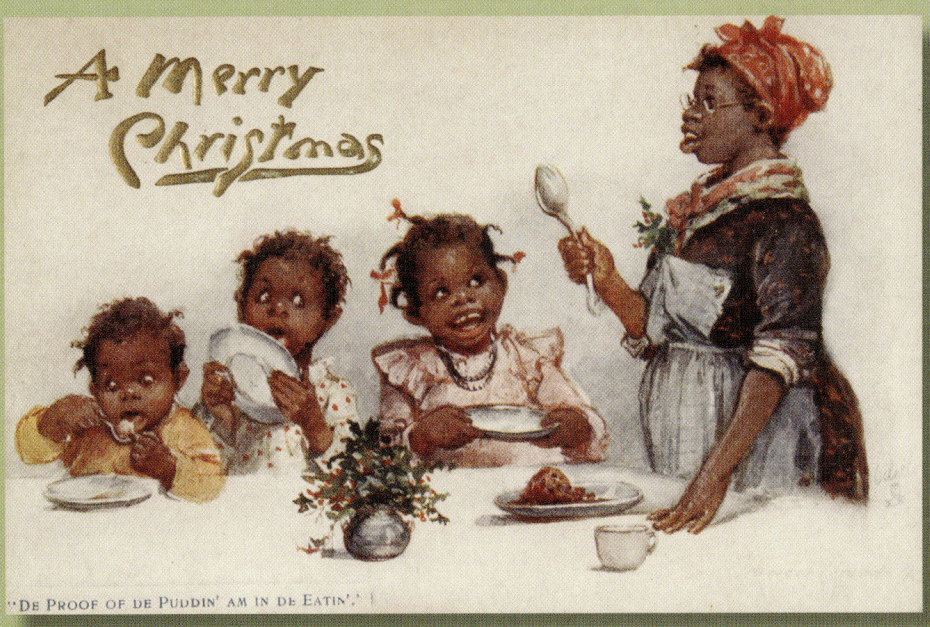

Views of African-Americans on early holiday cards are generally both rare and stereotypical.

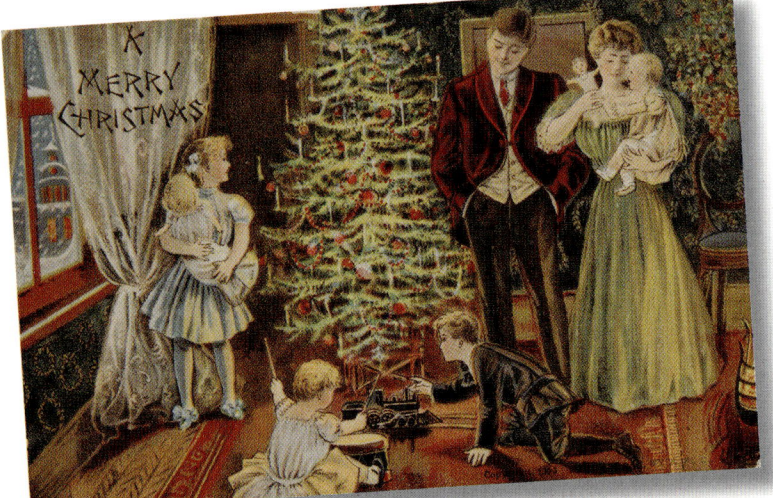

The Christmas tree became widely popular in America after it was introduced into British Royal society by Prince Albert, the German-born Consort of Queen Victoria, who reigned from 1837 to 1901. For a family to gather around a tree became the ultimate symbol of domesticity. To obtain a tree under adversity was viewed as an act of Christian charity and devotion. Poor children would be forgiven transgressions committed to allow them to be in the presence of a Christmas tree.

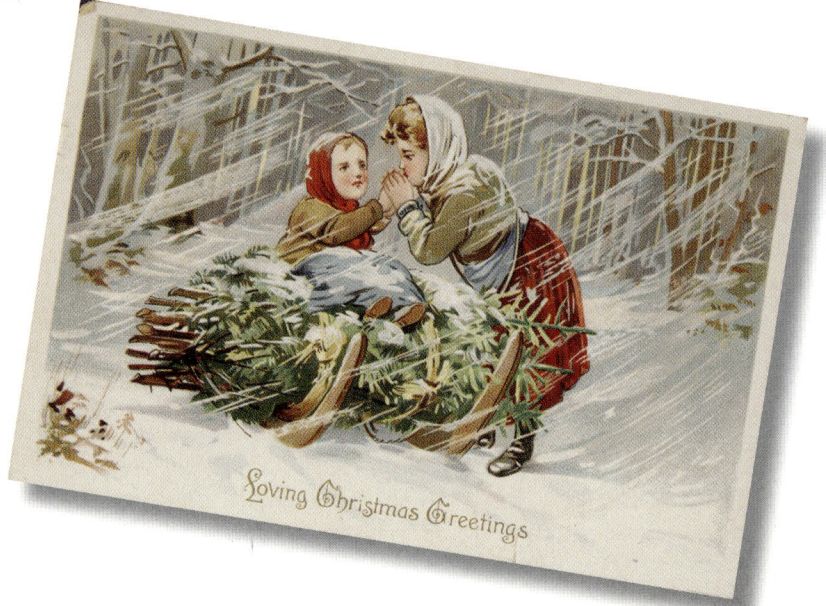

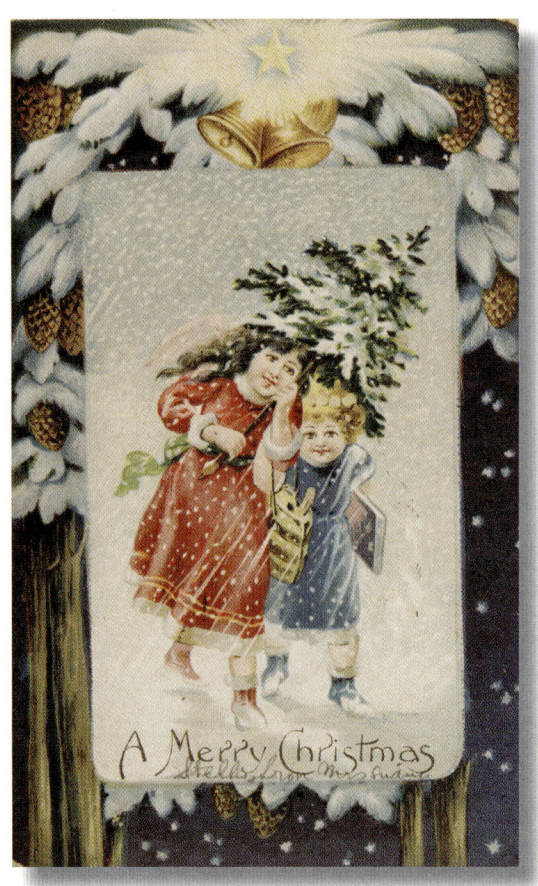

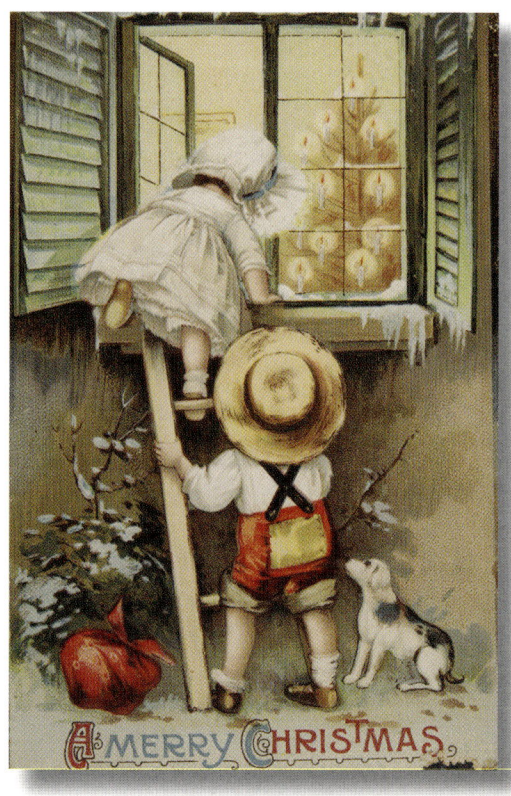

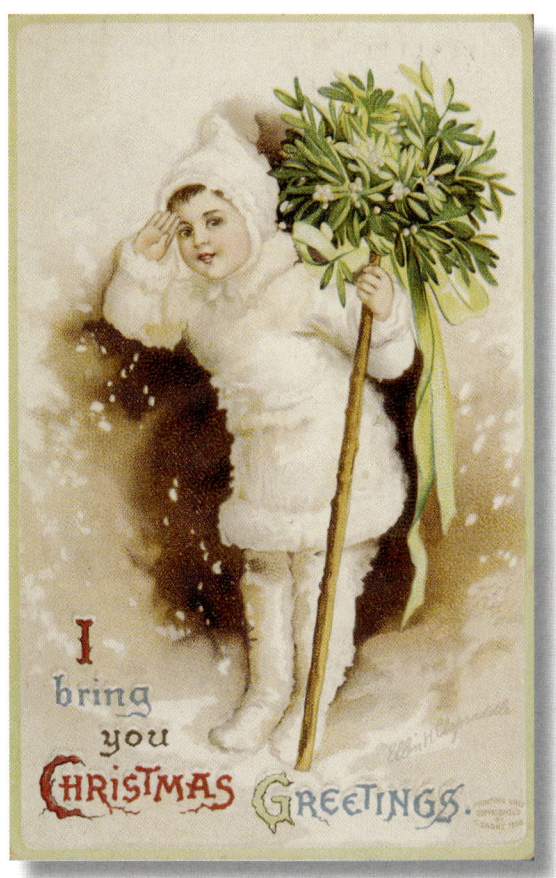

The use of mistletoe was popular at Christmastime. Mistletoe bears fruit at the time of the Winter Solstice, the birth of the new year, and may have been used in Druidic Britain as a symbol of immortality. The belief in the plant's magical powers goes back to the pagan past. The Druids, legend holds, only cut the plant with a golden sickle and took care that the plant would not touch the ground. Because mistletoe grows on oaks (the wood many believed the Cross was made of), it became an important Christmas symbol. Like the shamrock, there are botanically different plants that we call "mistletoe." In Europe it is *Viscum album* in America, *Pharadendron seretinum* is used. Bouquets of the plant, like those held by the fur clad young lady, are still sold in Britain.

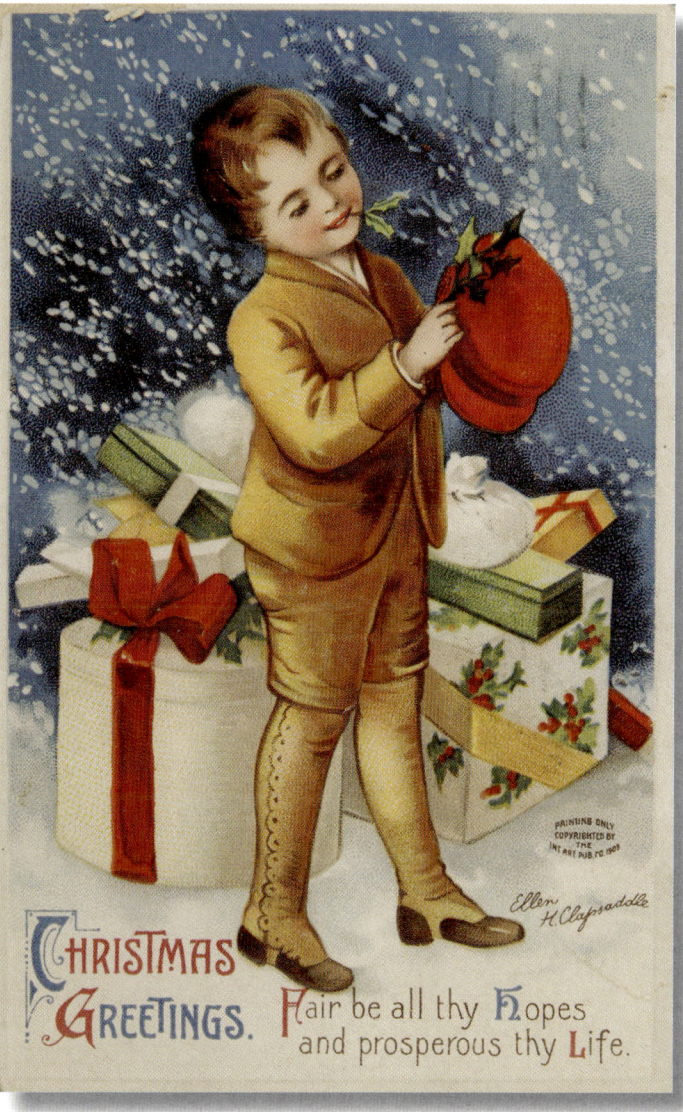

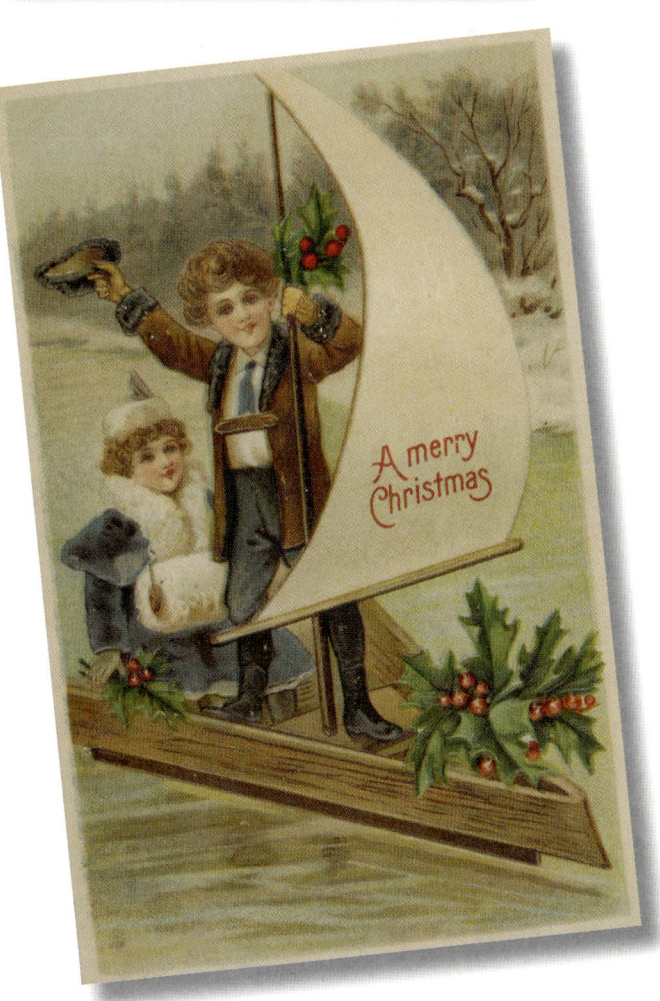

Prosperity and Christmas are linked on holiday greetings. A well dressed lad adorns his new hat with a sprig of holly. A very expensively dressed young couple goes ice-yachting on the holiday.

Unusual gifts can appear on Christmas. This card probably heralded a birth. I hope the roses were 'de-thorned."

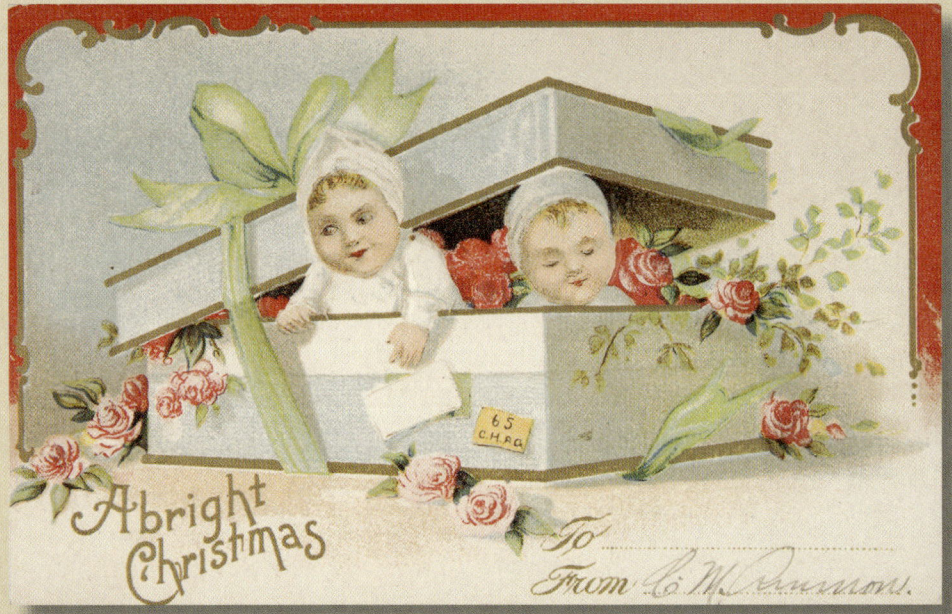

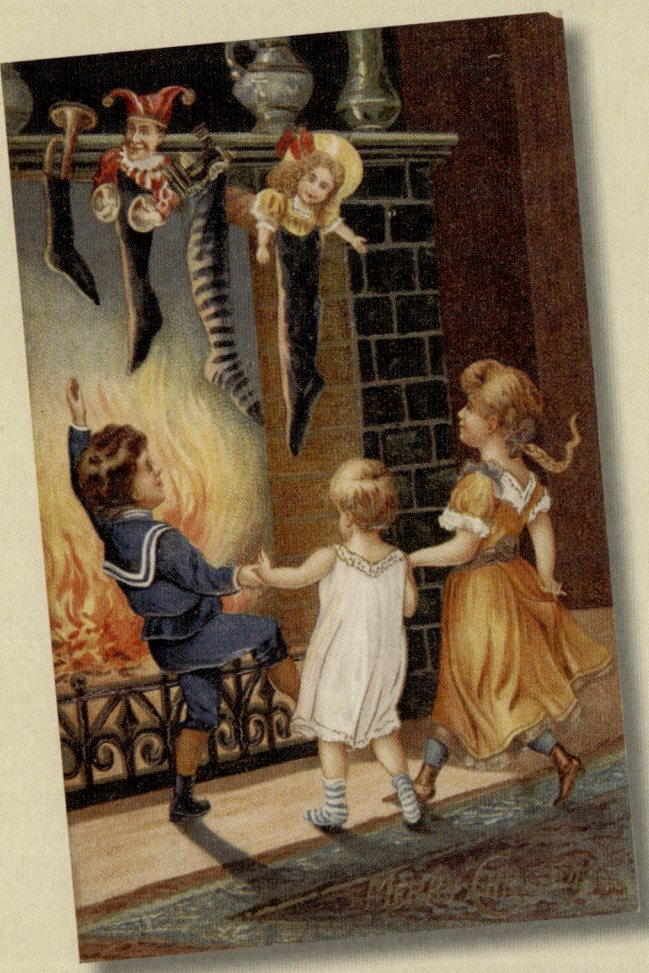

Children and Christmas stockings always make for a happy card. In simple homes the stockings might contain only an orange and nuts and candies. Naughty kids were threatened that they would only find lumps of coal or ashes in their stockings.

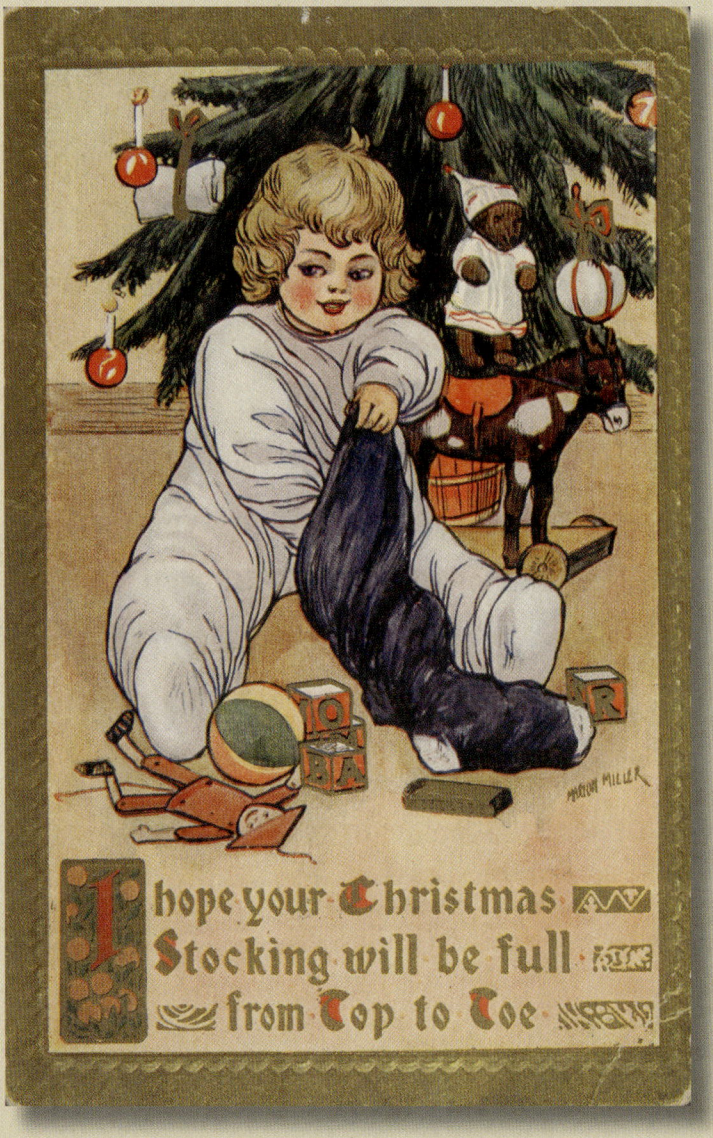

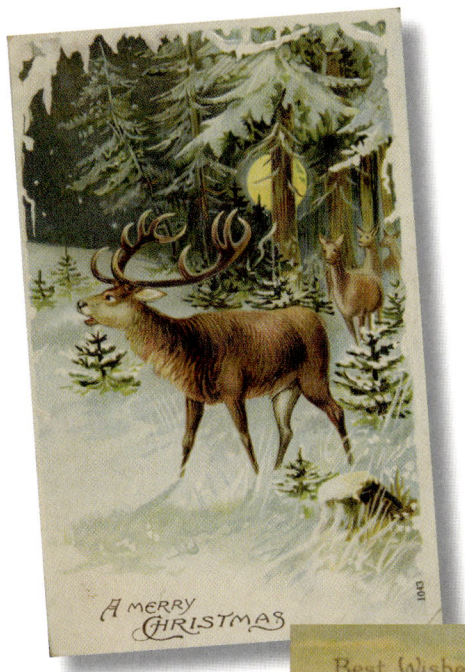

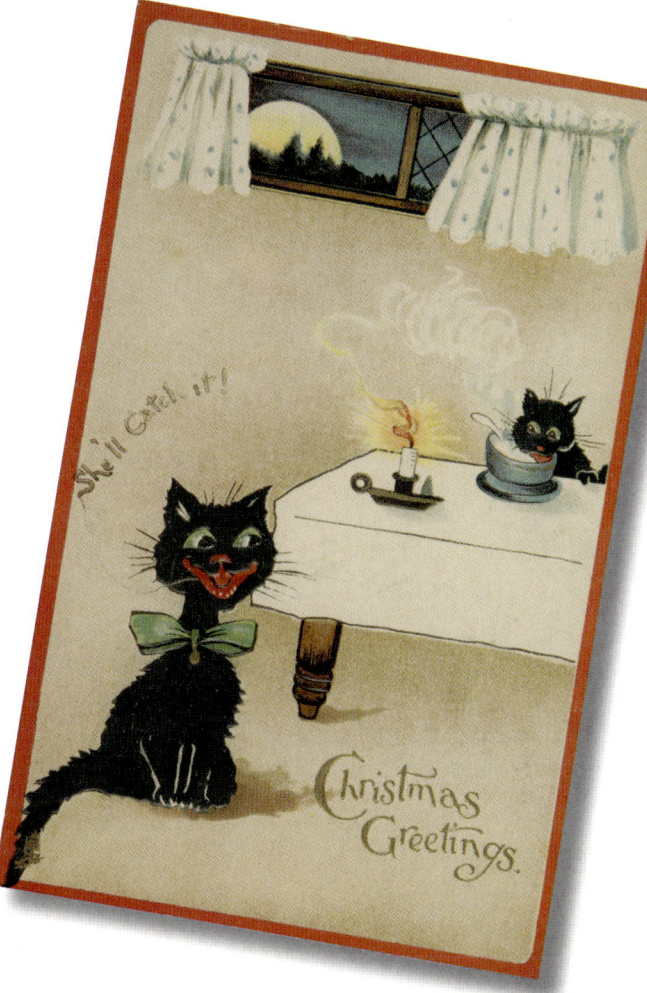

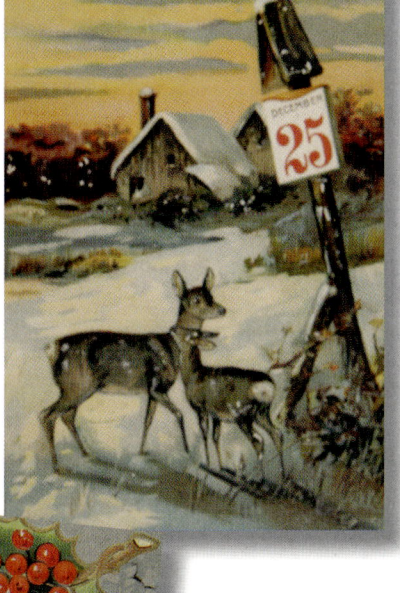

In many cultures animals were believed to be endowed with special attributes on Christmas. Many Germans, on Christmas Eve, would tell their animals of the birth of Christ. Others, including many English, believed that animals could speak at midnight. Wild animals like deer intuitively know something special has occurred. A dog is festooned for the holiday. A cat looks like he is left over from Halloween and well "Xmas Greetings From One [Ass] To Another." Not everything was holy.

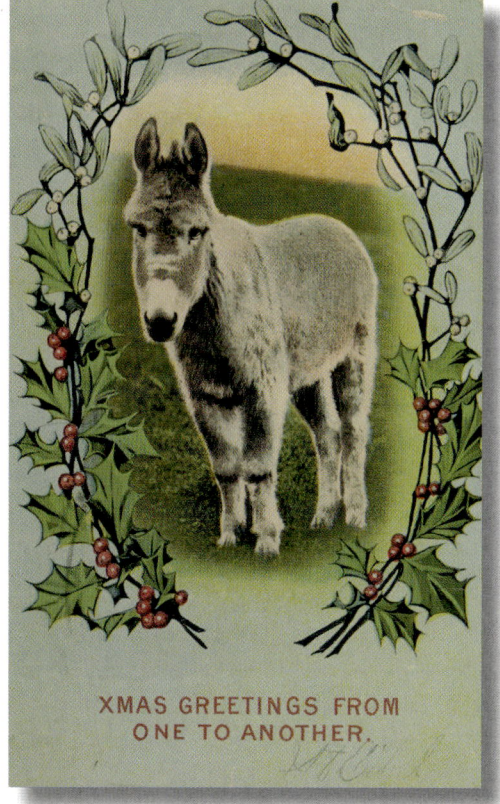

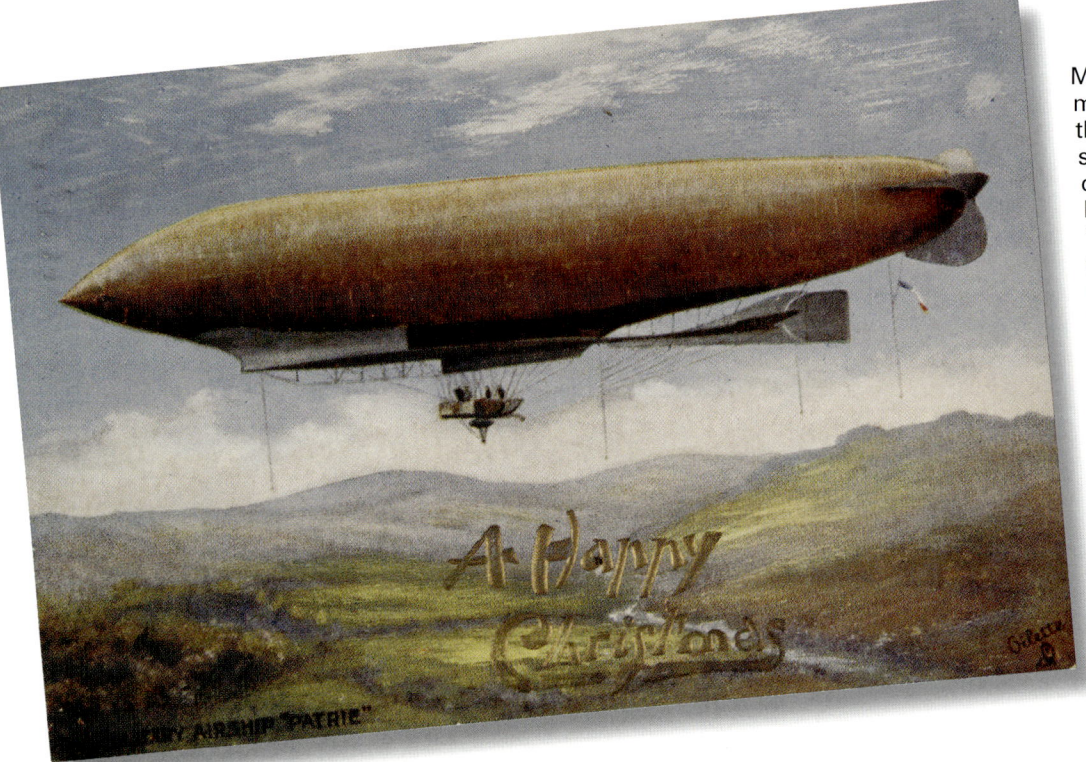

Modern Adventure. The message on the reverse of this card, mailed in 1908, says it all. Sent to Freddie Kershner in Reading, Pennsylvania, it reads: "Dear Freddie, How would you like to take me ariding in one of these instead of a pony cart or auto. I hope you have a Merry Xmas Come to see my Tree"

This celestial "A Merry Christmas" card is identical to "A Happy New Year" card illustrated in Chapter 2. Whatever the occasion, this image truly emphasizes the Weird as associated with holidays, sacred and profane.

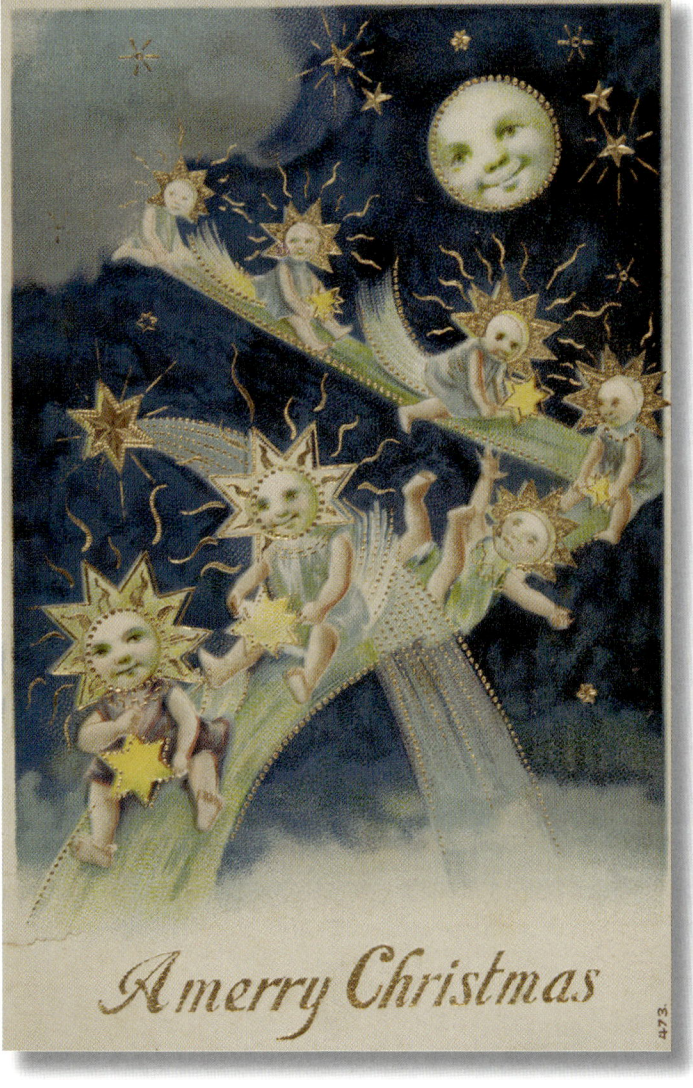

10
Weird Events

Can You Believe These?

Why would anyone want to record these subjects on a postcard? One might legitimately ask the question. Some cards reflect archaic ideas and many others speak to the changing nature of information, and how information is passed on. Humorous postcards can reflect dated humor or timeless themes. Other postcards portray events that we can find to be downright disturbing. But then the meaning and the use of postcards has changed.

Today the postcard is essentially a souvenir. It is something we send to friends or relatives to show that we are thinking of them or that we are proud to be where we are. "Wish you were here," is a phrase commonly used on travel cards. "Having a Wonderful Time, Wish You Were Here." Or, at least, turn green with envy knowing that we are here – and you are not. Accordingly, most cards today reflect their souvenir status: city views, museums, works of art, and quaint folks in quaint costumes are shown on the bulk of modern cards.

In the golden age of postcards, their function was far broader than merely being souvenirs. This was the time before images would inundate us. Motion pictures were new; newsreels were uncommon. Even newspapers and magazines used photographs sparingly. Postcards could be souvenirs, but they could also spread information. It is very common to find cards sent from one town to the next where the sender just wants to show off his or her town's new bank, bridge, school, or prison. Others might want to expose the horror of child labor.

Collecting postcards became a national obsession. Many would exchange cards, simply to add cards to their collections. Nettie May Landis (1879-1914), the sister of the founders of the Landis Valley Museum, mailed out literally thousands of postcards in the early years of the twentieth century, asking only that her correspondents reply in kind. The thousands of cards she garnered from all over America and the wider world are now preserved at the Landis Valley Museum as part of its vast holdings.

Judging from the many unsent cards that exist, it is clear that many postcards, and especially sets and series, were purchased as souvenirs or memory pieces. These might explain the cards that depict local disasters and other horrors.

Humorous cards had a life of their own. The author, who was born in 1937, clearly remembers as a kid buying novelty postcards just because they were funny – or perhaps a bit naughty.

While one can categorize many cards and attempt to decipher their meanings, there are still many others whose message and meaning are obscure or just plain weird. And probably always will be.

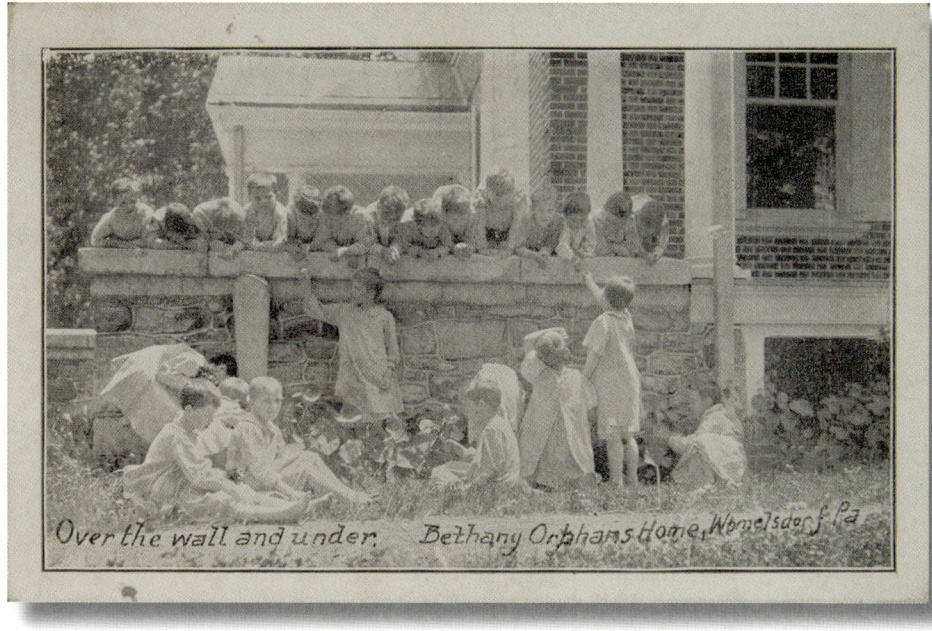

Orphanages printed postcards to show how happy and well cared for their charges were. Many of these were gifted to donors or prospective donors. The church-related Bethany Orphans Home in Womelsdorf, Pennsylvania, distributed cards with at least a dozen images. "Over the Wall and Under" was sent to "Master Carl Ernst" of Bethlehem, Pennsylvania, by "Aunt Maud." Was this to warn Carl or make him realize how lucky he was? *Collection: Mr. and Mrs. Michael Emery*

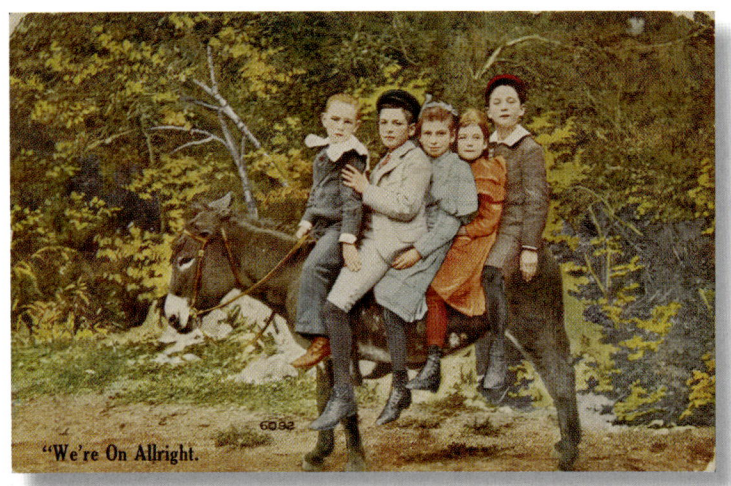

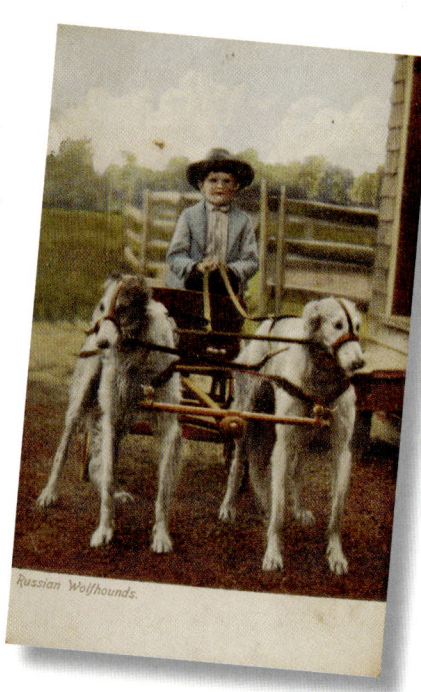

The card showing a boy in a dogcart being drawn by a pair of "Russian Wolfhounds" was given to Stella "from gram papa" about 1905.

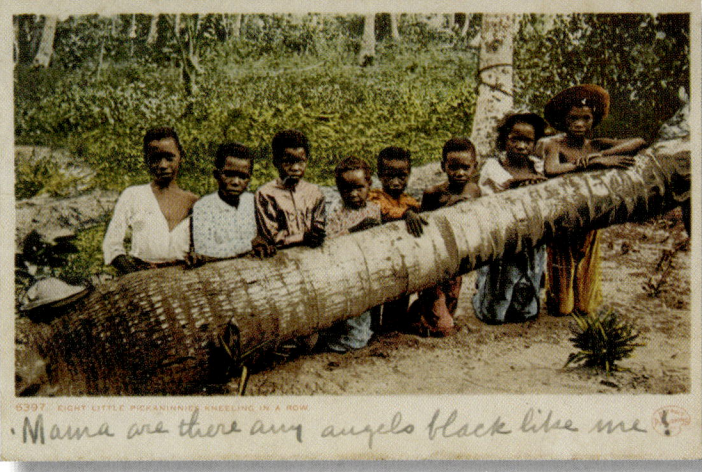

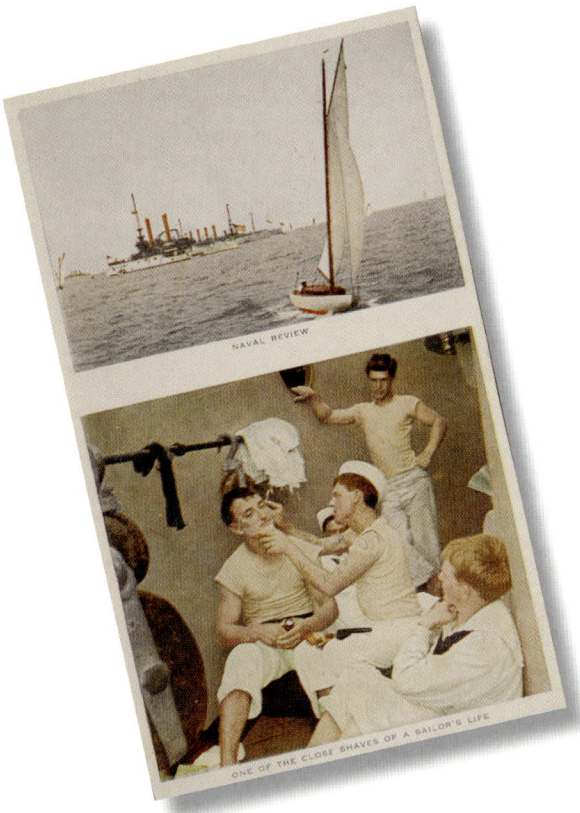

What do these images mean? Five bored-looking middleclass white kids sit on a donkey while eight African-American children pose behind a fallen log. The message on the one sent to "Master Henry B. Brown" of Mount Vernon, New York, reads: "Dear Henry, Jr, Big folks as well as little people like to ride these donkeys instead of walking or riding in a carriage. With love, Cousin Hattie" It must have been really strange to be in Manitou, Colorado, in 1914. The legend on the other card, mailed to "Miss Alice Viola Rabenold of Reading, Pennsylvania, is clearly racist and reflective of an earlier age. "Eight Little Pickaninnies," it reads, "Kneeling on a Log."

A large series of cards showed life in the pre-World War I American Navy. Have you ever wondered how sailors shaved at sea? *Collection: Dr. Russell Eaton*

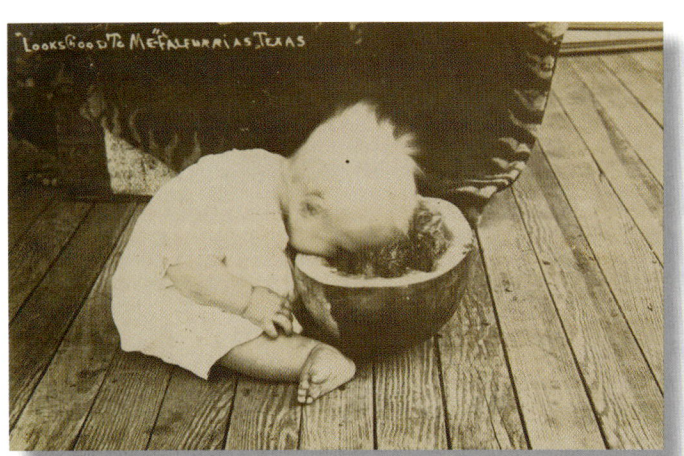

Kids like watermelon. "Looks Good to Me – FalFurrias, Texas" probably dates from about 1910. *Collection: Oscar D. Beisert, Jr.*

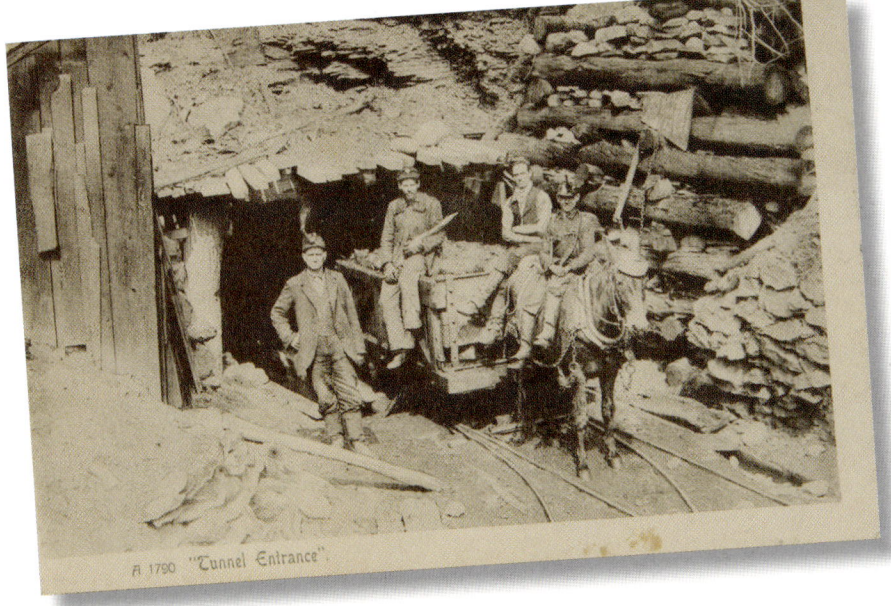

Today work scenes are hardly what we expect on postcards and the image of breaker boys at work causes dismay and pity, but early in the 20th century "Coal was King" and the industry was being celebrated. All three cards were mailed in Pennsylvania to Pennsylvania residents. A resident of Shamokin in the anthracite region thought the "Screen Room" scene a fine representative of her town's prosperity.

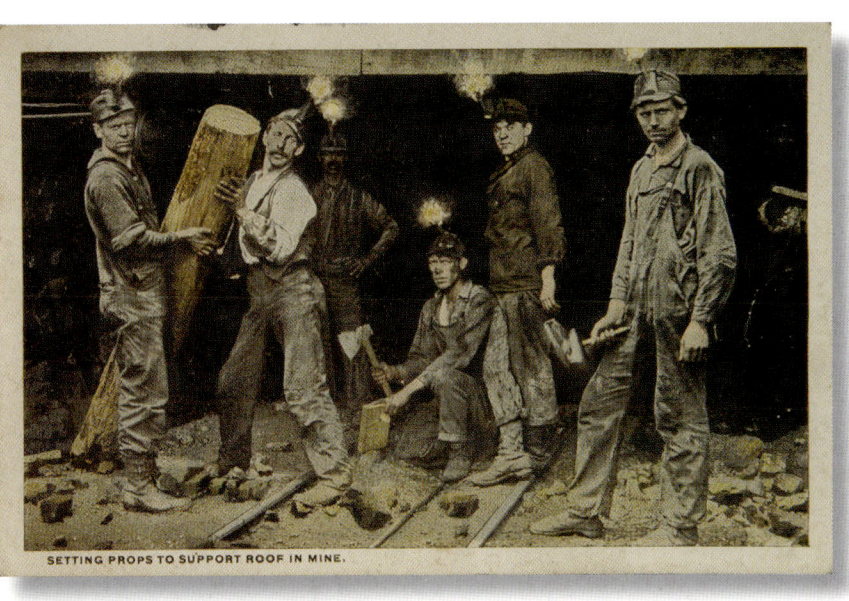

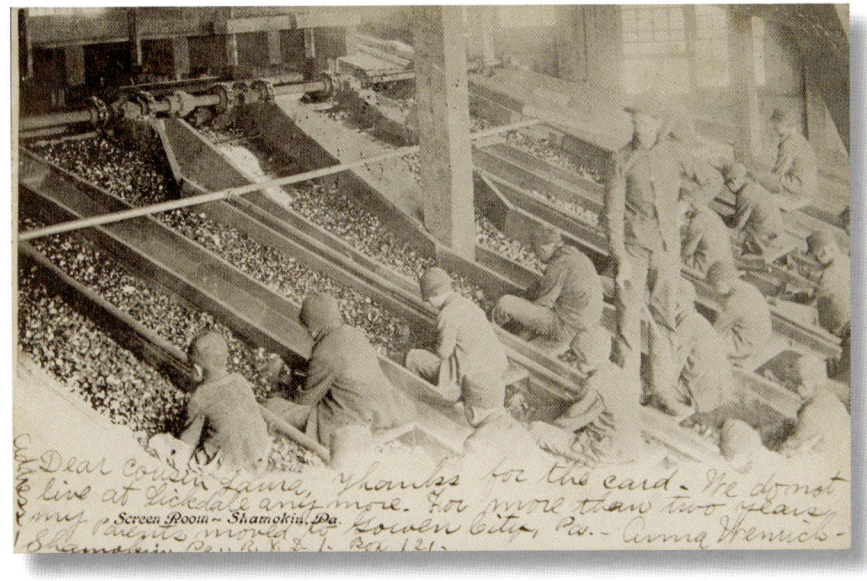

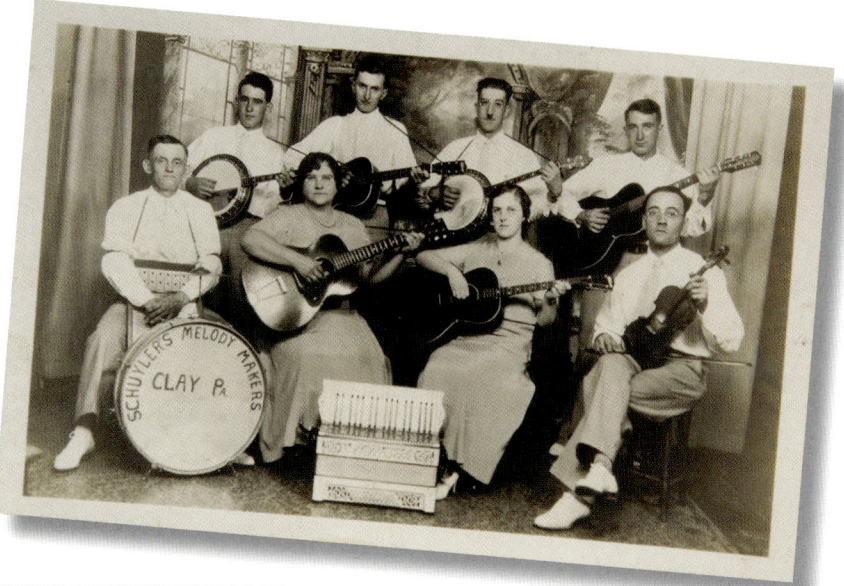

"Schuyler's Melody Makers" from Clay (Lancaster County) Pennsylvania, were, no doubt, a lively group, which included four guitars, two banjos and a fiddle. The drummer wears a musical washboard. He probably also played the accordion.

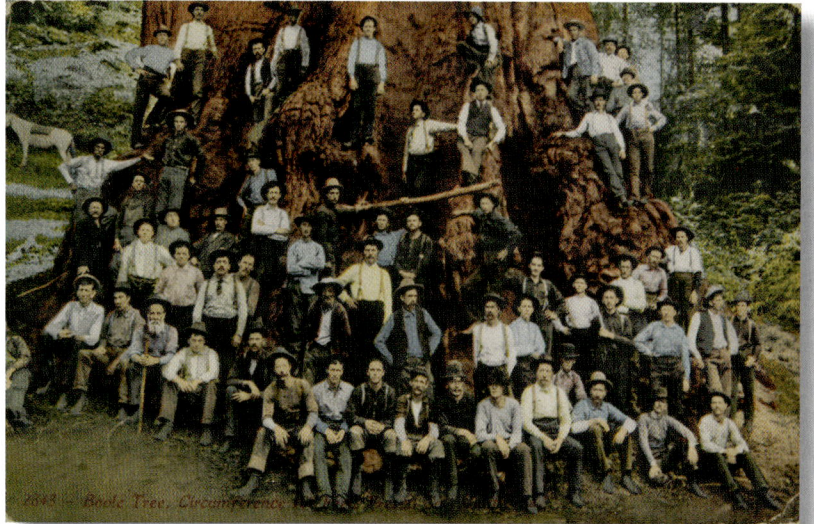

Proud lumbermen pose on a giant redwood on a card published in San Francisco by Edward H. Mitchell. Mailed to George Faust in Orwigsburg, Pennsylvania, by Aunt Dora in Reedley, California, the message reads: "This is the kind of trees we have in Calif. I wish you all could see the fruit that is raised just a few miles from Reedley. I never saw such big peaches, apples & grapes. I have been here two weeks ant like it very well. Give my love to mother & father."

"A good day for ducks." It certainly was. Obviously enhanced with the flying birds, this is a duck hunter's ultimate fantasy from the days before bagging limits.

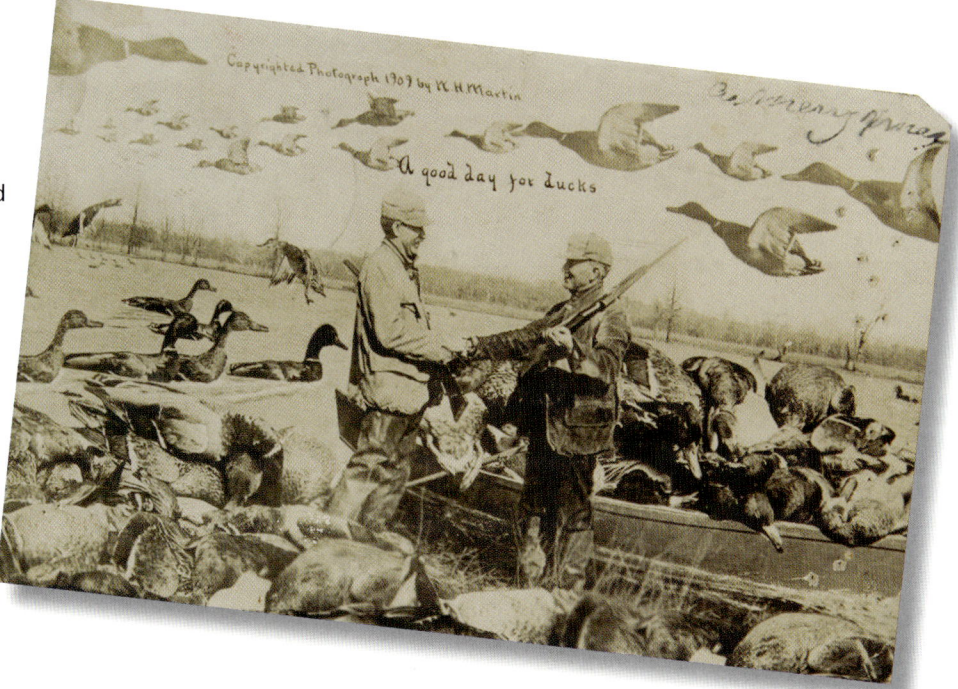

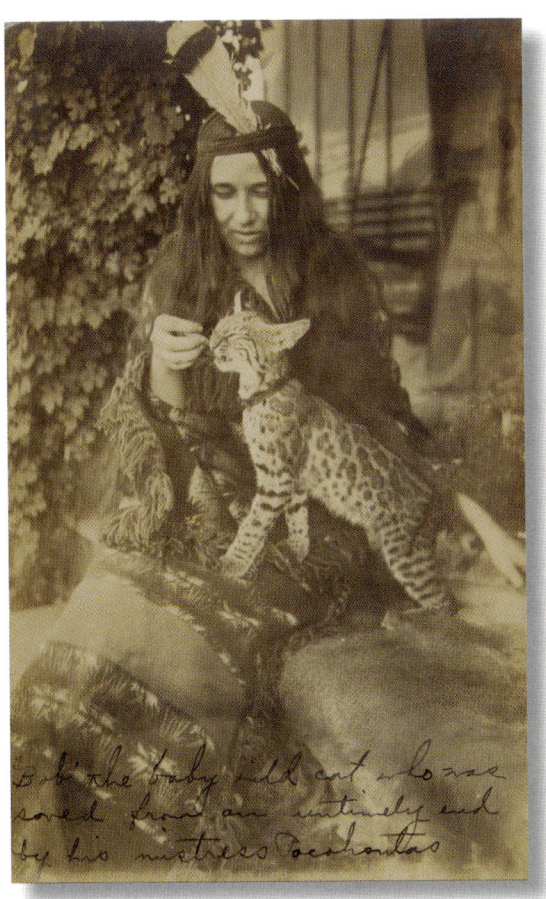

"Bob the baby wild cat who was saved from an untimely end by his mistress Pocahontas" is from a small series of bizarre and probably unique postcards originating in Lee County, Texas. *Collection: Oscar D. Beisert, Jr.*

Varied romantic interactions: one in a barrel and the other on the ball field. *Rifle view: Collection: Oscar D. Beisert, Jr.*

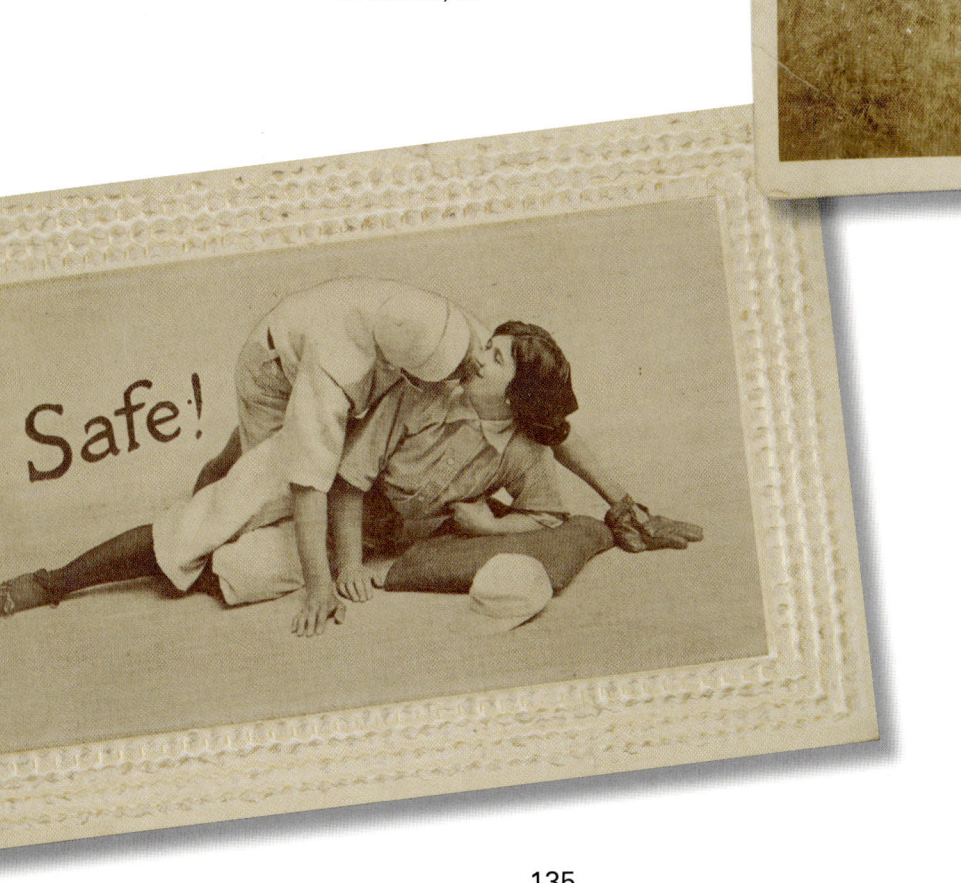

Parades, coast-to-coast, were and usually remain as strange events. The big shoe float adorned a parade in Pottsville, Pennsylvania, in 1906. The German mythology-themed floats were created for the Hudson Fulton Celebration of 1909, which commemorated Henry Hudson's discovery of that great river in 1609 and the first successful steamship launch in 1809. Like all floats in the Tournament of Roses Parade, only live flowers could be used as decoration for this elegant carriage.

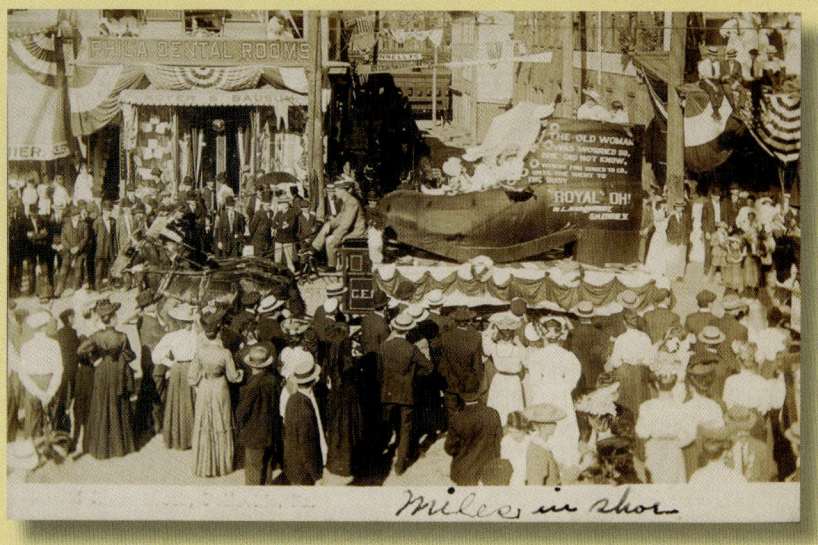

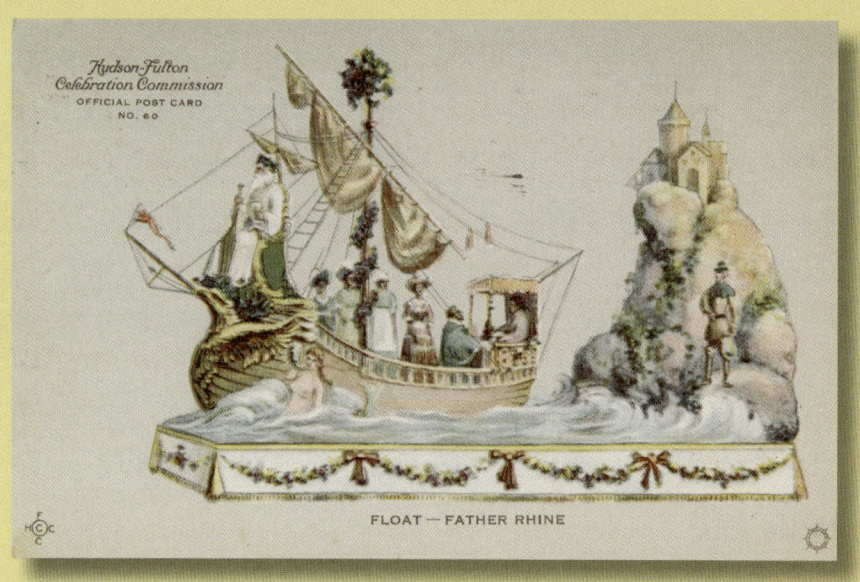

FLOAT—FATHER RHINE

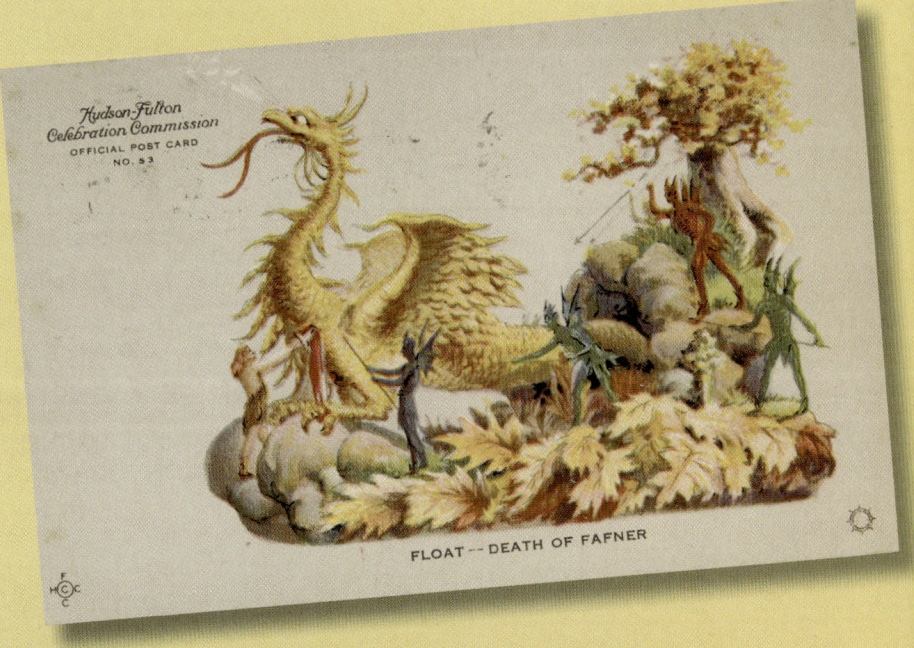

FLOAT—DEATH OF FAFNER

Index

Adams, John Quincy, 66
African Americans, 5, 125, 132
Amityville, PA, 141
Apples, 94-95, 99
Armistice Day, 78
Angels, 7, 8, 37, 40, 116
Ash Wednesday, 35
Automobile, 11, 31, 105, 122, 192
Balloons, Hot Air, 14, 30
Bats, 93, 95, 142
Beisert, Oskar H., 142
Belsnickle, 124-125
Berlin, Irving, 35
Bethany Orphans Home, 131
Birth Control, 13
Black Cats, 83, 88-91, 129
Blarney Castle, 65
Boats, 29, 34, 47, 79, 127, 140
Boyertown Opera House, 141
Brumalia, 114
California, 113, 123, 137
Capitol, U.S., 69
Capp, Al, 17
Cherries, 73-74
Cherubs, 18
Chicks, 46-49, 55, 58
Christ, Jesus, 6, 35-36, 114-115
Christmas, 114-130
Christmas Cards, 114
Christma Carols, 114-115, 117
Christmas Stockings, 121, 128
Christmas Trees, 116-123, 126, 128
Churches, 36, 42, 117, 121, 123
Champagne, 6, 11, 98
Circus, 138
Clapsaddle, Ellen H., 61, 69, 74
Coal, 133
Columbia, 67, 69, 70
Confederate Memorial Day, 5, 66
Corn, 99, 102, 105
Corpses, 141
Cupid, 18, 19, 22, 26-28
David, Jacques, 22
Day of the Dead, 81 96
Decoration Day: see Memorial Day
Devils & Demons, 89, 92
Devil's Night, 81
Dirigibles, 10, 130, 142
Disasters, 140-141
Dogs, 129, 132
Donkeys, 21, 129, 132
Doughboys, 78, 142
Doves, 20, 21, 38
Ducks, 46, 134
Eagles, 69, 71, 76-77, 109
Easter, 35-58
Easter Eggs, 39-45, 52-54
Easter Parades, 35
Easter Lilies, 36, 37, 53
Eisenhower, Dwight David, 78
Elves, 8, 43, 57
Father Time, 12
Fire engine, 140
Fireworks, 66, 67
Fitzgerald, John F., 65

Flag (U.S.), 65, 68-71, 75, 78-80, 110
Flag Day, 80
GAR, 66, 71-72, 80
Gays, 59, 81
Germany, 6, 7, 12, 48, 58, 142
Gettysburg Address, 78
Gibson, Charles Dana, 13
Gilbert, Conrad, 50
Hale, Sarah J., 97
Halloween, 5, 81-86
Hanukkah, 114
Harps, 60, 61, 65
Harvest Home, 97
Hearts, 21-27, 32
Holly, 122-125
Humpty-Dumpty, 43
Indians, 103
Independence Day, 66, 67-69
Jack-O-Lantern, 81-90, 92
Jews, 13, 15, 39, 48
Juneteenth, 66
Karenga, Maulana, 114
Kennedy, Thomas, 65
Kennedy, John F., 65
Kittens, 46
Kwanza, 114
Labor Day, 5
Lambs, 39, 51
Leprechauns, 63
Landis, George D., 17
Landis, Nettie Mae, 131
Leap Year, 16-17
Lincoln, Abraham, 76-78
Lincoln's Birthday, 66, 76-78
Lucy the Margate Elephant, 139
Luna Park, 138
Man-in-the-Moon, 7, 86, 90, 95, 130
Mistletoe, 127
Martin Luther King, Jr. Day, 5
Macy's, 96
Memorial Day, 5, 66, 69-72
Moravians, 35, 114
Mother-in-Law, 33
Mothers Day, 5
Mushrooms, 113
Nativity, 114-115
Navy, 8, 68, 132
Nests, 41, 44
New Years, Eve & Day, 2, 6-12,
New York City, 6, 136
Obama, Barack 5
Ostara, 35, 40
Owls, 89
Parades, 136-137
Pennsylvania Dutch, 35, 9, 125
Philadelphia, PA, 140
Photography, 54
Pilgrims and Puritans, 101-103
Pigs, 139
Pin Ups, 42, 88, 138, 139
Poinsett, Joel, 123
Poinsettia, 123
Potter, Harry, 20, 117
Prang, Louis, 114
Pre-existence, 12

Presidents Day, 5, 66
Providence, R.I., 80
Pumpkins, 99-101, 105
Pussy willows, 37, 38, 40, 51
Rabbits, 50-58
Redwood, 134
Reindeer, 117, 120
Rosh Hashanah, 15
Roosevelt, Franklin D., 97
Roosevelt, Theodore, 67, 140
Rough Riders, 78
Russia, 48
"Sadie Hawkins Day", 17
Salem, Massachusetts, 90
Safety Match, 22
St. Cyr, Lili, 139
St. Bridgit, 17
St. David, 59
St. George, 59
St. Gertrude, 59
St. Patrick, 17, 59
St. Patrick's Day, 5, 59-65
St. Patrick's Cathedral, 59
St. Urho, 59
Samhain, 81
Schuyler's Melody Makers, 134
Shamrocks, 62-65
Santa Claus, 117-122, 124-125
Shaugnessy's pig, 62
Shillelagh, 64-65
Skeletons and Skulls, 81-96
Snow Man, 10
Spanish American War, 78, 79, 140
Storks, 12-13, 33
Sukkoth, 97
"Super Bowl Sunday", 5
Telegram, 9
Texas, 124, 132, 136, 141-142
Telephone, 34, 47, 62, 122
Thanksgiving, 97-113
Thesmorphoria, 97
Truman, Harry S., 66, 80
Turkeys, 100-113
Uncle Sam, 65, 67-68
Valentine's Day, 5, 18-34, 38
Venus, 20
Vernal Equinox, 34, 64
Veterans Day, 78
Villa, Pancho, 141
"Village People", 14
Vulcan, 22
Washington, George, 66, 73-75
Washington, Martha, 75
Washington's Birthday, 66, 73-75
Weapons, 42, 58, 64, 78, 134, 135
Weems, Mason Locke, 73
Whales, 141
White House, 69, 76, 77
Wildcats, 135
Wilson, Woodrow, 5, 80
Wish Bones, 108, 111
Witches, 84-86, 88-92
Wreaths, 120

Sources and Suggestions for Additional Reading

Barth, Edna. *Hearts, Cupids, and Red Roses: The Story of the Valentine Symbols.* New York, New York: Clarion, 1974.

Barth, Edna. *Shamrocks, Harps, and Shillelaghs The Story of St. Patrick Day*. New York, New York: Clarion, 1977

Barth, Edna. *Witches, Pumpkins, and Grinning Ghosts: The Story of Halloween Symbols.* New York, New York: Clarion, 1972

Brenner, Robert. *Christmas Past.* 3rd ed. Atglen, Pennsylvania: Schiffer Publishing Ltd., 1996

Brenner, Robert. *Christmas Through the Decades*. Atglen, Pennsylvania: Schiffer Publishing Ltd., 1993

Brenner, Robert. *Valentine Treasury: A Century of Valentine Cards.*. Atglen, Pennsylvania: Schiffer Publishing Ltd., 1997

Cashman, Greer Fay. *Jewish Days and Holidays.* New York, New York: Adama, 1979.

Crippen, T. G. *Christmas and Christmas Lore*. Detroit, Michigan: Omni Graphics, 1990.

Doyle, Marian I. *Christmas Long Ago*. Atglen, Pennsylvania: Schiffer Publications, 2006.

Giblin, James Cross. *Fireworks, Picnics, and Flags*: The Story of the Fourth of July Symbols, New York, New York: Clarion 1983.

Golby, J.J. and W.A. Purdue. *The making of a Modern Christmas*. Athens, Georgia: University of Georgia Press, 1986.

Gulevich, Tanya. *Encyclopedia of Christmas*. Detroit, Michigan: Omnigraphics, 2000.

Gulevich, Tanya. *Encyclopedia of Easter, Carnival and Lent*. Detroit, Michigan: Omnigraphics, 2002.

Henderson, Helene and Sue Ellen Thompson. *Holidays, Festivals and Celebrations of the World Dictionary*. 2nd ed. Detroit, Michigan: Omnigraphics, 1997

Hobsbawm, Erik, and Terrence Ranger, eds. *The Invention of Tradition*. Cambridge: Cambridge University Press, 1983.

Humphrey, Theodore C. and Lin T. Humpfrey. *"We Gather Together:" Food and Festival in America*. Ann Arbor, Michigan: UMI Research, 1988.

Ickis, Marguerite. *The Book of Patriotic Holidays*. New York, New York: Dodd, Mead, 1962.

Kreider, Katherine. *One Hundred Years of Valentines*. Atglen, Pennsylvania: Schiffer Publishing Ltd., 1999.

Litwicki, Ellen M. *America's Public Holidays, 1865-1920*. Washington, D.C.: Smithsonian Institution Press, 2000.

Lord, Priscilla S. and Daniel J. Foley. *Easter Garland*. Reprint. Philadelphia, Pennsylvania: Chilton Books, 1999.

Lowe, James L. *Bibliography of Postcard Literature: A List of References Pertaining to the Publishing and Collecting of Picture Postcards*. Folson, Pennsylvania: Privately Printed, 1969.

Miller, Daniel, ed. *Unwrapping Christmas*. Oxford: Clarendon Press, 1993.

Monahan, Valerie. *An American Postcard Collector's Guide*. Poole, Dorset, United Kingdom: Blanford Press, 1981.

Reed, Robert M. *Christmas Postcards: A Collector's Guide*. Atglen, Pennsylvania: Schiffer Publishing, Ltd., 2007.

Richman, Irwin. *Lancaster County Pennsylvania Postcards*. Atglen, Pennsylvania: Schiffer Publishing, Ltd., 2008.

Rubin, Cynthia Elyce and Morgan Williams. *Larger than Life: The American Tall Tale Postcard, 1905-1915*. New York, New York: Abbeville Press, 1990.

Santino, Jack. *All Around the Year: Holidays and Celebrations in American Life*. Urbana, Illinois: University of Illinois Press, 1994.

Santino, Jack. *Halloween and Other Festivals of Death and Life*. Knoxville, Tennessee: University of Tennessee Press, 1994.

Santino, Jack. *New Old Fashioned Ways: Holidays and Popular Culture*. Knoxville, Tennessee: The University of Tennessee Press, 1996.

Schmidt, Leigh Eric. *Consumer Rites: The Buying and Selling of American Holidays*. Princeton, New Jersey: Princeton University Press, 1995.

Schneider, Stuart. *Halloween in America*. Atglen, Pennsylvania: Schiffer Publishing , Ltd., 1995.

Schneider, Stuart and Bruce Zalkin.. *Halloween Costumes and Other Treats*. Atglen, Pennsylvania: Schiffer Publishing, Ltd., 2001.

Shoemaker, Alfred A. *Christmas in Pennsylvania: A Folk Cultural Study*. Reprinted. Harrisburg, Pennsylvania: Stackpole Books, 1999.

Shoemaker, Alfred A. *Easter Tide in Pennsylvania: A Folk Cultural Study*. Kutztown, Pennsylvania: Pennsylvania German Folklife Society, 1960.

Staff, Frank. *The Picture Postcard and Its Origins*. New York, New York: Frederick A. Praeger, 1966.

Thomas, John Wesley and Sandra Lynn Thomas. *Thanksgiving and Turkey Collectibles; Then and Now*. Atglen, Pennsylvania: Schiffer Publishing, Ltd., 2004.

Thompson, Sue Ellen. *Holiday Symbols and Customs*, 3rd ed. Detroit, Michigan: Omnigraphics, 2003.

Tuleja, Tad. *Curious Customs: The Stories Behind 296 Popular American Rituals*. New York, New York: Galahad Books, 1987.

Waits, William B. *The Modern Christmas in America: A Cultural History of Gift Giving*. New York, New York: New York University Press, 1993.

Weiser, Francis X. *The Christmas Book*. New York, New York: Harcourt Brace and Co., 1952.

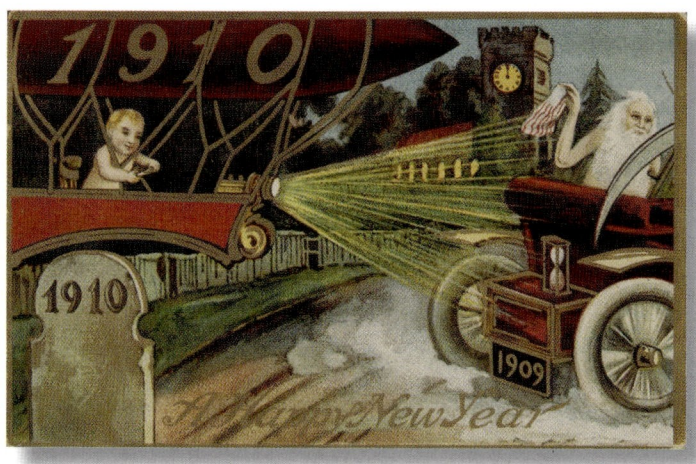
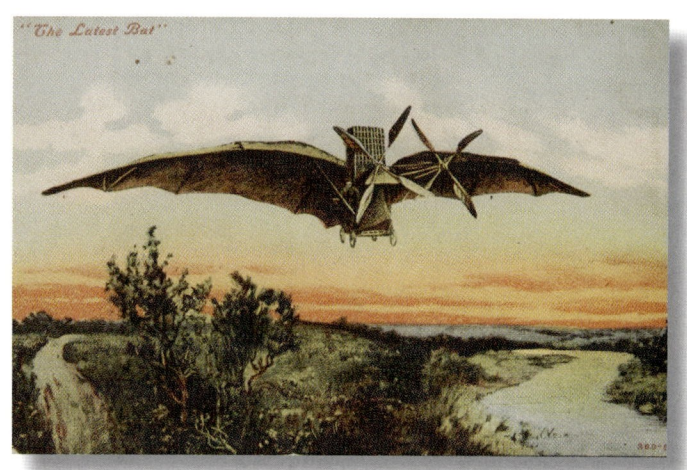

The latest in technology was always to be celebrated, sometimes to strange effect. The New Year's infant of 1910 steering an aircraft bids farewell to a flag-waving 1909 riding in an earlier sensation – the automobile. Once the skies were opened anything was believed to be possible, as seen in the pre-Wright Brothers' creation: "The Latest Bat!"

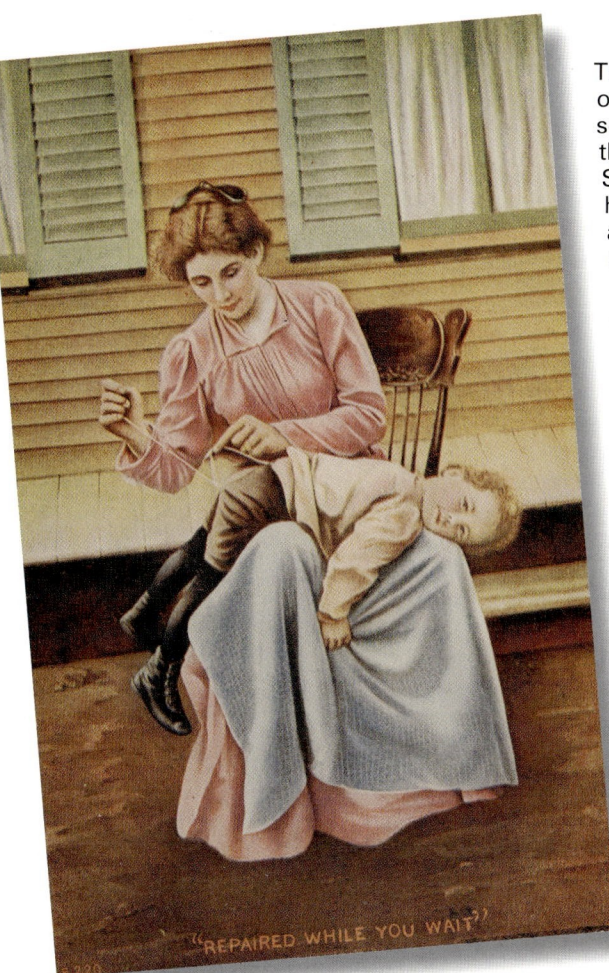

The End. A mother mends a split on her remarkably placid young son's knickers while she sits on the front porch. A determined U. S. doughboy spanks a doll-like helmeted German soldier with a shoe, "Getting at the bottom of all our troubles" on a card mailed June 15, 1918. Meanwhile, in Loebau, Lee County, Texas, a strange ritual is being performed. Did the one guy complain of constipation or was this the start of the Texas oil boom? Holding the auger is Oskar Herman Beisert (1901-1988). *Texas humor, Collection: Oscar D. Beisert, Jr.*

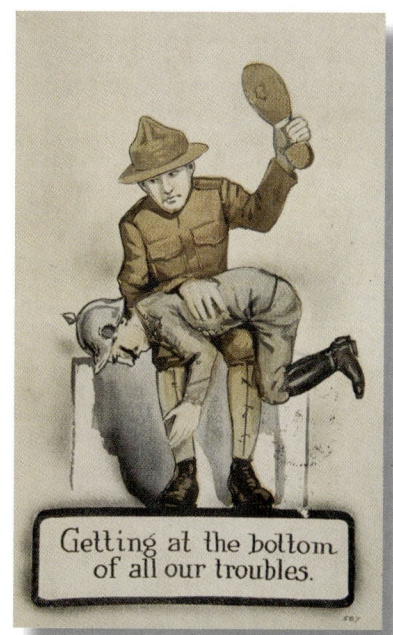
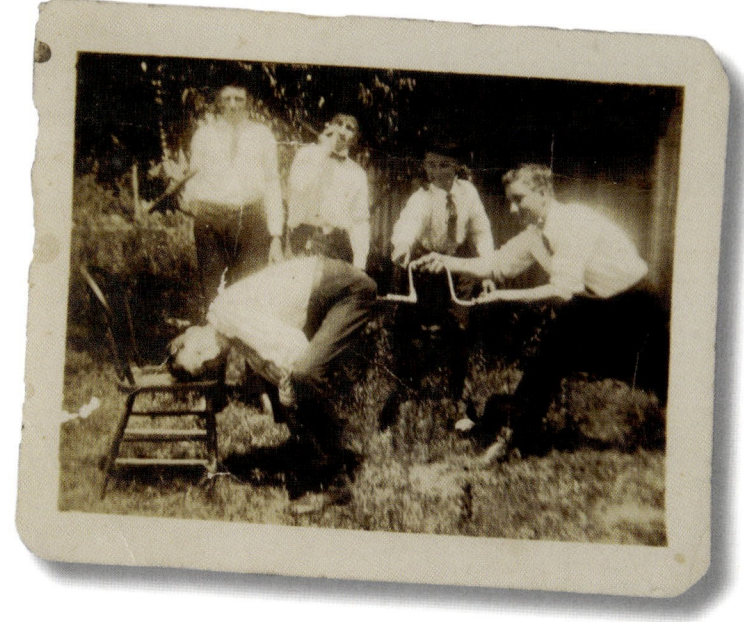

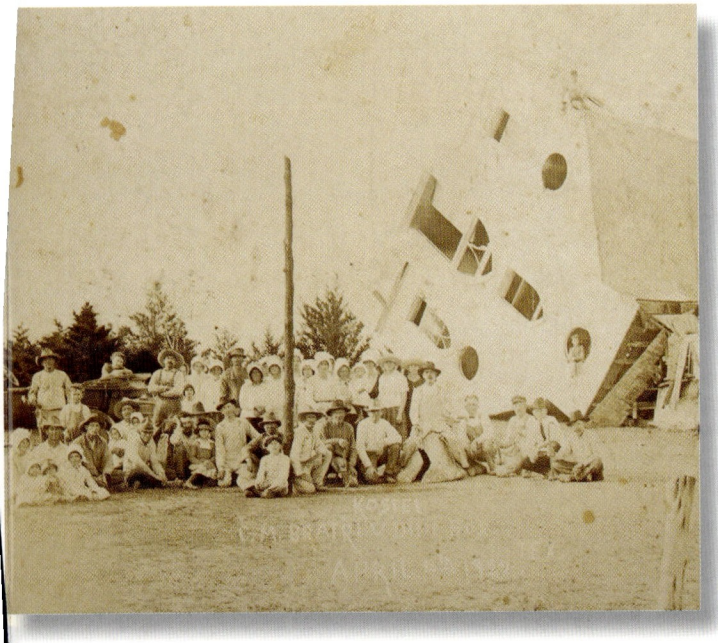
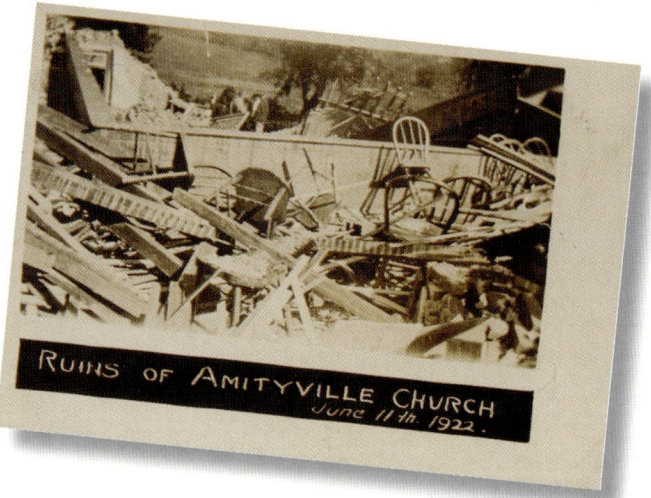

1922 was a bad year for American houses of worship. In that year tornados toppled a church in Dime Box, Lee County, Texas, and destroyed another in rural Pennsylvania. In the Texas scene note the man sitting on the bell with the Liberty-Bell-Crack. *Texas scene, Collection: Oscar D. Beisert, Jr.; Amityville scene, Collection: Mr. & Mrs. Michael Emery*

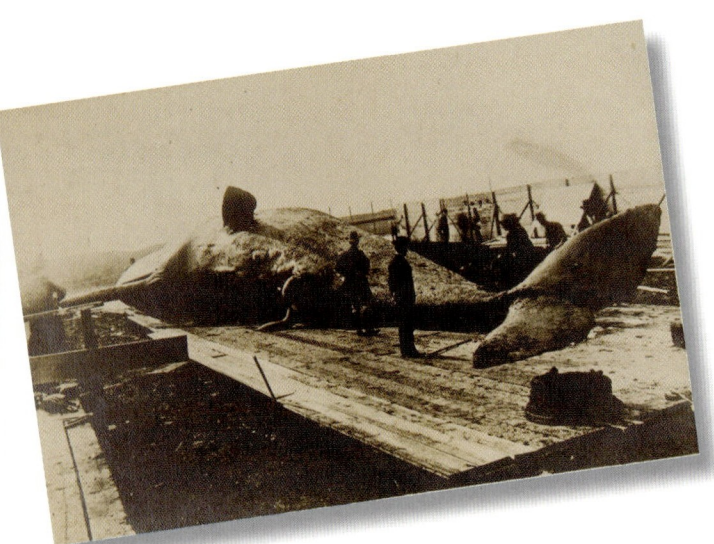
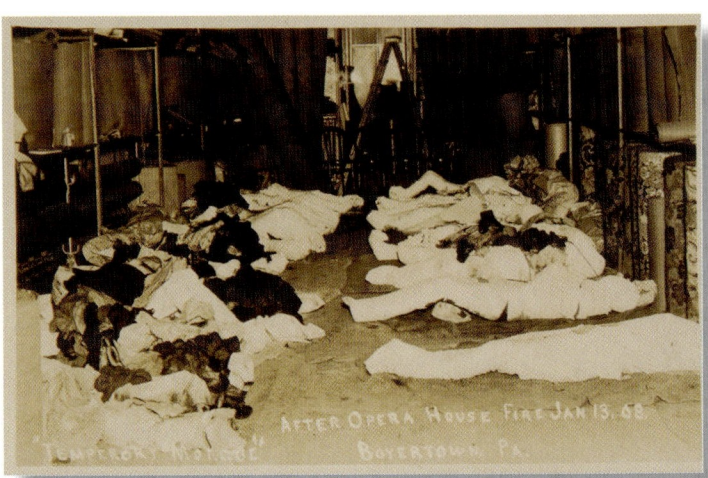

Death and postcards are a more common combination than one would imagine; this is seen in the animal world and the human realm. A whale on a dock awaits butchering and the shrouded bodies of just a few of the victims of a horrendous fire at the Boyertown, Pennsylvania Opera House of January 13, 1908 are laid out in a temporary morgue – a nearby carpet warehouse. Even more bizarre is the postcard showing the body of the notorious Pancho Villa (hero or villain), killed in Mexico in 1923, displayed like a macabre hunting trophy. *Boyertown card, Collection: Mr. & Mrs. Michael Emery*

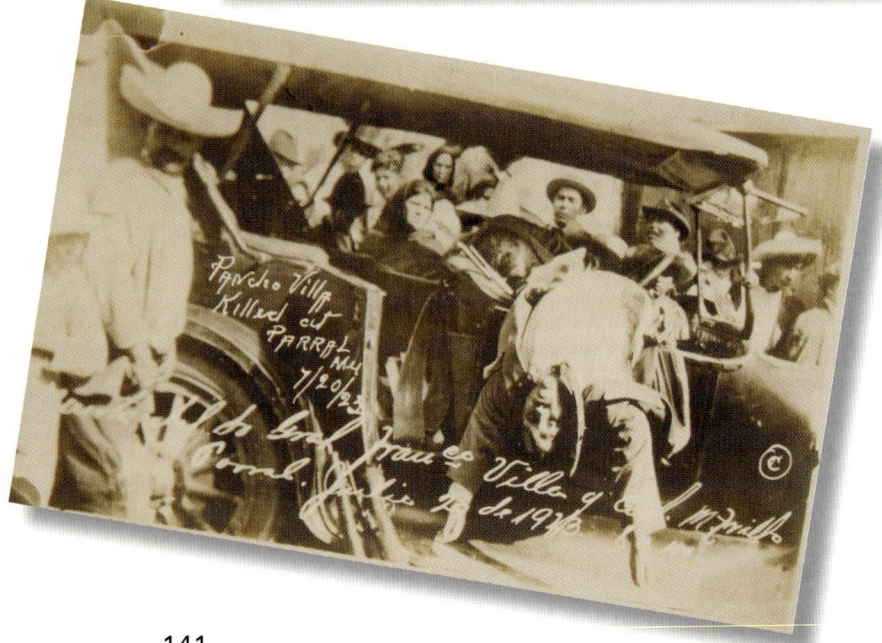

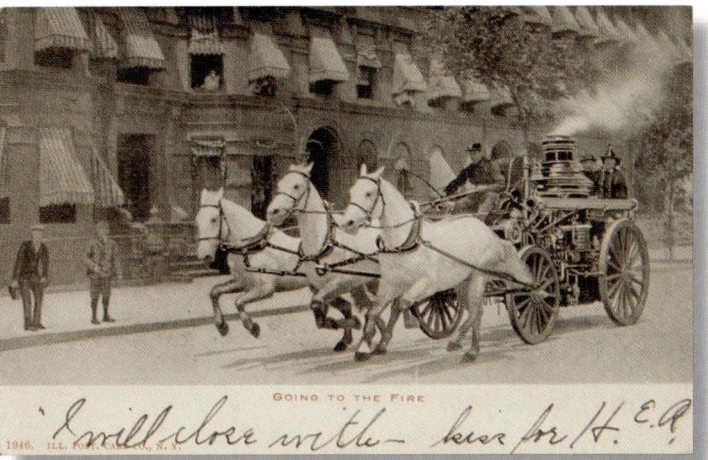

This view of a Philadelphia fire engine rushing on a call was mailed to a lady in Lancaster, Pennsylvania, in 1911.

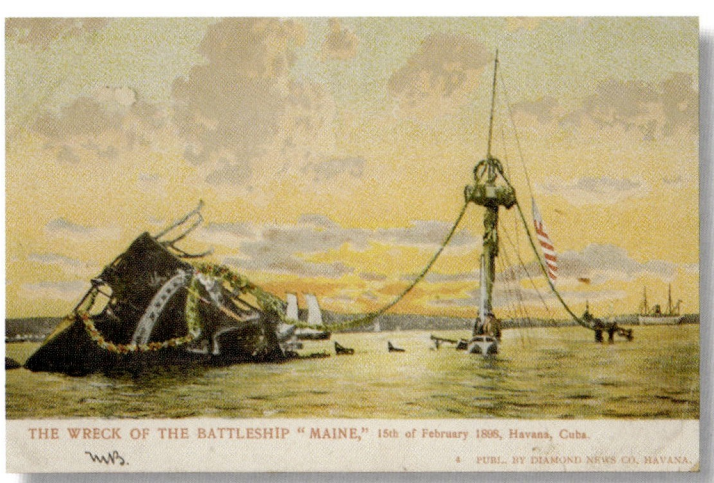

The wreck of the battleship "Maine, which was sunk in Havana, Cuba's harbor in 1898, was reproduced on thousands of cards. Because it was a hindrance to navigation, the remains were eventually removed. The sinking of the "Maine" led to the Spanish American War and the subsequent fame of Theodore Roosevelt, who would become one of the best of U.S. presidents. *Collection: Dr. Russell Eaton*

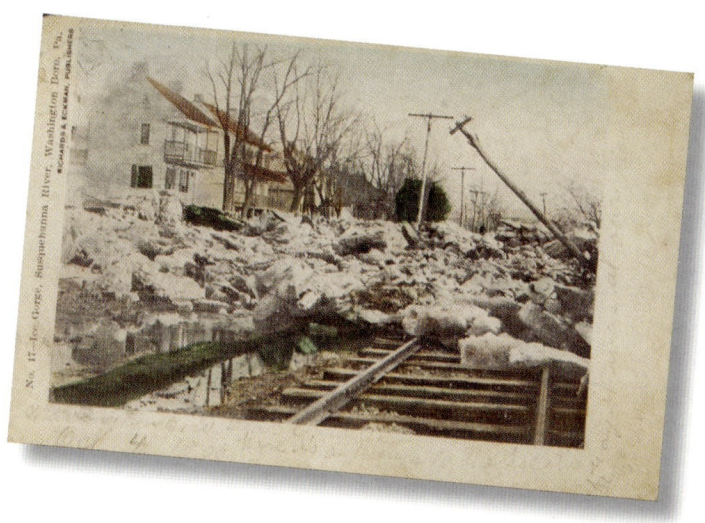

Disasters and accidents were popular subjects for postcard makers. Those involving railroads were especially popular. Ice overruns railroad tracks and knocks down telegraph poles in Washington Boro (Lancaster County, Pennsylvania) and a terrible train wreck near Chattanooga, Tennessee, were prime subjects as was a dreadful industrial accident at the York Rolling Mill in York, Pennsylvania. The engine is part of the clean-up effort.

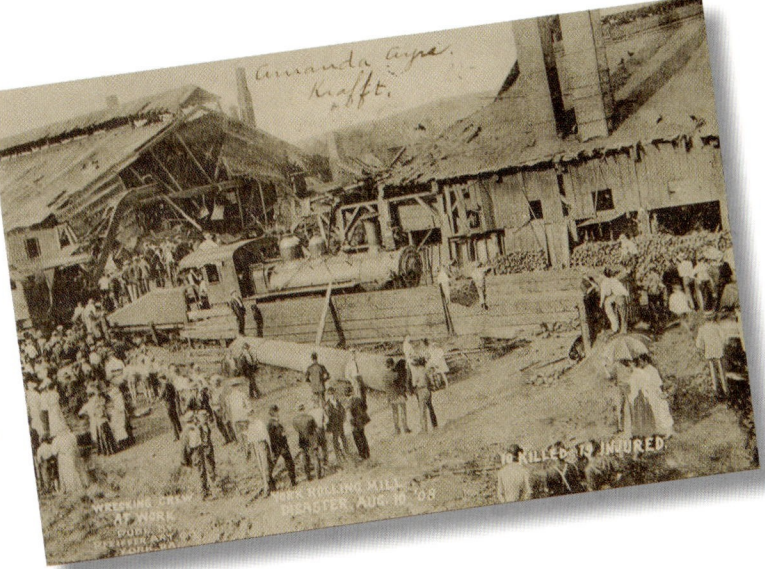

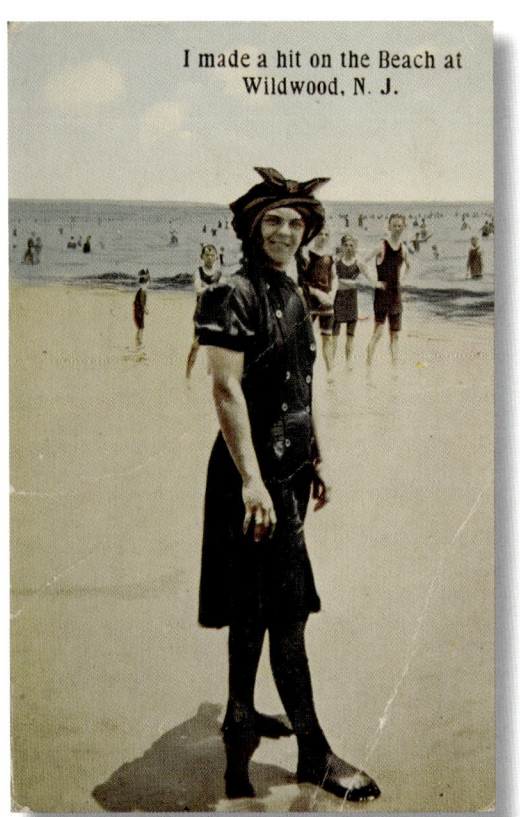
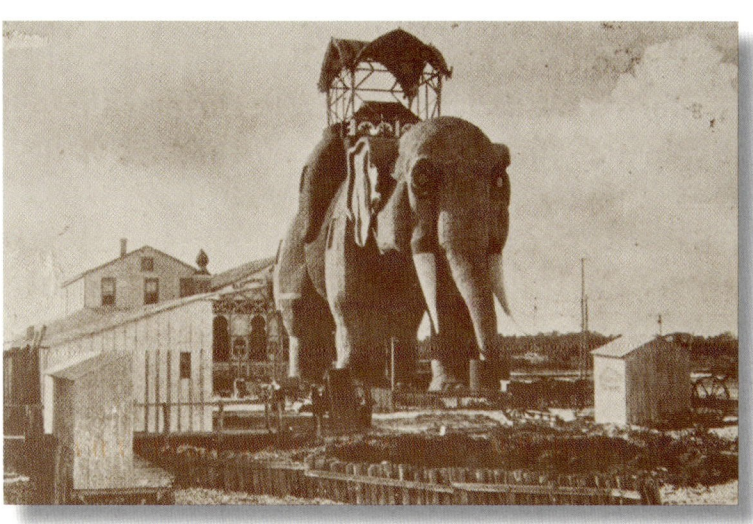
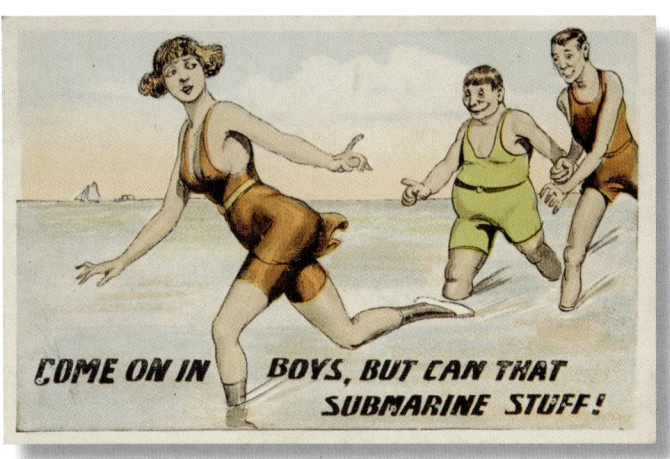
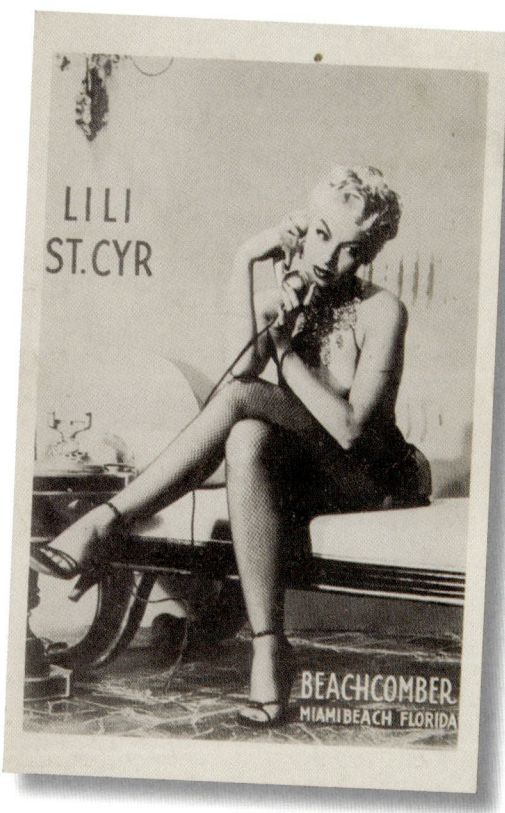
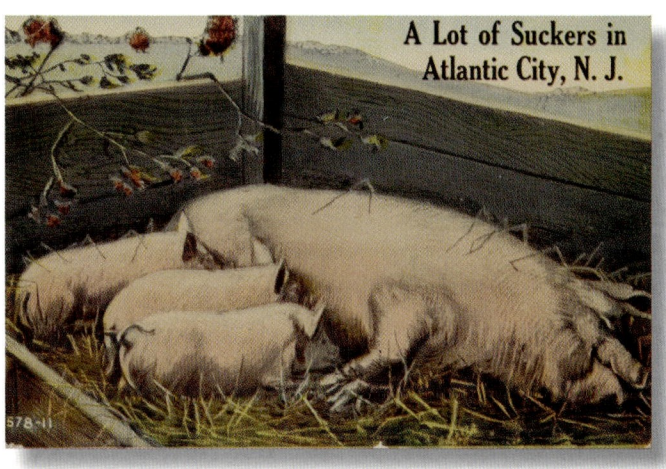

"By the Sea, By the Sea, By the Beautiful Sea," was the opening line of a popular early 20th century song. The guy in a woman's bathing suit would certainly have been noticed on any New Jersey beach, *circa* 1910. Of course, he would have been even more sensational in the more abbreviated costume of a decade later! Lucy, "The Margate (New Jersey) Elephant," was a hotel in 1881, now she is a National Historic Landmark. Atlantic City, Margate's near neighbor, always had a somewhat racier reputation. Heading further south, Len "Spent the evening here at the Beachcomber the show was Swell." Lily St. Cyr was a 1950s Queen of Burlesque when this card was mailed to Fred Brubaker back in "Reading Pa." Len had just witnessed the "Beachcomber's Million Dollar Review – SIN-CYR-ITIES of 1952 Starring LILI ST. CYR and Cast of 52."

Circuses are continual fantasies. The "Two Hemisphere" Band chariot was built for P. T. Barnum in 1896 at a reported cost of $40,000. Back in the days when the circus really was "The Greatest Show on Earth" it was drawn by a team of 40 matched horses!

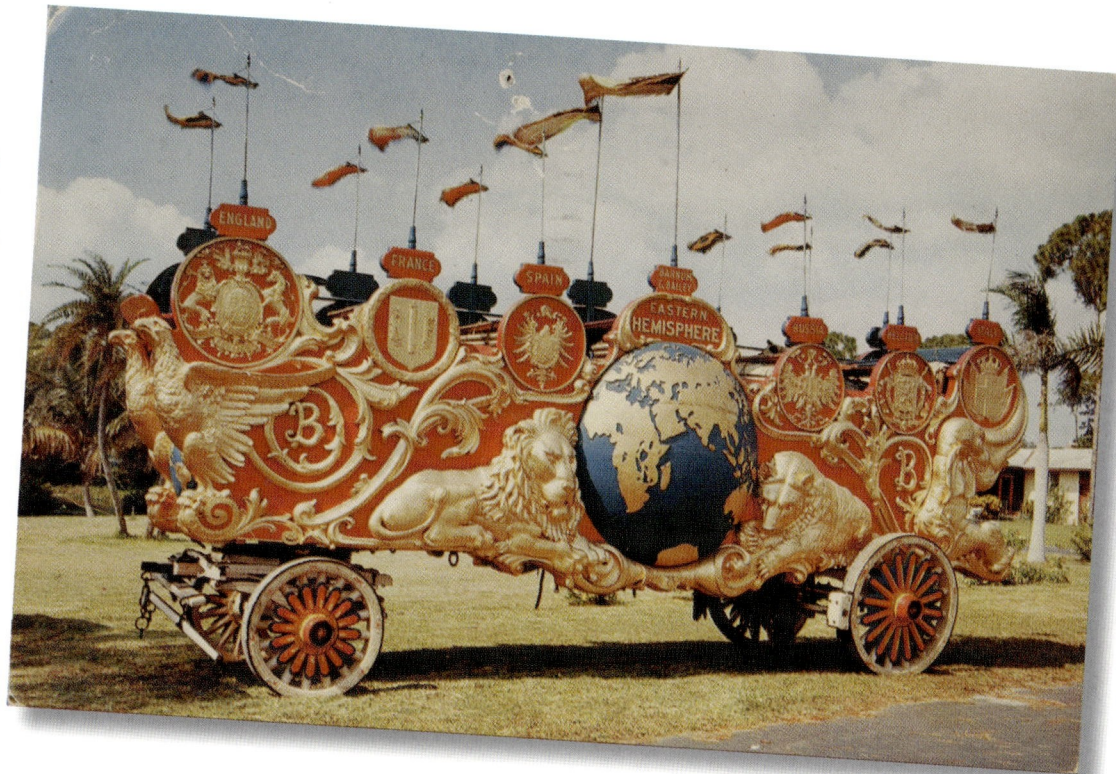

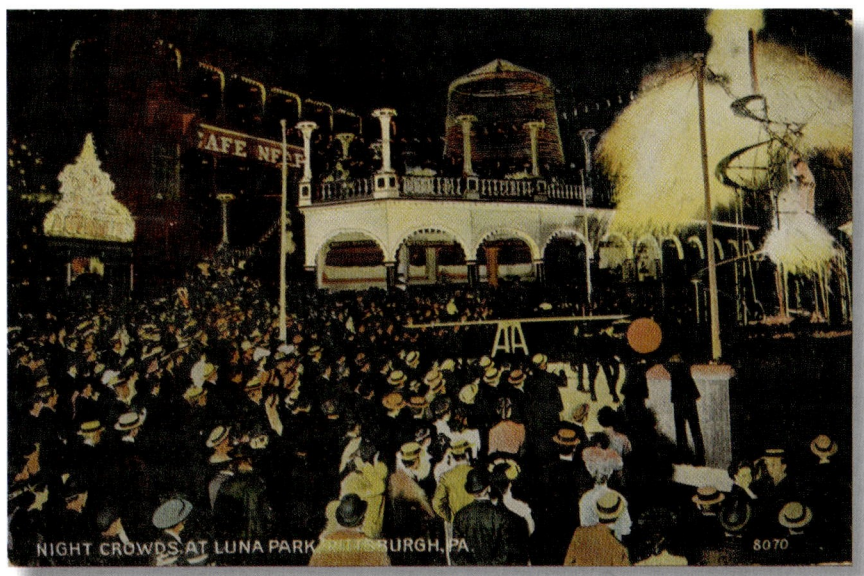

Electricity really created the magic that characterized early 20th century amusement parks. Luna Park in Pittsburgh was named for the famed Coney Island attraction, which would later burn. The message on the back speaks to an era. The sender writes to Ida Diller of Lancaster, Pennsylvania, in 1908, asking "How about exchanging a few postals with me."

Cheesecake always sells. The grotesque, over-sized leg shot dates from the 1930s.

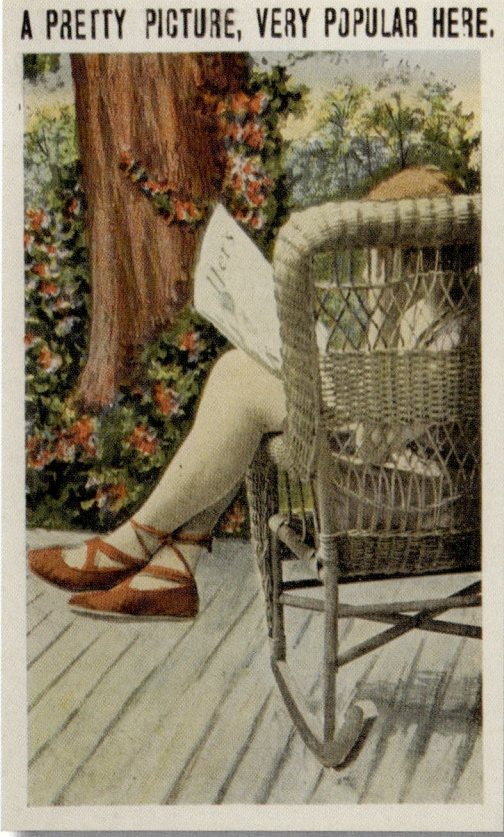

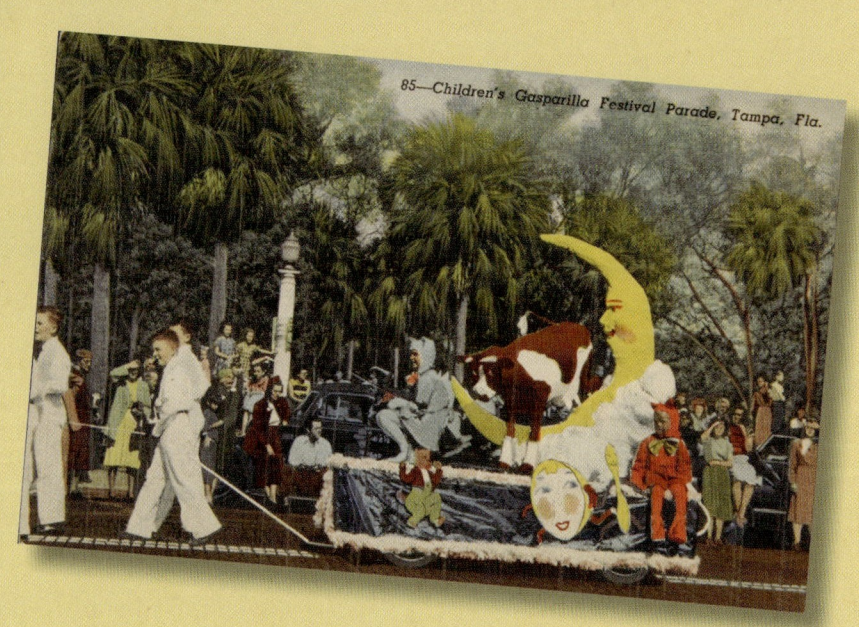

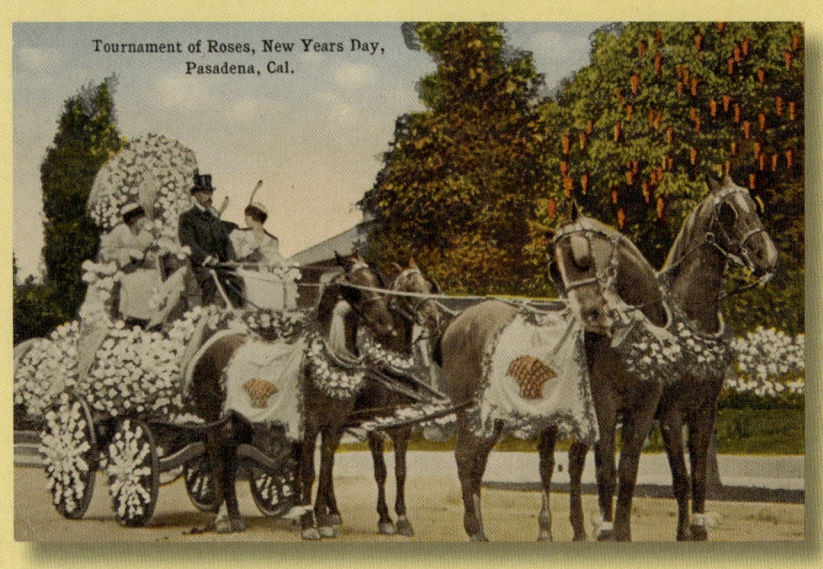

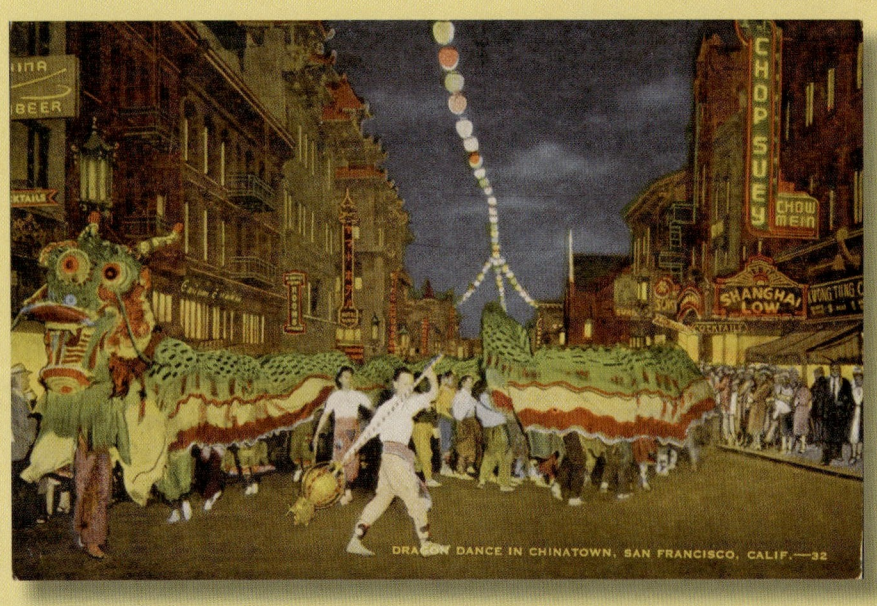